D0617338

THE LETTERS OF
A. E. HOUSMAN

THE LETTERS OF
A. E. HOUSMAN

EDITED BY
HENRY MAAS

HARVARD UNIVERSITY PRESS

Cambridge, Massachusetts

1971

FIRST PUBLISHED 1971
LETTERS © R. E. SYMONS 1971
EDITORIAL MATTER © HENRY MAAS 1971

Library of Congress Catalog Card Number 70–142222

SBN 674–52581–7

PRINTED IN GREAT BRITAIN

To S.M.M.

CONTENTS

PREFACE   *Page* xi

MANUSCRIPT AND OTHER LOCATIONS   xvii

BIOGRAPHICAL TABLE   xix

FAMILY CHART   xxiii

PART I

Early letters: 1875–1877   3

Oxford: 1877–1880   10

The Patent Office: 1885–1890   22

University College: 1892–1896   28

A Shropshire Lad: 1896–1910   35

Cambridge: 1911–1936   113

PART II

Letters on Classical Subjects   397

SELECT BIBLIOGRAPHY   439

INDEX OF RECIPIENTS   443

GENERAL INDEX   447

PLATES

Between pages 200–201

Letter to Lucy Housman, 9 January 1875

Letter to H. E. Butler, 28 June 1911

A. E. H. at 18

. . . at 35

. . . in his fifties

. . . at 70

Letter to S. C. Roberts, 17 July 1926

Postcard to Katharine Symons
(his last correspondence)

PREFACE

'There is no biography of Matthew Arnold, so there certainly need be none of me.' A. E. Housman was emphatic on this point and insisted that his very brief entry in *Who's Who* contained all that need be known about him.

None the less, since his death in 1936, in addition to numerous shorter studies, no fewer than six volumes of biography and recollection have been lavished on his memory. In spite of them all very little is known of the man. To that extent Housman succeeded in keeping his privacy; but his very reticence has done him a disservice. The biographers, starved of facts, have been driven to speculation, with results that are often ludicrous; while popular anecdote, fed chiefly by the gushing admirers he himself studiously repelled, dwells most often on his icy reserve.

The letters, though they reveal nothing startling, at least provide solid materials for the study of his life and character. With the continuing interest in Housman it is surprising that no previous attempt has been made to collect them; only two substantial sets of them (those to Grant Richards and to Laurence Housman) have been printed, and then with numerous omissions. I have been able to trace altogether some 1500 letters, and of these I print about half. With certain exceptions I have excluded only short notes dealing with appointments and minor matters of business, and letters whose content is repeated in others.

A small number of letters has not been available to me—notably those to Housman's great friend, Moses Jackson. I have seen a specimen of these, and it suggests that the others, though of the greatest interest, will not seriously affect what is already known of Housman's relations with Jackson. Should it later become possible to publish these letters and the few others that I have not been permitted to use, they will certainly form a valuable supplement to the present collection.

Housman always wrote carefully, and the letters are here printed almost exactly as he set them down. Unless I have said otherwise, the text is taken directly from the original or a photographic copy. I have omitted nothing; the rare editorial interpolations have been placed in square brackets; dates have been put into standard form—the form that Housman himself used most often—and addresses abbreviated after the first appearance of each; small numbers and some abbreviated forms of words have been spelled out; titles of books, plays and periodicals, as well as words underlined by Housman, have been put into italics, titles of poems and articles into inverted commas. Housman's rare slips of the pen have been corrected without comment.

The book is divided into two parts. The first contains the main body of Housman's letters in chronological order. In the second I have placed those letters that deal chiefly with the technicalities of classical scholarship. Very occasionally, rather than split a small set of letters to the same correspondent, I have allowed myself to put a letter in a section to which it does not properly belong.

It is a pleasure to record my gratitude to the many friends and correspondents whose help has made this edition possible. My first obligation is to Housman's literary executor, Mr Robert E. Symons, who authorised the publication of his great-uncle's correspondence; and to the Society of Authors, which acts as administrator of Housman's literary estate and has given its co-operation freely from the start.

Mr John Carter, the leading authority on the bibliography of Housman, has been tireless in his efforts on my behalf. He has secured permission to use many letters, traced many others which I should certainly not have found on my own, placed his expert knowledge at my disposal and in countless ways smoothed my path.

Before I began work on this book it was my special wish to assure myself that the project would have the concurrence of Mr A. S. F. Gow, Housman's close friend at Trinity College, Cambridge. It was he who wrote the first and the best book on Housman and who more than any other man may truly be called the guardian of Housman's memory. Had he objected, that would have been the end of the matter. He has instead been constantly kind and helpful, and I am happy to have this opportunity to express my sense of obligation.

The following libraries, institutions and private owners have most generously allowed me to use letters in their possession and supplied me not only with photocopies but with information and assistance of every sort: The Society of Authors, and Miss Anne Munro-Kerr; the City of Bath, and Mr Peter Pagan, Director of the Municipal Libraries and Victoria Art Gallery; the Henry W. and Albert A. Berg Collection, New York Public Library, and the late Dr John D. Gordan, the Curator; Birkbeck College, London; the Department of Rare Books and Special Collections, University of California, Berkeley, and Mr Leslie S. Clarke, the Assistant Head; the Bodleian Library, Oxford; the British Museum, and Mr T. C. Skeat, the Keeper of Manuscripts; the Brotherton Collection, University of Leeds, and Mr David I. Masson, Sub-Librarian in charge of the Collection;

Brown University Library, and Mrs Christine D. Hathaway, Special Collections Librarian; the Lockwood Library, State University of New York at Buffalo, and Mr David Posner, Curator of the Poetry Collection; the University Library, Cambridge, and the Emeritus Librarian, Mr H. R. Creswick; the Cambridge University Press, Mr R. W. David, the Secretary, and his predecessor, Mr R. J. L. Kingsford; the University of Chicago Library, and Mr Robert Rosenthal, Curator of Special Collections; the William L. Clements Library, University of Michigan, and Mr William S. Ewing, Curator of Manuscripts;

Colby College Library, and Professor Richard Cary, Curator of Rare Books and Manuscripts; the Butler Library, Columbia University, and Mr Kenneth A. Lohf, Assistant Librarian for Special Collections; the Library of Congress, Mr L. Quincy Mumford, the Librarian, Mr David C. Mearns, late Chief of the Manuscript Division and Mr Julian D. Mason, Jr., American Cultural History Specialist; the Baker Memorial Library, Dartmouth College, and Mr Kenneth C. Kramer, the Archivist; the Dorset County Museum and Miss E. M. Samuel, Assistant Curator; the Library of Trinity College, Dublin, and Mr William O'Sullivan, Keeper of Manuscripts; the Fitzwilliam Museum, Cambridge, and the Librarian, Miss Phyllis M. Giles; the University of Glasgow, and Professor C. J. Fordyce, the Clerk of Senate;

Harvard College, and Dr William H. Bond, Librarian of the Houghton Library; the Borough of Hove Central Library, and Mr Jack Dove, Borough Librarian; the University of Illinois Library, and Mr R. B. Downs, Dean of Library Administration; the Provost and Fellows of King's College, Cambridge, and Dr A. N. L. Munby, College Librarian; the University Libraries, Indiana University, Mr David A. Randall, the Librarian, and Miss Elfrieda Lang, Curator of Manuscripts; the University Library, Liverpool, and Mr D. H. Varley, University Librarian; Messrs Macmillan and Company, and Mr T. M. Farmiloe; the Memorial Library Archives, Marquette University, and the Rev. R. N. Hamilton, S.J., University Archivist; McGill University Library, and Mrs C. M. Lewis, Rare Book Librarian; the Warden and Fellows of Merton College, Oxford, and Mr R. Highfield, College Librarian; the Newberry Library, Chicago, and Mr Matthew P. Lowman II; the University Library, Newcastle-upon-Tyne, and Dr William S. Mitchell, the Librarian; the University Registry, Oxford, and Sir Folliott Sandford, the Registrar; the Oxford University Press, and Mr John Bell;

Princeton University Library and Dr Alexander P. Clark, Curator of Manuscripts; the Library of St John's College, Oxford, Mr H. M. Colvin, the Librarian and Mr Charles Morgenstern, Assistant Librarian; Shrewsbury School Library, and Mr J. B. Lawson, the Librarian; Somerset County Library, and Mr B. D. C. Totterdell; the University Libraries, Southern Illinois University, and Mr Ralph Bushee, Rare Book Librarian; the University of Sydney, and Mr David S. Macmillan, University Archivist; the University of Texas Library, and Mrs Mary M. Hirth, Librarian of the Academic Center; the Library of Trinity College, Cambridge, and Mr A. Halcrow, Sub-Librarian; the Library of University College, London, Mr Joseph W. Scott, the Librarian, and Miss Sheila Williams, Assistant Librarian; the Victoria and Albert Museum; the University of Virginia Library, and Miss Elizabeth Ryall, Assistant in Manuscripts; the University of

Wales, and the Registrar, Mr J. Gareth Thomas; Yale University Library, Miss Dorothy Bridgwater and Mr Kenneth Nesheim;

Mr Seymour Adelman; Mr Mark Bonham Carter; Sir Maurice Bowra; the late Lord Bridges; Mr J. H. Britton; Mrs Margaret L. Butler; Mr John Carter; Professor W. V. Clausen; Mr Cyril Clemens; Professor Patrick Duff; Mrs T. S. Eliot; Mr H. C. Gottoff; Mrs M. I. Henderson; Mrs Charles Hill; Mrs M. N. Hooper; Mr A. Hudson-Williams; Mr Douglas M. Jacobs; Mr Houston Martin; Mr Ian Samuels; Mr R. Shaw-Smith; Mr Walter Shewring; Professor O. Skutsch; Mr John Sparrow; Mrs P. M. Symons; Professor Geoffrey Tillotson; Professor W. S. Watt; Mr Kenneth Wellesley; Mr William White; Miss Monica Withers and Mrs Audrey Kennett.

Many others have contributed by tracing letters, checking details, carrying out research and providing expert advice: The late Sir Frank Adcock; Mr Alan S. Bell; Mr T. S. Blakeney; Mr Wilfrid Blunt; Dr F. Brittain; the Rev. Professor John Burnaby; Mr John Burns; the late Mrs Irene Cooper-Willis; Mr R. L. Coutts; Miss Diana Daniels; Miss Fiona Davidson; Miss Christabel Draper; Major-General A. C. Duff; Mr H. J. Easterling; Lord Evans; Professor G. B. A. Fletcher; Signor Giuseppe Giangrande; Mr Tom Burns Haber; Sir Rupert and Lady Hart-Davis; Frau Edith Herbig; Mr F. H. Hodges; Mr Neil Ker; Mr R. N. Kerr; Professor Günther Klaffenbach; Professor Georg Knauer; Professor Ludwig Koenen; the late F. L. Lucas; Lady Anne Lytton; Dr Hilde Maas; Mr Norman Marlow; the late John Masefield, O.M.; Mr Ernest Mehew; Mr T. W. Melluish; Mrs Katherine Lyon Mix; Professor S. G. Morley; Miss Stephanie Mullins; Mr J. C. T. Oates; Mr C. W. Orr; Mr George D. Painter; Mr Graham Pollard; Mr J. B. Priestley; Mr Brian Reade; Professor L. J. C. Richardson; the late A. F. Scholfield; Dr Karl Schultes; Mr Martin Secker; Mr Dominick Spencer; Mr N. V. H. Symons; Mr George L. Watson; Mr L. P. Wilkinson; Frau Lena Williger; Mr A. J. Woodman;

Mr M. D. Griffith of the Board of Trade; Mr A. L. Hutchinson of the British Broadcasting Corporation; Mr R. A. G. Carson, Deputy Keeper of Coins and Medals, British Museum; Mr B. F. Underwood, Librarian of Bromsgrove School; Miss H. E. Peek, Keeper of the Archives, University of Cambridge; Professor C. J. Fordyce and *The Classical Review*; Messrs J. Curwen and Sons Ltd; Mr Duncan Robinson, Assistant Keeper of Drawings, the Fitzwilliam Museum; Mrs E. Vaughan, Librarian of the Highgate Literary and Scientific Institution; Mr H. M. G. Baillie of the Historical Manuscripts Commission; Miss Doreen Arthur of the Vice-Chancellor's Office, University of Liverpool; the Librarian to the Corporation of London; Mr A. L. Maycock, Keeper of the Old Library, Magdalene College, Cambridge; Mr Charles Parish, Librarian of the Newcastle Literary and Philosophical Society; Mr Philip Hepworth of Norwich Central Library; Mr Henry Jones of Oswestry Public Library; The Secretary, Public Record Office;

Miss Patricia Palmer of Stanford University Libraries; Mr J. W. Ford of the Treasury; Mr A. ap Gwynn of the Library of the University College of Wales, Aberystwyth; Miss Monica Davies of the National Library of Wales; Mr Robert Mackworth-Young, Librarian of Windsor Castle; Mr A. A. C. Hedges of Great Yarmouth Central Library; and Mr H. W. Sharp, of Godden, Holme and Co., Solicitors to the Brewers' Society. There are many others who have courteously answered enquiries and given other help. My gratitude to them is no less for being expressed without their names.

Few editors, if any, can have been as fortunate as I in the expert assistance freely given by the scholarly helpers who have read the proofs of this book: Mr John Carter, Mr A. S. F. Gow, Sir Rupert Hart-Davis, Mr and Mrs Ernest Mehew, and Mr John Sparrow. Their contribution goes far beyond the correction of minor errors: they have subjected both the text and the editing to a minute scrutiny, traced references that defeated me, carried out additional research, and made countless improvements to the footnotes. I salute them, and thank the good fortune that gave me such collaborators.

My final debt, and my greatest, is to my wife, Susan Maas. She has undertaken much of the research and revised the typescript and the proofs. I have constantly relied on her judgment, and she has been in every way the partner that all editors long for and few find.

HENRY MAAS

MANUSCRIPT AND OTHER LOCATIONS

I. LIBRARIES AND INSTITUTIONS

Bath	City of Bath Municipal Libraries
Berg	Henry W. and Albert A. Berg Collection, New York Public Library
Berkeley	Library of University of California, Berkeley
Birkbeck	Birkbeck College, London
Bodley	Bodleian Library, Oxford
B.M.	British Museum, London
Brotherton	Brotherton Library, University of Leeds
Brown	Library of Brown University, Providence
Buffalo	State University of New York, Buffalo
Cambridge	University Library, Cambridge
C.U.P.	Cambridge University Press
Chicago	University of Chicago Library
Clements	William L. Clements Library, University of Michigan
Colby	Colby College Library, Waterville
Columbia	Butler Library, Columbia University, New York
Congress	Library of Congress, Washington
Dorchester	Dorset County Museum, Dorchester
Dublin	Library of Trinity College, Dublin
Feinberg	Charles Feinberg Collections, Southern Illinois University Library
Fitzwilliam	Fitzwilliam Museum, Cambridge
Glasgow	Senate of the University of Glasgow
Harvard	Library of Harvard University
Hove	Borough of Hove Central Library
Illinois	University of Illinois Library
King's	Library of King's College, Cambridge
Lilly	Lilly Library, Indiana University
Liverpool	University Library, Liverpool
Macmillan	Messrs Macmillan and Company, London
Marquette	Memorial Library, Marquette University, Milwaukee
McGill	McGill University Library, Montreal
Merton	Library of Merton College, Oxford
Newberry	Newberry Library, Chicago
Newcastle	University Library, Newcastle Upon Tyne

Oxford	University Registry, Oxford
O.U.P.	Oxford University Press, London
Princeton	Princeton University Library
St John's	Library of St John's College, Oxford
Shrewsbury	Shrewsbury School Library
Society of Authors	Society of Authors, London
Street	Somerset County Library, Street
Texas	University of Texas Library
Trinity	Library of Trinity College, Cambridge
U.C.L.	Library of University College, London
Victoria and Albert	Victoria and Albert Museum, London
Virginia	University of Virginia Library
Windsor	Royal Archives, Windsor Castle
Yale	Yale University Library

2. PRIVATE OWNERS[1]

Adelman	Mr Seymour Adelman
Bowra	Sir Maurice Bowra
Bridges	The late Lord Bridges
Britton	Mr J. H. Britton
Carter	Mr John Carter
Clemens	Mr Cyril Clemens
Eliot	Mrs T. S. Eliot
Gotoff	Mr H. C. Gotoff
Hudson-Williams	Mr A. Hudson-Williams
Jacobs	Mr Douglas M. Jacobs
Martin	Mr Houston Martin
Samuels	Mr Ian Samuels
Shaw-Smith	Mr R. Shaw-Smith
Sparrow	Mr John Sparrow
Symons	Mrs P. M. Symons
Wellesley	Mr Kenneth Wellesley
Withers	Miss Monica Withers and Mrs Audrey Kennett

3. PRINTED SOURCES NAMED IN THE HEADNOTES

Memoir	*A.E.H.* by Laurence Housman, 1937
Richards	*Housman: 1897–1941* by Grant Richards, 1941

[1] The headnote 'MS. Private' means that the owner has asked not to be named.

BIOGRAPHICAL TABLE

1859	26 March	A. E. Housman, eldest son of Edward and Sarah Housman, born at The Valley House, Fockbury
	24 April	Baptized in Catshill Church
1860		Family moves to Perry Hall, Bromsgrove
1870	September	Enters Bromsgrove School as day-boy
1871	March	Stays at Woodchester
	26 March	Death of Sarah Housman
1873	Spring	Family moves to Fockbury House
	26 June	Edward Housman marries his cousin, Lucy Housman
1875	January	A. E. Housman visits London
1877	Summer	Family moves back to Perry Hall
	October	A. E. Housman goes up to St John's College, Oxford
		Meets Moses Jackson
1879	April	Stays in London with A. W. Pollard
	July	First in Mods
1880	October	Takes rooms with Jackson and Pollard
1881	*circa* April	Edward Housman suffers stroke
	July	Fails in Greats and returns to Bromsgrove
	October	Returns to Oxford for one term to read for Pass Degree
1882		Passes Civil Service Examination
		His first paper, 'Horatiana', published
	December	Moves to London, takes rooms with Moses and Adalbert Jackson in Talbot Road, Bayswater
		Enters Patent Office
1885		Moves to Northumberland Place, Bayswater
	December	Text and apparatus criticus of Propertius completed
1886		Moves to North Road, Highgate
1887	April	Visits Woodchester, the first of a long series of annual visits
	13 August	Katharine Housman marries E. W. Symons
	December	Jackson leaves for India
1888		'Emendationes Propertianae' published, followed by numerous other papers every year till his death
1889		Joins Cambridge Philological Society
	October	Jackson on leave in England
	9 December	Jackson marries and returns to India
1892	June	Housman appointed Professor of Latin at University College, London

1892	3 October	Delivers Introductory Lecture
	12 November	Death of Adalbert Jackson
1894		Edits *Ibis* in Postgate's *Corpus*
	27 November	Death of Edward Housman
1895	January–May	'Continuous excitement' during which he wrote most of *A Shropshire Lad*
1896	March	*A Shropshire Lad* published
	September	Visits Shropshire
1897	August–September	Visits Paris, Rome and Naples
1898	May	Jackson home on leave
	14 September	Second edition of *A Shropshire Lad* published
1899	18 June	Meets Thomas Hardy in London
	August	Stays with Hardy at Dorchester
1900	September	Visits Milan and Venice
1901	September	Visits Paris, Pisa, Florence and Venice. Goes to France or Italy almost every year thereafter
	30 October	Herbert Housman killed in South Africa
1903	June	Manilius I published
1904	September	Visits Constantinople
1905	2 May	Death of Robert Housman
	July	Housman's edition of Juvenal published
	November	Moves to Yarborough Villas, Pinner
1907	12 November	Death of Lucy Housman
1911		Jackson leaves India and settles in Vancouver
	January	Housman appointed Kennedy Professor of Latin at Cambridge
	9 May	Delivers Inaugural Lecture
	September	Moves into Trinity College
	November	Visits W. S. Blunt in Sussex
1912	May	Manilius II published
1915	March	With Grant Richards on French Riviera
1916	February	Manilius III published
1919		Joins Family (dining club)
1920	September	Manilius IV published
	9 September	For the first time flies to Paris
1922	19 October	*Last Poems* published
1923	14 January	Death of Jackson
	March–May	Housman continuously ill
	December	Visits Robert Bridges in Oxford
1925	16 March	Death of Arthur Platt
1926	January	Housman's edition of Lucan published
1928	15 January	Pall-bearer at Hardy's funeral

1929	23 February	Refuses Order of Merit
1930	December	Manilius V published
1931	3 May	Death of Sophie Becker
1932	1 December	Death of Basil Housman
1933	9 May	Delivers Leslie Stephen Lecture
	June	Begins to suffer from heart trouble
1935	February	Becomes seriously ill
	August–September	Last visit to France
1936	30 April	Death of A. E. Housman in Evelyn Nursing Home, Cambridge

FAMILY CHART

Robert Housman of Lune Bank (1724–1800)

Rev. Robert H. (1759–1838)
Vicar of St Anne's, Lancaster

William H. (b. 1768)
West India merchant; bought Lune Bank
from his elder brother;
m. (1804) Sarah Fletcher of Halton Hall

Robert Fletcher H.
of Lune Bank (b. 1807)

Rev. Thomas H.
Vicar of Catshill, Worcestershire,
m. Ann Brettell of Bromsgrove

Edward H.
(1831–1894)
solicitor, m.
(1) Sarah Jane Williams; (2) Lucy Housman
(1828–1871)
daughter of
Rev. John Williams,
Rector of Woodchester

Rev. Joseph Brettell H.
Rector of Cheriton
Bishop, Devon

Mary Brettell H.

William H.,
solicitor,
m. Mary Vernon
of Hanbury

Rev. George Vernon H.
(1820–1887)
Dean of Quebec

Rev. Henry H.
(1832–1912)
Rector of Bradley

Mary Theophania H.

Helen Agnes H.
m. Sir William
Smith, Bt.

Lucy H.
(1813–1907)

Eva Vernon H.
m. A. P. Parker

Rev. Arthur Oslow H.

Robert Holden H.
(1860–1905)
electrical engineer

Clemence Annie H.
(1861–1961)
illustrator

Katherine Elizabeth H.
(1862–1945)
m. Edward William Symons
(1857–1932)
Headmaster of
King Edward's School, Bath

Basil Williams H.
(1864–1932)
Medical Officer of
Health, Worcestershire
County Council,
m. Jane (Jeannie) Dixon
of Tardebigge

Laurence H.
(1865–1959)
poet,
playwright
and illustrator

George Herbert H.
(1868–1901)
Sergeant in
King's Royal Rifles

Alfred Edward H.
(1859–1936)

Herbert Edward Symons
(1888–1939)

Arthur Denis S.
(1891–1951)

Clement Aubrey S.
(1893–1915)

Noel Victor Housman S.
(born 1894)

Part I

THE HOUSMAN family was descended from Flemish weavers who settled in England in the fourteenth century or earlier, and had lived since at least 1550 at Skerton in Lancashire. Farmers at first, they had later turned to cotton-spinning and brewing. In 1618 Richard Housman bought a house at Skerton, which his eighteenth-century descendant Robert Housman enlarged and renamed Lune Bank.

The next Robert, a prosperous brewer, had a younger son, also Robert, who proved a problem. Apprenticed at first to a local surgeon, he gave up everything to follow a religious calling which took him first to Cambridge, then to an Anglican curacy in Yorkshire, then for ten years to the privations of an itinerant Wesleyan preacher. In 1793 he returned to Lancaster to found the church of St Anne. Resented at first as an interloper, he lived to win the respect of a devoted congregation and fame for his sermons in the world outside.

His younger son, Thomas, like him went to St John's College, Cambridge, and was ordained priest in the Church of England at Chester in 1820. His marriage not long after brought him what his father never had—money and position. His bride was the descendant of two wealthy Worcestershire families, the Holdens and the Brettells. After a few years in Staffordshire the couple settled in one of her family homes near Bromsgrove, the Clock House, Fockbury, and Thomas Housman became Vicar of the neighbouring parish of Catshill.

Three of his sons survived infancy. The first became a parson and spent his life in Devon; the second was drowned as a young man in a shipwreck; the youngest, Edward, stayed at home, became a solicitor and established himself in practice in Bromsgrove. Much of his time was given to the affairs of a distant relative, Captain John Adams of Perry Hall, Bromsgrove, and on his death in 1860 Edward Housman inherited his property.

Not long before that date he had married. His wife, Sarah Jane Williams, was the daughter of the Rector of Woodchester, Gloucestershire. The match was arranged by Edward's cousin, Lucy Housman. Resolving that her favourite cousin should marry her closest friend, Lucy introduced them when he was on a visit to her family in Woodchester. The scheme succeeded, Edward Housman proposed and was accepted, and soon after brought his bride to live in The Valley House, close by his parents' home in Fockbury.

Their first child was born on 26 March 1859, and on 24 April was christened Alfred Edward. Six more children followed in the next nine years. Their careers proved unconventional for such a family: Robert became an engineer, Basil a doctor; Herbert abandoned his medical studies and enlisted as a private soldier. He rose to the rank of sergeant before dying in the Boer War. Katharine was the only one to have children; she married a schoolmaster, had four sons, and late in life wrote a scholarly history of her husband's school in Bath. Clemence Housman became an illustrator and won fame with a popular mystery novel, *The Werewolf.*

Laurence Housman was probably the most variously talented member of the family. Starting as an illustrator in the early eighteen-nineties he soon achieved a distinguished reputation. His interests however turned increasingly to writing, and in the course of a long life he produced many volumes of poems, stories and plays. He was virtually the inventor of a new dramatic form, the miniature play, complete in itself but constituting part of a set to be performed together. He achieved his greatest success in this medium with his Victorian *Palace Plays*, which made him briefly rich in the years before the Second World War. In addition to his prolific output of books, he gave nearly a lifetime of active devotion first to the women's suffrage movement and later to the cause of pacifism.

Alfred resembled Laurence only in the ability to write. Otherwise he was a complete contrast. Where Laurence was diffuse, impulsive and warm-hearted, Alfred was precise, disciplined and reserved. Laurence lavished his gifts on too many books, Alfred constricted his poems within the bounds of a tiny *oeuvre*. Laurence was always getting into trouble, Alfred carefully kept out of it. Laurence was a visionary and idealist, to whom his elder brother must at times have seemed a reactionary pedant.

The Housman family was orthodox—High Church, Tory, and, outwardly at least, somewhat puritanical. But despite a conventional upbringing in comfortable though unostentatious circumstances and amid pleasant surroundings, Alfred was early to be acquainted with trouble.

Soon after the birth of her seventh child, Sarah Housman became ill, probably with cancer. As she grew weaker and the pain increased, she was confined to her room, where Alfred, then ten or eleven years old, became her regular companion. He read to her, took letters at her dictation, talked with her, and received her confidences.

Meanwhile Edward Housman had turned from the misery of his wife and the clamour of his children to the pleasures of country sports and alcohol. He shut himself in his study, neglected his work, and lost all purpose.

In the Easter holidays of 1871 Alfred was given a break from the strain of home life and sent to stay with his mother's friends, the Wises of Woodchester. After a few days of delight with the three children of the family and their loved German governess, Sophie Becker, he was greeted by the news that his mother had died on his twelfth birthday. Though he was spared the pain of returning for her funeral, the weeks that followed it must have been an appalling period for him.

Two years later Edward Housman married his cousin Lucy. She was close on fifty at the time—eight years older than her husband—and must have been more than usually endowed with a sense of duty to take on a husband in decline and seven young children. Alfred, in whom the sense of duty was also strong, promised her his best help in bringing up the others, and so long as he remained at home he devoted much of his spare time to organising entertainments—usually instructive ones—for them. Lucy came to rely on him, and for the rest of her life he was her trusted friend and adviser.

At the age of eleven Alfred had become a day-boy at Bromsgrove School. He was well taught, and showed ability in Latin and Greek. In January 1875 he spent a few days away from his family on holiday in London, and it is from there that his first surviving letter is written.

To Lucy Housman

MS. U.C.L.

9 January [1875]   *London*

My dear Mamma,

I have now seen Oxford Street, Regent Street, Holborn, Cheapside, Cornhill, Piccadilly etc, but not much of the Strand. On Wednesday we went to Waterloo Place, Pall Mall and St James's Park, where I saw the band of the Grenadier Guards and some of the 1st Life Guards. We went to the Chapel Royal for service, — the queen's present was given by an attenuated person in gorgeous trimming, who Cousin Mary[1] thinks is an earl, as there was one of those coronets on his carriage. Then we went to Trafalgar Square, which is quite magical, and to Westminster. I explored the north transept where the statesman are, I looked at Pitt's and Fox's monuments and went into Poets' Corner. Service was at three, with an anthem by Greene which was like a boa constrictor—very long and very ugly. We had a beautiful one by Goss at the Chapel Royal in the morning.

On Thursday we went by omnibus to Holborn Viaduct, got out and walked about the City, we saw the little boy in Panyer Alley[2] and crossed Paternoster Row, which is not so narrow as you told me, after all; at St Paul's I went up to the golden gallery but Cousin Mary did not wish to repeat the experiment which she had tried before [and] remained on terra firma. They would not allow me to go into the iron gallery inside. The day was so foggy that one could scarcely see the other side of the river from the

---

[1] Lucy Housman's sister, Mary Theophania.
[2] Statue of a boy astride a bread basket, set up in 1868 to mark the highest ground in the City; now in the precincts of St Paul's Cathedral.

dome; and the mist had got into the Cathedral. We saw the Guildhall, Mansion House, Bank and Exchange, then the Monument, London Bridge and London stone. In the evening I went to *The Creation*[1] at the Albert Hall. Mme Lemmens-Sherrington, Vernon Rigby and Lewis Thomas. I think what charmed me most was 'By thee with Bliss'. Mme Lemmens-Sherrington has a most exquisite voice, so completely unaffected, but Mr Vernon Rigby's voice has not nearly power enough for that great building. I saw nothing more than the outline of the Albert Memorial. Though I was half an hour early, I could not get a seat in the shilling places, so I stood for the first part, and sat or lay on the floor for the rest. I was exactly opposite the orchestra and heard very well.

Yesterday I went to the British Museum and spent most of my time among the Greeks and Romans. I looked at your Venus—the Towneley Venus—in the alcove, but I do not admire her. What delighted me most was the Farnese Mercury. I examined some of the Nineveh bulls and lions, and I went through the zoological gallery. I met Cousin Henry[2] there, but he had only ten minutes to spare,—and those were of course geological. I have come to the conclusion, which you may tell the readers of *The Centre of the Earth*, that if the Mastodon and Megatherium were to fight it would decidedly be a very bad job for the Megatherium. I may also remark that the Ichthyosauri and Plesiosauri are by no means so large or terrific as those met by Professor Hardwigg[3] and Co.

To-day I am going to the Houses of Parliament, and to a ballad concert in the afternoon. On Monday the Zoological Gardens, and on Tuesday the South Kensington Museum.

I like the view from Westminster Bridge, and Trafalgar Square best of all the *places* I have seen, and I am afraid you will be horrified to hear that I like St Paul's better than Westminster Abbey; The Quadrant, Regent Street, and Pall Mall are the finest streets; but I think of all I have seen, what has most impressed me is—the Guards. This may be barbarian, but it is true.

I hope your cold is getting better. I am serenaded every morning by some cocks who crow as if their life depended upon it. If they were in my hands their life would depend upon it.

With love to my father and all I remain your affectionate son

A. E. HOUSMAN

[1] By Haydn.

[2] Lucy Housman's brother, the Rev. Henry Housman (1832–1912), at this time Curate of All Saints', Notting Hill, London; Lecturer at Chichester College, 1879–1912; Rector of Bradley, Worcestershire, 1898–1912.

[3] The reference is to Jules Verne's *Journey to the Centre of the Earth*. Professor Hardwigg is one of the main characters.

To Lucy Housman

MS. LILLY

Friday [postmark 29 January 1875]   *[Bromsgrove School][1]*

My dear Mamma,

I am very much obliged to you for sending 'Sir Walter Raleigh'[2] which I return, as you wished, now that I have copied it. I am also very much obliged for the *Standard* you sent me, though I am sorry to say that I did not go to that concert, for though I arrived there in plenty of time, all the shilling places were full, and I did not happen to have two shillings with me. However I went to Baker Street and saw Madame Tussaud's,[3] which I should not otherwise have had time to see, though of course I should have preferred the concert. It was however, in a great measure, a repetition of the one which I heard on the Saturday after I went to London; Santley,[4] especially, sang exactly the same songs.

Please thank Clemence for her letter and tell her that I am glad to hear that she has begun 'H', and that I hope she progresses with it. I hope that the glandular swellings of your two patients are abating, and that cook's appetite is reviving.

Yesterday I went into the churchyard, from which one can see Fockbury quite plainly, especially the window of your room. I was there from two o'clock till three. I wonder if you went into your room between those hours. One can see quite plainly the pine tree, the sycamore and the elm at the top of the field. The house looks much nearer than you would expect, and the distance between the sycamore and the beeches in the orchard seems very great, much longer than one thinks it when one is at Fockbury.

Give my love to my Father, and to my brothers and sisters and believe me, your affectionate son

ALFRED

To Lucy Housman

MS. U.C.L.

[Postmark 22 April 1875]   *[Fockbury House, Bromsgrove]*

My dear Mamma,
I cannot say
That much, since you have gone away,

---

[1] Housman boarded at Bromsgrove School while members of the family were in bed with scarlet fever.

[2] Housman's unsuccessful entry for the Bromsgrove School English verse prize, 1873. He won the competition in 1874 with 'The Death of Socrates'.

[3] The waxworks museum.

[4] Charles Santley (1834–1922), the most eminent baritone of the day; knighted, 1907.

Has happened to us, so of course
I must fall back on that resource,—
That great resource, which o'er the earth
Precedence holds, and which is worth
All other topics put together,
I mean, (I need not say) THE WEATHER.
The weather has been clear and bright,
The sun has shed a vivid light
So hot and torrid, that my stout
Aunt Mary[1] has not ventured out,
Until the shades of evening fall
And gentle moonbeams silver all,
When lunatics are wont to prowl
As also are the bat and owl.
Then to the shadowy garden fly
My relative and Clem and I.
Clemence becomes a fancied knight
In visionary armour dight
And waves her lance extremely well,
Terrific but invisible.
I turn into a dragon dire
Breathing imaginary fire,
Obscuring all the starry sky
With vapours seen by fancy's eye.
Aunt Mary is a hapless maid
Imprisoned in a dungeon's shade,
And spreading streams of golden hair
Impalpably upon the air.
Such is she 'neath the moon's pale ray,
But during all the burning day
At open window she has heard
The notes of many a chattering bird,
Receiving quite an education
From all this feathered conversation.
'Look here! Look here!' one of them cries,
'Peter' another one replies
(Perhaps a Roman Catholic bird),
And scarcely has he said this word
When one of more ferocious mind
Screams out in fury 'Whip behind!'
And scarcely has his clamour ceased
When shrieks arise of 'You're a beast!'

---

[1] Probably Edward Housman's sister, Mary Brettell Housman.

Another, rest one moment brings,
Saying, in French, pacific things,
Then one (piano) 'Pretty Dick!'
One more (crescendo) 'Quick! Quick! Quick!
(Forte) Look here! Look here!' once more,
And so da capo, as before.

Far other sounds thine ears delight,
Far other shapes are in thy sight,
Where the pellucid Thames flows by
The towers of English liberty,
Where he of Stoke[1] brays forth his din,
(That famous ass in lion's skin),
Waves his umbrella high in vain
And shakes off dewdrops from his mane.
Or where, high rising over all,
Stands the Cathedral of St Paul
And in its shadow you may scan
Our late lamented ruler, Anne;
Or where the clouds of legend lower
Around the mediaeval Tower,
And ghosts of every shape and size
With throttled throats and staring eyes
Come walking from their earthy beds
With pillow cases on their heads
And various ornaments beside
Denoting why or how they died.
Or where all beasts that ever grew
All birds, all fish, all reptiles too
Are congregated at the Zoo.
Where singing turtles soothe the shade,
And mackerel gambol through the glade,
Where prisoned oysters fain would try
Their wonted flight into the sky,
And the fierce lobster in its rage
Beats its broad wings against its cage.
Or where soft music's rise and fall
Re-echoes through St James's Hall,
Or where of painting many a one
Adorn the House of Burlington,

---

[1] Edward Vaughan Kenealy, Irish barrister (1819–1880), notorious for his violent conduct of the case of Orton, the Tichborne claimant, was elected to the House of Commons for Stoke-on-Trent in February 1875. On 23 April he moved for a Royal Commission on the Tichborne case, but failed to win a single supporter.

Or where the gilded chariots ride
Resplendent through the Park of Hyde.
Or where, when he's been doomed to feel
Death from Laertes' poisoned steel,
The lifeless corpse of Hamlet draws
Resuscitation from applause;
Or where—
        You will perceive perhaps
These 'wheres' have come to a collapse;
'The waxen wings that flew so high'
Etcetera.

        Mamma, goodbye.

You will be glad to hear it told
Father has almost lost his cold,
Miss Hudd is *healthy*, and all we
Are well as we could wish to be.
Our love for you we all declare
And our relations at Kildare,[1]
Hopes for your pleasure in Lond**ó**n,
And I remain your loving son.

                  A.E.H.

At the age of seventeen Housman was elected to a scholarship at St John's College, Oxford, and in the autumn of 1877 he became an undergraduate.

His first years at Oxford were entirely successful; he worked hard, made friends and enjoyed life. In Honour Moderations, 1879, he was placed in the First Class. Lectures were of little interest to him, and he was horrified at the slapdash scholarship of some of the dons. He was already immersing himself in the study of textual criticism, and early in his time at the university he began the ambitious task of editing Propertius. During these years he was in correspondence with the great Cambridge Latinist, H. A. J. Munro, the only English critic of the time he whole-heartedly admired.

With his strong Conservative and High Church background, Housman found the antics of the Oxford Union and of Oxford Anglicanism continuously amusing. His sense of fun showed not only in his letters home but also in his contributions to *Ye Rounde Table*, an undergraduate periodical in which his first humorous verses appeared.

The impression he made on those around him was that of a well-behaved young man, studious and orderly, and anything but the commoner type of

[1] The house in Hereford belonging to Lucy Housman's family; she went to live there after her husband's death in 1894.

drinking, hunting and whoring rowdy. In fact he passed through Oxford
without getting into trouble or debt.

To Lucy Housman

MS. U.C.L.

Sunday [*21 October 1877*]   *St John's College, Oxford*

My dear Mamma,

The ceremony of Matriculation, which you want to hear about, was as
follows. At a quarter to five on the Saturday afternoon all the freshmen of this
college, twenty-two in number, were collected in Mr Ewing's[1] rooms, and
were there instructed how to write our names in Latin in the Vice-
Chancellor's book. Alfred, he said, became Alfredus, Edward, Edvardus, and
so on; the surnames of course remaining unchanged. Then he marched us off
to New College, where we found the Vice-Chancellor[2] seated in dim
religious light at the top of the hall. Another college was just concluding the
ceremony, and when they had finished, we one by one inscribed our names
in a large book, in this wise. 'Alfredus Edvardus Housman, e Coll. Di. Joh.
Bapt. Gen. Fil. natu max.' which is, being interpreted, 'A. E. Housman, of the
College of St John the Baptist, eldest son of a gentleman'. Sons of clergymen
write 'Cler. Fil.' and sons of officers write 'arm. fil.' Then I wrote my name
in English in a smaller and less dignified book, and then paid £2 10s. 0d. to
a man at the table, and then we sat down one by one in a row till all had
written their names and paid their fee. Then an attendant brought in twenty-
two copies of the Statutes of the University, bound in violet, and piled them
on the table, hiding the Vice-Chancellor from the eye. Presently his head
appeared over the top, and we got up and stood in a sort of semicircle in front
of him. Then he called up each of us by name and presented each with a copy
of the Statutes, and with a paper on which was written in Latin, or what
passes for Latin at Oxford:—

'At Oxford, in the Michaelmas term A.D. 1877, on the 13th day of the
month of October: on which day Alfred Edward Housman of the College
of St John the Baptist, gentleman's son, appeared in my presence, and was
admonished to keep the laws of this University, and was enrolled in the
register (matricula) of the University.

> J. E. Sewell
> Vice-Chancellor'

[1] Robert Ewing (1847–1908), Tutor of St John's College, 1872; Rector of Winterslow,
Wiltshire, 1889; Canon of Salisbury Cathedral, 1905.
[2] James Edwards Sewell (1810–1903), Warden of New College, 1860–1903; Vice-
Chancellor of the University, 1874–1878.

Then he settled his gown over his shoulders and said, 'Gentlemen of St John's College, attend to me.' We attended. He said, in Latin, 'Allow me to inform you that you have this day been enrolled in the register of the University, and that you are bound to keep all the statutes contained in this book' (with the violet cover) 'as far as they may concern you.' Then we went. As to keeping the statutes contained in the violet cover, you may judge what a farce that is when I tell you that you are forbidden to wear any coat save a black one, or to use fire-arms, or to trundle a hoop, among other things.

I went to Mr Warren[1] at Magdalen yesterday. I am going to him three times a week. Then I have nine lectures a week in college besides. Two men have invited me to breakfast next week, and Mr Ewing has asked me to tea to-day along with several others, apropos of some Sunday-Night Essays, which are read by him and others in his rooms and at which he invites us to attend. Reginald Horton[2] called on me the other day: he is a Commoner a Worcester, and lives in the vicinity, with his wife and children. He asked me to remember him kindly to my father.

I hear that the gale did dreadful damage at the School. I am very glad that we suffered so comparatively little. I was afraid those beeches in the orchard would go. With many thanks for your letter, which is dutifully burnt, and with love to my father and all, I remain your loving son

ALFRED E. HOUSMAN, or, as the Vice-Chancellor with superior scholarship writes,—Al*u*redus Edvardus etc.

To Lucy Housman

MS. U.C.L.

Thursday [*Postmark 29 November 1877*]　　　　　　　　*St John's College*

My dear Mamma,

Thanks for the Bromsgrove papers. This letter is indited at the Union, pending the beginning of the debate; please therefore excuse its probable disjointedness. Nothing very remarkable has happened. I go to Ruskin's lectures, which end on Saturday.[3] I have received the great-coat, which is

---

[1] Thomas Herbert Warren (1853–1930); Fellow of Magdalen College, 1877; President, 1885; Vice-Chancellor of the University, 1906–1910; knighted, 1914.

[2] 1852–1914; son of a Bromsgrove doctor; educated at Bromsgrove School; assistant curate at St Barnabas, Oxford, 1880; Vicar of Dymock, 1883; Canon of Gloucester Cathedral, 1902.

[3] John Ruskin (1819–1900) was Slade Professor of Fine Art at Oxford, 1870–1879.

very nice: though the weather has not been such as to cause me to use it. It has been raining a little at unexpected times, but nothing much recently; about a fortnight ago a great deal of rain fell, and the Cherwell and then the Isis were flooded, as they still remain, altering the landscape to a great extent, and making Oxford look very picturesque from the Berkshire side. In times when the floods were more frequent than they are now, it must have been almost a moated fortress.

This afternoon Ruskin gave us a great outburst against modern times. He had got a picture of Turner's, framed and glassed, representing Leicester and the Abbey in the distance at sunset, over a river. He read the account of Wolsey's death out of *Henry VIII*. Then he pointed to the picture as representing Leicester when Turner had drawn it. Then he said, 'You, if you like, may go to Leicester to see what it is like now. I never shall. But I can make a pretty good guess.' Then he caught up a paintbrush. 'These stepping-stones of course have been done away with, and are replaced by a be-au-ti-ful iron bridge.' Then he dashed in the iron bridge on the glass of the picture. 'The colour of the stream is supplied on one side by the indigo factory.' Forthwith one side of the stream became indigo. 'On the other side by the soap factory.' Soap dashed in. 'They mix in the middle—like curds,' he said, working them together with a sort of malicious deliberation. 'This field, over which you see the sun setting behind the abbey, is now occupied in a *proper* manner.' Then there went a flame of scarlet across the picture, which developed itself into windows and roofs and red brick, and rushed up into a chimney. 'The atmosphere is supplied—thus!' A puff and cloud of smoke all over Turner's sky: and then the brush thrown down, and Ruskin confronting modern civilisation amidst a tempest of applause, which he always elicits now, as he has this term become immensely popular, his lectures being crowded, whereas of old he used to prophesy to empty benches.

How he confuted the geological survey, and science in general, by the help of the college cook I have no time to tell you, but remain, with love to father and all, your affectionate son

ALFRED E. HOUSMAN

To Edward Housman

MS. U.C.L.

12 February [1878]   *St John's College*

My dear Father,

As this is likely to be a long letter, and as I have a good deal to tell you, I had better begin with a few little things that I may forget at the end. Please thank Mamma for the two *Bromsgrove Messengers* which I got this morning.

13

I sent a copy of the *Round Table*[1] to Mrs Wise, and the other day I had a letter from her, inviting me to go to Woodchester in the Easter Vacation. The weather is now clearer, though rather cold, and the roads are dry at last: the mud here is quite à la Gloucestershire.

Last Thursday a motion was brought on at the Union, to the following effect—That the Eastern policy of Lord Beaconsfield[2] has been from the first, and remains, utterly unworthy of the confidence of the country. This was moved by a Balliol Liberal. Mr Gladstone had been in Oxford a few days before, and a meeting was held at the Corn Exchange, where Mr Gladstone spoke, and, I believe, moved some motion or other. A good many undergraduates in the hall held up their hands against this motion. Some of them were turned out, but I suppose Mr Gladstone was disconcerted, for thereupon uprose Thorold Rogers,[3] who holds, or rather has just vacated, the Professorship of Political Economy, and can therefore perhaps be scarcely held accountable for his actions,—he rose from Mr Gladstone's side, and bade the rt. hon. gentleman be of good cheer, and pay no attention to 'dissipated undergraduates'. Now undergraduate Oxford was rather riled at this, and Professor Thorold Rogers, who goes by the name of the Beaumont Street Gorilla, was considerably groaned for at the anti-Russian demonstration last Saturday, of which more anon,—and on Thursday this opprobrious epithet was rankling in our hearts, and most were disposed to do anything to spite W.E.G. Owing to the excited state of the public mind, the attendance at the debate was tremendous: and then at the last moment before it began came those telegrams that the Russians were in Constantinople, and that Mr Forster[4] had withdrawn his amendment. The crush and the frantic excitement were such as the oldest inhabitant etc.

The debate began with most of the House perpendicular, and some floating off their legs. Private business was got through in speech and silence; and then the terms of the motion were read. Then ensued seven good minutes of storm and tempest, and the cheering and groaning were such that neither could roar down the other, and they ceased from pure exhaustion. Then the speech began. It was not violent, which was a mercy, and not rhetorical, which was a greater mercy still. The man was nothing of the

[1] An undergraduate periodical to which Housman contributed humorous verses. The first number was published on 2 February 1878.

[2] War between Russia and Turkey broke out in 1877. The policy of Lord Beaconsfield's government was to prevent Russian control of the Dardanelles by supporting Turkey; Mr Gladstone and the Liberals condemned the Turks for their persecution of the Armenian and Bulgarian Christians.

[3] James Edwin Thorold Rogers (1823–1890), Drummond Professor of Political Economy, 1862–1867 and 1888–1890; Member of Parliament, 1880–1886.

[4] William Edward Forster (1819–1886), Liberal Member of Parliament for Bradford, former member of the Cabinet and author of the Elementary Education Act, 1870, had put down an amendment to the Vote of Credit. He withdrew it on 7 February at the news that the Turks had surrendered the defences of Constantinople.

orator, but he was fluent, and very cool and impudent. The speech lasted an hour, but the greater part of this time was occupied by the speaking of the House, and not of the honourable member. I should not say that his remarks took more than twenty minutes, but they only cropped up as islets in the oceanic demonstration of opinion. About the middle of the speech, chairs were set on the dais usually reserved for speakers; then the back ranks made a rush forward, and more pressed in at the door: the poor new president[1] was always on his legs to maintain order, and only the orator's head could be seen, which occasioned suggestions that he should stand on the table:—rejected however, as savouring of stump oratory. There came then three other speakers, one for the motion and two against; the two were baldly bad, and the one was gaudily bad. Perhaps one bye-cause of the great throng was the belief that Baumann,[2] who is the best Union speaker, a Conservative, was going to speak. But he did not: the crowd diminished a little after the third speech: then, after the fourth speech, came the only glimmer of light in the darkness of debate: Burrows,[3] the popular buffoon. He was better than I have heard him. It was rather ludicrous to hear him say that this was not the first time it had been his duty to vindicate Lord Beaconsfield's character, and that he hoped it would not be the last. Not that he did, in reality, vindicate it at all. He merely stated that Lord Beaconsfield's fame was a thing that would come—and come—and come, when the honourable mover was gone—and gone—and gone. He then said that the honourable mover would rot. We must all rot. He did not however anticipate any precipitate action in that direction on the part of the honourable mover. Etc. etc.—sometimes slightly coarse, as you see, and sometimes really slightly witty. Then there came a priest from Keble, with an amendment which was precisely the same as the motion. He was a Liberal. Then a Conservative priest from Christ Church, in reply: then vociferations for a division. But there were several more speakers all the same. Then it was half past eleven. Then someone proposed the adjournment of the debate, and someone else seconded it. The President stated that twelve honourable members had informed him they wished to speak on the question, and that some of them had left the House in anticipation of the adjournment of the debate. This struck us as highly insolent on their part, and we determined to serve them out by refusing to adjourn, especially as we had our majority on the spot. The last straw was laid on the camel's back by Lord Lymington,[4] an ex-president, who stated that he

[1] The Hon. W. St John Brodrick (1856–1942); Member of Parliament, 1880–1906; Secretary of State for War, 1900–1903; for India, 1903–1905; Viscount Midleton, 1907.
[2] Arthur Anthony Baumann (1856–1936); President of the Union, Easter 1877; Member of Parliament, 1885–1886; editor of *The Saturday Review*, 1917–1921.
[3] Francis Robert Burrows (born 1856); Treasurer of the Union, 1878; President, 1879; assistant master at Blackheath School, 1883; author of books on the teaching of Geography.
[4] Newton Wallop, Viscount Lymington (1856–1917); Member of Parliament, 1880–1891; sixth Earl of Portsmouth, 1891; Under-Secretary for War, 1905–1908.

15

wanted to speak. His oratory is generally considered the one thing worse than death, and so the adjournment was negatived by a vast majority. The amendment was lost without a division. The division on the motion was—for the motion 68; against the motion 146,—majority against the motion—unheard in the transports of enthusiasm, and the general rush back to college; for you can only understand the patriotic state of excitement in which we were, when you consider that the division took place between ten and five minutes to twelve: and if you are not back in college at twelve the penalties, I believe, are something very fearful indeed.

I did not go to Gladstone: I did not discover he was in Oxford till the moment before. He was rather feeble, as he tried to be humorous, which was very unwise. I believe he was very fine at the Palmerston Club, in the passage where he described his antagonism to Lord Beaconsfield.

On Saturday night an anti-Russian demonstration was held in the Corn Exchange. I went, because Sir Robert Peel[1] was coming: he did not come; but I heard Alfred Austin.[2] The hall was crammed. The orators were late. First 'Rule Britannia' was sung by the crowd; latent English Liberalism testified by scattered hisses its decided objection to the marine rule of Britannia. Then we took up our parable and sang that we didn't want to fight, but by jingo, if we did, we'd got the ships, we'd got the men, we'd got the money too.[3] As a matter of fact we had not got the money yet, but that was immaterial; and growing impatience soon made it clear, by several 'mills' in the body of the hall, that when we *did* want to fight we could perfectly well dispense with money, and ships too, for the matter of that, in the attainment of our desire. When it was getting towards eight, the orators came. Then there was great cheering, and the Mayor was unheard, and Mr Hall,[4] member for the city of Oxford, (along with Sir William Harcourt!)[5] began to speak. Then there was much cheering again, and much desultory ejection of malcontent Liberals, at intervals, between which the orator struggled on. I was close to the platform, so I heard well. He said nothing worth remark, except that the Christians of Turkey hated one another with a hatred passing the love of woman. This I relished very much, especially as his wife was sitting beside him. Then came Sir Henry Drummond

---

[1] 1822–1895, son of Sir Robert Peel, the Prime Minister; Member of Parliament since 1850, originally Liberal, but since 1874 Liberal–Conservative, supporting Disraeli's Eastern policy.

[2] Poet and Conservative propagandist (1835–1913); Poet Laureate, 1896–1913.

[3] A music hall song by G. W. Hunt, made famous by G. H. Macdermott.

[4] Alexander William Hall (1838–1919), Conservative Member of Parliament for Oxford, 1874–1880 and 1885–1892.

[5] William George Granville Venables Vernon Harcourt (1827–1904), Liberal Member for Oxford since 1868; knighted on his appointment as Solicitor-General, 1873; Home Secretary, 1880–1885; Chancellor of the Exchequer, 1886 and 1892–1895; Leader of the Liberal Party, 1896–1898.

Wolff,[1] weak; then Mr Hanbury,[2] frantic, but gentlemanly: then Alfred Austin, pointed and clever, but insufficiently audible. These speeches formed the interlude to about a dozen patriotic ejections,—one being that of an eminent Liberal undergraduate who speaks much at the Union, and on this occasion attempted to scale the platform with an amendment. These ejections were vigorously prompted by a man on the platform with a long black beard. This I thought bad taste, so, as I was close to the platform, I caught hold of Sir Drummond Wolff,—selecting his left hand, because he wore a large gold ring upon it, and was therefore likely to consider it the most valuable portion of his frame—and told him that I thought we should have scored off Gladstone if we had abstained from following the ejective example set by this meeting, and I asked him whether he could not suppress the man with the black beard. But Sir Drummond Wolff was in a helpless state of imbecility, and could do nothing, and as Mr Hanbury looked as if he was going to faint after his oratorical exertions, and Alfred Austin was bent upon sitting immoveable and looking as much like Mr Disraeli as he could manage,—there was nothing to be done. But the result was a rather rowdy meeting. The motion—Conservative and Turk—was of course carried with acclamation, and then the meeting fought itself out of doors and culminated in the combustion of an effigy of Mr Gladstone just outside our college.

On the Sunday before last, Canon King[3] of Christ Church preached at St Mary's on 'binding and loosing'—a counterblast to Dean Stanley in the *Nineteenth Century*.[4] The sermon was unconscionably long, and considerably over our heads, brimming as it did with patristic learning, until, at the end of an hour and a quarter, he concluded with an apology to his younger brethren for having bored them, and giving as his reason that Our Lord grieved Peter,[5] which I did not quite see the force of. But I felt it was quite worth sitting still for an hour and a quarter to watch such an interesting personality. He is tall, but stoops; and haggard in the face but without grey hair; and his sermon was most masterly here and there. The exquisitely deprecating way and affected timidity with which he put his strongest points, and the mournful and apologetic modulation of his voice where he was pulling Dean Stanley to pieces, were really almost worthy of Disraeli, and not altogether unlike, were it not for the deadly earnest, which was rather detrimental to the oratorical effect.

[1] Henry Drummond Charles Wolff (1830–1908), former Civil Servant; knighted 1862; Conservative Member of Parliament, 1874–1880; subsequently Ambassador to Persia, Rumania and Spain.

[2] Robert William Hanbury (1845–1903); Conservative Member of Parliament, 1872–1880 and 1885–1903; President of the Board of Agriculture, 1900.

[3] The Rev. Edward King (1829–1910), a prominent High Churchman; Regius Professor of Pastoral Theology, 1873–1885; Bishop of Lincoln, 1885–1910.

[4] 'Absolution' by Arthur Penrhyn Stanley (1815–1881), Dean of Westminster, in *The Nineteenth Century*, January 1878.

[5] See St John 21. 18.

Last Sunday, Dean Church[1] in the morning. Dean Church, I regret to say it, is dull. He is very nice to look at, and particularly ethereal in countenance, and he speaks in earnest, and everything, but he is certainly tedious. I thought so last term, and now I am confirmed. In the afternoon, the Bishop of Manchester,[2] who commenced operations by blowing his nose, which is a rhetorical device he has apparently just found out, and which in the first ecstasy of novelty he uses with injudicious profusion. In the bidding prayer he prayed that this country might not be drawn into war. He took a text to the effect that when he saw devils being cast out, the Kingdom of God would be at hand. As he went on it became apparent that the first devil was the Turk. The second devil was the Pope, over whose death-bed the Bishop uttered a wild whoop of triumph,[3] and then proceeded to inveigh against the Romish Church, which inspired him with much despair, as it did not seem inclined to die. This part of the sermon was garnished with several quotations from Macaulay's essay on von Ranke's history of the Popes.[4] Now Canon Liddon[5] was present, and up to this point of course he must have found himself in unexpected sympathy with the Bishop,—on both the Turk and Rome. This was particularly kind on Dr Fraser's part, as, in the morning, Canon Liddon, in getting into the pew at the end of which the Bishop sat, had almost taken his seat on his Lordship's knees, for which the Bishop had rewarded him with a smile of such Christian forgiveness that Canon Liddon hastily made his way to the middle of the pew, and, taking up a prayer book, began to read it with an avidity and apparent sense of novelty which that interesting work does not often excite in the clergy of the Established Church of England. Well, the Bishop, having shown us a great deal of reason why the church of Rome was unlikely to go down quick into the pit, now began to give us a few slight crumbs of consolation, on which we might base a hope, though not a belief, that she would do so. And then he somehow got upon the subject of Ritualism and the Confessional in England. Poor Canon Liddon! He always sits with his hand over his face, so I could not see his emotions; but the revulsion of feeling must have been great, when the sermon which began so promisingly developed into this. But the Bishop was now far above Canons and all the inferior clergy. He began to plunge into eloquence, in which he rather staggered. He even began a sentence with 'Methinks,'—but got rather bewildered towards the end of it, and so found it time to conclude with a remark about freedom of conscience, which was calculated to bring down the house, and then blew his nose in the middle of the

---

[1] Richard William Church (1815–1890), Dean of St Paul's, 1871–1890.

[2] James Fraser (1818–1885); Tutor of Oriel College, 1842–1847; Bishop of Manchester, 1870–1885.

[3] Pope Pius IX died on 7 February 1878 after a Papacy of 32 years.

[4] In volume III of *Critical and Historical Essays*, 1850.

[5] Henry Parry Liddon (1829–1890), Canon of St Paul's Cathedral and the leading preacher there.

doxology or whatever you call it, to show how little trouble it had all cost him.

Here it is time to conclude these irrelevant recitals, which I hope will interest you a little. With love to Mamma and the rest, I remain your loving son

ALFRED E. HOUSMAN

P.S. The Union authorities decline to supply one with stamps up to more than a certain weight. Such is my wiliness that I intend to frustrate their parsimony by posting this letter in *two* envelopes, differently directed. I have numbered the sheets of this letter, that you may not be confused.

To Lucy Housman

MS. U.C.L.

[*15 March 1878*]   *St John's College*

My dear Mamma,

It was very good of you to write, for I believe as a matter of fact I owed you a letter. The reason why I have been so remiss lately is that I have been in for the Hertford,[1] the result being that I am among the first six, which is better than anyone else thought I should do, and better than I myself fancied I had actually done. I enclose Kate's letter which I have copied out with scrupulous accuracy, reproducing even the erasures of the marvellous work. If she chooses to compare it with my answer she will see how very closely and humbly I have trodden in her footsteps.

I am glad you are well enough to be about again. Lucky, considering youthful Louisas and unprotected dinner-plates. I expect I shall come back on Lady Day. I have called on Mrs Sankey.[2] The third *Round Table* will be out to-morrow. There will be a considerably larger number of writers in it than heretofore.

With best love I remain your loving son

ALFRED E. HOUSMAN

To Lucy Housman

MS. U.C.L.

Monday [*postmark 10 May 1880*]   *St John's College*

My dear Mamma,

You have seen by now that the strife is o'er, the battle done, the triumph

---

[1] The University Latin Scholarship.

[2] Mother of Housman's contemporary at Bromsgrove School, G. M. Sankey.

etc.[1] Last week of course has been a scene of great excitement: the campaign opened by the Vice-Chancellor announcing that any undergraduate who should take part in any political meeting would be fined £5, which was gall and wormwood to a pretty large number of Liberals especially, who had been promising themselves the honour and glory of standing by Sir William Harcourt on the platform and spreading the wings of the University over him: Conservative undergraduates were less hard hit, as they none of them can speak decently. Hall himself however is an undergraduate, the senior undergraduate of Exeter; whether they have fined him £5 I can't say. We had great fun with Mr Ewing who is one of the pro-Proctors this year; we told him we knew of an undergraduate who had spoken at every Conservative meeting during the election, which wrought him up to wild excitement till we mentioned the name Alexander William Hall, after which his ardour seemed to cool. All the nights there have been crowds of both parties promenading the streets and singing on the one hand Rule Britannia and on the other the following new and lovely lyric, composed I believe at the general election:—

> 'Hurrah! Hurrah!
> Two Liberals there shall be!
> Hurrah! Hurrah!
> For Harcourt and Chit*tee*!'[2]

On Friday they were chairing Harcourt from the station to a mass-meeting at the Martyrs' Memorial, just outside college; we kept shouting out of the front windows Hurrah for Hall, at which the crowd looked up and made the scathing rejoinder—'Yah! yer aint got no votes!' which I daresay however was just as true for them as for us. On Saturday (election day) both the candidates were driving about all over the town: Hall had got his infant sons in an open carriage with him, by way of appealing to the feelings. About midday there came out a flaming poster in the Liberal colour (red) announcing that 'Frank Hedges had been detected endeavouring to record his vote twice and was now in custody.' This I believe was true: but there instantly came out a blue placard that 'Frank Hedges had *not* recorded his vote twice and was now pursuing his ordinary avocations' which was also true, as Frank Hedges, whoever he may be, had of course only *tried* to record his vote twice, and had since been bailed off. At about a quarter to seven the poll was declared with a

[1] An allusion to the well-known hymn by Francis Pott (1832–1909). The General Election of March–April 1880 had been won by the Liberals. Sir William Harcourt, who had held Oxford, now submitted himself for re-election on his appointment as Home Secretary and was defeated by A. W. Hall.

[2] Joseph William Chitty (1828–1899); Fellow of New College, 1852; called to the Bar, 1856; Member of Parliament for Oxford 1880; appointed a Judge of the High Court and knighted, 1881; Lord Justice of the Court of Appeal, 1897.

Conservative majority of 54, and immediately afterwards the numerous spectators crowded round the front of the Roebuck, Hall's headquarters, observed an exciting scene. This was Mr Hall at the centre window endeavouring to burst on to the balcony, and restrained by arm after arm thrown round his chest by his committee-men who dare not let him speak a word in that state of excitement. At intervals you saw him saying 'I will speak to them!' and breaking from his keepers halfway out of the window, and then he would be overwhelmed again and disappear. Finally one of his committee came out instead: this gentleman's eloquence was confined to taking off his hat and whirling it round his head, and directing frightful grimaces of scorn and derision at the Randolph where Sir William Harcourt was. That evening we were forbidden to leave college after seven; but a good many got over that by leaving before seven: and we were also forbidden to look out of the windows or in any way attract the attention of the mob; however we blew horns out of the windows in great profusion, and on one of the dons coming round to demand the offending instrument he was presented with an aged and decrepit horn which had no inside and would not blow: so that in the morning he restored it with an apology, saying that he thought he must have made a mistake, as he could not make it give out any sound at all. We heard Sir William Harcourt booming away from the Randolph opposite, and he drove off for the first train with a bodyguard of six policemen, but we could not make out what he said; he said however that he bore no ill-feeling etc. etc., so I suppose there will not be a petition, though of course this morning everyone is talking about bribery, just as I believe they did after the last Election.[1] The Searanckes[2] are in Oxford; they arrived in the thick of it on Saturday afternoon and were conveyed to the Randolph in a scarlet-streamered omnibus intended for voters: Mr Searancke contrived to make his way into Harcourt's committee room while he was making his speech at the window: he says he looked utterly upset and taken aback and was even on the verge of tears (taken aback by the poll, I mean, not by Mr Searancke's entrance). I am going to dine with them to-morrow: they stay here probably till Thursday. At the Randolph they have fallen in with a Mr Moss,[3] member for Winchester, who turns out to be an old friend of Mr Searancke's, and who says that the Provost of Eton[4] told him that Princess Christian[5] told him that 'Mr Gladstone had forgotten that mamma was a lady, and had forgotten that she was his queen.' They were in Italy about seven weeks and came home

[1] A commission of inquiry into corrupt practices was appointed and Hall's election declared void on petition.
[2] Not identified.
[3] Richard Moss (1823–1905), Secretary (later Chairman) of the Country Brewers' Society; Member for Winchester, 1850–1885 and 1888–1892.
[4] The Rev. Charles Old Goodford (1812–1884); Headmaster of Eton College, 1853; Provost, 1862.
[5] Princess Helena (1846–1923), daughter of Queen Victoria, wife of Prince Christian of Schleswig-Holstein.

earlier than they intended for the Elections. Have they made Mr Vernon[1] a baronet yet as the wages of sin? I see by the papers you sent you have been having a fine exciting fire, and Stillman[2] tells me Edith Sanders[3] is engaged to be married: so? As I don't see a letter-weight anywhere in sight and am not clear about the weight of one of these sheets of paper, I shall employ two envelopes and put the Union Society to the expense of an extra penny. Give my love to my father and all and believe me ever your loving son

ALFRED E. HOUSMAN

The gap of five years which falls before the next letter covers the unhappiest time of Housman's life. 'The troubles of my early manhood', he later said, 'were real and great.'

In his last year at Oxford Housman shared lodgings with two friends, A. W. Pollard and Moses Jackson. Jackson was a brilliant scientist, certain of a First, tall, well-built, handsome and self-confident. Housman, short, shy and undistinguished in appearance, worshipped him. Too clear-headed and honest to deceive himself about the nature of this absorption, he was also too well trained in conventional morality to accept it with resignation. The evidence of his poetry suggests that he was overwhelmed with shame. His Christian faith had gone at the age of thirteen, when he became a deist; by twenty-one he was an atheist. At heart he defied the world; but outwardly, circumstances and a naturally conformist temper of mind preserved an appearance of rigid propriety. He hid his emotions and for the rest of his life felt the bitterness of the frustration.

How far this trouble affected Housman's work cannot be known. He was much occupied with Propertius, but the ancient history and philosophy which he had to read for Greats did not interest him at all, and he simply ignored them.

If this was a calculated risk, it was very badly calculated; if it was mere thoughtlessness, it is almost incredibly out of character. But whatever the reason for his folly, his judgment was no doubt undermined by depression at the news of his father's illness. In the examinations Housman barely attempted to answer the questions on the neglected work, and he was automatically failed.

It was a terrible disaster. Housman had to leave Oxford without a degree. His family, reduced to bare respectability by the fecklessness of Edward

[1] Harry Foley Vernon of Hanbury Hall, Droitwich (1834–1920), Member for East Worcestershire, 1861–1868, created a baronet in 1885. He was a cousin of Lucy Housman.
[2] William Beaufoy Stillman (1857–1903), Housman's contemporary at Bromsgrove School, at this time an undergraduate of Worcester College, Oxford; Rector of Downham Market, Norfolk, 1894.
[3] Not identified.

Housman (who in the spring of 1881 suffered a stroke from which he never fully recovered), had made sacrifices for Alfred's education, confident that when it was completed he could earn enough to help to pay for that of his younger brothers. He now had to return home without a job or any great prospect of one, to face the silent reproaches of his family as best he could, while reading to pass the Civil Service examination.

He stayed for a year, earning at least his keep by helping with Sixth Form teaching at Bromsgrove School. In 1882, equipped with a humble pass degree, he obtained a Higher Division Clerkship in the Patent Office at a salary of £100 a year.

Moving to London he settled in lodgings with Moses Jackson and his younger brother Adalbert in Bayswater. Moses Jackson also was in the Patent Office as an Examiner of Electrical Specifications. The arrangement seems to have worked well, and it lasted for three years. Why it ended is not known, but by December 1885 Housman had moved from 82 Talbot Road to another part of Bayswater, and in the following year he took lodgings in Highgate which he retained until 1905.

Meanwhile Housman resumed his classical researches with determination. Denied the possibility of a college fellowship and the leisure to write as he pleased, he now gave all his time after office hours to work in the British Museum. He had already produced his first paper, 'Horatiana', published in *The Journal of Philology* in 1882. His next task was to complete his edition of Propertius. After three years the text and apparatus criticus were ready. The book was rejected by Macmillan, the first publisher to whom it was offered, and after that Housman seems to have done nothing more about it, though he published the most important of his conjectures in 1888. From that date onwards he produced a magisterial series of papers on both Greek and Latin subjects, and within a few years he had become widely known among scholars, abroad as well as in England, as the author of many brilliant emendations and a widely read and penetrating critic.

To Lucy Housman

MS. U.C.L.

29 March 1885 *82 Talbot Road, Bayswater*

My dear Mamma,

I was delighted to get your long letter on the 26th: it was quite the best epistle I have ever seen, with the possible exception of the second of the apostle Paul to the Corinthians. The violets also were very sweet: I don't know whether St Paul used to enclose violets. Also please thank my father for his letter. Clemence and Laurence sent me a postcard with a very lovely drawing on the

23

back, representing Cherubim and Seraphim continually crying, and an inscription in Spanish or Portuguese, I think.

I saw the boat race yesterday, from the Thames boat house at Putney this time, so that I saw the start. It was a perfect day, beautiful sunshine but not too hot. There were many objects of interest on the river besides the crews: especially boats with brilliantly coloured sails displaying advertisements of various newspapers and theatres. There were much fewer people than usual, at least at Putney, and *very* little wearing of colours. Palm branches seemed to be the commonest decoration among the lower orders. The blue which they wore was a very artful shade, which could be made out to be either Oxford or Cambridge with equal plausibility, whichever might happen to win.[1]

Last Sunday morning there was a rather deep fall of snow here, but it soon melted. It is almost the only specimen of snow we have had all the winter.

The juvenile son of a friend of mine at the Office has the loftiest ambition I ever heard tell of. When he goes to heaven, which he regards as a dead certainty, he wants to be *God*, and is keenly mortified to learn that it is not probable he will. However his aspirations are now turning into another channel: it has come to his knowledge, through the housemaid, that the devil has horns and a tail; and in comparison with these decorations the glories of heaven have lost their attractiveness.

I will go and see Basil when he comes to town. I suppose he is going to stay with C. and L. I should think his most convenient place to dine when at the College would be the restaurant of the Inns of Court Hotel, just on the opposite side of Lincoln's Inn Fields. I daresay he will not be too much occupied to go to a theatre with me some evening.

An elaborate new Index of Trade Marks is being compiled at the Office. It goes on very remarkable principles which I do not quite understand. Under the head of 'Biblical Subjects' is included an old monk drinking out of a tankard; and the Virgin Mary and St John the Baptist are put among 'Mythical Figures'.

I hope you and your household are well; and with love to my father and all I remain your loving son

A. E. HOUSMAN

To Lucy Housman

MS. U.C.L.

10 June 1885   *82 Talbot Road*

My dear Mamma,

You would never guess what I was doing on Tuesday week: serving on a Coroner's Jury. This comes of having one's name on the register of voters.

[1] Oxford won by a length and a quarter.

Civil Servants I believe are exempt from serving on ordinary Juries, but not on Coroners'. Of course for once in a way it is rather amusing, and it is not likely to happen oftener than about once in four years. We sat on five bodies: one laundryman who tied a hundred-weight to his neck and tipped over into the water-butt; one butcher's man who cut his throat with a rusty knife and died a week after of erysipelas (moral: use a clean knife on these occasions); one old lady who dropped down in a fit; one baby who died in convulsions; and one young woman who died of heart disease after eating spring onions for supper. I really do not know what is the good of a jury or of witnesses either: the Coroner does it all: his mind seemingly is lighted by wisdom from on high, so he tells the Jury what their verdict is and the witnesses what their evidence is: if they make mistakes he corrects them. The butcher's man had a brother-in-law: he looked radiantly happy: a member of his family had distinguished himself, and he was revelling in the reflected glory.

I think if there were an Inquest held on this Government of ours the verdict would have to be deliberate suicide: there does not seem to have been the least reason why they should have been beaten unless they wanted it.[1] I should say whether they go out or not the whole affair will do a lot of damage to the Conservatives, because if they take office before the election they will have a fearful muddle to deal with, and if they do not, everyone will call them unpatriotic.

Who is the Mr Seymour who is your vicar elect?[2] I had not heard of the appointment.

There was a mild sort of scare at the Office the other day: a loud bang which collected quite a crowd. Civil Servants in these days of course live in hourly expectation of being blown up by dynamite for political reasons,[3] and the Patent Office has the further danger of the ingenious and vindictive inventor of explosives, who might try to lay the place in ruins if his patent did not go on smoothly. The room I sit in is considered the likeliest place, because it has a charming deep area outside which looks as if it was made to drop dynamite into; so when this explosion was heard, several people came trooping into the room in hopes of finding corpses weltering in their gore. However they had to go empty away: I believe the noise was really the firing of a charge of powder in a neighbouring chimney to bring the soot down.

I hope you have not been drowned in the last few days: the state of

---

[1] Mr Gladstone's Government was defeated by twelve votes in the Budget division on 8 June 1885, seventy-six Liberals having failed to attend. The Government resigned the next day. The Conservatives formed a Government under Lord Salisbury but lost the General Election held in November–December 1885.

[2] The Rev. Albert Eden Seymour became Vicar of Bromsgrove in 1885.

[3] In 1884–1885 Irish terrorists campaigning for independence organised a series of dynamite explosions in London. In January 1885 they tried to blow up the House of Commons and the Tower.

London you will have seen from the papers. Love to my father and the rest and believe me always your loving son

A. E. HOUSMAN

To Messrs Macmillan and Company[1]

MS. MACMILLAN

11 December 1885 *39 Northumberland Place,*
Bayswater

Gentlemen,

I propose that you should, if you think fit, publish my recension of the text of Propertius, a specimen of which, consisting of the first book with its apparatus criticus, I send by the same post with this letter. There are few authors for whose emendation and explanation so much remains to be done. The collation by Baehrens, in his edition of the text in 1880, of four important MSS previously overlooked has in a measure rendered obsolete all texts preceding or simultaneous with his own; while he himself was prevented, partly by haste and partly by a very natural bias of judgment, from making a really scientific use of his materials. No commentary possessing original value, with the exception of Mr Postgate's *Selections*,[2] has been published since Hertzberg's of 1845. Six years ago I formed the design of producing an edition and commentary which should meet the requirements of modern critical science, and have now completed the first of these two tasks:—the emended text accompanied by a register of such among the MS readings as are of import for constituting the words of the author or for classifying the MSS themselves. The collection and arrangement of materials for the commentary will naturally demand further time and labour; and I therefore judge it best that the text with its apparatus criticus should be issued separately, especially as I annually find not a few of my corrections anticipated by German scholars in philological periodicals.

I am, Gentlemen, Yours faithfully A. E. HOUSMAN[3]

[1] The distinguished firm of publishers, who ten years later were to reject *A Shropshire Lad* and, in 1924, Housman's edition of Lucan.

[2] *Select Elegies of Propertius*, edited by J. P. Postgate, 1881.

[3] The firm replied on 14 December that 'after due consideration' they could not accept the book. Housman seems to have made no further attempt to publish it. His emendations appeared, together with a commentary on Book I 1, in *The Journal of Philology*, 1888; his studies of the manuscripts were published *ibidem* and in *The Classical Review*, 1893–1895. The text and apparatus criticus were found among Housman's papers after his death and destroyed in accordance with his directions.

To Mrs Wise[1]

MS. LILLY

30 July 1890   *Byron Cottage, 17 North Road, Highgate*

My dear Mrs Wise,

Here I am (or, as our lively neighbour the Gaul would say, me voilà arrivé). I had a very good journey (bon voyage), as the weather improved and I found a through carriage to London (Londres) so that there was no need to change at Swindon (Swindres), after which the train stopped nowhere, not even at Reading (Lisant). My stay at Woodchester was 'brief but delightful' like the lady in Byron who died young.[2] Please make my apologies to Sarah and Martha for going away without saying goodbye: but I was told that Martha was upstairs, which from what I know of her character probably meant on the roof, whither I did not venture to follow her; while Sarah was said to be amongst her fowls, where I sought her in vain. I enclose a cloak room ticket for Miss Becker[3] and also a poem which I have written in her own beautiful language: please tell her this, because otherwise perhaps she may not know it: I assure her that it is the fact. Give my love to all, or at least to all to whom it may with propriety be given, and believe me yours affectionately

A. E. HOUSMAN

To the Registrar of Trade Marks[4]

MS. CAMBRIDGE

9 October 1890   *Trade Marks Branch, H.M.*
Patent Office

Sir,

The Administrative Principal, Mr Webb,[5] has to-day taken up the comparison of Trade Mark applications. We beg most strongly to protest against his assumption of work in this Branch of the Office. We believe that it is quite

---

[1] Mother of Housman's three friends, Edith, Minnie and Edward Wise of Woodchester. She was the close friend of Housman's mother, during whose last illness he had stayed with her. He continued to visit the house regularly for many years.

[2] See *Don Juan* IV. lxxi. 6.

[3] Sophie Becker (died 1931), a German governess employed by the Wise family. She became Housman's close friend and confidante. She returned to Germany before the First World War.

[4] This letter, written in Housman's hand, was clearly drafted by him on behalf of the other signatories. It appears to be the only surviving specimen of his Patent Office correspondence.

[5] Philip George Lancelot Webb (1856–1937); Clerk in Patent Office, 1880; Principal, 1890; Assistant Comptroller, 1920. His *Poems* appeared in 1927, and he also published three volumes of translations from Goethe and Heine.

unusual that an officer should, without the most formal authorisation, take up a position in a Department other than that to which he belongs. In the present case such a course seems to us particularly objectionable because the position as Principal held by Mr Webb would give him a status not justified either by length of service or by acquaintance with the details of the work of this Branch. The present moment, moreover, seems particularly inopportune, since of late the amount of comparison work has not been sufficient to occupy the ordinary staff, one of whom has in consequence been filling up his time with other work. You are also aware that the question is now before the Comptroller whether one of the three present First Division men in the Trade Marks Department can be spared for transfer to another Office, and it therefore does not appear probable that the Department would be considered entitled to the services of a fourth.

We have the honour to be, Sir, Your obedient servants

F. W. H. DAVIES

FRANCIS WM. HODGES

A. E. HOUSMAN

H. C. A. TARRANT

During the later eighteen-eighties Housman's life had undergone some important changes. In 1887 Moses Jackson had left the Patent Office to become headmaster of a school in India. The parting with Housman was stiff and dry (*More Poems* XXXI); they met again when Jackson returned two years later to marry before settling for the rest of his life in India and Canada.

Housman's growing reputation brought an invitation to join the Cambridge Philological Society in 1889 and the friendship of a leading member, Henry Jackson, Fellow of Trinity College.

It would probably have been possible for Housman to have obtained some sort of academic employment much sooner, but he chose to wait until one of the better posts became vacant before making any attempt. In 1892 he applied for the Chair of Latin at University College, London, and despite his unconventional career he was recognised as the best candidate.

The news evoked a tribute from one of his Patent Office colleagues that Housman treasured to the end of his life:[1] 'I got your testimonials this morning, and shortly afterwards I found that your name was in *The Times* as Professor of Latin to London University. I am as delighted with your success as though I had got something for myself. Now mind, that's saying as much as one can say for anyone else's good fortune. W[ebb]'s remark that your success was a score for the Office excited my anger. I told him that it was a score for you, and that it was nothing at all for the infernal Office. It is funny

[1] Text from *Memoir*. The writer, John Maycock, died in 1910.

28

to think how I used to chaff you about your work producing no money, and all the time you were working silently on, with that strength of purpose which I can admire but can't imitate . . . As a rule English people never allow themselves to say or write what they think about anyone, no matter how much of a pal he may be. Well, I am going to let myself loose. I like you better than any man I ever knew. There is, as far as I could ever discover, absolutely no flaw in your character as a man. I don't say this only on my own account, but I have seen how you can stick to a friend like you have to Jackson. I mean not stick to him in the sentimental sense of not forgetting him although he is right out of your reach. I have always, besides liking you so much, had a great respect for your learning. I always do respect a man that can do anything well. Now your work has produced for you substantial honour, I feel proud of your success, and I hope that you will be much happier altogether. I know you must naturally feel proud. If you don't, you are a duffer. One doesn't get too many moments of elation in this life, so don't check the feeling when you have it. The testimonials are wonderfully good. At one o'clock or thereabouts, Kingsford and I will drink a glass of the old Falernian to your long life and increasing prosperity. Dear old pal, I'm as pleased as if I'd done something good myself.'

In accordance with the custom of University College it fell to Housman as junior professor to deliver an address to mark the opening of the academic year to the assembled lecturers and undergraduates. It was the first time he had had to speak in public, and composing the lecture troubled him through-out the summer. But when he came to deliver it he was immediately recog-nised as an excellent speaker, and the College paid him the compliment of having the speech printed and distributed.

To the Council of University College, London[1]

19 April 1892   *H.M. Patent Office, London*

My Lords and Gentlemen,

I have the honour to present myself as a candidate for the vacant Professor-ship of Latin in University College. If however the Latin chair should be conferred on another I would ask to be considered as an applicant in that event for the Professorship of Greek.[2]

I am thirty-three years of age. I entered the University of Oxford as a scholar of St John's College in 1877; in 1879 I was placed in the first class in

[1] The text of this letter is taken from the pamphlet, printed by the Cambridge Univer-sity Press, containing also the testimonials in support of Housman's application.
[2] The Chairs had been held jointly by Alfred Goodwin. On his death the Council decided to separate the two appointments. Housman's candidature was supported by an imposing array of scholars including Robinson Ellis, Henry Jackson, A. W. Verrall and N. Wecklein. The Professorship of Greek was given to William Wyse.

the Honour School of Classical Moderations; in 1881 I failed to obtain honours in the Final School of Litterae Humaniores. I have since passed the examinations required for the degree of B.A., and am of standing to take the degree of M.A. in the event of my appointment to a Professorship. In 1881 and 1882 I was for some time engaged in teaching the sixth form at Bromsgrove School, and in the latter year I obtained by open competition a Higher Division Clerkship in Her Majesty's Patent Office, which I now hold. During the last ten years the study of the Classics has been the chief occupation of my leisure, and I have contributed to the learned journals many papers on ancient literature and critical science, of which the following are the most important.

Latin. In the *Journal of Philology*: 'Horatiana', vols. X, XVII and XVIII; 'Emendationes Propertianae', vol. XVI; 'On a Vatican Glossary', vol. XX. In the *Classical Review*: 'Notes on Latin Poets', vols. III and IV; 'Adversaria Orthographica', vol. V. In the *Transactions of the Cambridge Philological Society*: 'Emendations in Ovid's Metamorphoses', vol. III.

Greek. In the *Journal of Philology*: 'The Agamemnon of Aeschylus', vol. XVI; 'Sophoclea', vol. XX. In the *American Journal of Philology*: 'On certain corruptions in the Persae of Aeschylus', vol. IX. In the *Classical Review*: 'Σωφρόνη', vol. II; 'Emendations in the Medea of Euripides', vol. IV.

I have also published translations from the Attic tragedians into English verse in Mr A. W. Pollard's *Odes from the Greek Dramatists* (Stott, 1890).[1]

If I am honoured by your choice I shall give my best endeavours to the fulfilment of my duties and to the maintenance of accurate learning in University College.

I have the honour to be, My Lords and Gentlemen, Your obedient servant,

A. E. HOUSMAN

To the Editor of The Standard[2]

12 March 1894   *17 North Road*

Sir,

In August 1886 Highgate Wood became the property of the Mayor and Commonalty and Citizens of the City of London. It was then in a very sad state. So thickly was it overgrown with brushwood, that if you stood in the centre you could not see the linen of the inhabitants of Archway Road

---

[1] A volume of verse translations by English scholars. A. W. Pollard (1859–1944), one of Housman's close friends at Oxford, entered the Department of Printed Books in the British Museum in 1883; Keeper, 1919–1924; Professor of Bibliography at King's College, London, 1919–1932.

[2] Text from *The Standard*, 14 March 1894.

hanging to dry in their back gardens. Nor could you see the advertisement of Juggins's stout and porter which surmounts the front of the public house at the south corner of the wood. Therefore the Mayor and Commonalty and Citizens cut down the intervening brushwood, and now when we stand in the centre we can divide our attention between Juggins's porter and our neighbours' washing. Scarlet flannel petticoats are much worn in Archway Road, and if anyone desires to feast his eyes on these very bright and picturesque objects, so seldom seen in the streets, let him repair to the centre of Highgate Wood.

Still we were not happy. The wood is bounded on the north by the railway to Muswell Hill; and it was a common subject of complaint in Highgate that we could not see the railway from the wood without going quite to the edge. At length, however, the Mayor and Commonalty and Citizens have begun to fell the trees on the north, so that people in the centre of the wood will soon be able to look at the railway when they are tired of the porter and the petticoats. But there are a number of new red-brick houses on the east side of the wood, and I regret to say that I observe no clearing of timber in that direction. Surely, Sir, a man who stands in the centre of the wood, and knows that there are new red-brick houses to the east of him, will not be happy unless he sees them.

Sir, it is spring: birds are pairing, and the County Council has begun to carve the mud-pie which it made last year at the bottom of Waterlow Park. I do not know how to address the Mayor and Commonalty; but the Citizens of the City of London all read the *Standard*, and surely they will respond to my appeal and will not continue to screen from my yearning gaze any one of those objects of interest which one naturally desires to see when one goes to the centre of a wood.

I am, Sir, your obedient servant   A.E.H.

To Laurence Housman

TEXT: MEMOIR

14 December 1894   *17 North Road*

My dear Laurence,

I have got your poems[1] into what seems to me a rough order of merit. "Love-bound Time" I think is the most original, and it is very well written and quite as lucid as one can expect; though I rather doubt if the English language will allow the stanza beginning 'Beauty may to beauty err' to mean anything in particular: however, it sounds nice. "Prisoner of Carisbrooke"

---

[1] The manuscript of Laurence Housman's first volume of poems, *Green Arras*, published in 1896.

31

ought certainly to be included, as it has more root in earth than most of its author's lays, and occupies the proud position of distinctly meaning something from beginning to end: also I think it good in itself, though 'well-water' is rather neiges d'antan. "The Three Kings" is very good verse, except the end of the 12th stanza and the second line of the 13th; in the 14th too I don't like 'this tells', though I am afraid that cannot be altered without sacrificing 'Earth, Earth, Earth', on which you have probably set your young affections. Poems on pictures seem to me an illegitimate genre, but "Autumn Leaves" is a favourable specimen. . . . 'At the undarkening of days' might be made into something, but it would take a lot of making: at present it is not only so obscure as to suggest that the poet does not quite know what he would be at, but fearfully untidy into the bargain: for instance, one cannot put an accent on the first syllable of 'interrogation'; and if 'hopen' means 'holpen' it does not rhyme with 'open'. I doubt if "The Sleep of the Gods" signifies much. "Blind Fortune" and "The King's Gifts" I should decidedly leave out, and, for my own part, the remaining pieces; these show a certain proficiency, in a certain style, which shall wax old as doth a garment:[1] still, I daresay some will admire them: your Scotch friend very likely, who draws large cats. I would die many deaths rather than use such words as 'a-croon' and 'a-saw'; but that holy man St Jerome very truly observes 'nemo tam imperitus scriptor est qui lectorem non inveniat similem sui' (the worst hand at writing in the world is sure to find some reader of his own kidney).

What makes many of your poems more obscure than they need be is that you do not put yourself in the reader's place and consider how, and at what stage, that man of sorrows is to find out what it is all about. You are behind the scenes and know all the data; but he knows only what you tell him. It appears from the alternative titles "Heart's Bane" and "Little Death" that in writing that precious croon you had in your head some meaning of which you did not suffer a single drop to escape into what you wrote: you treat us as Nebuchadnezzar did the Chaldeans, and expect us to find out the dream as well as the interpretation.[2] That is the worst instance; but there are others where throughout the first half of a poem the hapless reader is clawing the air for a clue and has not enough breath in his body to admire anything you show him. Take "The Stolen Mermaid": I was some time in discovering who was talking, whether it was the stolen mermaid or the robbed merman. There matters might be made clearer by altering the crabbed lines 'O, heart to captive be', etc., into something like 'This land-bound heart of me Hears sound its mother-sea', only better expressed I hope. In "The Great Ride", to begin with, you had better add place as well as date to the title, or the allusion may easily be missed. You start off 'Where the merciful waters *rolled*': the reader sees the past tense, and instead of thinking of the heavenly

[1] Psalm 102. 26.   [2] See Daniel 2. 5.

Jordan, as you want him to, he is off to Abana and Pharphar, rivers of Damascus,[1] and expects to hear you tell him about some historical crossing of a river where a lot of people were killed: all which you would avoid by saying '*roll*'. Further: how soon do you imagine your victim will find out that you are talking about horses? Not until the thirteenth of these long lines, unless he is such a prodigy of intelligence and good will as I am: there you mention 'hoofs', and he has to read the thirteen lines over again. 'Flank' in line six is not enough: Swinburne's women have flanks. And as line six is at present a foot too short I advise you to introduce hoofs into it; or tails?

Now I will go through some details. You will find here and there some marginal suggestions in pencil which may help to shew in what direction I think improvements might be made . . .

"The Fire Worshippers" is surely a very bad title and rather helps to confuse. "Man, Truth, and Beauty" would be, not good I daresay, but better. 'Bowels': if terrific sublimity is what you are after, say 'guts'; which has the further advantage of being one syllable, and not two, like 'bowels', though I am aware that Aytoun rhymes the latter with 'howls'.[2] But nobody rent Prometheus' bowels that I know of, so I should say 'side' like an ordinary creature. '*Speak the word* which spells' will suggest d-o-g, c-a-t, etc. The first two lines of the fourth stanza I can't very well advise about, not knowing what they mean.

"The Stolen Mermaid". 'To the bay's *caves*' is where the upward not the downward tide would go. 'If, ah, but if' displays with almost cynical candour its mission to rhyme with 'cliff'. It might be 'hill' and 'if still, if still'. . . .

"Under the Rose" I call a bad title; because I suppose you don't mean it to signify "Clandestinely", yet how can the reader think anything else? It strikes me too that, as you tell the tale, the hero gets his roses cheap, for we don't hear that he did give much mirth to earth: apparently he merely lay under the rose and chuckled, and earth said 'how that boy is enjoying himself!'

"The Great Ride": 'in *tragic* accord'. I suspect Miss A. Mary F. Robinson[3] began with *tragic*: then in the fulness of time she got to *insensate*: be warned and pause. What are 'gods of Mammon'? I thought Mammon was a god, since Spenser and Milton: in the other sense the newspapers have got it. . . .

"The Sleep of the Gods". Does one put one's head either to one's own heart or to another person's (for it is not clear which this god did) in order to hear the beat of feet? The last stanza of this poem is one of your triumphs of obscurity. I have come to the conclusion, which may be wrong, that the last

[1] See 2 Kings 5. 12.

[2] In 'The Massacre of the Macpherson' (*Bon Gaultier Ballads*, 1850).

[3] Agnes Mary Frances Robinson, poet and miscellaneous writer (1857–1944). The reference is probably to her poem 'The Conquest of Fairyland' (in *The New Arcadia*, 1884): '. . . Cursed the insensate longing for life in the heart of a sick old man.'

two lines are uttered by Deep to Deep, and not sung by the gods, because the pronoun 'their' appears to require this interpretation; but if so, what black inhumanity on your part not to say 'whispered' or the like instead of 'trembled'.

"Heart's Bane" alias "Little Death" alias "White Rabbits": If you print this, better *not* employ the last title, but keep your rabbits for an agreeable surprise in the last verse.

I daresay I have left out some things I meant to say, but here is the paper at an end. . . .

Your affectionate brother   A. E. HOUSMAN

To Laurence Housman

TEXT: MEMOIR

31 March 1895   [*17 North Road*]

My dear Laurence,

. . . I think Le Gallienne[1] has picked out the four or five best. "The Blue Eyes of Margret" would be as good as any, if the words 'while heart's memories met' conveyed any meaning, which to me they don't; and I think the poem would gain if they vanished . . . "Lord Paramount" is superior in execution to anything I have seen of yours; though I think I said before that men were not created to write poems about pictures. "The Keepsake", with its beautiful moral lesson, is clever and striking; though your Muse is apt to preoccupy herself unduly with the phenomenon of gestation. "The Queen's Bees" is about as good in another way; but on the last page the two lines about fashion and passion are evidently not meant literally: then how in the world are they meant? and their phraseology is precious cheap. I don't know if it wouldn't improve the poem to run straight on from 'a poor man's way' to 'Then would I give'. Another point: do you really know what the Queen did to the poor man? If she bent him flat, as you said at first, that explains his resentment, though it sounds rather comic; but in the second version she gives him nothing to cry about. "The Cornkeeper" may go along with these. I don't care for any of the others I now see for the first time. I return the list of Le Gallienne's rejections, etc.: I have put a cipher to what I think should be left out and underlined what I think should be printed: where I have put no mark I have no definite opinion. As to "The Great Ride", Le Gallienne truly says that it is in another key than the rest, but I don't know if that is altogether an objection: it may find its way to hearts from which White Rabbits run off like water from a duck's back. Its faults seem to me rather its length, and its theme, which I don't think really very well suited to poetry.

---

[1] Richard Le Gallienne, poet and man of letters (1866–1947), at this time literary adviser to Laurence Housman's publisher, John Lane.

34

A few details.

"The Keepsake." 'She waits by the windowsill and whistles.' Do you think so, Jim? The accomplishment is rare among women . . .

"The Bleeding Arras." This fails to impress, all the more because of the evident intention to impress. By the way, arras, embarrass and harass are brazen effrontery . . .

"The House of Birth." This is less indecent than Rossetti and less comical than W. E. Henley, but that is all I can say for it.

"The Two Debtors." I do not understand this, and perhaps that is why I think it perfectly odious.

"King B's Daughter." Nor this; but that may be the fault of my ignorance in not knowing who the monarch was.

The Dedication is pretty, especially the end of the second verse. In some places it lumbers by reason of having heavy syllables where light ones ought to be: 'Is each bird that *here* sings', 'Where *dim* lights and *dark* shadows belong *Hangs* that arras of song'. The beginning of the last verse I think is doggerel, especially the third line; and the third stanza is weak except at the end. But the chief objection is not merely the Swinburnian style of the whole but the fact that Swinburne has twice used almost this same metre for a dedication . . .

Your affectionate brother   A. E. HOUSMAN

Besides the comic verses, which he produced with ease, Housman occasionally wrote serious poems, but too rarely to contemplate publishing a volume until, in the spring of 1895, he was unexpectedly seized by an intense excitement, which evoked some fifty poems in the space of a few weeks.

The reasons are uncertain. He himself associated the poems with a persistent throat trouble and with an annoying controversy on the manuscripts of Propertius; but it is at least possible that the death of Edward Housman in November 1894 contributed to the removal of old inhibitions, while the scandal of Oscar Wilde's downfall in April 1895 revived long-suppressed conflicts in Housman's emotions.

When he had enough satisfactory poems, he assembled them under the title *Poems by Terence Hearsay* and asked A. W. Pollard to look through them. Pollard disliked the title and proposed *A Shropshire Lad*. At his suggestion Housman offered the book to Macmillan and Company, who refused it; he then arranged with Kegan Paul to publish it at his expense.

A Shropshire Lad appeared in March 1896. The book had obvious merit and was highly praised, but sales were nothing out of the ordinary, and it took two years before the edition of 500 copies was exhausted. It was only when a new publisher, Grant Richards, who was enthusiastic about the book, reprinted it in 1898 that it began slowly to establish itself.

35

At University College Housman made some lifelong friends, notably W. P. Ker, the Professor of English, and Arthur Platt, who was appointed to the Chair of Greek in 1894. In their company, and with a few other chosen colleagues, he relaxed, as he had done in his Oxford days. He became known as an after-dinner speaker and a contributor of witty papers on the English poets to the College Literary Society.

When the need arose he could be a capable organiser. In the summer of 1900 University College was plunged into a financial crisis brought on by incompetent administration. Housman played a decisive part on that occasion in reorganising the College and establishing the new régime.

Although he enjoyed the popular fame of his poems, Housman's only real concern was for his classical work. In addition to the numerous papers he wrote every year, he had in 1894 edited the text of the *Ibis*, and towards the end of the decade he began to prepare his great edition of Manilius. He was formidably equipped for the task by wide reading, precise memory and acute judgment. He had been preceded in his labours by Scaliger and Bentley, and had the sense to avoid suggestions which they must have considered and rejected. But since their times textual criticism had acquired proper scientific foundations, and Housman, the first editor to take account of all the major manuscripts, and the best equipped in knowledge of ancient astrology, wrote with an authority and decisiveness that make his edition an outstanding achievement of modern scholarship.

To Laurence Housman

TEXT: MEMOIR

[*April 1896*]   [*17 North Road*]

Yes, the cover and title-page[1] are my own. Blackett[2] was very amusing. He was particularly captivated with the military element; so much so that he wanted me at first to make the whole affair, with Herbert's assistance,[3] into a romance of enlistment. I had to tell him that this would probably take me another thirty-six years. Then the next thing was, he thought it would be well to have a design on the cover representing a yokel in a smock frock with a bunch of recruiting-sergeant's ribbons in his hat: this too I would not. Everything has its drawbacks, and the binding seems to me so extraordinarily beautiful that I cannot bear to lose sight of it by opening the book: when I

---

[1] Of *A Shropshire Lad*, just published, at Housman's expense, by Kegan Paul. It was bound in pale blue boards with a white spine.

[2] Spencer Blackett, Manager of Kegan Paul.

[3] Herbert Housman, A.E.H.'s youngest brother, on leaving school became a medical student, but in 1889 enlisted in the King's Royal Rifles. He was killed in South Africa in 1901.

take it down with the intention of reading it, the cover detains me in a stupor of admiration till it is time to go to bed.

To Laurence Housman

TEXT: MEMOIR

27 April 1896   [*17 North Road*]

My dear Laurence,

. . . Why am I being reviewed in semi-religious papers like the *New Age*[1] and the *British Weekly*?[2] and how does that sort of literature find its way to Marloes Road?[3] and where do you suppose did the *British Weekly* learn my antecedents?

There is rather a good notice in last week's *Sketch*.[4]

I thought the *New Age* review very nice, except the first paragraph disparaging the other chaps.

Kate writes to say that she likes the verse better than the sentiments. The sentiments, she then goes on to say, appear to be taken from the book of Ecclesiastes. To prefer my versification to the sentiments of the Holy Ghost is decidedly flattering, but strikes me as a trifle impious. . .

Your affectionate brother   A. E. HOUSMAN

Testimonial for R. W. Chambers[5]

MS. U.C.L.

16 June 1896   *University College, London*

Mr R. W. Chambers was a member of my Senior Latin Class in the College from 1892 to 1894, and was placed first in the examinations at the end of each Session. I have no hesitation in saying that he possesses a knowledge of Latin which is not only adequate to the post of Assistant Librarian in the Gray's Inn Library, but probably much in excess of any requirements which will be made of him in that capacity. He is in fact a student of unusual accuracy. His methodical industry always struck me greatly, and appears to

---

[1] Unsigned review of *A Shropshire Lad* by Hubert Bland in the issue for 16 April 1896.

[2] Review by 'Claudius Clear' (pseudonym of William Robertson Nicoll) in the issue for 23 April 1896.

[3] Where Laurence and Clemence Housman lived in Kensington.

[4] Signed O.O., in the issue for 22 April.

[5] Raymond Wilson Chambers (1874–1942), a member of Housman's first Latin class at University College; College Librarian, 1901; Quain Professor of English, 1922–1941. He left a sympathetic account of Housman in *Man's Unconquerable Mind*, 1939.

me a very valuable qualification for such an office as that which he seeks; and I sincerely wish that he may be successful in his application.

A. E. HOUSMAN
Professor of Latin

To Laurence Housman

TEXT: MEMOIR

26 September 1896   [17 North Road]

My dear Laurence,

... I have *Green Arras* and thank you very much for it. Of the poems I think I have seen all but one or two before. Of the illustrations I like 'The Queen's Bees' the best, with its distant view and its kidney bean sticks: the scarecrow is full of life and is perhaps the best of your wind-blown pillow-cases to date; and the figure in the foreground wins upon one when one realises that what one at first took for his nose is really and truly his chin. 'The Corn-keeper' looks much better than it did in *Atalanta*.[1] The central or principal figure in 'The Housebuilders' strikes me as very good indeed, if his right arm were a trifle shorter; but if I were the employer of those bricklayers I should take care to pay them by the piece and not by the day.

I am much disappointed to find no illustration to 'White Rabbits'. I have attempted to supply this deficiency and I enclose the result. You will see that I have had some difficulty with the young lady's arm; and the gentleman is not quite as tall as I could have wished. The moon (together with the weathervanes and everything else which I could not draw) is behind the spectator, and accounts for the vivid illumination of the principal figures. You may remark that the rabbits are not running: true; but they have been running, and they are just going to begin again.

The other enclosure is not one of my finished works: I should hardly call it more than a sketch. It depicts the meeting at the end of 'The Keepsake'.

I think I would have put either 'The Keepsake' or else 'The Queen's Bees' nearer the beginning of the volume, as these are the two pieces I should expect to attract most attention; and 'The Comforters' does not strike me as a very ingratiating poem to put so early. Otherwise I think the arrangement is good ...

I think you will probably be able to congratulate yourself on having brought out this autumn at the Bodley Head a much better book than Davidson,[2] if the whole of his *New Ballads* are at all like those he has been publishing in the magazines. Not that this is a very lofty compliment ...

Your affectionate brother   A. E. HOUSMAN

[1] In the issue for October 1892.

[2] John Davidson, Scottish poet, novelist and playwright (1857–1909), well known since the publication of his *Fleet Street Eclogues*, 1893.

To Laurence Housman

TEXT: MEMOIR

5 October 1896 [*17 North Road*]

My dear Laurence,

. . . I was in Bridgnorth for several hours. In the churchyard there I remembered having heard our mother describe it and the steps up to it, which I had absolutely forgotten for more than 25 years.

I ascertained by looking down from Wenlock Edge that Hughley Church could not have much of a steeple.[1] But as I had already composed the poem and could not invent another name that sounded so nice, I could only deplore that the church at Hughley should follow the bad example of the church at Brou, which persists in standing on a plain after Matthew Arnold has said that it stands among mountains.[2] I thought of putting a note to say that Hughley was only a name, but then I thought that would merely disturb the reader. I did not apprehend that the faithful would be making pilgrimages to these holy places.

Morris dead![3] now Swinburne will have something to write about. He wrote 12 epicediums on P. B. Marston,[4] so Morris ought to be good for at least 144.

Reading your poems in print I was a good deal struck by 'Gammer Garu', which I don't remember noticing much in manuscript. The last stanza is really quite beautiful.

A new firm of publishers[5] has written to me proposing to publish 'the successor' of *A.S.L.* But as they don't also offer to write it, I have had to put them off . . .

Your affectionate brother   A. E. HOUSMAN

[1] See *A Shropshire Lad* LXI:
    'The vane on Hughley steeple
      Veers bright, a far-known sign.'
[2] In 'The Church at Brou', 1853.
[3] William Morris, poet, weaver, fabric designer, printer and socialist (1834–1896), died on 3 October.
[4] Algernon Charles Swinburne (1837–1909) had produced little verse of any value for the past twenty years. His twelve poems in memory of the blind poet Philip Bourke Marston (1850–1887) were published in *Astrophel and Other Poems*, 1894.
[5] Grant Richards, whose firm began in business in January 1897.

To Laurence Housman

TEXT: MEMOIR

4 December 1896 [*17 North Road*]

My dear Laurence,

... There has been no notice in the *Bookman* yet.[1] I feel sure you are wrong in thinking that A.M.[2] stands for Mrs Meynell;[3] partly because of the style, which is neither sufficiently correct nor sufficiently pretentious, and partly because the sub-editor's name is A. Macdonnell.

I have been reading your latest work,[4]—probably by this time it is not your latest work, but I can't read as fast as you write. What I chiefly admire in your stories, here as on previous occasions, is the ingenuity of the plan: this particularly applies to "The King's Evil", which I thought a good deal the best of the set. The pieces of poetry interspersed seem to me better in point of diction than any in *Green Arras*. The sentiments are a bit lurid. 'Long through the night', 'Amid this grave-strewn', and 'You the dear trouble' struck me as the best; but there are a number of good verses in the others . . .

Your affectionate brother   A. E. HOUSMAN

To Laurence Housman

TEXT: MEMOIR

24 December 1896 [*17 North Road*]

... I am extremely anxious that you should spend a happy Christmas; and as I have it in my power,—here goes. Last night at dinner I was sitting next to Rendall,[5] Principal of University College Liverpool and Professor of Greek there, a very nice fellow and a great student of Marcus Aurelius and modern poetry. He was interested to hear that you were my brother: he said that he had got *Green Arras*, and then he proceeded, 'I think it is the best volume by him that I have seen: the *Shropshire Lad* had a pretty cover.'

I remain

Your affectionate brother (what a thing is fraternal affection, that it will stand these tests!)

A. E. HOUSMAN

---

[1] Of *Green Arras*. The *Bookman* reviewed *A Shropshire Lad* very favourably in June and published a biographical article on Housman in August 1896.

[2] The initials at the end of the review, which was written by Annie Macdonnell.

[3] Alice Meynell, poet and essayist (1847–1922), at this time a leading reviewer.

[4] *All-Fellows*, a book of imaginary legends.

[5] The Rev. Gerald Henry Rendall (1851–1945); Professor of Greek at Liverpool from 1880; Headmaster of Charterhouse, 1897–1911.

P.S. After all, it was I who designed that pretty cover; and he did not say that the cover of *Green Arras*[1] was pretty. (*Nor is it.*)

P.P.S. I was just licking the envelope, when I thought of the following venomed dart: I had far, far rather that people should attribute my verses to you than yours to me.

To Laurence Housman

TEXT: MEMOIR

12 May 1897   [*17 North Road*]

My dear Laurence,

... There is a notice of *Gods and their Makers*[2] in last week's *Athenaeum*: I don't know if it is depreciatory enough to suit your taste.

George Darley was the writer of the excellent sham 17th century song 'It is not beauty I demand' which Palgrave printed as genuine in the second part of the *Golden Treasury*. Because it was so good I read another thing of his, a sort of fairy drama whose name I forget,[3] and was disappointed with it and read no more. But the piece you quote about the sea[4] is capital. He was also the chief praiser of Beddoes' first play,[5] and a great detester of Byron's versification when it was all the vogue.

The sea is a subject by no means exhausted. I have somewhere a poem which directs attention to one of its most striking characteristics, which hardly any of the poets seem to have observed. They call it salt and blue and deep and dark and so on; but they never make such profoundly true reflexions as the following:

> O billows bounding far,
> How wet, how wet ye are!
>
> When first my gaze ye met
> I said 'Those waves are wet'.
>
> I said it, and am quite
> Convinced that I was right.
>
> Who saith that ye are dry?
> I give that man the lie.
>
> Thy wetness, O thou sea,
> Is wonderful to me.

[1] Designed by Laurence Housman.
[2] A mythological novel by Laurence Housman. The review is in the issue for 8 May 1897.
[3] *Sylvia, or the May Queen*, 1827. Darley lived from 1795–1846.
[4] Probably Canto III of *Nepenthe*, 1836, which was reprinted in 1897.
[5] *The Bride's Tragedy*, 1822.

41

It agitates my heart,
To think how wet thou art.

No object I have met
Is more profoundly wet.

Methinks, 'twere vain to try,
O sea, to wipe thee dry.

I therefore will refrain.
Farewell, thou humid main.

Farewell thou irreligious writer . . .

   Your affectionate brother   A. E. HOUSMAN

To Lucy Housman

MS. U.C.L.

25 June 1897   *University College*

My dear Mamma,

I suppose that whether you went to Marloes Road or not you will now be at Chichester. I came back to town yesterday. The time I had at Bromsgrove was not bad, as either the morning or afternoon of every day was sunny. The Valley is decent enough, though the cooking is not up to much. I saw both the Millingtons[1] and the Kidds.[2]

On the evening of the 22nd[3] I started at eight in the evening for Clent, and got to the top of Walton Hill about 9.20. The sky was fairly clear, and so was the air to the north, but hazy southwards: Malvern had been invisible all day. (On Saturday when the rain was about I saw as good a view from Walton Hill as I ever saw, the Sugar Loaf and Black Mountain and Radnor Forest quite plain.) One or two private bonfires started before the time, but most of them waited for 10 o'clock. Five minutes or so after the hour I easily counted 67. Some of these were small affairs in the near neighbourhood, which soon died down; but at half-past there were 52 burning merely on the south and west, from the Lickey on the left to the Wrekin on the right. Northward I did not attempt to count, as it was hard to tell the beacons from the ordinary illuminations of the Black Country. Of the distant fires Malvern was much the largest: the pile was sixty feet high and could be seen with the naked eye by daylight: through a telescope it looked like the Eiffel tower, as it was much higher than its width and held together with iron. But it had been so saturated with paraffin that it burnt out in an hour. The Clent fire was on the further

[1] Herbert Millington (1841–1922) was Headmaster of Bromsgrove School, 1873–1901.
[2] H. Cameron Kidd, a Bromsgrove doctor, who had two sons at Bromsgrove School.
[3] The day of the official celebration of Queen Victoria's Diamond Jubilee.

hill, and not on the top but on the south-western face. By midnight the number of fires had very much decreased, and only four, besides the Clent one, were visible at two o'clock: two distant ones somewhere by the Brown Clee, and two nearer,—one Droitwich way, and one on Kinver Edge which burnt till daylight brilliantly. It was a fine night, and at midnight the sky in the north had enough light for me to see the time by my watch. At two I heard a cuckoo, and immediately afterward the larks began to go up and make a deafening noise, and some person at Kingswinford, possibly wishing to stop the row, sent up a sky-rocket. (There had been a number of rockets at Birmingham before ten.) About this time the first tinge that you could call blue came in the sky, which had turned buff and green soon after one: at three the clouds were red. I stayed to see the sun get above the mists and clouds, which was just four o'clock, and then I went back to bed at 5.15. There was a fair crowd round the Clent fire, but a policeman, who told me at three that he had been on duty ever since 6 a.m. the day before, said that it was not near so large as in 1887.

Bromsgrove was still gay as I came through yesterday to the station, and had kept its Jubilee flags and festoons to enhance the splendour of the fair-day. The chief thing was a triumphal arch at the Strand.

Love to Cousin Henry and the family. I remain your loving son

A. E. HOUSMAN

To Lucy Housman

MS. U.C.L.

22 September 1897   *17 North Road*

My dear Mamma,

I came home yesterday after having been just a month away, at Paris, Rome and Naples. I stayed in Paris a week, then went to Rome (two nights in the train) and stayed there three or four days, then to Naples, in order that my ticket might not expire. At Naples I stayed about ten days, and then came back by the same route, stopping four or five days at Rome and one at Paris.

I think I saw most things that are to be seen at Paris in the week, and I also went to Versailles. I should have liked also to see St Germain and Fontaine-bleau, but that week was rainy and not very propitious for distant excursions. What most strikes one in Paris is the countless number of handsome streets, any five of which would constitute a fine town in England: imagine a place as well built as Edinburgh or Bath and practically about as large as London. Notre Dame is hardly equal to Westminster Abbey, and none of the modern churches are anything like St Paul's, but the number of such buildings, interesting or beautiful, is much greater than in London; and London has

43

nothing at all equivalent to the Louvre. The Bois de Boulogne is wilder and more picturesque than any of our parks, and the garden of the Tuileries is more sumptuously laid out. They make a deal more of their river than we do of ours: it is all edged with handsome quays and crossed with handsome bridges.

When I got into Italy the weather was very hot, and remained so all the while I was there. The Neapolitans themselves were amazed at it; for though the first week of September is one of their hottest times, the heat generally ends on the 8th. The Sirocco was blowing part of the time: this is a very damp and enervating wind, which makes fish go bad six hours after they are caught. I went to Pompeii, which is more extensive than I thought, and to Vesuvius. You drive most of the way up; then you ride about a mile where the lava has buried the road; then you go up a cable-railway on the side of the cone, and then it is about ten minutes' walk to the top. The lower part of the hill is covered with vineyards and the like: then you come to coppices of chestnut; then to the lava, which is various shades of grey and brown and has just the shape which is taken by melted lead when you drop it into cold water. When you get to the cone the lava is mostly buried under ashes: at the top the ground is streaked with sulphur, and steam issues from cracks and mingles with the smoke from the crater and the clouds which hang on the hill (it is about the height of Ben Nevis), so that it wants a guide to tell you which is which. Here you begin to hear an angry sound such as water will sometimes make in pipes, as if the mountain were gargling, or were trying to talk but had stones in its mouth; which indeed it has. This is the lava boiling inside. The volcano was unusually quiet, so that I was able to go quite to the edge of the crater, which is often impossible. This is a great pit, sending out so much smoke that you hardly catch a glimpse of the other brim; the sides are ashes, with smears of sulphur and of an orange-coloured stuff which I believe is arsenic; in the centre there starts up at intervals a tall narrow fountain of red-hot stones, which then fall rattling back again into the funnel with a noise like a wave going down the beach. It is much the highest hill in the neighbourhood, so you see all the country, vineyards and oliveyards and woods of young trees, dotted with white or pink houses: into this green carpet the lava runs out on every side in long grey tongues, as if you had spilt an inkpot. There had been an overflow about a month before I was there: part was still red-hot, and visible from Naples as smoke by day and a spot of fire by night. I went to the place: the surface had mostly turned grey, but the red-hot part could be seen through cracks, and the heat in some parts was like a furnace. The guides fasten coins to the ends of long sticks, plunge them into these cracks, and withdraw them with the hot lava adhering to them; I have brought one of these home for you, as I believe such things amuse women and children. The best view near Naples is from the monastery of Camaldoli, on a hill behind the town: here you get not only the view of the bay to the south, which you see from Naples itself, but also the view to the north-west, the bay of Baia, which I think more beautiful. I went to most of the places along the coast, and to the two islands of Capri and Ischia. Autumn is not the time for flowers in Italy any more than in England, but in one wood I found cyclamen blooming almost as thick as wood anemones in April. The chief ornament of gardens at this season is the oleander, which grows about the size of a lilac and is covered with trusses of rose-coloured flowers like carnations. The plumbago also grows and blooms very well, and so does the purple convolvulus. The town of Naples has a fine museum and a good palace, but not much else. Here I have said nothing about Rome, which I liked much best of the three; but I have to go into town this morning, so I will stop here for the present. Many thanks for your letter. Love to cousin Mary.

Your loving son   A. E. HOUSMAN

To Lucy Housman

TEXT: MEMOIR

[circa *1897*]   [*17 North Road*]

I shall be interested to see the Devotional Poems.[1] Perhaps I myself may write a Hymn-book for use in the Salvation Army:

There is Hallelujah Hannah
  Walking backwards down the lane,
And I hear the loud Hosanna
  Of regenerated Jane;
And Lieutenant Isabella
  In the centre of them comes,
Dealing blows with her umbrella
  On the trumpets and the drums.

Or again:

'Hallelujah!' was the only observation
That escaped Lieutenant-Colonel Mary Jane,
When she tumbled off the platform in the station,
And was cut in little pieces by the train.
  Mary Jane, the train is through yer:
  Hallelujah, Hallelujah!
We will gather up the fragments that remain.

It seems to come quite easy.

[1] Laurence Housman's *Spikenard*, 1898.

45

To Grant Richards[1]

21 February 1898   *17 North Road*

My dear Sir,

My brother Laurence has sent me a proposal from you to take over the remaining copies of *A Shropshire Lad* and publish a second edition at your own risk.

I suppose no author is averse to see his works in a second edition, or slow to take advantage of an infatuated publisher; and it is impossible not to be touched by the engaging form which your infatuation takes. But there are two points to consider at the outset.

I should not like the second edition to differ from the first in form, nor to be sold at a higher price. But, so far as I can judge from the finances of the first edition,[2] unless it were produced cheaper or sold dearer, the sale of an entire edition of 500 copies would not pay for the printing and binding and advertising; and so, apart from the royalty, which I do not care about, you would be out of pocket.[3]

Also I should have to ask Kegan Paul if their feelings would be lacerated by the transfer. I do not think very much of them as men of business, but their manager has been nice to me and takes a sentimental interest in the book, like you.

At the present moment I can think of nothing else to damp your ardour.

I am yours very truly   A. E. HOUSMAN

To Lucy Housman

TEXT: MEMOIR

21 March 1898   *[17 North Road]*

. . . The end of term is now in sight, and I am quite ready for it; twelve weeks on end is not nice. I hope to see a good many of the hedges green by the time the holidays begin, as the spring is early in these parts . . .

---

[1] Franklin Thomas Grant Richards (1872–1948), son of Franklin Richards, Fellow of Trinity College, Oxford; left school at sixteen; on the staff of *The Review of Reviews*, 1890–1896; founded his publishing firm in 1897; published the second edition of *A Shropshire Lad*, 1898, Housman's editions of Manilius, 1903–1930, and Juvenal, 1905, and *Last Poems*, 1922; novelist and miscellaneous writer; his *Housman: 1897–1936*, 1941, gives a detailed record of their business dealings and friendship.

[2] Which was sold at 2*s.* 6*d.*

[3] Richards replied the next day inviting Housman to discuss arrangements for the second edition, but nothing further was done until Richards wrote again in July.

The only poem that I can find is this.

> I knew a Cappadocian
> Who fell into the Ocean:
> His mother came and took him out
> With tokens of emotion.
>
> She also had a daughter
> Who fell into the Water:
> At any rate she would have fallen
> If someone hadn't caught her.
>
> The second son went frantic
> And fell in the Atlantic:
> His parent reached the spot too late
> To check her offspring's antic.
>
> Her grief was then terrific:
> She fell in the Pacific,
> Exclaiming with her latest breath
> 'I have been too prolific.'

To Lucy Housman

MS. U.C.L.

26 April 1898   *17 North Road*

My dear Mamma,

This is the first day of term; so, as the holidays are over, I sit down to write a letter. I have to thank you for two, one on my birthday and one later. You will see that yours was not the only one I received on my birthday: I believe you collect the epistles of this amiable madman,[1] so I enclose this one for you. He must have discovered the date from a publication called *Who's Who*.

I did go into Hampshire for five days at Easter; but it was not the south but the north, near Whitchurch. Since I came back I have been having good walks about the country to see things coming out in the sunshine, and I feel very well. I suppose Cousin Henry is settled in his rectory by this time. I see from looking through your letters that Eva[2] is to be married to-morrow; so give her my benediction.

Marriage, and the necessity of filling this sheet of paper, remind me of one of my occasional poems, which I may or may not have told you before:

[1] An unknown admirer who wrote to Housman every year on his birthday.
[2] Lucy Housman's niece.

47

When Adam day by day
Woke up in Paradise
He always used to say
'Oh, this is very nice.'

But Eve from scenes of bliss
Transported him for life.
The more I think of this
The more I beat my wife.

I remain your loving son   A. E. HOUSMAN

To Grant Richards

MS. ILLINOIS

20 July 1898   *Grosvenor Arms Hotel, Shaftesbury*

Dear Sir,
    I am much obliged to you for your letter; but I have thought it proper to
write to Kegan Paul and Co. before taking any immediate step. When I hear
from them I will write to you again.
    Yours very truly   A. E. HOUSMAN

To Grant Richards

MS. ILLINOIS

22 July 1898   *Shaftesbury*
Dear Sir,
    As Kegan Paul and Co. say that their feelings would not be lacerated, and
as I suppose Mr Archer's article[1] may create some sort of demand, I shall be
very willing that you should bring out a second edition of my poems.[2] I only
stipulate for simplicity of get-up and moderateness of price. Your former
proposals I have not by me at the moment, but I think you offered to pay me
a royalty, or, in case I did not care for it, to hand the amount to a charity. I
should prefer that it should go to reduce the price at which the book is to be
sold.
    I shall not be in town till 3 August. I expect to be here till Wednesday,
and then at the King's Arms, Dorchester.
    I am yours very truly   A. E. HOUSMAN

---

[1] In *The Fortnightly Review*, 1 August 1898; reprinted in William Archer's *Poets of the Younger Generation*, 1902.
[2] This was published in a printing of 500 copies on 14 September 1898 and sold at 3s. 6d.

To Grant Richards

MS. ILLINOIS

24 July 1898   *Shaftesbury*

Dear Sir,

I think it best not to make any alterations, even the slightest, after one has once printed a thing. It was Shelley's plan, and is much wiser than Wordsworth's perpetual tinkering, as it makes the public fancy one is inspired. But after the book is set up I should like to have the sheets to correct, as I don't trust printers or proof-readers in matters of punctuation.[1]

3/6 is perhaps the largest sum which can be called moderate, but I suppose it deserves the name.

I am yours very truly   A. E. HOUSMAN

To Grant Richards

MS. ILLINOIS

11 December 1898   *17 North Road*

Dear Mr Richards,

I rather like the notion of a pocket edition.[2] Large paper and illustrations are things I have not much affection for. In any case I should like to correct the proofs and to have them printed as I correct them. Last time someone played games with the punctuation.

It does you infinite credit that the sale should be so good:[3] I wonder how you manage it.

Yours very truly   A. E. HOUSMAN

To Grant Richards

MS. ILLINOIS

8 February 1899   *17 North Road*

Dear Mr Richards,

I do not want any profits.[4] They had better go towards paying that long bill which Mr G. B. Shaw[5] sent in to you the other day.

Yours very truly   A. E. HOUSMAN

[1] Housman was not given proofs, and the text of the second edition contains over forty unauthorised variants.

[2] This was eventually produced in 1904.

[3] 397 copies of the second edition were sold by the end of the year.

[4] Housman continued to refuse royalties on *A Shropshire Lad* until 1922.

[5] George Bernard Shaw (1856–1950), whose *Plays Pleasant and Unpleasant* Richards published in 1898, had been infuriated at being charged for 'author's alterations' in the proofs. He sent Richards a mock bill for 'Services rendered as Typographical Expert by Author to Publisher' which Richards sent for publication in *The Academy*.

To Paul Lemperly[1]

Dear Sir,

The second edition contains nothing new except a few misprints. I have not published any other book.

I am much obliged by your letter and bookplate. I think yours is the only letter containing no nonsense that I have ever received from a stranger, and certainly it is the only letter containing an English stamp that I have ever received from an American. Your countrymen generally enclose the stamps of your great and free republic.

I am yours faithfully   A. E. HOUSMAN

To Mrs Platt[2]

MS. U.C.L.

12 March 1900   *17 North Road*

Dear Mrs Platt,

I shall be very pleased to come to dinner on the 22nd.

The reason why you so seldom see me is that when the weather is bad on Sundays I am afraid to come so far, and when the weather is good, the country, being both nearer and larger, drags me north. Platt, who knows everything, even Greek, will explain to you that every particle of matter in the universe attracts every other particle with a force directly as their masses and inversely as the square of the distance which separates them.

Moreover, at the last at-home I came to, you treated me very ill. I had hidden under the piano, or in it, I forget which; and you came and pulled me out.

I am yours sincerely   A. E. HOUSMAN

To Grant Richards

MS. ILLINOIS

26 March 1900   *17 North Road*

Dear Mr Richards,

I am much obliged by the copies of the third edition[3] you have sent me. The new get-up is very pretty.

Yours very truly   A. E. HOUSMAN

[1] American collector. Text from the Lemperly Sale Catalogue and A. Edward Newton, *This Book-Collecting Game*, 1931.

[2] Mildred Barham, daughter of Sir Edward Bond, Librarian of the British Museum; wife of Housman's friend and colleague Arthur Platt (1860–1925), Professor of Greek at University College, London, since 1894.

[3] 1,000 copies were printed, half of them being sold by the end of the year. The new price was 3*s*.

Testimonial for Miss A. M. B. Meakin[1]

MS. BODLEY

26 March 1900   *University College*

Miss A. M. B. Meakin has during the last three years attended many of my Senior and Junior Latin classes in this College. She has displayed not only much intelligence but also an interest in and even an enthusiasm for her work such as I have seldom known. Her progress in general grasp of the subject has been steady and in some respects rapid. I have been particularly struck by the zeal with which she applied herself to Latin composition, not only in prose but in verse. It was at her own wish that she began the study of the latter art, which is not usually practised by students here; and she soon attained a fair degree of proficiency in more than one of the metres. If Miss Meakin should herself engage in the teaching of Latin, I have no doubt that she will be found both a careful and an effective teacher.

A. E. HOUSMAN, Professor of Latin

Postcard to Grant Richards

MS. ILLINOIS

30 March 1900   *17 North Road*

I have just found your note of the 17th which I had overlooked. I am afraid there is no chance of another book from me yet awhile.

Yours   A. E. HOUSMAN

To Gilbert Murray[2]

MS. BODLEY

23 April 1900   *17 North Road*

Dear Murray,

I have put off thanking you for the Andromache[3] till I could send the Euripidea.[4] It is very interesting, very unlike anything one could have anticipated, and the end of it really moving. The piece of verse on p. 70 is so

---

[1] Annette Meakin, author of thirteen books, including three travel books on Russia, published between 1901 and 1932. She contributed a note on Housman's reputation among German scholars to *The Times*, 7 May 1936.

[2] Gilbert George Aimé Murray (1866–1957); Professor of Greek at Glasgow, 1889–1899; Regius Professor of Greek at Oxford, 1908–1936; appointed to the Order of Merit, 1941; celebrated for his translations of Greek drama.

[3] Murray's play on the murder of Pyrrhus, just published.

[4] Housman's unpublished conjectures, which Murray used in his Oxford edition, 1902–1909.

51

good that I wish you would write more. Ancient Greece, as you depict it, is rather more medieval than I thought it was, but I don't know how far this may be due to the notions I attach to words: the word 'lord' always carries me into the middle ages, and even 'castle', though I suppose it ought not. I rather doubt if man really has much to gain by substituting peace for strife, as you and Jesus Christ recommend. Sic notus Ulixes?[1] do you think you can outwit the resourceful malevolence of Nature? God is not mocked, as St Paul long ago warned the Galatians.[2] When man gets rid of a great trouble he is easier for a little while, but not for long: Nature instantly sets to work to weaken his power of sustaining trouble, and very soon seven pounds is as heavy as fourteen pounds used to be. Last Easter Monday a young woman threw herself into the Lea because her dress looked so shabby amongst the holiday crowd: in other times and countries women have been ravished by half-a-dozen dragoons and taken it less to heart. It looks to me as if the state of mankind always had been and always would be a state of just tolerable discomfort.

The Bacchae, Iph. Taur., and Medea are the only three plays I have really studied. I don't know if you are editing the fragments, so I don't send my conjectures on them. I enclose my own essay at an Andromache, only it is an Alcmaeon.[3]

When are we going to the music-hall?

Yours very truly   A. E. HOUSMAN

To Lily Thicknesse[4]

TEXT: MEMOIR

11 June 1900   [*17 North Road*]

Dear Mrs Thicknesse,

. . . I am sorry to hear Ray has been so ill, and I hope he continues to improve. I trust it was not the mention of my farewell interview which gave a bad turn to his illness.

I ordered the *Londoner* some days ago, but W. H. Smith and Sons have not yet sent it: I don't know whether this is pure negligence on their part, or whether they have detected in it anything which they think would be likely to demoralise me.[5]

On Saturday Karl Pearson[6] and I are going for a walk in Buckinghamshire,

---

[1] See Virgil, *Aeneid* II. 44. 'Is this the Ulysses we know?'
[2] See Galatians 6. 7.
[3] 'Fragment of a Greek Tragedy', originally published in *The Bromsgrovian*, 1883; reprinted in *The University College Gazette*, 1897.
[4] Wife (died 1952) of Ralph Thicknesse, solicitor and writer on law (1856–1923). Her *Collected Poems* were published in 1954.
[5] The issue for 2 June 1900 contained her poem 'Invocation'.
[6] 1857–1936; Professor of Eugenics at University College, London.

to find a farmer who lays a particular kind of eggs, which tend to prove that there is no God . . .

Yours sincerely   A. E. HOUSMAN

To Lucy Housman

MS. U.C.L.

27 September 1900   *17 North Road*

My dear Mamma,

I got home on the evening of the 25th, and have just received your letter this morning.

The crossing to Calais was the windiest and rainiest I have ever had, and the rain or drizzle kept on right across France till nightfall. Artois, Picardy and Champagne are all very flat; large arable fields without hedges, only occasional groves and avenues of black poplar; and rain does not make them look cheerful. Just after sunset we came to Laon, which is built against a solitary ridge of hill, on the middle of which stood the cathedral, looking very fine with its five towers in the twilight; though not finer than the view of Canterbury from the Chatham line. Before we got to Rheims it was quite dark, so I saw nothing of the cathedral there. When the day broke we were in Switzerland approaching Basle, a country of very green meadows and bold but not very lofty hills with woods of the spruce fir. At Basle there is an hour's wait and a change of train: afterwards the same sort of country till you pass beside a small lake and then come to Lucerne, a biggish town with some picturesque bits of fortifications. The lake of Lucerne is in shape something like a clover leaf, only more so: it, and the neighbouring lake of Zug, keep the railway company for more than an hour, during which you are always coming across fresh bays of it and new views. The water is a strong opaque blue: the scenery, though it is not what I consider the best sort of scenery, must be quite the best of its sort: any number of cliffs falling straight to the water, pine trees and cottages adhering to them in impossible places, and narrow white waterfalls streaming all down them with a noise to be heard above the clatter of the train. After you quit the lake and draw near to the St Gothard the country is still interesting and in some respects beautiful: the valleys are often surprisingly soft and pretty, full of smooth meadows and orchard trees and foaming streams of yellowish water; but many of the mountains would be better for having their tops taken off them. Some of their tops actually were taken off, so far as I was concerned, by the clouds and mist, and I saw no snow at all. The tunnel lasted seventeen minutes, and we came out into a sort of hazy sunshine. It is still Switzerland for two hours more, and the form of the landscape is much the same; but trees, especially firs, grow fewer and smaller, and the fig makes its appearance, and even once

53

or twice the olive; and the towns and churches look Italian. The streams flow in the other direction, and have clearer water, and the waterfalls on the hills are more in number and less in volume; when I came back a month later they were most of them dry. The lake of Lugano, part Swiss and part Italian, is much like Lucerne in its broken outline; but its hills are less bold and less wooded, and its water a sort of burnished green. We pass the town of Como, but cannot see the lake; then the hills die into the plain of Lombardy, and you come to Monza, where the king was killed,[1] and then to Milan.

I suppose Milan is the least Italian town in Italy; it considers itself the intellectual capital of the country, and probably hopes to go to France when it dies. Much of it is new, with the ordinary fine wide streets, and its older parts are not very picturesque as wholes, though many of the single buildings are. There seem to be arches, some very old, at all the numerous gates. The castle, now a barracks overlooking a new park, is very huge and solid and medieval: two of the churches, St Ambrogio and St Eustorgio, are of the old Romanesque architecture from which our Norman is copied, and the former is a very fine example, with a square colonnaded court in front of it. In one street stand sixteen pillars of a Roman bath, with a tramway on each side. Next to the cathedral, the tramway seems to be the thing on which the Milanese chiefly pride themselves. The Cathedral, though one cannot call it good architecture if compared with French or English or even German or the best Italian Gothic, is certainly impressive from its mere size and magnificence and completeness, except the west front, which has a mean effect and actually looks small, thanks to the stupid Italian notion that the proper outline for a west front is the same as that for a dog-kennel. From other points of view the building looks full its size, and indeed looks larger than St Peter's at Rome, though in fact it is much less. The ornament, the pinnacles and statues and finials at the top, and the niches at the side, looks rich at first, but it soon begins to look poor: the recesses are shallow, the usual Italian fault, the succession of upright lines is monotonous, and the buttresses and pinnacles, though marble, look almost like the ironwork of a drawing-room fender, owing to the thinness and stiffness of their ornament. The guide calls your attention to the fact that no two statues and no two flowers of the carving are alike; but they might just as well be alike; they could not produce a greater effect of sameness. The inside is very dark, a fault on the right side, and so the defects in details do not trouble one much, and the general effect is fine. The central aisle is half as high again as our highest, York and Westminster, and is quite English in its breadth,—not the narrow French proportion: there are double aisles on each side, the lowest of which I calculate are as high as the nave of Winchester. The clerestory is small, and there is no

[1] King Umberto I of Italy was assassinated by an anarchist named Bresci at Monza on 29 July 1900.

triforium, so fully three quarters of the height of the nave is merely pillars and arches: the pillars are crowned, not by capitals, but by octagonal stilts consisting of niches with statues in them, on the top of which the arches are perched: I suppose all this adds to the effect of height, but it is disproportioned and fatigues the eyes: if you look straight before you there is only column after column: you cannot help looking up, and then there is nothing to see except the arches and the roof at a distance where you lose their outlines. There is much stained glass, some of it old and fine: the three great east windows have good tracery and are very rich and gorgeous.

Here I must stop at present. I am sorry the festival has knocked you up. The enclosed is what the Venetians call the flower of the sea: it grows all over the salt marshes in the lagoon. Love to Cousin Agnes.[1]

Your loving son   A. E. HOUSMAN

To Lucy Housman

MS. U.C.L.

2 October 1900   *17 North Road*

My dear Mamma,

I was in Milan on the day of Bresci's trial:[2] at first I could not make out why the ends of all the streets round the Court of Justice were occupied by cavalry who let no wheeled traffic pass, but this accounted for it. I went to the top of the cathedral to see the view: the distance was not very clear, so that only the nearest Alps and Apennines were visible, not Mount Rosa. All round extends the plain of Lombardy as flat as a carpet, and very green with pollard trees and shrubs, red and white towns and towers here and there: the great Carthusian monastery and church of Pavia looks like a ship on the sea. Going from Milan to Venice at first you have merely this plain, cut up into small and narrow fields of Indian corn in all stages of growth (they make it into 'polenta' and a cheap sort of bread: they call it Turkish corn, and to put matters straight they call a turkey an Indian fowl, poor benighted Papists); these fields are separated not by hedges but by rows of small trees, black poplar, willow, and especially mulberry: they also plant the mulberry among the corn and in orchards by itself: they grow it for silk, not fruit. You cross many rivers, and at this time of the year you can tell by their condition where they come from: those which flow from the lakes have plenty of water, but those which have to rely on their own springs are merely brooks amidst broad white beds of sand and stones. When you are getting towards Brescia the Alps come down from the north to keep the railroad company: this part is very picturesque, the hills have towns and churches and forts and convents

---

[1] Lucy Housman's sister, Helen Agnes, wife of Sir William Smith.
[2] 29 September 1900. He was sentenced to life imprisonment.

perched here and there; but there is a great lack of large trees: I believe there are not half a dozen large trees in Italy except in gardens and parks. The Lombardy poplar does not seem to be common in Lombardy: it grows badly, and they often lop it like a Worcestershire elm. The railway runs close to the lake of Garda, the largest and much the broadest of the lakes, and this is the most beautiful part of the journey; the water is bright blue, and retreats into the mountains on the north; on the south, where the shores are flatter, the landscape begins to be ornamented with the cypress, the most telling of all trees. Now we pass into the Venetian provinces, and between Verona and Vicenza the Alps recede into the north again: the country is much like Lombardy, but the fields are larger and farms and towns seem fewer; but every town and village, even more than in Lombardy, seems to have built itself a lofty brick bell-tower, which in Venetia generally has a short sort of spire on the top (you know the great campanile of St Mark's at Venice): also the poplar becomes more frequent: people who live in very flat countries (Lincolnshire for instance) must have tall towers and such things to cheer them up. As the sun went down we came to what is called the dead lagoon, where the sea and land begin to mix, but there is more land than sea: the live lagoon, where there is more sea than land, is what Venice stands in. The scene was very dreary at that hour: pools and canals, and marshes all overgrown with that purple flower I sent you; and the last touch of mystery and desolation was provided by three large staring red tramcars about a quarter of a mile away which were being rapidly drawn, by one very small horse apiece, into the Adriatic sea. (I found afterwards that they go to a spot on the coast whence there is a steamer to Venice.) Then the railway runs out on to the water to Venice over a bridge two miles and a half long: Venice itself is not very well seen, and looks something like an English manufacturing town with the chimneys transformed into towers. Entering Venice itself, especially at nightfall, when most of the canals are empty, the first impression is its stillness: you get a gondola at the landing place by the station, and are taken to the other end of the Grand Canal, where the hotels are, chiefly by short cuts through lesser canals: the Grand Canal is like an S.

I hope your health is going on all right.

Your loving son   A. E. HOUSMAN

To Lucy Housman

MS. U.C.L.

15 October 1900   *17 North Road*

My dear Mamma,

I suppose I had better take the contents of Venice in the order of date. The first is the best: the Byzantine architecture as represented by the cathedral of

St Mark, which I should think is the most beautiful, not the grandest, building in the world. It might be possible to erect in the Gothic style a more beautiful building, but I doubt if such a one exists. It is not lofty, and not large, except that it is broad for its length; but every square yard of it is worth looking at for an hour together. I used to go there nearly every day; but it would take years to exhaust it. It is all covered with coloured marble and alabaster, except where it has gold mosaics, or richly carved stone capitals to the pillars; and yet it does not look a bit like a piece of patch-work: everything helps towards the general effect. The preciousness of the material and the delicacy of the workmanship make it look almost more like jewellery than architecture, and one feels as if it ought not to be left out of doors at night. The inside is equally costly in material but not so good in general effect: the five domes with their gold mosaics are well enough, but the walls are of a brown alabaster which gives a rather dingy effect at a distance, though it is very beautiful to examine closely; and the building looks more like a cave hewn out of the solid than a building such as we are accustomed to, resting its weight on walls and pillars. The few remaining palaces of the same architecture I did not think much of, though Ruskin cries them up a great deal. Of Gothic they had two sorts in Venice: one for the churches, very thin and poor, with naked red brick on the outside; another for their palaces, exceedingly rich and elegant, but rather timid and monotonous. Of this the Doge's palace is the great example: you know its stupid general design, like a clothes-horse with a blanket on it: I am bound to say the reality is better than the pictures, because one can see that the flat and tame upper half of it is composed of red and white marble, although the pattern is no better than you see on the cottages in the Stourbridge Road at Bromsgrove. The lower part, the two colonnades, are as beautiful and as full of fine carving as you could wish. There is a much smaller palace on the Grand Canal, called the Casa d'Oro, which is almost richer in effect. But the majority of the Gothic palaces are not satisfactory: they are all on the same pattern, part of the surface consisting of very rich arcades and windows, and the rest of painfully flat wall, made worse by being painted. The earliest Renaissance work in Venice is very peculiar and very charming in detail, with much inlaying of coloured marbles, a device which they borrowed from the old Byzantine architecture: there was a family of architects called the Lombardi, who built the little church of St Maria dei Miracoli and one or two palaces in this style, with beautiful foliated carving: in point of general design however they are not good or effective. Then comes the regular Renaissance, which we all know: the most imposing building of that date is the church of the Salute, with a large and a small dome, which always figures in pictures of the Grand Canal and is really very fine outside: inside, all the Renaissance churches are merely St Paul's on a smaller scale and with more ornament on the walls. The church of the Redentore, by Palladio, has a charmingly pretty and simple exterior to its east (or rather its south) end, which nobody except me seems to notice or admire.

The painter best represented in Venice is that lurid and theatrical Tintoret, whom I avoid, and Paul Veronese, whom one soon sees enough of. There are surprisingly few Titians, though two of them are very fine and famous. The best paintings to my thinking are those of Giovanni Bellini, who belongs to the previous generation, and his pupil Cima da Conegliano, mostly Madonnas and groups of saints; also two painters both called Bonifacio Veronese. The picture gallery really pleased me more than any I have seen, because of the beautiful glow of colour on all the walls, except of course where Tintoret was scowling Paul Veronese out of countenance in the large room which they have had given them to sprawl about in. Many of the best paintings are in the churches: there is a very interesting series by Carpaccio (scenes in the lives of St George and St Jerome) in St Giorgio dei Schiavoni, covering all the walls of the little building.

Often at sunset I used to go up the great bell-tower in St Mark's Place. Venice looks like one large island (the canals cannot be seen): the lagoon lies all round, dotted with the stakes which mark out the navigable channels, and the water declares its depth or shallowness by its colour: as the sun goes down it turns partly a golden green and partly a pale vermilion.

My gondolier expressed a wish that he were your son. He wanted me to come to Venice next Christmas, and I explained that at Christmas I went to see you; and then he made this remark. The reason is, that if he were your son he would be well off and would have no family to provide for: so at least he says. At present he has to earn a living for one wife, two sisters, one mother, one mother-in-law, and half an uncle (who was once a champion oarsman and is now paralysed); which is pretty good for a young man of twenty-three who has had one eye kicked out by a horse.

On the other side of the island of Lido, which is the chief bulwark against the Adriatic, there is a great bathing place on the open sea with splendid sands, where I went several times. On this same island I also discovered a bit of real country; grass and a grove of trees round about the fort of St Nicolo, where the Venetians have their great picnic in May. In addition to the usual English autumn wildflowers there was purple salvia and the evening primrose. There were also very attractive grasshoppers two inches long, which they call by the name 'salto-martino'. I went also to Mestre on the mainland, and saw for the first time in my life a swallow-tail butterfly on the wing: in England I believe it survives only in a few spots in the eastern counties.

Your loving son   A. E. HOUSMAN

To Horatio F. Brown[1]

Dear Mr Brown,

I shall be very pleased to lunch with you and Mrs Brown on Sunday. Apparently I nearly encountered you both yesterday afternoon, for Andrea[2] tells me you were on one side of Lido while I was on the other.

Yours very truly   A. E. HOUSMAN

To Lucy Housman

MS. U.C.L.

13 September 1901   *[Castelfranco]*

My dear Mamma,

This is written in pouring rain at the town of Castelfranco, which most likely you never heard of, and no more did I till four or five days ago. The pen and ink are too awful, so I must go on in pencil, which is all the better as there is no blotting paper. This is about twenty miles inland from Venice: it is celebrated as the birthplace of Giorgione, and as containing the only picture which is known with certainty to be his. It is a smallish place which once was smaller, for it stands partly within and partly without the fine old walls and moat: the walls are partly in ruins, and the space between them and the moat is now a sort of garden-bank, something like the castle at Hereford. I have been at Paris, Pisa and Florence, and now lastly at Venice. Pisa is a rather handsome and very sleepy town, with all its chief buildings, the Cathedral, Baptistery and leaning tower, packed in one corner on an open space of grass, surrounded on two sides by the ancient walls of the city, which still run right round it. The weather was very hot and bright, and by daytime one could hardly open one's eyes to look at things; for although the Cathedral etc. are about as old as any Norman architecture that we have got in England, they are chiefly built of Carrara marble, which in process of time does indeed become smeary and untidy, but never becomes mellow and venerable; and under an Italian sun it blazes like a dusty highroad. The cathedral is quite a failure, high-shouldered and almost mean-looking outside, handsome and roomy inside, but not a bit religious: bands of black marble on white, looking painfully spick and span, in spite of its antiquity. The Baptistery, a large dome, is a beautiful building outside, much improved

---

[1] Horatio Robert Forbes Brown (1854–1926), author of many books on Venice; literary executor, editor and biographer of John Addington Symonds. The text of this letter is taken from *The Dalhousie Review* XXIX, 1950.
[2] His gondolier.

by the addition of some Gothic gables and pinnacles to the Romanesque original; the inside is quite uninteresting. By daylight the Baptistery is much the finest of the group of buildings, but in twilight and moonlight I think the leaning tower is superior, with its six rows of pillars picked out in light and shade. The country immediately around Pisa is flat, much of it having been deposited by the sea within human memory: the nearest hills are about five miles off, but the Apennine and other mountains are well in sight. I went out for a drive to the west to the park of the royal villa, which is a great game-preserve, planted with woods and avenues of the stone pine. The Arno at Pisa, being penned within embankments, is a respectable stream by moonlight, when you cannot see that it is liquid mud: however, after all it is not so bad as the Exe at Exeter: the Arno is like pea-soup, but the Exe is like tomato-soup. Between Pisa and Florence the Arno at present is merely a shallow brook meandering along a wide bed of pebbles: at Florence they try to make it look decent by a series of dams, but in this dry summer it does not succeed. I have only one candle, which is bothering to my eyes, and Florence would take up more space than I could fill before I go to bed, so here I will stop, and try to address the envelope legibly with the abandoned pen and ink.

Your loving son   A. E. HOUSMAN

To Grant Richards

MS. ILLINOIS

12 October 1902   *17 North Road*

Dear Richards,

If I may drop the Mr. I am sending simultaneously by parcel post the text and notes of the edition of Manilius I,[1] and also a specimen of the Teubner classics[2] to show what sort of book I have in my mind's eye. The notes should be printed at the foot of the text, and should run right across the page, not stand in two columns: the type of the notes should be smaller in proportion to that of the text than is the case in the German book: the paper should be thicker, I think. As to my manuscript, the curved line ∼∼∼ under words and figures and letters is meant to indicate Clarendon type (I am not sure if it is the correct sign); and the spaces which I have left between sentences are meant to be preserved in printing. In the text, I want the numbers in the *left*-hand margin, as I have put them: and the letters 'j' and 'v', wherever they occur in the type-written copy, are to be altered into 'i' and 'u' respectively: I suppose this is a change which may be left to the printer.

[1] The first volume, published in 1903, of the *magnum opus* that continued to occupy Housman for the next thirty years.
[2] The well known series of scholarly editions, containing only text and apparatus criticus, published in Leipzig since 1824.

60

When the next edition of the *Shropshire Lad* is being prepared, it would save trouble to the compositor as well as to me if he were told that the third edition is almost exactly correct, and that he had better not put in commas and notes of exclamation for me to strike out of the proof, as was the case last time.

I think this is all I have to say.

I remain yours sincerely   A. E. HOUSMAN

To Grant Richards

MS. ILLINOIS
8 November 1902   *17 North Road*

My dear Richards,

4/6 is my notion of the proper price, for several reasons: firstly because I want the book to be read abroad, and continental scholars are poorer than English; secondly as a protest against the usual English prices—e.g. 12/6 for a single play of Sophocles by Jebb[1]—which I have always supposed to be due to the cloth binding and gilt lettering; thirdly because I hardly like to ask more for a single book of a poem which contains five, when Lachmann's celebrated commentary on the whole of Lucretius[2] only costs 7/6. The Teubner which I sent you as a specimen is priced at 4/–; true, it is a shocking bad book, but that makes no difference. Still, if 4/6 is one of those prices which publishers and booksellers for some mysterious reason dislike, and if your heart is set on 5/–, I have no strong objection, as I see that my notes in print are more voluminous than I imagined.[3]

The division of the notes in the proofs sent is satisfactory: the important thing is that the note on any verse should *begin* on the page which contains that verse. As to the Greek σ, I wish the letter to have this form at the end as well as in the body of words: fifty years hence all Greek books will be printed so.

I am hoping to receive from Rome in about a week's time some information about manuscripts in the Vatican which may involve additions or alterations in the notes on the first 80 lines.

Yours sincerely   A. E. HOUSMAN

[1] Richard Claverhouse Jebb (1841–1905); Professor of Greek at Glasgow, 1875–1889; Regius Professor of Greek at Cambridge, 1889–1905; knighted, 1900. His edition of Sophocles appeared in seven volumes, 1883–1896.
[2] Published in 1850.
[3] The book was sold at 4*s.* 6*d.* It was published at Housman's expense.

To Grant Richards

MS. ILLINOIS

20 November 1902   *17 North Road*

Dear Richards,

I return the proofs,[1] in which I have made corrections on pages 18, 19, 21, 35, 52 and 92. What I want on pages 18 and 19 is to have the seventh line of each stanza put level with the second and fourth: I don't know if I have expressed this desire in the correct form.

My attempt to get the readings of the Rome manuscript through the British School there seems to have had no effect; but I am making another effort through another channel, the friend of a friend of mine, and I hope to succeed shortly.

Yours sincerely   A. E. HOUSMAN

To Grant Richards

MS. ILLINOIS

30 November 1902   *17 North Road*

Dear Richards,

I have got the collation of the Vatican MSS, so I return the proof corrected. As I have not yet had my manuscript returned from the printers (except page 4) it is possible that slight further corrections will be necessary, but nothing to affect the arrangement of the printed matter on the pages, I hope.

The alterations to be made in the remainder of the first 80 verses (the part affected by the Vatican MSS) are not so formidable as in these first 37.

There is one general instruction which had better be given to the printers. When a colon or semicolon comes at the *end* of a quotation in italics, it ought to stand upright, not to slant (I have written 'rom.' in the margin, but I am not sure if that is the correct way to signify what I mean). With notes of interrogation, if they belong to the sense of the quotation, the case is different.

Yours sincerely   A. E. HOUSMAN

To Grant Richards

MS. ILLINOIS

5 January 1903   *17 North Road*

Dear Richards,

I return corrected the proofs which I have received.

[1] Of the fourth edition (2,000 copies) of *A Shropshire Lad*, 1903.

As regards long notes, like those on 226 and 245, I see no objection to having a whole page, or two if necessary, filled with annotation, without any text at the top.

Either the type or else the printing of these slips is rather bad, and trying to the eyes to correct by lamplight.

I have made a good many changes in the title page, which ought to be as Latin as possible, I think; and I must confess that I don't know the Latin for Leicester Square.[1] I hope you will approve.

Yours sincerely   A. E. HOUSMAN

To Grant Richards

MS. ILLINOIS

27 January 1903   *17 North Road*

Dear Richards,

I return the last portion of the text and notes corrected; and I enclose the manuscript of the matter which is to follow them at the end of the book. I have marked the two parts A and B to show their order.

As I was unwell in the Christmas holidays, the preface is still only partly written, and I do not get on with it very fast now that the work of the term has begun again.

Yours very truly   A. E. HOUSMAN

To H. E. Butler[2]

MS. ST JOHN'S

7 February 1903   *University College*

Dear Sir,

I am very willing that you should include in your selection the poem you wish.[3]

I do not know if it is necessary that you should also obtain the consent of the publisher (Grant Richards, 48 Leicester Square), but no doubt he would readily give it.

I am yours faithfully   A. E. HOUSMAN

[1] The address of Richards' office; it was omitted from the title-page.

[2] Harold Edgeworth Butler (1878–1951); Lecturer at New College, Oxford, 1901; Fellow 1902; Professor of Latin at University College, London, in succession to Housman, 1911–1943.

[3] '1887' (*A Shropshire Lad* I), for inclusion in *War Songs of Britain*, 1903.

To Grant Richards

MS. ILLINOIS

12 February 1903   *17 North Road*

Dear Richards,

With regard to your note of to-day, I don't quite know the meaning of 'the preliminary', but I enclose the dedication[1] which is to follow the title page. I suppose it had better be printed in italics. If it will not all go on one page, it should be broken at the point I have marked, and a catch-word should be added.

After this, and before the text and notes, there will come a long introduction, which, as I said, is not yet finished; but there is nothing else of the nature of a preliminary.

Many thanks for the copies of the *Shropshire Lad* which I received to-day. The colour attracts the eye, and the convolvulus-leaf detains it in fascinated admiration.[2]

Yours sincerely   A. E. HOUSMAN

To Grant Richards

MS. ILLINOIS

15 March 1903   *17 North Road*

Dear Richards,

In your announcement of my Manilius there are two misprints: *instruit* should be *instruxit* and *amendationes* should be *emendationes*. They do not cause me any piercing anguish, and I only write about it because I thought you might like to know.

The preface proceeds very slowly now that it is term-time. I hope I shall be able to send you an instalment of it in a fortnight or so.

Yours sincerely   A. E. HOUSMAN

To Henry Jackson[3]

MS. TRINITY

4 May 1903   *17 North Road*

My dear Jackson,

I write to inform you of the safe arrival of Platt: my own you will probably

---

[1] To Manilius I; a Latin poem of 28 lines in elegiac couplets, inscribed to Moses Jackson.

[2] The fourth edition, which was sold at 1s., had scarlet paper covers, and a small convolvulus leaf ornament was added at the end of each poem.

[3] Greek scholar (1839–1921); Fellow of Trinity College, Cambridge, 1865; Regius Professor of Greek, 1906; appointed to the Order of Merit, 1908; Vice-Master of Trinity, 1914; editor of *The Journal of Philology*, 1879–1921; a leading University liberal.

infer by some logical process derived from the study of Aristotle, so I need not explicitly record it.

I think, in spite of the weather, I have enjoyed this visit to Cambridge more than any other.

Yours very truly   A. E. HOUSMAN

To Witter Bynner[1]

MS. HARVARD

3 June 1903   *University College*

My dear Sir,

You seem to admire my poems even more than I admire them myself, which is very noble of you, but will most likely be difficult to keep up for any great length of time.

However it is not for me to find fault with you; and naturally there is a pleasure in receiving such ardent letters as yours.

As to your inquiries: I wrote the book when I was thirty-five, and I expect to write another when I am seventy, by which time your enthusiasm will have had time to cool. My trade is that of professor of Latin in this college: I suppose that my classical training has been of some use to me in furnishing good models, and making me fastidious, and telling me what to leave out. My chief object in publishing my verses was to give pleasure to a few young men here and there, and I am glad if they have given pleasure to you.

I am yours very truly   A. E. HOUSMAN

To Grant Richards

MS. ILLINOIS

5 June 1903   *17 North Road*

My dear Richards,

There is no American publication which regularly reviews classical books, but the *American Journal of Philology* (Johns Hopkins University, Baltimore) reviews a certain number, and I have no objection to your sending them a copy. But I doubt if they would review it; American scholars are mere grammarians and collectors of statistics, and what we call critical scholarship hardly exists there.

Yours sincerely   A. E. HOUSMAN

The Classical Review circulates in America and has American sub-editors.

[1] American poet and playwright (born 1881) at this time poetry editor of *McClure's Magazine*, in which he printed thirteen poems from *A Shropshire Lad* in the next five years.

To Grant Richards

MS. ILLINOIS

22 June 1903   *17 North Road*

Dear Richards,

I have no objection to Mr Ettrick[1] setting the verses to music; but I have not exacted fees from other people who have set other pieces, so I don't want to begin now. Vanity, not avarice, is my ruling passion; and so long as young men write to me from America saying that they would rather part with their hair than with their copy of my book, I do not feel the need of food and drink.

Yours sincerely   A. E. HOUSMAN

To Grant Richards

MS. ILLINOIS

24 June 1903   *17 North Road*

My dear Richards,

As I started with a vague notion that the book would cost about £100, I regard anything short of that as clear gain.[2] Also my classes have been unusually large this year, and the extra fees may possibly balance this extra expenditure; which tempts me to believe in the existence of Providence. I rather think that the difference between the printers' estimate and the actual cost is caused not merely by my additions and alterations but also by an initial miscalculation on their part as to the amount of matter contained in the manuscript.

Would you add to the list of people to whom copies are to be sent—J. W. Mackail Esq.,[3] 6 Pembroke Gardens, Kensington, W.

Yours sincerely   A. E. HOUSMAN

To Grant Richards

MS. ILLINOIS

24 July 1903   *17 North Road*

My dear Richards,

I can only give the *full* address of two of the enclosed;[4] but I suppose the names of the towns where they are published will be enough.

---

[1] Henry Havelock Ettrick. I have not traced any Housman setting by him.

[2] The printing of the edition of 400 copies of Manilius I cost Housman £83 9s. Richards made no charge for office and distribution costs.

[3] John William Mackail (1859–1945); classical scholar, literary critic and translator; biographer of William Morris; Professor of Poetry at Oxford, 1906–1911.

[4] Learned journals to receive review copies.

Mackail congratulates me on my publisher, 'who has produced quite an elegant book'; and he is quite an authority.

I rather gather, from some letters which I have received, that the copies sent to my friends were not accompanied by an indication that they were sent by me.

Yours sincerely   A. E. HOUSMAN

To Grant Richards

MS. ILLINOIS

26 July 1903   *17 North Road*

My dear Richards,

I should like the two morocco-bound copies[1] to have the edges cut all round and gilt all round. No gilt should be put on the edges of the inter-leaved copy, which is merely for me to scribble in.

I am obliged to you for Ellis's[2] letter, which I return.

I should be glad if you would take such steps as may seem good to you for collecting press-cuttings from the learned journals of the Continent.

Yours sincerely   A. E. HOUSMAN

To Laurence Housman

TEXT: MEMOIR

9 August 1903   [*17 North Road*]

My dear Laurence,

. . . To write a paper on Patmore would be an awful job, especially in the holidays, so I send you two poems, of which you can print whichever you think the least imperfect.[3]

I hope you won't succeed in getting anything from Meredith,[4] as I am a respectable character, and do not care to be seen in the company of galvanised corpses. By this time he stinketh: for he hath been dead twenty years . . .

Your affectionate brother   A. E. HOUSMAN

[1] One of these copies of Manilius I was for Moses Jackson, the other probably for Lucy Housman.

[2] Robinson Ellis (1834–1913), Corpus Professor of Latin at Oxford, 1893–1913; formerly Professor of Latin at University College, London; a friend of Richards' father and uncle and of Richards himself; editor of *Noctes Manilianae*, 1891. Housman later wrote of his corrections to Manilius: 'One or two of them were very pretty, but his readers were in perpetual contact with the mind of an idiot child.'

[3] Laurence Housman had asked for an essay on Coventry Patmore for *The Venture. An Annual of Art and Literature*, which he edited with Somerset Maugham, 1903. In place of the essay he published A.E.H.'s 'The Oracles', reprinted in *Last Poems*.

[4] George Meredith (1828–1909) did not contribute to *The Venture*.

67

To Grant Richards

MS. ILLINOIS

11 August 1903   *17 North Road*

My dear Richards,

I don't want to appear impatient, but I shall leave for the continent in about a week's time, and I particularly desire to have one of the morocco-bound copies of the Manilius before then, in order to send it to India to the friend to whom the book is dedicated. I suppose it must be nearly ready now.

The Duchess of Sutherland is under the impression that I not only gave her my consent to print some verses of mine in a novel of hers, but also wrote her a kind letter about it;[1] neither of which things did I ever do. I have no doubt that you gave her my consent, as you have given it to other people; and I have no particular objection: but when it comes to writing kind letters to Duchesses I think it is time to protest.

Yours sincerely   A. E. HOUSMAN

Postcard to Grant Richards

MS. ILLINOIS

[10 September 1903][2]   *Venice*

If I can find sufficient industry I hope to go on with the Manilius; but not immediately, because at this moment I am rather sick of writing and want to read; moreover book II is the most serious job of the whole lot. I am sure your father's annotations would be valuable.[3]

Either you or I or the Duchess of Sutherland seems to have a treacherous memory: let us hope it is the Duchess.

Yours   A. E. HOUSMAN

To Gilbert Murray

MS. BODLEY

22 September 1903   *17 North Road*

Dear Murray,

I have just come back from Italy and found your letter here, and as regards the Music Hall I hasten to observe that it is your own fault if I have not taken

---

[1] *Wayfarer's Love: Contributions from Living Poets*, 1904, edited by the Duchess of Sutherland, contained Housman's poem 'Astronomy', reprinted in *Last Poems*. The book was published in aid of the Newcastle and Potteries Cripples' Guild. The Duchess of Sutherland later insisted that Housman had given her written permission.

[2] The postmark is illegible; the date is given by Richards.

[3] Manuscript notes in his copy.

you there already: the last time I saw you in London you had armed yourself with tickets for Duse's *Magda*[1] and were not amenable. If you will let me know a little beforehand when you think of being next in town, and what evening or evenings you will be free, I will get you to come and dine somewhere with me, and try to find some other educated person to keep us company. Next month? I am bound to say however that on the last three occasions of going to a Music Hall I found the entertainment of the most harrowing dulness: I don't know whether it is that the Halls are deteriorating or that I am improving.

Radicalism in textual criticism is just as bad as conservatism; but it is not now rampant, and conservatism is. Radicalism was rampant thirty or forty years ago, and it was then rebuked by Madvig[2] and Haupt:[3] now it is conservatism that wants rebuking. Similarly in social morality, puritanism is a pest; but if I were writing an Epistle to the Parisians I should not dwell on this truth, because it is not a truth which the Parisians need to consider: the pest they suffer from is quite different.

Some time ago I saw somewhere an extract from a prelude of yours to a tale of chivalry, in heroic couplets, which struck me as very rich and fine: I should be glad to hear any more news of it.

Yours very truly   A. E. HOUSMAN

To Gilbert Murray

MS. BODLEY

13 October 1903   *17 North Road*

Dear Murray,

Many thanks for the Introduction.[4] I have also been reading your translations from Euripides.[5] With your command of language and metre you are really a noble example of ἐγκράτεια,[6] in that you don't produce volumes of original poetry.

I don't think I have anything on the plays you mention.

Yours very truly   A. E. HOUSMAN

---

[1] Play by Hermann Sudermann (1857–1928); its first London production was in 1896. Eleanora Duse, the great Italian tragic actress (1859–1924), appeared in London frequently from 1893 until her death.
[2] Danish classical scholar (1804–1886).
[3] German classical scholar (1808–1874).
[4] Possibly *Prolegomena to the Study of Greek Religion* by Jane Harrison, 1903, to which Murray contributed an appendix.
[5] *Hippolytus* and *The Bacchae*, in *Euripides*, 1902.
[6] Self-control.

To Witter Bynner

MS. HARVARD

14 December 1903   *University College*

Dear Mr Bynner,

I have never taken money for any of my verses, and accordingly I return you, with many thanks, the draft which you have kindly sent me.

I have no copy of the piece called 'The Olive', which is not particularly good: it was published on the conclusion of the peace in June 1902, in the *Outlook*.[1] I enclose however a poem which I have contributed to a collection which the Duchess of Sutherland is bringing out for charitable purposes; only, as the book is not yet published, you must not go printing it in America.

I am much obliged for the copies of the magazine, and remain yours very truly

A. E. HOUSMAN

To P. Habberton Lulham[2]

MS. HOVE

28 June 1904   *17 North Road*

Dear Sir,

I have received your kind gift and have been reading it with much pleasure. The pieces 'Red Dawn', 'Now', 'Forbid', 'A Sorrow in Spring', 'Birds', and 'Stricken', particularly took my fancy, as well as many passages in the other poems, such as the opening of 'Between the Tides'. If I may make one criticism, it is that although I knew that *morn* and *dawn* rhymed in London, I cherished the hope that it was not so in Kent, at least in Thanet.

With sincere thanks I remain yours very truly

A. E. HOUSMAN

To Grant Richards

MS. ILLINOIS

27 July 1904   *17 North Road*

My dear Richards,

Thanks to your treatment last night I am quite restored to health this morning.

I enclose a copy of our joint work.[3] The results of your collaboration are

---

[1] The poem was not reprinted until 1939, when it appeared in *Collected Poems*.

[2] Edwin Percy Habberton Lulham, author of *Devices and Desires*, 1904.

[3] The fifth edition of *A Shropshire Lad*, in Richards' 'Smaller Classics' series, sold at sixpence (cloth) and one shilling (leather). Housman was not sent proofs.

70

noted on pages 4, 22, 45, 55, 71, 77, 78, 92, 116 (this last occurred also in the previous edition, where I overlooked it). I don't mark details of punctuation. I am bound to say however that the leather binding makes a very pretty book.

Yours sincerely   A. E. HOUSMAN

To Grant Richards

MS. ILLINOIS

18 August 1904   *17 North Road*

My dear Richards,
    The text and notes of the Juvenal[1] which you are burning to publish are now finished, and I think the printers had better have them to play with while I am writing the introduction; so as I expect to go abroad on the 27th, I propose to send you the manuscript some time next week.
    My notion is that the book should be identical in form and print with the Manilius, which is so much admired by people who are connoisseurs in these matters. The text is about four times as long as the Manilius, but the notes are on a very much smaller scale, and the introduction will be much shorter too; so that the whole volume would probably be rather slimmer.

Yours sincerely   A. E. HOUSMAN

To Grant Richards

MS. ILLINOIS

5 September 1904   *Péra-Palace, Constantinople*

My dear Richards,
    I have not received an acknowledgement of the priceless manuscript I sent you when I left England ten days ago. Anxiety is preying on my health, and if the Sultan next Friday observes my haggard countenance in the crowd, he will certainly suppose me to be a conspirator and order me to be thrown into the Bosphorus: then you will have to intervene, as John Lane did in the case of William Watson;[2] and that will cost you more than a postage stamp. If my money holds out I shall be here long enough to hear from you.

Yours sincerely   A. E. HOUSMAN

[1] Critical edition 'editorum in usum', published in 1905, based on Housman's text of Juvenal in Postgate's *Corpus Poetarum Latinorum*, volume II, 1905.
[2] The reference is to a caricature in Max Beerbohm's *The Poets' Corner*, 1904. Watson's violent attacks on Turkey in *The Purple East*, 1896, had caused considerable embarrassment to the Foreign Office. The caricature shows him 'in the nick of time saved from the trap-door to the Bosphorus by the passionate intercession of Mr John Lane'.

To Grant Richards

MS. ILLINOIS

9 September 1904   *Péra-Palace, Constantinople*

My dear Richards,

Your letter addressed to Highgate has just reached me here. I advised you not to produce the book at your own expense, and now you recognise my superior wisdom. I will pay for it. Will you get from the printers an estimate of the cost? In addition to what I have sent there will be an introduction of some 30 pages or more. It will not be anything like £84, as that amount was reached in the case of the Manilius largely because of unforeseen alterations.

Yours sincerely   A. E. HOUSMAN

I shall be home in about ten days.

To Lucy Housman

TEXT: MEMOIR

[September 1904]   *Constantinople*[1]

The ruins are not nearly so lofty as some of our English castles, but what strikes one is their immense extent and the loneliness around. Inside, the skirts of the city are thinly peopled, more market gardens than houses; outside, the country is rolling downs and graveyards, with cultivation only here and there. A Turkish graveyard is a forest of cypresses with an undergrowth of tombstones, which dies much sooner than the trees; for a Turkish tombstone is no thicker and no broader than a plank, and is ill fixed in the ground, so that they soon begin to lean in all directions, and finally lie down flat upon the earth. The Jews bury their dead on the bare hillside under slabs: the great cemetery is west of Pera, above the Golden Horn, and makes the downs look as if they were sprinkled with large hailstones or coarde-grained salt.

Constantinople is famous for its sunsets, and I used to watch them from the western edge of the hill that Pera stands on, looking over the cypresses of what was once a graveyard but now contains only dust and dogs and is beginning to be built over. From here you look across the Golden Horn and west, where the sun goes under. The sky would be orange and the hillside of the city would be dark with a few lights coming out, and the Golden Horn would reflect the blue or grey of the upper sky; and as there was a new moon, the crescent used to come and hang itself appropriately over the mosque of Muhammad the Conqueror.

[1] The address is given on Laurence Housman's authority, but it seems clear that this letter was written after Housman's return to England.

It was a great comfort to me not to have you with me in Constantinople: it would have been 'poor doggie!' every step of the way, and we should never have got a hundred yards from the hotel. They lie all about the streets and the pavement, mostly asleep, and almost all have got something the matter with them. They are extremely meek and inoffensive: Turkey is a country where dogs and women are kept in their proper place, and consequently are quite unlike the pampered and obstreperous animals we know under those names in England. The Turkish dog spends his life much like the English cat: he sleeps by day, and at night he grows melodious. He does not bark over his quarrels so much as English dogs do, and when he does bark it is sometimes rather like the quacking of a soprano duck; but he wails: whether he is winning or losing seems to make no difference, so dejected are his spirits. I soon got used to the noise, however, and it did not spoil my sleep. The people are very good in not treading on them, and so are the beasts of burden; but wheeled vehicles, which have got much commoner of late years, are less good to them, and the trams are not good to them at all. One night in the dark I trod on a dog lying exactly in the middle of the road: he squealed in a bitterly reproachful tone for a certain time; when he had finished, the next dog barked in an expostulatory manner for the same period, and then the incident was closed. Carts drawn by white oxen or by black buffaloes are pretty frequent in the streets; and once my carriage was stopped by a train of camels, but these are not common. The sheep, many of which are horned, have the whitest and prettiest wool I have ever seen. The Turks keep fighting rams as pets, and make matches between them: these lively creatures may sometimes be met in the streets, invading the greengrocers' shops and butting at the boys, who catch them by the horns.

The population is very mixed, and largely descended from kidnapped Christians. Pure Turks are rather rare, Greeks and Armenians common: a man is an Armenian when his nose is like this $\mathcal{C}$. I have come across the handsomest faces I ever saw: their figures are not so good. Some of the Greeks make you rub your eyes; their features and complexions are more like pictures than realities: though the women unfortunately bleach themselves by keeping out the sun. The Turks, when they are good-looking, I like even better; there is an aquiline type like the English aristocracy very much improved: if I could send you the photograph of a young man who rowed me to the Sweet Waters of Asia, and asked you to guess his name, you would instantly reply 'Aubrey de Vere Plantagenet'. But unless they take to outdoor work they get fat at an early age.

FRAGMENT OF A SUBSEQUENT LETTER

It is the great place to see the view from, as it commands the whole city, and shows you parts of the Bosphorus and Golden Horn and Sea of Marmora and the coast of Asia opposite. It is now used as a watch-tower for fires, which are common and dangerous in a city mostly built of wood. The watchmen pace round and look out of the eight windows continually for smoke or fire; then they signal by hanging out a flag by day or a lamp by night from the window which looks towards the fire, and this sign is seen by all the fire-stations. The fire-engines then go to the spot indicated and gaze at the conflagration: if the owner of the property likes to hire them, they will put out the fire for him, but not otherwise.

To Grant Richards

MS. ILLINOIS

23 September 1904   *17 North Road*

My dear Richards,

The printers' estimate for the Juvenal seems absurd, and they don't appear to understand the facts.

They say that 'the extent of both books is nearly the same'. That is true if they are talking about the amount of paper, but false if they are talking about the amount of print. The chief expense of the Manilius must have been the voluminous notes: the notes in the Juvenal, I should think, are not one quarter of what the Manilius notes were. The *text* of the Juvenal is about four times the text of the Manilius; but the text, though it fills a lot of paper, cannot be expensive to set up;—it is merely 4000 lines or so. The only thing that I can think of to explain their estimate is that the Juvenal notes will require a much larger proportion of Clarendon type, which perhaps is expensive.

Moreover the cost of the Manilius was largely due, I had supposed, to the rather numerous alterations which I made in proof. The original estimate for the Manilius was nothing like £84: it was something less than £50. (True, this was when I thought the introduction would be only 25 pages, and it afterwards ran to 75 pages; but they now say that introductions are cheap to print, so this won't explain the difference.) Possibly you have the original estimate for the Manilius in your archives: if so, it would be useful and instructive to compare it.

You understand what my point is: a page of the Manilius consisted on the average of less than 12 lines of text (large print) and more than 35 lines of notes (small print). In the Juvenal the proportion, I should think, will be more like 25 lines of text to 15 lines of notes, or often less: I remember one place (at the end of the fifth satire) where there are 30 lines of text without a single note.

I *can* pay the sum they ask,[1] but I very much object to, as Constantinople

---

[1] The printers' estimate of £84 was later reduced to £69 7s., which included the binding of the first 200 copies.

and the Orient Express are both pretty expensive, and I want to go to Italy next spring.[1]

Yours sincerely

A. E. HOUSMAN

If they are now printing the text and notes, as I understand they are, it ought to be quite easy to ascertain the proportion they bear to one another.

To Gilbert Murray

MS. BODLEY

13 October 1904   *University College*

Dear Murray,

If you would send me two tickets[2] for the 21st or 28th I should be pleased to make use of them.

You cannot deny that you are now in London, therefore your long-impending music-hall can no further be delayed. When is it to be? I am engaged to-morrow and on Saturday, but not later, except that Tuesdays and Wednesdays are less convenient than other evenings.

I received some weeks ago a letter from South Africa whose contents may interest you. The writer, whose name I forget, divides poetry into two classes: that which is tainted with the spirit of Le Gallienne, and that which is not. The latter class is small, and indeed appears to comprise only the following examples. First, and seemingly foremost, *A Shropshire Lad*. Secondly, Shakespeare's songs (not, it appears, anything else of his). Thirdly, a few early English poems. Fourthly, Goethe's 'Ueber allen Gipfeln'.[3] Fifthly a translation from a fragment of Euripides, about woods, which he once heard read by Professor Murray of Glasgow.[4]

Yours very truly

A. E. HOUSMAN

To Gilbert Murray

MS. BODLEY

25 October 1904   *17 North Road*

Dear Murray,

I went to the Court on Friday with your tickets and with a good deal of apprehension, as I find it generally a trial to hear actors and actresses reciting

---

[1] He did not go then, but went instead in September 1905.
[2] For Murray's translation of Euripides' *Hippolytus*, which opened at the Court Theatre, after a run at the Lyric, on 16 October 1904.
[3] i.e. 'Wanderers Nachtlied', written in 1780.
[4] Probably the first messenger's speech from *The Bacchae*, 1902.

75

verse. But though I can't say that witnessing the play gave me as much pleasure as reading it, it did give me pleasure and indeed excitement. I thought Theseus[1] on the whole the best. Phaedra is one of the parts which I used to plan out in detail a long while ago, and Miss Olive's[2] plan, though it may be as good, is rather different from mine, and so I was not quite happy with it. Ben Webster[3] is not Hippolytus, but who is? The most effective and unexpected thing to me was the statue of Cypris standing there quiet all the time.

Your lyrics, which are the most alluring part to read, were of course only imperfectly audible when sung: on the other hand some of the rhetoric in the dialogue came out very well indeed, especially the close of the messenger's speech. I hear that although you have not quite repeated Aeschylus' triumph with the Eumenides,[4] you have caused members of the audience to be removed in a fainting condition.

Yours very truly   A. E. HOUSMAN

To Grant Richards

TEXT: RICHARDS

24 November 1904   [*17 North Road*]

Almost immediately after I wrote to you last week, I heard, and was very sorry to hear, that there is a crisis in your affairs.[5] I hope that this will come out straight, and in the meantime I do not want to worry you with correspondence. I only write just to let you know, as is proper, that I propose to try to find someone else to undertake the publishing of the Juvenal, though I shall not find anyone to do it for nothing, as you were good enough to say you would. I suppose I may assume that you have no objection, and I will take silence to mean consent.

I don't know if you would have leisure or inclination to come and dine with me somewhere next week, but I should be very pleased if you would: say Friday 2 December. Perhaps I could get my brother to come.[6]

---

[1] Alfred Brydone (1864–1920).

[2] Edyth Olive (died 1956) began on the stage in 1892 in F. R. Benson's company. She later appeared in two other of Murray's translations.

[3] 1864–1947, acting since 1887.

[4] At the first performance, according to tradition, the children fainted and women in the audience miscarried.

[5] Richards found himself unable to meet his liabilities and was made bankrupt. His firm was sold, but he resumed business, initially under his wife's name, E. Grant Richards, in 1905.

[6] They dined at the Café Royal, then went on to a music-hall and the Criterion Bar.

To Wallace Rice[1]

MS. NEWBERRY

15 February 1905   *University College*

My dear Sir,

You are very welcome to include in your selection the piece 'To an athlete dying young';[2] but I object to the inclusion of the other two extracts, because one is only a fragment[3] and the other merely mentions football and cricket as palliations of misery.[4] If I may offer advice, I should recommend you not to insert poems containing mere casual allusions to athletics.

I am obliged by the kindness of your letter, and also by the graceful book of poems which you have been good enough to send me.

 I am yours very truly   A. E. HOUSMAN

To William Stewart[5]

MS. GLASGOW

17 February 1905   *University College*

Dear Sir,

 I gratefully acknowledge the flattering offer of the Honorary Degree of Doctor of Laws which in your letter of yesterday's date you have kindly communicated to me from the Senate of the University of Glasgow. But, for reasons which it would be tedious and perhaps difficult to enumerate, though they seem to me sufficient and decisive, I long ago resolved to decline all such honours, if they should ever be offered me. I have already, with feelings of equal embarrassment, excused myself from accepting a similar title at the hands of another University;[6] and if I ever in the future receive the same compliment I shall return the same reply. I can only beg to express my high appreciation of the kindness which has prompted the Senate of your University to offer me this valued distinction, and my regret that I am not able to accept it.

 I am your obedient servant   A. E. HOUSMAN

---

[1] Wallace de Groot Cecil Rice, American author and lecturer (1859–1939), editor of *The Athlete's Garland*, 1905.

[2] *A Shropshire Lad* XIX.

[3] Probably verses 3 and 4 of *A Shropshire Lad* XXVII.

[4] *A Shropshire Lad* XVII.

[5] 1835–1919; Professor of Divinity at Glasgow, 1873–1910; Clerk of Senate of the University, 1876–1911.

[6] It is not known which. Housman was subsequently offered honorary degrees at St Andrews, Liverpool, Oxford and the University of Wales. He refused them all in similar terms.

To Grant Richards

1 March 1905   *17 North Road*

My dear Richards,

The applicant may publish the songs so far as I am concerned, but I had rather you should tell her so, as I do not want to write letters to a lady whose name is Birdie.[1]

I told my solicitors to tell your Trustee the state of things about *A Shropshire Lad*.[2] As to the Manilius, they advised me to take possession of the copies, and offered to store them for me temporarily; and I believe this is now being done.[3] Thank you for the statement of accounts which you sent me the other day.

      Yours sincerely   A. E. HOUSMAN

To Grant Richards

17 April 1905   [*17 North Road*]

I am very sorry to see your father's death in to-day's paper; both for the loss to scholarship of his simple and disinterested love of learning, and also that this grief should come upon you in addition to your other troubles.

To Mrs Wise

25 April 1905   *17 North Road*

My dear Mrs Wise,

Here you see the effects of Woodchester air. I am not yet, perhaps, so great an artist as Laurence, but it seems to me that the enclosed sketch[4] (for it is little more) has a simple beauty of its own, and that the likenesses are lifelike.

      Yours affectionately   A. E. HOUSMAN

[1] Not traced.

[2] Since Housman had refused a contract for the book, Richards had no rights in it which could be sold with his other assets. Housman left the book for the time being in the hands of Richards' trustee. In April 1906 Richards issued as a sixth edition the remaining sheets of the 1903 printing bound in white.

[3] The stock of Manilius I was held by the binders, to whom Richards owed money. It was however Housman's property, and was recovered for him by Richards a year later.

[4] Of the Wises' dachshund Minka. Housman had stayed with Mrs Wise from 20 to 25 April.

To Mrs Grant Richards[1]

MS. ILLINOIS

8 June 1905   *17 North Road*

Dear Mrs Grant Richards,

Many thanks for your letter: I am proud to be your first author. I have told the printers to send you the 94 bound copies[2] which remain of the 100, six having been sent to me. I will send in a few days a list of the individuals and the reviews to which I want to have copies forwarded.

    I am yours sincerely   A. E. HOUSMAN

I am sending, to your address, a letter to G.R. which I want him to receive as soon as possible.

To Grant Richards

MS. ILLINOIS

8 June 1905   *17 North Road*

My dear Richards,

As I hear that you want to see me soon, it occurs to me to send you the enclosed,[3] in case you may be willing and able to use it. If you go, I shall be there about 9 o'clock, just drunk enough to be pleasant, but not so incapable as a publisher would like an author to be. If you don't go, you will probably escape a very tiresome entertainment.

    Yours sincerely   A. E. HOUSMAN

To Grant Richards

MS. ILLINOIS

13 June 1905   [*17 North Road*]

Your flamboyant production is not on any account to be printed. The following might serve:

'A critical edition of Juvenal by Mr A. E. Housman, intended to make good some of the principal defects in existing editions, and especially to supply a better knowledge of the manuscripts, will be published by . . .' (No nonsense about Shropshire lads).

    Yours   A. E. HOUSMAN

---

[1] Richards' first wife, nominal proprietor of the reorganized firm, of which he was manager.
[2] Of Juvenal.   [3] A theatre ticket.

To Grant Richards

MS. ILLINOIS

27 June 1905   *17 North Road*

My dear Richards,
  I suppose the delay is more annoying to you than to me, so I will not declaim about it.

    Yours sincerely   A. E. HOUSMAN

To Katharine Tynan Hinkson[1]

MS. TEXAS

4 July 1905   *University College*

Dear Mrs Hinkson,
  You have my permission to use the verses you require, and I daresay my brother will not be disagreeable.

    I am yours sincerely   A. E. HOUSMAN

To Grant Richards

MS. ILLINOIS

3 August 1905   *17 North Road*

My dear Richards,
  My competent or incompetent hand is quite innocent of any intention to edit Catullus; but Nonconformist ministers will say anything.[2] They believe in justification by faith, and act accordingly.

    Yours sincerely   A. E. HOUSMAN

Thanks for the German review (very hostile) of the Manilius. It is written by a young man who makes false quantities.

---

[1] Prolific Irish novelist and poet (1861–1931). She included three short extracts from *A Shropshire Lad*, and one stanza by Laurence Housman, in *A Book of Memory. The Birthday Book of the Blessed Dead*, 1905.
[2] Richards later thought that the reference was to the Rev. W. Robertson Nicoll, editor of *The British Weekly*; but I have not traced the paragraph in question. See also p. 144.

To Grant Richards

TEXT: RICHARDS

[circa *23 September 1905*]   *17 North Road*

... If you will let me take you to dine somewhere, I will let you take me to a music hall or theatre afterwards, on Wednesday or any later evening of the week. As I am just back from France and Italy, I am feeling British, and unless you protest I will take you to the Holborn and order the one good dinner which I know how to order there (there is only one): it is very simple and straightforward and distinctly British; so if you don't think you can stand it, say so. I leave you to fix the day, and also the hour.

To Grant Richards

MS. ILLINOIS

5 October 1905   *17 North Road*

My dear Richards,

Don't send a copy of the Juvenal to the *Oxford Magazine*. The request merely means that Owen[1] would like to write a second anonymous review.

Yours sincerely   A. E. HOUSMAN

To Grant Richards

MS. ILLINOIS

31 October 1905   *17 North Road*

My dear Richards,

After our failure to meet last week I am afraid that I forgot, together with many other things, that you wanted to see me; my excuse is the bother and discomfort of a change of house which is now going on.[2] On Thursday after 2 o'clock I can meet you where you like.

Yours sincerely   A. E. HOUSMAN

[1] Sidney George Owen (1858–1940), Student of Christ Church, Oxford, since 1891, had in 1903 edited the Oxford text of Juvenal, a work that Housman contemptuously ignored in his own edition.

[2] Housman's landlady, Mrs Trim, was moving out to Pinner. Housman went with her.

To Grant Richards

MS. ILLINOIS

14 November 1905   *1 Yarborough Villas, Pinner*

My dear Richards,

It afflicts me very much that I cannot come to your lunch and meet your attractive company of guests, but I have got much too bad a cold and cough. I have been in the country, and reached here only last night, when I found your note.

Yours sincerely   A. E. HOUSMAN

To Grant Richards

MS. ILLINOIS

15 November 1905   *University College*

My dear Richards,

I have come up to the College to do what is necessary, but I am not fit for company. My colds are always bad ones. I am very much annoyed on your account as well as my own. I send you my best wishes.

Yours sincerely   A. E. HOUSMAN

My books are in confusion at present, but I will look out a copy of the *Shropshire Lad*.

To Grant Richards

MS. ILLINOIS

15 November 1905   *1 Yarborough Villas*

My dear Richards,

Here is a copy of the first edition;[1] but if you are going to publish a new one, let me see the final proofs. There is no other way to ensure accuracy.

Yours sincerely   A. E. HOUSMAN

The Clarks[2] tell me that they have sent you 100 bound copies of Juvenal.

[1] Of *A Shropshire Lad*.
[2] R. & R. Clark, the printers.

82

To Grant Richards

MS. ILLINOIS

20 December 1905   *1 Yarborough Villas*

My dear Richards,

John Lane wrote to me about a week ago, asking if I could give him the publication of *A Shropshire Lad* in England and America, or in America only.[1] I replied that I had given the publication in England to E. Grant Richards and that I could not do anything about America without consulting that firm. Then he writes me the enclosed, on which I should like to have your views. Please return the letter.

Thanks for Drummond's *Cypress Grove*,[2] which is new to me. The cover, if you want my opinion, is both ugly and silly; but you probably have a just contempt for my artistic taste and will not allow this remark to embitter your Christmas.

Yours sincerely

A. E. HOUSMAN

To Grant Richards

MS. ILLINOIS

17 January 1906   *1 Yarborough Villas*

My dear Richards,

Lane is pressing for a reply: how about McClure's?[3]

Thanks for Hyde's illustration, which I think very nice.[4] I have read the Parisian part of *The Sands of Pleasure*:[5] it is interesting and well written.

Yours sincerely

A. E. HOUSMAN

P.S. The above remark about the novel is not to be regarded as an entry for your prize competition.

---

[1] Up to this time *A Shropshire Lad* had been distributed in the United States by the John Lane Company, New York, who bought the sheets from Kegan Paul and Richards. The book was not copyright in America, and Lane had no rights in it.

[2] Published by Richards in his 'Venetian Series' of sixpenny booklets.

[3] McClure, Phillips and Company, whose *McClure's Magazine* had already reprinted several poems from *A Shropshire Lad*.

[4] William Hyde, an artist whom Richards engaged to illustrate *A Shropshire Lad*, 1908. Richards had sent Housman a specimen drawing.

[5] By (Alexander Bell) Filson Young (1876–1938), published by Richards.

To Grant Richards

MS. ILLINOIS

24 January 1906   *1 Yarborough Villas*

My dear Richards,

I ought to tell you at once, as it may affect your plans, what I hear from John Lane this morning:—that John Lane Company of New York have informed him that they intend to make plates and reprint *A Shropshire Lad* in America. The history of the matter is this. Lane, as I told you, wrote to me on 12 December, asking to be given the publication of the book, or its publication in America, and adding that of course there was nothing to prevent him from reprinting the book there, but that he would not 'commit this act of piracy'. I replied that I must consult E. Grant Richards, but that if, on second thoughts, he could bring himself to turn pirate, it would inflict no injury on me personally, as I should not in any case accept royalties. John Lane Company say that they regard my kind letter as tantamount to permission to do what they intend to do.

It may interest my publisher to learn that she has broken all the traditions of the trade by making arrangements with another publisher in New York[1] without giving John Lane Company the opportunity of taking the new edition: that company is reluctantly, in self-defence, compelled to issue an edition of its own. There is etiquette, I daresay, even in Pandemonium.

Yours sincerely   A. E. HOUSMAN

To Henry Jackson

MS. TRINITY

30 January 1906   *1 Yarborough Villas*

My dear Jackson,

I wished that you should get the Greek professorship[2] in order that you might cease to sit up till four in the morning preparing lectures and looking over essays; but as your most intimate friends assure me that you do this because you like it, I do not see any reason why I should congratulate you. In any case, do not take any notice of this letter, as your mass of correspondence must be only second to that of your friend Chamberlain[3] when he got in for West Birmingham.

Yours sincerely   A. E. HOUSMAN

[1] Mitchell Kennerley, whose edition appeared in 1907.
[2] Jackson was elected to the Regius Professorship in succession to Sir Richard Jebb.
[3] Joseph Chamberlain (1836–1914) was Mayor of Birmingham, 1873–1875. He became Liberal Member of Parliament for Birmingham in 1876, and was President of the Board of

To Grant Richards

MS. ILLINOIS

10 February 1906   *1 Yarborough Villas*

My dear Richards,

Thanks for cheque for £3 2s. 3d.

As to the Manilius, I have no objection to incurring any publicity which may be entailed by your suing the binders as you propose. I will neither pay anything nor risk paying anything (because enough copies have been sold to make known what I wanted to make known, and my spare money I prefer to spend on producing other works). But when you say that it is of course understood that you pay the bill, I do not see why you should want to pay it, and I do not see what particular advantage you would gain by the rescue of my property from Leighton.

Yours sincerely   A. E. HOUSMAN

To Grant Richards

TEXT: RICHARDS

11 March 1906   [*1 Yarborough Villas*]

When I found your letter on the breakfast-table this morning, it reminded me that I had been dreaming about the subject in the night. I suppose that your amiable interest had been acting on me by telepathy. Anyhow I dreamt that I met the friend who introduced me to the wine, and asked him for its name, and he told me, and it was right; but alas, that is just the part of the dream that I have forgotten. It was a longer name than Corvo or Syracuse . . . I have been looking at the map of Sicily and I think it was *Camastra*.

To Grant Richards

MS. ILLINOIS

17 March 1906   *1 Yarborough Villas*

My dear Richards,

Please let me know when you are in possession of the Manilius, in order that I may close accounts with the lawyers I employed.

Yours sincerely   A. E. HOUSMAN

Trade, 1880–1885. He was elected Member for West Birmingham in the General Election of December 1885 after a vigorous campaign on his radical 'unauthorized programme'.

To Grant Richards

MS. ILLINOIS

29 March 1906   *1 Yarborough Villas*

My dear Richards,

Thanks for your news about Manilius and for your efforts in the matter, now crowned with success.[1]

I have ascertained that the name of the wine *is* Camastra, for the other day I was turning out a pocket and came upon the note I had made at the time. It appears that this benighted metropolis, full as it is of execrable Capri, contains none; but mind you order it if you find yourself at the Cavour in Milan.

I am afraid there is no chance of my being in Paris, at any rate so early as Easter Tuesday.

Yours sincerely   A. E. HOUSMAN

To Grant Richards

MS. ILLINOIS

7 April 1906   *1 Yarborough Villas*

My dear Richards,

Thanks for the copies of *A Shropshire Lad*. I suppose it is the edition of 1903 put into a white cover instead of a red, as it seems to have only the few misprints which distinguish that issue. The get-up, to my untutored eye, is nice.

If I am in Paris at all, it will be, roughly speaking, from the 19th to the 24th.

Yours sincerely   A. E. HOUSMAN

To Henry Jackson

MS. TRINITY

29 April 1906   *1 Yarborough Villas*

My dear Jackson,

I enclose a paper for the *Journal of Philology*.[2]

I hope I am doing correctly and acceptably in still directing to you as 'Dr'. I have been told by some authority that it is the higher title.

I may be in Cambridge this day week, and if so I will come and look you up.

Yours sincerely   A. E. HOUSMAN

---

[1] Recovery of the stock from the binders.

[2] 'Corrections and Explanations of Martial', printed in *The Journal of Philology*, 1907.

86

To Messrs Alexander Moring[1]

MS. LILLY

17 August 1906   *1 Yarborough Villas*

Dear Sirs,

Mr Grant Richards included my book *A Shropshire Lad* in his series of *The Smaller Classics* without consulting me, and to my annoyance. I contented myself with remonstrating, and did not demand its withdrawal; but now that I have the chance, I take it, and I refuse to allow the book to be any longer included in the series. I hope that you will not be very much aggrieved; but I think it unbecoming that the work of a living writer should appear under such a title.

I am yours faithfully   A. E. HOUSMAN

To Grant Richards

MS. ILLINOIS

17 August 1906   *1 Yarborough Villas*

My dear Richards,

Alexander Moring Ltd. have written to me asking to be allowed to continue to include *A Shropshire Lad* in *The Smaller Classics*. I have refused, and have told them how atrociously you behaved in ever including the book in the series, and how glad I am to have a chance of stopping the scandal.

I suppose you won't be in Paris between next Tuesday and Saturday. I shall be at the Normandy.

Yours sincerely   A. E. HOUSMAN

18 August. Mr Balfour Gardiner[2] may publish 'The Recruit' with music if he wants to. I always give my consent to all composers, in the hope of becoming immortal somehow.

To William Rothenstein[3]

MS. HARVARD

14 January 1907   *1 Yarborough Villas*

Dear Rothenstein,

Will you dine with me at the Café Royal on Friday, 1 February, at 7.30?

[1] The firm which had bought Richards' business after his bankruptcy.
[2] English composer (1877–1950). His setting of 'The Recruit' (*A Shropshire Lad* III) was published in 1906.
[3] English painter (1872–1945) best known for his portrait drawings; knighted 1931. He made three drawings of Housman in 1906, and two more in 1915.

The form which these orgies take is that after dinner we go to a music hall, and when the music hall closes, as I have no club, we are thrown on the streets and the pothouses: so you know what to expect.

On the evening when I last saw you, you were stricken with illness, and I afterwards heard that you had gone to Brighton to recruit. I hope you are well now. My kind regards to Mrs Rothenstein.[1]

Yours very truly

A. E. HOUSMAN

To Laurence Housman

TEXT: MEMOIR

1 February 1907   [*1 Yarborough Villas*]

My dear Laurence,

. . . I have induced Dr Morris[2] to tell me, on condition that Mamma does not hear that he told, the amount of his bill for last year. It is about £70 0s 0d; and I want to find out, if possible, what this will mean to Mamma. I have no clear notion of what her income is and what margin it generally leaves her; and perhaps you or Clemence can give me some notion. I am anxious to prevent her feeling any severe pinch for the bill, but on the other hand I don't want to be extravagant or ostentatious; so if you can help me to judge what I should give her in order to effect these two ends I should be much obliged.

Your bad behaviour in the theatre[3] I first heard of from your letters which were read to me at Hereford; I had seen nothing in the papers. I see the play is now taken off, but I suppose it will go into the provinces.

Rothenstein has made me a present of one of his three portraits of me. Perhaps when the weather is warmer and the spring more advanced you and Clemence will come out here and look at it . . .

Your affectionate brother

A. E. HOUSMAN

[1] Alice Knewstub (died 1958) married Rothenstein in 1899.
[2] Lucy Housman's doctor in Hereford, where she was now living.
[3] Laurence Housman had collaborated with Harley Granville Barker in writing a libretto for Liza Lehmann's *The Vicar of Wakefield*. He disapproved of alterations made in rehearsal, withdrew his name from the production, and, after imprudently going to the first performance at the Prince of Wales's Theatre on 12 December 1906, was forced to leave in order to avoid a fight with the manager. The latter was interviewed by the newspapers and gave a lurid account of Laurence Housman's behaviour in the theatre.

To Grant Richards

MS. ILLINOIS

17 April 1907   *Normandy Hotel, Paris*

My dear Richards,

On receiving your letter this morning I have sent you off a telegram, asking you, or rather commanding you (as is the manner of telegrams) to come and dine on Friday or lunch on Saturday. Perhaps it is impossible for you, however obedient, to get here on Friday; but, if you can, name your own dinner-hour, no matter how late.

I may be still here on Sunday, but it is uncertain.

Yours   A. E. HOUSMAN

To William Rothenstein

MS. HARVARD

23 April 1907   *1 Yarborough Villas*

My dear Rothenstein,

I am returning to you by Parcel Post Hudson's *El Ombu*,[1] which I have kept longer than I ought. I have read it with respect rather than admiration: the last story, the supernatural one, I thought the best. A piece like 'El Ombu' itself, hateful characters and harrowing events, showing man and God at their worst, is good to some extent if it is true, because then it is a weighty indictment of the nature of things.

I also send a copy of my poems which I promised you a long while ago. I think it is practically free from misprints, except one in the last piece, which I have corrected. The copy now in your possession I beg you to throw in the fire while there is a fire, before Mrs Rothenstein has had her spring cleaning and put Brunswick black on the grate.

Would you come and dine with me at the Café Royal on Friday 10 May at 7.30?

Yours sincerely   A. E. HOUSMAN

To Grant Richards

MS. ILLINOIS

7 May 1907   *1 Yarborough Villas*

My dear Richards,

Thanks for cheque for £1 10s. 5d.

[1] Published in 1902.

Wednesday is my best day for lunch, or else Friday.

The Athenaeum had previously reviewed both the Manilius and the Juvenal some time ago: to the Manilius they gave quite a long review in large print.[1]

Thanks for the *Triumph of Mammon*,[2] which is much more interesting to read than the *Theatrocrat*; but as for his knowledge which is going to change the world, it is just like the doctrine of the Trinity: probably false, and quite unimportant if true. The five lines at the top of p. 17 are the sort of thing he does really well.

Yours sincerely   A. E. HOUSMAN

To Grant Richards

MS. ILLINOIS

23 May 1907   *1 Yarborough Villas*

My dear Richards,

On pages 1, 8, 13, 24, 46, 72, 73, 83, I have marked for correction, if possible, certain ugly over-running of words from one line to another. Since these over-runnings existed in neither the 1896 nor the 1900 edition, it seems absurd that they should be necessary in this, which has smaller print than the former and a larger page than the latter. Moreover, on general grounds, a person like me, who habitually writes in metres which have short lines, ought not to be deprived by printers of the neatness which it is easy, in such metres, to preserve.

The further over-runnings which I have marked on pages 68, 82, 101, occurred in one or other of the two other editions, and therefore I do not so much object to them; but I suspect that they are really unnecessary. The over-runnings on page 48, on the other hand, may be necessary, as they occurred in the first edition and were only avoided in 1900 by not indenting the lines; but I am disposed to think that non-indentation would be preferable.

I feel that I did not earn my lunch the other day by the amount of information I was able to afford.

Yours sincerely   A. E. HOUSMAN

[1] *The Athenaeum*, 27 April 1907, reviewed Manilius I and Juvenal as though they were newly published.
[2] By John Davidson, 1907. *The Theatrocrat* had been published in 1905.

To Grant Richards

MS. ILLINOIS

29 June 1907   *1 Yarborough Villas*

My dear Richards,

Pray who gave Mr E. Thomas[1] leave to print two of my inspired lays in his and your *Pocket Book of Poems and Songs*? I didn't, though he thanks me in the preface. Just the same thing happened in the case of Lucas' *Open Road*,[2] issued by the same nefarious publisher. You must not treat my immortal works as quarries to be used at will by the various hacks whom you may employ to compile anthologies. It is a matter which affects my moral reputation: for six years back I have been refusing to allow the inclusion of my verses in the books of a number of anthologists who, unlike Mr Thomas, wrote to ask my permission; and I have excused myself by saying that I had an inflexible rule which I could not transgress in one case rather than another. Now these gentlemen, from Quiller-Couch[3] downward, will think I am a liar.

Mr Thomas thanks me for 'a poem', and prints two: which is the one he doesn't thank me for?

My temper, as you are well aware, is perfectly angelic, so I remain yours sincerely   A. E. HOUSMAN

To Grant Richards

MS. ILLINOIS

2 July 1907   *1 Yarborough Villas*

My dear Richards,

Thanks for your letter. What you have got in your head is the fact that I allow composers to set my music to words without any restriction. I never hear the music, so I do not suffer; but that is a very different thing from being included in an anthology with W. E. Henley or Walter de la Mare.

I did not remonstrate about *The Open Road*: I was speechless with surprise and indignation.

Yours sincerely   A. E. HOUSMAN

[1] Edward Thomas, poet, journalist and miscellaneous writer (1878–1917), edited Richards' *Pocket Book of Poems and Songs for the Open Air*, 1907. This anthology contained 'Reveille' and 'The Merry Guide' (*A Shropshire Lad* IV and XLII).

[2] E. V. Lucas, journalist and essayist (1868–1938), was literary adviser to Richards, who published his anthology *The Open Road* in 1899.

[3] Arthur Quiller-Couch, essayist and critic (1863–1944), edited *The Oxford Book of English Verse*, 1900. He was knighted in 1910 and became Professor of English at Cambridge in 1912.

To the Editor of Country Life[1]

7 November 1907   *University College*

Dear Sir,

I am obliged by your proposal, but several causes, of which barrenness is the chief, prevent me from contributing verses to periodical publications.

I am yours faithfully   A. E. HOUSMAN

To Alice Rothenstein

MS. HARVARD

9 February 1908   *1 Yarborough Villas*

Dear Mrs Rothenstein,

I am sorry for the misunderstanding and shall be very pleased to come on the 19th.

When Rothenstein gave me his portrait of me he also lent me (not *gave*) a portfolio to carry it away in. This ought long ago to have returned to him, but it has been swallowed by the man who framed the portrait, or otherwise vanished; so I have sent another, which I hope has now reached the artist and will occasionally remind him of me when he uses it.

Yours sincerely   A. E. HOUSMAN

To Laurence Housman

TEXT: MEMOIR

17 February 1908   *[1 Yarborough Villas]*

My dear Laurence,

. . . I should be very glad to look through your selections.[2] Did I ever say anything abusive about *Spikenard*?[3] I think on the whole it is about the cleverest of your poetry books . . .

So overpowering is your celebrity that I have just received an official letter from my own college addressed to 'Professor L. Housman' . . .

Your affectionate brother   A. E. HOUSMAN

[1] Text from *The Dalhousie Review* XXIX, 1950.
[2] For Laurence Housman's *Selected Poems*, 1908.
[3] He had described it as 'nonsense verse'. (Laurence Housman's note.)

To Grant Richards

MS. ILLINOIS

17 February 1908   *1 Yarborough Villas*

My dear Richards,
   I am told that a young lady[1] whom I have met once or twice in Gloucestershire, and who 'wants to take up black and white drawing' (having done
watercolours hitherto, I think) and who 'has lately been studying under
Cameron,[2] and he says that her architectural drawings are wonderful', wants
an introduction to my publisher. (I rather gather that she is under the deplor-
able impression that my publisher is Macmillan, but let that pass.) As you
were talking the other day about some architectural book, I wondered if you
would care to see her. She is tall and beauteous, but let that pass too.
   And pray what is the exact process of introducing people to one's publisher? Does one provide them with a letter, which they present at the door
of the spider's parlour?

Yours sincerely   A. E. HOUSMAN

To Grant Richards

MS. ILLINOIS

20 February 1908   *1 Yarborough Villas*

My dear Richards,
   I showed your picture to our professor of Archaeology,[3] who says that it is
most fanciful, and the rowing arrangements impracticable. Representations
of triremes exist at Pompeii and have been reproduced in several books, the
best of which is probably Baumeister's *Denkmäler*.[1]
   Thanks for your reply about Miss Frood, for such is her name, and also
for Filson Young's book,[5] which is pretty.

Yours sincerely   A. E. HOUSMAN

---

[1] Hester Frood (born 1882). She was duly employed by Richards as an illustrator, and
subsequently exhibited at the Royal Academy and held several one-man shows.
[2] David Young Cameron (1865–1945); elected Royal Academician, 1920; knighted, 1924.
[3] Ernest Arthur Gardner (1862–1939).
[4] Published in three volumes, 1884–1888.
[5] Probably *When the Tide Turns*, published by Richards in 1908.

To J. P. Postgate[1]

MS. NEWCASTLE

22 February 1908   *1 Yarborough Villas*

Dear Postgate,

I return Headlam's pamphlet,[2] for which I am much obliged, and hope I have not kept it an unconscionable time. He has the comic phraseology and vocabulary at his fingers' ends, and keeps a sharper eye on the metre than Wilamowitz;[3] but he does not see so far as he ought into the situations and the action, and this has led him into some strange mistakes.

Yours sincerely   A. E. HOUSMAN

To Alice Rothenstein

MS. HARVARD

26 February 1908   *1 Yarborough Villas*

Dear Mrs Rothenstein,

During the last week I have been engaged on a special piece of work which has interested me and caused me to postpone as much of my ordinary work as could be postponed; so that now I have arrears which must be got rid of, and will not allow me to be with you to-night. I am very sorry.

Yours sincerely   A. E. HOUSMAN

To Laurence Housman

TEXT: MEMOIR

1 March 1908   [*1 Yarborough Villas*]

My dear Laurence,

. . . With your inclusions from *Spikenard* I agree, except that I have very decidedly struck out one. In the other books I have not actually struck out anything (except once) and have even made one or two additions, which I think quite as good as the average of the inclusions. The pieces which I think your best, apart from *Spikenard*, are, in *Rue*, "Long through the night",

---

[1] John Percival Postgate (1853–1926), Professor of Comparative Philology at University College, London, 1880–1908; Professor of Latin at Liverpool, 1909–1920; editor of the *Corpus Poetarum Latinorum* (two volumes, 1894 and 1905), to which Housman contributed the texts of Juvenal and Ovid's 'Ibis'.

[2] 'Restorations of Menander', 1908, by Walter George Headlam (1866–1908), Fellow of King's College, Cambridge.

[3] Ulrich von Wilamowitz-Moellendorf (1848–1931), the outstanding Greek scholar of the day.

94

"Amid this grave-strewn", "What know ye of", and "Dark to its nest"; in *Mendicant Rhymes*, "The Settlers"; and in *The Little Land*, "The Elfin Bride": so I think these should in any case go in. "Mendicant Rhymes" itself, though rather obscure and untidy, is decidedly pretty, but the stanza where 'Chloe' rhymes to 'Evoe' would have to be altered, because Evoe is a word of two syllables, εὐοῖ, and the *oe* is a diphthong, and you might put two million dots on the top of it instead of two without changing its length. Speaking generally, I think the inclusions at present too many and too monotonous: I should not put in all the sonnets of *The Little Land* (sonnets stodge up a book more than anything, even blank verse), nor so much of *Rue*. The strong point of your poetry seems to me to be a lively fancy: you seem rather to value the pieces on account of thoughts or emotions which suggested them, without enough considering whether they are really reproduced in the words. Thus "Across these barren clods" is much more attractive and in- telligible to a reader than a great deal of its surroundings, which you prefer; and similarly "A Garden Enclosed" is more successful than "The Man in Possession", though I don't understand 'life's a fault' in the last verse. "The New Orpheus" I should call too long, and by no means so good in its way as "Advocatus Diaboli", though this wants making clearer and neater in parts.

I should be glad to look over the text when the selections are made, especially as you have a way of treating words like 'Messiah' and 'royal' as if they were a syllable shorter than they are—possibly in the vain hope of making amends for 'Evoë' . . .

A. E. HOUSMAN

Your affectionate brother

To Grant Richards

MS. ILLINOIS

16 May 1908   *1 Yarborough Villas*

My dear Richards,

Mr I. B. Gurney[1] (who resides in Gloucester Cathedral along with St Peter and Almighty God) must not print the words of my poems in full on concert programmes (a course which I am sure his fellow-lodgers would disapprove of); but he is quite welcome to set them to music, and to have them sung, and to print their titles on programmes when they are sung.

If you can lunch with me on Wednesday I will come down about one o'clock.

Yours sincerely   A. E. HOUSMAN

[1] Ivor Bertie Gurney, composer and poet (1890–1937), assistant organist at Gloucester Cathedral, 1906–1911, composed two song cycles with words from *A Shropshire Lad*: *Ludlow and Teme*, 1923, and *The Western Playland*, 1926.

To Laurence Housman[1]

26 May 1908   1 Yarborough Villas

My dear Laurence,
I enclose cheque for five guineas which Kate has asked me to send you towards the sundial in Bathwick cemetery.[2] I was down there last Saturday: the stone looks well enough, but the dial is conspicuously marked with an advertisement of the Birmingham Art Company, or whatever it is, which will have to be erased. The sign of our redemption, which has also been added, is less obnoxious, except that its addition is due to a lying priest . . .

To Grant Richards

MS. ILLINOIS

27 May 1908   1 Yarborough Villas

My dear Richards,
I have written to R. & R. Clark.
The fates seem to be against our meeting, but after all I don't know that it is necessary we should meet about Hyde's drawings.[3] I did not know that they were to be in colour, and should have preferred black and white; but the colour has a good effect in the autumnal scene on Wenlock Edge. As to the four I saw, I liked three of them; but the one entitled 'On the Teme' had nothing distinctive about it and might have been anywhere: the crescent moon, for instance, is a cosmopolitan embellishment, and I have seen it in France. He might have got a much more striking and characteristic view of the Teme under Whitecliff just opposite Ludlow. But the three views of Clee Hill and Ludlow and Wenlock Edge are quite the sort of thing required.

Yours sincerely   A. E. HOUSMAN

To Grant Richards

MS. ILLINOIS

6 June 1908   1 Yarborough Villas

My dear Richards,
1. I do not in the least want the crescent moon *removed* from the drawing 'On the Teme', as Mr Hyde seems to think.

[1] Text from *A. E. Housman: Man Behind a Mask* by Maude M. Hawkins, 1958
[2] On the outskirts of Bath, where Robert Housman died in 1905. The sundial was intended as a family monument. The vicar, regarding the design as pagan, had insisted on the addition of a cross.
[3] For the illustrated edition of *A Shropshire Lad*, 1908.

96

2. I suppose it was you who sent him on his wild goose chase to Hughley. I carefully abstained from suggesting that subject.

A view of the Wrekin from the neighbourhood of Much Wenlock, as he suggests, would do quite well.

4. I have no objection to his proposal about the frontispiece.

5. Long years ago I warned Laurence that if ever I wrote a book I would never let him decorate it.

Yours sincerely   A. E. HOUSMAN

To Henry Jackson

MS. TRINITY

26 June 1908   *1 Yarborough Villas*

My dear Jackson,

No doubt you are snowed up with congratulations:[1] do not take any notice of this. There is something to be said for a Liberal government after all.

If you experienced a sudden access of salubrity about 1.45 to-day, that was caused by Rothenstein and me drinking your health.

Yours sincerely   A. E. HOUSMAN

To Laurence Housman

TEXT: MEMOIR

27 June 1908   [*1 Yarborough Villas*]

My dear Laurence,

... I enjoyed parts of your play[2] very much, especially the first transformation of the picture, which was so effective that I think the act ought to have ended there. Olangtsi is very good and very well acted, and Mee Mee too is quite nice, and the Jews, especially the opulent one, are amusing. The acting of the students on the other hand, especially their voices and intonation, I thought almost the worst I had ever come across; and the words they have to say and sing seem to me to contain a good deal of your wet wit. And then there is the infernal music.[3] Theatres are beginning to exhibit notices asking ladies to remove their hats; my patronage shall be bestowed on the theatre which goes a step further and requests the orchestra to be silent. The sleep-walking scene ought to have been good; but it left me faint and weak from the effort of straining to hear the human voice through the uproar of pussy's bowels.

[1] On his appointment to the Order of Merit.
[2] *The Chinese Lantern*, which opened at the Haymarket Theatre on 16 June 1908.
[3] By Joseph Moorat.

Rothenstein asked me to express to you his great pleasure and admiration. He also explained to me the moral; which is that if one wants to be a great artist one must be *absorbed* in a work of art. He very politely assumed that I saw it myself; but alas, I did not.

Both Millington and George Fletcher[1] want to see me at the Bromsgrove dinner on the 8th, so I am going; but I have announced to Bunting[2] that I shall not make a speech.

I read an article on your work[3] by a most affected writer in a magazine whose name I forget, though I have got it in the next room; and I have sufficient artistic taste to be aware that the drawing of a lady and a tortoise is good. About the 'Night' I should not have felt sure; not that I have anything against it . . .

Your affectionate brother   A. E. HOUSMAN

To Grant Richards

MS. ILLINOIS

27 June 1908   *1 Yarborough Villas*

My dear Richards,

On the title page the three words *A Shropshire Lad* should be in one line, as in all the editions except the atrocious production of 1904. I have also marked small details on pp. vii and 13. The repetition of p. 3 as p. 11 is one of those sacred mysteries with which I don't interfere.

The corrections apply also to the American edition; but I am retaining the proofs of that unless you want them back.

Bywater[4] is resigning the Greek chair at Oxford, and Herbert Richards[5] ought to succeed him. Whether he will is quite another question. It is a Regius professorship, and the King generally asks the advice of one or two persons whom he supposes to be good judges. He has not applied to me: possibly because we have not been introduced.

Yours sincerely   A. E. HOUSMAN

Have I changed my publisher? What has become of E. Grant Richards?[6]

[1] 1848–1933; son of a Bromsgrove doctor; at Bromsgrove School, 1857–1866; at this time in medical practice in Highgate.
[2] William Louis Bunting (born 1873) taught at Bromsgrove School, 1897–1904. He was now secretary of the Old Bromsgrovian Club.
[3] By Charles Kains-Jackson in *The Book Lover's Magazine*, 1908.
[4] Ingram Bywater (1840–1914), Fellow of Exeter College, Oxford, had been Regius Professor since 1893.
[5] Herbert Paul Richards (1848–1916), uncle of Grant Richards; Fellow of Wadham College, Oxford, and one of the examiners who had failed Housman in Greats in 1881.
[6] Richards now reverted to publishing under his own name.

98

To Grant Richards

MS. ILLINOIS

4 July 1908   *1 Yarborough Villas*

My dear Richards,

The manuscript is numbered M 31 in the Biblioteca Nacional at Madrid. It contains Manilius and the Silvae of Statius.[1] What I really want is to have photographs of the first 107 pages, on which the Manilius is written. The cheapest process is one called (I think) *rotary-bromine*, in which no negative is used: whether this is practised in Madrid I can't be sure. The sums one is charged for photographs vary greatly in different towns and countries: I am prepared to go to £20, though it ought to be less, and in Rome at any rate would be very much less, probably about £5.

Yours sincerely   A. E. HOUSMAN

To Gilbert Murray

MS. BODLEY

17 October 1908   *1 Yarborough Villas*

Dear Murray,

I see in the paper the confirmation of what has been common rumour for some time past,[2] and I congratulate you on having survived a Scotch professorship long enough to obtain what I hope will be consolation even for that.

I think you are now well on your way to take that place in the public eye which used to be occupied by Jowett[3] and then by Jebb; and as you are a much better scholar than the one and a much better man of letters than the other, the public will be a gainer without knowing it, and good judges (by which I mean myself) will be less at variance with the public.

I am yours sincerely   A. E. HOUSMAN

You will be buried under letters of congratulation, so take no notice of this.

---

[1] Housman was now at work on his edition of Manilius II. It was published in 1912.
[2] His appointment as Regius Professor of Greek at Oxford.
[3] Benjamin Jowett (1817–1893); Regius Professor of Greek at Oxford, 1855–1893; Master of Balliol College, 1870–1893; well known for his translations of Plato and Thucydides.

To Laurence Housman

TEXT: MEMOIR

3 November 1908   [*1 Yarborough Villas*]

My dear Laurence,

... On page 11[1] 'when first knighted' sounds very prosy, though I don't think my suggestion much better, as it is ambiguous.[2] I have not found much else to note. The pieces on pp. 18 and 28 are really quite nice: I don't remember noticing them before.

I was at Cambridge a week or two ago, and met a lady who asked if I were the author of *Gods and their Makers*. Always honest, I owned that I was not: I said I was his brother. 'Oh, well,' said she, 'that's the next best thing.' It appears that the work is a household word with them: they have a dog or a cat called after one of your divinities ...

      Your affectionate brother   A. E. HOUSMAN

To Laurence Housman

TEXT: MEMOIR

8 November 1908   [*1 Yarborough Villas*]

My dear Laurence,

... The changes in 'Advocatus Diaboli' are very judicious.

The line on p. 52 is as bad as ever. I think you should try what you can do with *default* or *assault*; for I am afraid that salt and malt and cobalt are no good. There is however a kind of stiff clay called gault, in which I daresay sepulchres are sometimes dug.[3]

On p. 71, last line but one, I should restore the old reading, because it is not good to have two lines with their last halves so much on the same model as *the pangs he bore* and *the wound he wore*.[4]

The misprint on p. 101 is eloquent of the printer's cockney pronunciation ...

      Your affectionate brother   A. E. HOUSMAN

[1] In the page proofs of Laurence Housman's *Selected Poems*.
[2] The version printed is 'newly knighted'.
[3] The printed version reads: 'Or open to the skies a vault/Where basking sunnily I lie,/And negligent to Time's assault,/With foot in earth prepare to die.'
[4] This suggestion was not adopted.

To Grant Richards

MS. ILLINOIS

8 November 1908   *1 Yarborough Villas*

My dear Richards,

I do not care for the new edition;[1] but as it was brought out simply to please you and not me, that does not matter. Coloured plates always strike me as vulgar (though I understand that they are the fashion at present), and these drawings of Hyde's do not seem to me nearly so good as those in his London book. The end papers, on the other hand, I rather like, though the horses seem to be letting the man do all the ploughing. It lies, I find, on drawing-room tables, so all is well.

To the fate of the widows and orphans whom it appears that you have been introducing to outside brokers I am totally indifferent, having no spirit in my body.[2]

    Yours sincerely   A. E. HOUSMAN

To William Rothenstein

MS. HARVARD

15 January 1909   *1 Yarborough Villas*

My dear Rothenstein,

Will you dine with me at the Café Royal on Friday 5 February at 7.45?

I am anxious to know what it is that you think British Art requires in order to regenerate it: whether it is ribald laughter going up to heaven, or a river of laughter coming down from heaven; for the papers are not agreed.[3]

Remember me to Mrs Rothenstein.

    Yours very truly   A. E. HOUSMAN

To Grant Richards

MS. ILLINOIS

15 January 1909   *1 Yarborough Villas*

My dear Richards,

Miss or Mrs Jewell may be told that she can set and publish to her heart's content.[4] If you like to add that she displays an honourable scrupulousness

---

[1] The illustrated edition of 2,000 copies of *A Shropshire Lad*.

[2] Richards had been attacked in *The Academy* for allowing book-marks advertising the business of an outside broker to be inserted in books published by his firm.

[3] In their reports of Rothenstein's lecture at the London Institution. He had argued that art would remain second-rate 'until a great river of laughter comes down from Heaven at . . . the pictures which are daily shown as works of serious importance.'

[4] Lucina Jewell (born 1874) does not appear to have published any settings of Housman.

which is doubly remarkable inasmuch as it makes its appearance in a woman and an American; or if you like to quote the opinion of a doctor which I see in to-day's paper, that there are more people with unbalanced minds in Boston than anywhere else, do so: but don't say that I put you up to it.

Will you dine with me at the Café Royal on Friday 5 February at 7.45? I am also asking Rothenstein.

Yours sincerely   A. E. HOUSMAN

I will remember about the Cheshire Cheese.[1]

To Grant Richards

TEXT: RICHARDS

23 January 1909   [*1 Yarborough Villas*]

I have received your noble present of Montaigne, and I only wish the rest of my library were fit to keep it company. I have never read him yet in Florio's translation:[2] as a boy I used to study Cotton's,[3] which is good, but less good, I suppose. Thank you also for the guide to Paris.[4] The question whether I ever go to Vienna depends on the question whether you produce a similar guide to it.

The pudding was not only palatable but digestible.[5]

To Alice Rothenstein

MS. HARVARD

28 May 1909   *1 Yarborough Villas*

Dear Mrs Rothenstein

I hope that my conversation through the telephone yesterday did not sound brusque. I am very little accustomed to using that instrument. I was very sorry not to be able to come to the theatre with you, but I had an engagement out of town for the evening, and I was just leaving the college to catch my train when the beadle told me that someone had been enquiring for me.

Please tell Rothenstein that all my Jewish students are absenting themselves from my lectures from Wednesday to Friday this week on the plea that

---

[1] A Fleet Street inn, well known for its association with Dr Johnson and, later, with the Rhymers' Club of the eighteen nineties.

[2] First published in 1603; now reprinted by Richards in his Elizabethan Classics series.

[3] First published in 1685.

[4] *The Waistcoat Pocket Guide to Paris* by Leonard Williams. Richards did not publish a guide to Vienna.

[5] The beef-steak, lark, kidney and oyster pudding at the Cheshire Cheese.

these are Jewish holidays. I have been looking up the Old Testament, but I can find no mention there of either the Derby or the Oaks.[1]

Yours sincerely   A. E. HOUSMAN

To Grant Richards

MS. ILLINOIS

6 July 1909   *1 Yarborough Villas*

My dear Richards,

I am very much indebted to you for sending me Royall Tyler's *Spain*,[2] which is a capital straightforward business-like book, exactly the sort of thing I like and find *exciting*. How the public will bear the absence of the usual twaddle I don't know.

My only objection is to the title, as I think Spain is a neuter noun.

Yours sincerely   A. E. HOUSMAN

To Lily Thicknesse

TEXT: MEMOIR

11 August 1909   [*1 Yarborough Villas*]

Dear Mrs Thicknesse,

. . . My blood boils. This is not due to the recent commencement of summer, but to the Wrongs of Woman, with which I have been making myself acquainted.[3] 'She cannot serve on any Jury'; and yet she bravely lives on. 'She cannot serve in the army or navy'—oh cruel, cruel!—'except'—this adds insult to injury—'as a nurse'. They do not even employ a Running Woman instead of a Running Man for practising marksmanship. I have been making marginal additions. 'She cannot be ordained a Priest or Deacon': add *nor become a Freemason*. 'She cannot be a member of the Royal Society': add *nor of the Amateur Boxing Association*. In short your unhappy sex seem to have nothing to look forward to, except contracting a valid marriage as soon as they are 12 years old; and that must soon pall.

Thanks for the picture card. I did not know, or had forgotten, that you were at Woodbridge.[4] If you can find an old hat of Edward FitzGerald's they

---

[1] Run at Epsom on 26 and 28 May 1909. The Jewish Feast of Weeks in 1909 fell on 26 and 27 May.

[2] *Spain: A Study of Her Life and Arts*, just published by Richards.

[3] Mrs Thicknesse had sent him a copy of her husband's Suffragist pamphlet *The Rights and Wrongs of Women*.

[4] In Suffolk, home of Edward FitzGerald (1809–1883), poet and translator of Omar Khayyam.

will let you write three columns about it in the *Athenaeum*. But some literary people are so proud that they despise these avenues to fame . . .

     Yours sincerely   A. E. HOUSMAN

To Alice Rothenstein

MS. HARVARD

11 August 1909   *1 Yarborough Villas*

Dear Mrs Rothenstein,
    I am glad you have found such a pleasant spot and are enjoying yourselves. I have been rather industrious and have only been away for short visits. I may perhaps be going for another to Swanage, where my married sister and her family are, or *were*; for I hear nothing from them, and they have probably perished in the water-famine which you just escaped.
    I don't expect to come to France much before September, and then I shall not stay very long; and all the time that I can spare from the vices of Paris (as to which, consult William) I expect to spend in visiting cathedral towns which I have not yet seen. The life you sketch at Vaucottes-sur-mer, and kindly invite me to join you in, is very attractive, but when it is gone it is gone, and has not stored one's mind (except of course with the instructive conversation of the Rothenstein family, including John's[1] views on the soul and our future life) and one cannot boast about it afterwards. Though, after all, that is equally true of the vices of Paris.
    Remember me to all who remember me, and believe me yours sincerely

                                  A. E. HOUSMAN

To Grant Richards

MS. ILLINOIS

8 October 1909   *University College*

My dear Richards,
    I have noted the day and hour at which I am to go and have my teeth taken out by Lamb,[2] but I find that I have not got his address.

---

  [1] The Rothensteins' elder son, born 1901; Director of the Tate Gallery, 1936–1963; knighted, 1952.
  [2] Henry Lamb (1883–1960), well known portrait painter; elected Royal Academician, 1949. Richards had commissioned a drawing of Housman as the first of a series of portraits of friends whose work he published. Lamb made a second drawing, which is now in the possession of Trinity College, Cambridge. It was first reproduced in *The Trinity Review*, 1967.

I like Masefield[1] very much. Who was the other young man, who reads Manilius?[2]

Yours sincerely   A. E. HOUSMAN

To Gilbert Murray

MS. BODLEY

12 October 1909   *1 Yarborough Villas*

Dear Murray,

I shall be very pleased to stay with you the night of 26 November. I have work at the College in the morning, and will come down in the afternoon.

I have chosen a dry subject for my paper,[3] as I have no doubt that scholarship at Oxford is taking on an excessively literary tinge under the influence of the new Professor of Greek.

I am yours sincerely   A. E. HOUSMAN

To Grant Richards

MS. ILLINOIS

16 October 1909   *1 Yarborough Villas*

My dear Richards,

I can sit to Lamb again next Thursday at the same hour, if that will suit him. Why was I ever born? This question is addressed to the universe, not to you personally.

Yours sincerely   A. E. HOUSMAN

To Grant Richards

MS. ILLINOIS

11 November 1909   *1 Yarborough Villas*

My dear Richards,

'The terms' on which Mr Lambert[4] may print my words with his music are that he should spell my name right.

[1] John Masefield (1878–1967), poet, novelist and playwright; Poet Laureate, 1930.
[2] Eric Robert Dalrymple Maclagan (1879–1951); son of Dr William Maclagan, Archbishop of York; employed in the Victoria and Albert Museum, 1905; Director, 1924–1945; knighted, 1945.
[3] 'Greek Nouns in Latin Poetry', read to the Oxford Philological Society in New College on 26 November.
[4] E. Frank Lambert published a setting of 'The Street Sounds to the Soldiers' Tread' (*A Shropshire Lad* XXII) in 1914.

As to Mr Vaughan Williams,[1] about whom your secretary wrote: he came to see me, and made representations and entreaties, so that I said he might print the verses he wanted on his programmes. I mention this lest his action should come to your ears and cause you to set the police after him.

Yours sincerely   A. E. HOUSMAN

To Grant Richards

MS. ILLINOIS

27 November 1909   *1 Yarborough Villas*

My dear Richards,

Well, I will go to Lamb next Thursday if he likes, and I have written to tell him so: I have addressed the letter to 8 Fitzroy Street, though I am not quite sure if that is the number: if not, let me know.

I hope you will relate the incident to Mrs Richards, in order that she may see what a false notion of my temper she has, and how angelic it really is.[2]

I met your uncle[3] in Oxford yesterday, and returning here I find his last book, for which I am much obliged to the author or publisher, whichever is the donor: the enclosed slip says that it is sent for review and will not be published till the 29th of last month.

Yours sincerely   A. E. HOUSMAN

To Gilbert Murray

MS. BODLEY

9 December 1909   *1 Yarborough Villas*

Dear Murray,

I have read Mrs Taylor's poems,[4] that you were kind enough to give me, with a good deal of pleasure and interest. There are phrases and lines that are quite beautiful, and she has not only technical skill but impulse; and yet there is a curious indistinctness about the general impression, and hardly a poem that rings clear. She is rather like the second Lord Lytton;[5] susceptible to the beauty of other people's poetry, and giving out an answering note, beautiful in its way; and she is not so terribly fluent as he was, not such a

[1] Ralph Vaughan Williams (1872–1958), the foremost English composer of his generation. His song cycle *On Wenlock Edge* (settings of poems from *A Shropshire Lad*) was published in 1909.
[2] Lamb had missed an earlier appointment.
[3] Herbert Richards.
[4] *Rose and Vine*, 1909, by Rachel Annand Taylor (1876–1960).
[5] English poet (pseudonym Owen Meredith), (1831–1891).

106

bare-faced thief. The appeal to the optic nerve is almost shameless, and becomes monotonous. I like best some of the short pieces, like "The Young Martyrs". The poem on the Magi, as you said, is also good.

Will it be possible to break female poets of using such words as 'passional' and feeling proud of it?

Yours sincerely   A. E. HOUSMAN

To Grant Richards

TEXT: RICHARDS

15 February 1910   [*1 Yarborough Villas*]

As you are so good, I could come down on the 26th by the 5.50 from Paddington (I am writing with only a rather obsolete Bradshaw[1] at hand), and I should be very glad to stay till the Monday morning. Let me know the name of your house, unless your own celebrity in the neighbourhood is sufficient.

In Venice I almost always go to the Europa, which has absolutely the best possible situation and is not too large. In dignity, according to my gondolier, it ranks next to Danieli's, where the food and drink are better, but which is noisy, and not central enough, and dearer. A cheaper hotel, which I hear well spoken of, is the Luna, close to the royal palace; I have been inside it, and it struck me as well managed.

The best restaurant to my thinking is the Vapore, and my gondolier tells me that all foreigners say the same. From the piazza you go under the clock and along the Merceria till you come to a high bridge over a canal: there, instead of crossing it, you turn sharp to the left. Much greater simplicity is to be had at either of the two Giorgiones, one near San Silvestro and one near the Santi Apostoli; but the food is not very appetising, except the *Baccalà pizzicato* (salt cod mashed up with milk and pepper) which they have on Fridays.

At Milan I always stay at the Cavour, which I believe is really the best hotel, and certainly the most pleasantly situated. It is rather far from the cathedral, but fairly near to the picture gallery. The Hotel de la Ville, in the centre of the city, is, according to Horatio Brown, the best in Italy, but Ashburner[2] dislikes it: you have met them both, so you can choose which to believe. The Cavour is not cheap, but nothing outrageous. The restaurants of Milan I know nothing about: I suppose I have been in one or two, but if so I have forgotten them.

---

[1] The railway guide, published from 1842 until 1961. Richards had invited Housman to visit him at Cookham Dean in Berkshire.

[2] Walter Ashburner (1864–1936), American-born lawyer; Professor of Jurisprudence at Oxford, 1926–1929.

To Witter Bynner

MS. HARVARD

28 February 1910   *1 Yarborough Villas*

Dear Mr Bynner,

I was glad to hear from you and to learn that you are well and active; but as to your enquiry, I have not published any poem, since the last that you have seen. The other day I had the curiosity to reckon up the complete pieces, printed and unprinted, which I have written since 1896, and they only come to 300 lines, so the next volume appears to be some way off. In barrenness, at any rate, I hold a high place among English poets, excelling even Gray.[1]

I am yours sincerely   A. E. HOUSMAN

To Mrs Platt

MS. U.C.L.

2 March 1910   *1 Yarborough Villas*

Dear Mrs Platt,

I shall be very pleased to come on Monday. Gin is defined in the dictionary as 'a trap or snare', but it is quite unnecessary in this case.

Yours sincerely   A. E. HOUSMAN

To Alice Rothenstein

MS. HARVARD

4 March 1910   *1 Yarborough Villas*

Dear Mrs. Rothenstein,

People are asking me out a great deal too often, and you are one of the chief offenders. I am not a social butterfly like you: nature meant me for solitude and meditation (which frequently takes the form of going to sleep): talking to human beings, whether 'lovely ladies' or not, for any length of time leaves me in a state of prostration, and will finally undermine my health unless I take care. By declining your invitation for next Wednesday I calculate that I shall make you very indignant, and then you will leave me severely alone for a long time, which may save me from premature decease,—at least, if other people do the same, as I will try to make them.

Yes, I had a very fine and pleasant Sunday at Marlow, or rather Cookham Dean.

I am, though you may not think so, yours sincerely   A. E. HOUSMAN

---

[1] Thomas Gray (1716–1771), author of the 'Elegy', wrote little, refused the appointment of Poet Laureate, and declined payment for his poetry. He was Professor of History and Modern Languages at Cambridge, 1768–1771.

108

To William Rothenstein

MS. HARVARD

22 March 1910   *1 Yarborough Villas*

Dear Rothenstein,

I am much obliged to you for sending me Mrs(?) Cornford's poems.[1] I do not call them exactly good, except in phrases here and there; but they are really interesting and I am glad to have them. The verses about the horse and donkey are quite capital, and the triolet about the unhappy lady in gloves has moved me to the imitation on the opposite page. I hope Mrs Rothenstein does not languish.

Yours sincerely   A. E. HOUSMAN

O why do you walk through the fields in boots,
Missing so much and so much?
O fat white woman whom nobody shoots,
Why do you walk through the fields in boots,
When the grass is soft as the breast of coots
And shivering-sweet to the touch?

To Grant Richards

MS. ILLINOIS

12 April 1910   *1 Yarborough Villas*

My dear Richards,

Whatever the result may be, I am very much obliged both to Maclagan and you for your warfare against the Spanish character.[2]

I also have to thank you for Masefield's two novels, of which I have read *Captain Margaret*.[3] Quite readable, and containing a number of interesting details; but bad.

Yours sincerely   A. E. HOUSMAN

---

[1] Frances Crofts Cornford (*née* Darwin) (1886–1960), wife of F. M. Cornford, Fellow of Trinity College, Cambridge (see p. 246, note 1), published her first book, *Poems*, at the insistence of Rothenstein in 1910. Housman's parody is identical with the original except that *boots, shoots* and *coots* replace *gloves, loves* and *doves*.

[2] In their attempts to get photographs of the Madrid manuscript of Manilius.

[3] Published by Richards in 1908. The other novel was *Multitude and Solitude*, 1909.

To Alice Rothenstein

MS. HARVARD

17 May 1910   *1 Yarborough Villas*

Dear Mrs Rothenstein,

Many thanks for the card,[1] which I shall probably utilise on the 27th rather than the 26th, as I shall have more time at my disposal.

I hope to find some of the works which Rothenstein executed last August, with you holding his chair to save him from being blown over the cliff; and I shall be interested in trying to discover if the strokes of the artist's brush show any traces of the struggle between Love and Death which was raging around him.

Yours sincerely   A. E. HOUSMAN

To Laurence Housman

MS. MCGILL

9 June 1910   *1 Yarborough Villas*

My dear Laurence,

I would rather not sign your memorial;[2] chiefly because I don't think that writers as a class are particularly qualified to give advice on the question; and moreover it is certain to be signed by Galsworthy[3] and Hewlett[4] and everyone I cannot abide. Also I cannot say that 'the solution of this question appears to me to be urgent'. Even if I were actually in favour of women's suffrage in the abstract I think I should like to see some other and less precious country try it first: America for instance, where the solution ought to be just as urgent as here.

Thanks for the pamphlet.[5] I see you have another just published;[6] but as that costs 6*d*. I recognise that it is my duty to buy it; which indeed I am quite able to do, as your literary activity has fallen off of late, and my finances are recovering from the strain it used to put on them.

Love to Clemence: I hope she has read, or will read, *Ann Veronica*[7] (the prison scenes).

Your affectionate brother   A. E. HOUSMAN

[1] Ticket for the private view of an exhibition of Rothenstein's paintings and drawings (including one of Housman) at the Goupil Gallery.
[2] A declaration by authors in favour of Women's Suffrage. (Laurence Housman's note.)
[3] Novelist and playwright (1867–1933).
[4] Novelist and poet (1861–1923).
[5] Not traced.
[6] *Articles of Faith in the Freedom of Women.*
[7] By H. G. Wells, 1909. The heroine is a 'new woman' and a suffragist.

To Eric Maclagan

TEXT: RICHARDS

15 July 1910   *1 Yarborough Villas*

Dear Mr Maclagan,

I have received and examined the photographs, and find them complete and quite satisfactorily clear; and I assure you that it is a great comfort to possess them, and that as I shall constantly be using them I shall constantly be feeling gratitude to you for your trouble and your success. I must also thank you for the rather surprisingly low price at which you have managed to secure them.

I will write as you suggest to Dr G. de Osma.[1] I enclose cheque for £2 15s. 0d., and am yours sincerely and gratefully

A. E. HOUSMAN

To Grant Richards

TEXT: RICHARDS

15 July 1910   [*1 Yarborough Villas*)

I have received the photographs, which are quite satisfactory, and I am very grateful to you as well as to Maclagan and his hidalgo, for I should never have got them without your assistance.

Also I must thank you for Masefield's plays,[2] which are well worth reading and contain a lot that is very good; only he has got the Elizabethan notion that in order to have tragedy you must have villains, and villains of disgusting wickedness or vileness.

To Alice Rothenstein

MS. HARVARD

18 July 1910   *1 Yarborough Villas*

Dear Mrs Rothenstein,

It is a pleasure to hear that anyone is as happy as you appear to be, and when you say that no one can possibly be so happy in England I am not in a position to contradict you. I am engaged in composing an erudite work, which you will refuse to read, and my feelings do not rise much above tranquil satisfaction and the consciousness of virtue. I am afraid there is no chance of

---

[1] Guillermo de Osma, Oxford-educated Spanish diplomatist (1853–1922); founder of the Instituto de Valencia de Don Juan in Madrid.
[2] *The Tragedy of Nan and Other Plays*, 1909.

my sharing your raptures, as I shall not get away till the end of August, and then shall most likely go to Belgium.

I went to Rothenstein's show with the ticket, and admired particularly the farmyard and the quarry, which I had seen before, and the piece called "Spring", which I had not; but particularly and extremely the picture "Night", though I fear that the subject may have something to do with this, and that a dark tree with the moon rising behind it might produce much the same effect on me even if it were painted by Mr B. W. Leader.[1] The *Standard* called it a great picture; and I suppose that a picture which is praised by the *Standard* and admired by me must have something wrong with it, and that Rothenstein will reel under this double blow. I find on looking at my catalogue that I have supplied alternative titles to some of the pictures: opposite '57. A Study' I have written 'Mrs Rothenstein detected in a prevarication', and opposite 42 the elucidation 'Lady, watching her first husband die of poison administered by herself, reflects, with melancholy, that her second may be no better'. Tell Rothenstein that while standing before the portrait of the artist I heard another visitor say, with just an instant's pause between the utterances, 'Very unkind,—very like'.

At the end of this month I am going for a few days to Swanage, which reminds me that I have never seen a picture of what I think one of the most wonderful views I know, Egdon Heath, seen from the hills south of it, with the heather in bloom and Poole Harbour reaching its arms into the midst of it. But this is such a summerless year that I doubt if the heather will be properly out when I get there. It may be better in France: if so I congratulate both of you.

I am yours sincerely   A. E. HOUSMAN

To *Grant Richards*

MS. CONGRESS

5 September 1910   *Normandy Hotel, Paris*

My dear Richards,

I am going home on Wednesday, so we have accurately timed our visits so as to miss one another, which is annoying, but cannot be helped. The first thing I was told when I got here was the recent departure of my friend M. Gran' Reesharr.

Yours sincerely   A. E. HOUSMAN

[1] Benjamin Williams Leader, popular landscape painter (1831–1923); elected Royal Academician, 1898.

To Grant Richards

MS. ILLINOIS

15 November 1910   *1 Yarborough Villas*

My dear Richards,

Mr Hemsley may print the verses he wants in his Latin book.[1] As to the Manilius, tell the enquirer that you have no information.

I have just been lunching with Frank Harris,[2] who came down on me at the College like a wolf on the fold.

Yours sincerely   A. E. HOUSMAN

Housman had been happy at University College, but the heavy load of routine teaching left him little leisure in term-time. He must sometimes have thought of returning to Oxford, and could well have waited to succeed Robinson Ellis, who was twenty-five years his senior; but when the Cambridge Professorship fell vacant on the death of J. E. B. Mayor in 1910, and Housman was invited to stand, he allowed his name to go forward. The electors waived the customary trial lectures and simply offered Housman the appointment, and Trinity College elected him to a fellowship. After delivering his inaugural lecture on 9 May 1911 Housman divided the rest of the summer term between Cambridge and London, and in September moved into the rooms in Whewell's Court which remained his home for the next twenty-four years.

His conditions there were far from comfortable. The three rooms, situated in a remote corner of the College, lay at the top of a steep staircase; they were poorly furnished, dark and cold. But Housman never paid much attention to his surroundings, and was probably content that they should discourage visitors.

For the rest of his life his routine changed little. He lectured once or twice a week, sat on the Faculty Board and College committees, produced a new volume of Manilius every few years and kept up an unbroken stream of articles and reviews. In the afternoons he went for long solitary walks; in the vacations he visited members of his family and a few friends, and usually spent a few weeks in France or Italy.

During these years *A Shropshire Lad* enjoyed a boom. It was constantly reprinted, illustrated, set to music and plagiarised. By 1922, when its successor, *Last Poems*, eventually appeared, Housman was widely regarded as a great poet.

---

[1] *Latin Elegiac Verse-Writing* by W. J. Hemsley and John Aston, 1911, contains *A Shropshire Lad* XX under the title 'Reflections' for translation into Latin.

[2] Author, editor and adventurer (1856–1931). His account of this interview appeared in his *Latest Contemporary Portraits*, 1928.

113

To Grant Richards

MS. CONGRESS

17 January 1911   *1 Yarborough Villas*

My dear Richards,
   Will you dine with me at the Café Royal on Friday 3 February at 7.45 ?[1] I am asking Platt, whom you have already met under other circumstances.[2]

   Yours sincerely   A. E. HOUSMAN

To Mrs Platt

MS. U.C.L.

19 January 1911   *1 Yarborough Villas*

Dear Mrs Platt,
   Yours was the first letter, so I will answer it first and thank you for your congratulations, which show a very Christian and forgiving spirit, considering my remissness in attending your at homes. The prospect of exchanging you for Mrs Frazer[3] is one of the clouds on my horizon; but please do not repeat this remark to all your Cambridge acquaintances.
   I should be very pleased to dine with you any day next week but Tuesday.

   Yours sincerely   A. E. HOUSMAN

To Edmund Gosse[4]

MS. BROTHERTON

19 January 1911   *University College*

My dear Gosse,
   Many thanks for your kind letter. In most respects, though not quite in all, I think the change is matter for congratulation. If the exhalations of the Granta[5] give me a relaxed sore throat, more poems may be expected.[6]

   Yours sincerely   A. E. HOUSMAN

---

[1] To celebrate Housman's appointment.
[2] In connection with the publication of his translation of the *Agamemnon*.
[3] Lilly (*née* Grove), wife of J. G. Frazer (see p. 184, note 2), the eminent anthropologist, Fellow of Trinity College, Cambridge. She was the author of French text-books for schools.
[4] Poet and critic (1849–1928); friend of Rossetti and Swinburne; Librarian of the House of Lords, 1904–1914; knighted, 1925.
[5] Cambridge river.
[6] Housman believed that the poetic impulse was associated with ill-health. Much of *A Shropshire Lad* was written while he was suffering from a persistent sore throat early in 1895.

To Grant Richards

MS. CONGRESS

20 January 1911   *1 Yarborough Villas*

My dear Richards,

First, many thanks for your congratulations. Then, as to the dinner, Platt is an easy-going character and will not mind having the date shifted if you cannot come on the 3rd. Next week will be quite time enough to let me know. Thirdly I am afraid there is no safe immediate prospect of my finding my way to your French cook, as next Saturday I lunch in town, and expect to be at Godalming on the next after that. Thank you all the same.

Yours sincerely   A. E. HOUSMAN

To Alice Rothenstein

MS. HARVARD

22 January 1911   *1 Yarborough Villas*

Dear Mrs Rothenstein,

I thank you sincerely for your kind letter. I expect I shall see you and Rothenstein sometimes in Cambridge, as I know you have friends there. Besides, the Cambridge terms are agreeably short, and I shall most likely spend some part of each year in London.

To have less work and more pay is always agreeable, and that will be the case with me. The drawback is that I shall be obliged to be less unsociable. I am glad to hear your news from Benares.[1]

I am yours sincerely   A. E. HOUSMAN

To Lady Ramsay[2]

MS. U.C.L.

26 January 1911   *1 Yarborough Villas*

Dear Lady Ramsay,

Many thanks for your kind congratulations. Joy does predominate over sorrow, as I am fond of money and fond of leisure; but as I am also fond of solitude, and shall not have it at Cambridge, there is some sorrow mingled with the joy; apart from leaving friends and the College.

I am yours very truly   A. E. HOUSMAN

---

[1] Rothenstein was painting in India, 1910–1911.

[2] Margaret (*née* Buchanan), wife of Housman's colleague Sir William Ramsay, Professor of Chemistry at University College, London, from 1887. See p. 147, note 1.

To Laurence Housman

TEXT: MEMOIR

30 January 1911   [*1 Yarborough Villas*]

My dear Laurence,

. . . I thank you both for your congratulations. It is not by any means certain that I could have secured the Oxford chair by waiting for it;[1] and on the whole I think I prefer Cambridge.

I spent one of my hard-earned half-crowns on the *English Review* containing the trial-scene of your play:[2] it interested me, but I did not think it would interest most people without the Censor's assistance.

Disraeli visited the villa where your heroine resided in Italy,[3] soon after the trial. Its decorations, he says, were of such a character that it was painful to view them in company with a lady. The local Italians regarded the tumult in London as a great joke . . .

      Your affectionate brother   A. E. HOUSMAN

To Grant Richards

MS. ILLINOIS

7 March 1911   *1 Yarborough Villas*

My dear Richards,

The Wolsey Hall[4] people do not know what they are talking about: my Juvenal would be no use to students whatever. The proper Juvenal for English students is Duff's, Cambridge Press.[5]

When Blackwell[6] says 'Eriphyle' he means the 'Fragment of a Greek Tragedy' which appeared in *Cornhill*[7] about ten years ago.

      Yours sincerely   A. E. HOUSMAN

---

[1] Robinson Ellis retained the Corpus Professorship of Latin at Oxford until his death in 1913. He was succeeded by A. C. Clark.

[2] The issue for November 1910 contained Act III of Laurence Housman's *Pains and Penalties*, describing George IV's attempt to divorce Queen Caroline. The play was refused a licence by the Lord Chamberlain but was published in 1911.

[3] The Villa d'Este on Lake Como. Disraeli was there in 1826.

[4] Oxford correspondence college, founded in 1894.

[5] Published in 1898.

[6] Oxford bookseller and publisher.

[7] In the issue for April 1901.

To Laurence Housman

TEXT: MEMOIR

27 April 1911 [*1 Yarborough Villas*]

My dear Laurence,

. . . This is to say that I am not coming to hear your seditious play,[1] and I shall not make any attempt to see you, as your time will probably be taken up with more whole-hearted admirers. For the same reason I suppose you will not be coming to see me, though I shall be glad to see you if you do . . .

Your affectionate brother   A. E. HOUSMAN

To Witter Bynner

MS. HARVARD

17 May 1911 *Trinity College, Cambridge*

Dear Mr Bynner,

It is true that I am now professor of Latin here, and I thank you for your congratulations. Of course it is nonsense when they talk about my 'steadily refusing to write any more poetry': poetry does not even *steadily* refuse to be written by me; but there is not yet enough to make even a small book. I am glad to hear of you and your projects.

Yours very truly   A. E. HOUSMAN

To Sydney Cockerell[2]

MS. PRINCETON

26 May 1911 *32 Panton Street, Cambridge*

Dear Mr Cockerell,

It is very good of you to offer to show me over the Museum, and I should be glad to avail myself of your kindness some morning between 10 and 1. I think I had better leave you to fix the day, as your time is probably much more occupied than mine: the only professorial function I am discharging this term is that of residing.

I am yours very truly   A. E. HOUSMAN

[1] Laurence Housman gave a public reading from *Pains and Penalties* as an act of defiance of the Lord Chamberlain.

[2] Sydney Carlyle Cockerell (1867–1955); Director of the Fitzwilliam Museum, Cambridge, 1908–1937; knighted, 1934.

117

To Laurence Housman

TEXT: MEMOIR

11 June 1911   *[Trinity College]*

My dear Laurence,

. . . Although I had very few official duties during the Cambridge term I was much occupied with social duties, which are a deal worse, and either from the climate or the heat was generally tired when I was not occupied, so that I have not thanked you for the proofs of your play. It interested me, but I should not have thought it would interest most people, nor be effective on the stage. However, everyone who heard it was loud in praise of your reading, and apparently swallowed Caroline whole.

An undergraduate came to me to get your address, which I gave him, after exacting assurances that he was not bent on avenging the glorious house of Hanover . . .

Your affectionate brother   A. E. HOUSMAN

To H. E. Butler

MS. ST JOHN'S

28 June 1911   *1 Yarborough Villas*

Dear Butler,

I did not see at the time the announcement, which I understand has been made, of your appointment as my successor, so that I am rather belated in sending my best wishes for your success and happiness. I think you will find at University College pleasant colleagues and tractable pupils.

If there is any information about the work that you think I could supply, I shall be very pleased to do so; but you will very likely be able to get all you want from Platt, whose classes are in many respects parallel to the Latin.

I am yours very truly   A. E. HOUSMAN

To Alice Rothenstein

MS. HARVARD

4 August 1911   *Woodchester*

Dear Mrs Rothenstein,

It unfortunately happens that I am away, and paying a series of visits. This is about six miles from Bisley, near which you once spent a summer holiday.

118

I had not heard about New York,[1] but I suppose it is a natural revulsion after India. I hope Rothenstein will find subjects equally inspiring. I may be going to Belgium and making the acquaintance of the van Eycks, who were, when I last received information on the subject, *the* painters.

Yours sincerely   A. E. HOUSMAN

To Grant Richards

MS. ILLINOIS

15 August 1911   *1 Yarborough Villas*

My dear Richards,
This is rather a miscellaneous letter.

1. The Second Book of Manilius is nearly finished, and a large portion of it will be ready for the printers by the end of this month, so I want them to start upon it while I am abroad in September. It had better be published on the same arrangement as the First, if you have no objection.

2. I expect to be in Paris in the first week of September and again in the third: about the 24th I shall take up my abode permanently in Cambridge, of which I will send you due notice when the time comes.

3. Can you tell me anything definite of the Hôtel de Crillon as to expense? e.g. whether one would get a bedroom and bathroom for 20 francs or so. I shall most likely go either there or to the Continental.

Yours sincerely   A. E. HOUSMAN

To Grant Richards

MS. ILLINOIS

28 August 1911   *1 Yarborough Villas*

My dear Richards,

1. I have just despatched to you by Parcel Post the text and notes of the Manilius. If you will be good enough to acknowledge receipt of them, I can go abroad with a mind at ease.

2. This second book is to be printed in just the same form as the first, of which the printers had better have a copy to guide them.

3. It will be convenient to me if at first, in slip, the text and notes are printed separately, not together as in the former occasion.

4. The type-written text contains the letters:
    J (cap.)   j (l.c.)   v (l.c.)
These are everywhere to be changed to
    I   i   u.
The compositor's simplest way to avoid error will be to put lids on the

---

[1] Rothenstein had arranged to visit the United States for exhibitions of his work in New York, Boston and Chicago.

receptacles containing the types of the forbidden forms, so that his hand cannot get into them; but no doubt he is too proud to take advice from me.

5. As to errors of the press. On former occasions the proofs have come to me full of the usual blunders,—numerals wrong, letters upside-down, stops missing, and so on. I have then, at the cost of much labour, removed all these errors. Then, when the last proof has left my hands, the corrector for the press has been turned on to it, and has found nothing to correct; whereupon, for fear his employers should think he is not earning his pay, he has set to work meddling with what I have written,—altering my English spelling into Webster's American spelling, my use of capitals into his own misuse of capitals, my scientific punctuation into the punctuation he learnt from his grandmother. What ought to be done is the reverse of this. The errors which are introduced by the printer should be removed by the press corrector, who will do it more easily and rapidly, though not more efficiently, than I; then and not till then the proofs should come to me, and after that no corrections should be made except by me.

I am yours sincerely   A. E. HOUSMAN

P.S. Because my hand is particularly good and clear, printers misread it whenever they can; but there is only one letter which they can misread, and that is the letter *r*. At the end of a word they pretend they think it is *s*, and in other positions they pretend they think it is *v*. If they would just notice how I write it, and not expect to find *ι*, it would save trouble.

To Grant Richards

MS. PRINCETON

30 August 1911   *1 Yarborough Villas*

My dear Richards,

It is a sine qua non that Book II of the Manilius should be identical with Book I in type, arrangement, paper, and get-up generally. If this can be secured, I have no *decisive* objection to changing the printers.

But still I should prefer Clark, unless you have some decided reason on the other side. They are more accurate than Maclehose or anyone who has ever printed the *Classical Review*; and when the Juvenal was finished they wrote to me to say that they hoped I would employ them for any similar work in future: though I don't suppose this was due to any sentimental affection for me. Moreover I am a conservative, and do not like changing anything without due reason, not even a printer,—nay, not even a publisher.

Your *Athenaeum* notice is quite chaste in style. I have put in a word or two.

I am off to Paris to-morrow, and shall be at the Continental for a week. Any letter after that had better be addressed here.

Yours sincerely   A. E. HOUSMAN

To H. W. Garrod[1]

MS. SPARROW

24 October 1911   *Trinity College*

My dear Sir,

I have no wish to prevent other scholars from editing Manilius, but rather the reverse; and I think the world is probably wide enough for both our books, as each contains a good deal which the other does not. I congratulate you on your addition to our knowledge of the cod. Venetus.

I am yours very truly   A. E. HOUSMAN

To Katharine Symons

MS. TRINITY

30 December 1911   *Trinity College*

My dear Kate,

I am staying here through the vacation as I am seeing a book through the press and found that I could not do much at it during the term. Being conscientious, I took a great deal of time to prepare my lectures; and being a new-comer, I was much asked out to dinner. People here are very hospitable and friendly. The attendance at my lectures was from 20 to 30 (which, though not large, is from 20 to 30 times greater than the attendance at my predecessor's), several of whom were lecturers themselves. I believe the lectures are considered good (as indeed they are).

I don't know that the climate exactly suits me, and probably I have drunk too much port at College Feasts; but I am not feeling stupid, which is the great thing.

The twins of Mrs Martin of Hereford called on me the other day, when they were up for scholarships. They were as fluent and self-possessed as ever, and conversed affably on subjects which they thought likely to interest me. I see that each got a scholarship or exhibition, though only for £40, Cambridge being less munificent than Oxford and they less intellectual than Gadd.[2]

I was glad to have your letter at Christmas: I also heard from Jeannie.[3] Love to all.

Your affectionate brother   A. E. HOUSMAN

[1] Heathcote William Garrod (1878–1960), Fellow of Merton College, Oxford; editor of *The Oxford Book of Latin Verse*, 1912; Professor of Poetry at Oxford, 1923–1928. His commentary on Manilius II, with a translation, was published in 1911. Housman declined to write a review but in the preface to Manilius V (1930) criticised Garrod's book ferociously.

[2] S. S. and T. L. Martin were elected to scholarships at King's College and Peterhouse respectively. Cyril John Gadd (born 1893), a pupil at King Edward VI School, Bath (where Katharine Symons' husband was head), won a scholarship to Brasenose College, Oxford. He was Keeper of Egyptian and Assyrian Antiquities at the British Museum, 1948–1955.

[3] Basil Housman's wife.

To Grant Richards

31 December 1911   *[Trinity College]*

I return the seven drawings of diagrams for the Manilius, and I return also my own original drawings, *which must also be returned to the printers.* The work is very nicely executed, and the only fault I find with it is that the artist has imitated too closely my own imperfect draughtsmanship. I have failed in several cases to put II and Ω on the same level, and in the diagram c (hexagona) the inequality is unpleasing to the eye and should be corrected somewhat as I have pencilled on the tissue paper.

As to the size of the blocks, the chief matter to be considered is the following. It is important that the diagrams should be inserted exactly at those points which I have indicated in my MS. But when the preface is put into pages, it may happen that the end of a page will cut a diagram in two; and the greater the perpendicular height of the diagram, the oftener this is likely to happen, and the more difficult it will be to remedy.

The printers must remember to place under the diagrams the titles shown in my drawings.

To Grant Richards

4 January 1912   *Trinity College*

I return pp. 17–48 of the Manilius notes corrected. The printers have introduced two new errors, *aque* for *quae* on p. 25 and II for I on p. 33: this last is a perfectly atrocious action, and I cannot imagine how such a thing could come to pass. I wonder where they will stop if they once begin altering numerals: it will be impossible for me to detect them except by chance.

I want to have pp. 1–16 again, as I overlooked some things which were wrong.

To Grant Richards

12 January 1912   *[Trinity College]*

I hope that the Manilius may appear before the end of February, and it occurs to me that it might avoid delay if they already began to prepare the cover: they know the number of pages (text and notes and preface combined) well enough to be able to judge of the size: the only addition will be about three pages of index, which I cannot complete till the preface is paged. I therefore enclose a rough pattern: the type and colour to be just the same as vol. I. The label on the back to be

MANILII II. HOVSMAN

To Grant Richards

TEXT: RICHARDS

11 February 1912 [*Trinity College*]

I enclose the last corrections of proofs. I do not want to see them again, and so far as I am concerned all is now ready for publication. I suppose I can trust them to make the binding the same colour as Book I.

To Grant Richards

TEXT: RICHARDS

29 February 1912 [*Trinity College*]

When will the precious work be published? The Cambridge term ends on 15 March, the coal-strike begins to-morrow, and the destruction of the national wealth is a question of days.[1]

Telegram to Grant Richards

TEXT: RICHARDS

4 March 1912 [*Trinity College*]

I expressly said no corrections required Housman.

To P. G. L. Webb

MS. LILLY

19 April 1912 *Trinity College*

Dear Webb,

I have just come back from abroad and found here the translations from Heine[2] you have been kind enough to send me. I have been dipping into them, and was very much pleased with the piece in p. 33. The conclusion of *Faust* I don't like any better than the original. I am very glad to have the book.

I have been in Sicily, where the weather and the wild flowers were all that could be desired.

Yours sincerely A. E. HOUSMAN

[1] The national strike of miners, in support of their demand for a minimum wage, continued until 11 April.
[2] *Translations from Heine and Goethe*, 1912.

To Grant Richards

TEXT: RICHARDS

28 April 1912 *[Trinity College]*

A month ago you wrote to say that you were informed that Manilius II was
on the sea. Where are you now informed that it is? at the bottom? or is the
vessel approaching London via Yokohama?

To Grant Richards

TEXT: RICHARDS

1 May 1912 *[Trinity College]*

. . . Two months ago I sent you a list of the persons and newspapers to
which I wished copies of the Manilius to be sent. Probably you have lost it,
in which case please let me know at once and I will draw up a new one; don't
keep the poor wretches waiting another couple of months.

Whether I can lunch with a person who is so far from being what he should
be is a question which I will consider between now and my next visit to
London.

To Grant Richards

TEXT: RICHARDS

30 July 1912 *[Trinity College]*

I remember the name of Graham Peel as a composer to whom I gave some
permission.[1] If he mentions the name of the author I don't think he is bound
to mention the name of the book; and he probably altered the title because
'Bredon Hill' has been set to music by so many composers and he wanted to
differentiate, which I think is harmless.

It was not Bourg but Bourges that I went to.

I saw your case in the paper[2] and wondered what exactly it was about. I
don't think any of my letters are very incriminating.

[1] Gerald Graham Peel (1877–1937), published a setting of 'Bredon Hill' (*A Shropshire Lad* XXI) under the title 'In Summertime on Bredon' in 1911.

[2] Richards' injunction to stop the sale of letters to him from Housman, Meredith, Shaw and other authors. They were in the files of his original firm, sold to Alexander Moring in 1906, and had been passed to a dealer. Richards, by a compromise, recovered Housman's letters.

To Grant Richards

TEXT: RICHARDS

7 September 1912   *Hôtel de l'Europe, Venice*

Your gift[1] came just as I was starting, and prevented me from paying
W. H. Smith and Son six shillings for some much less entertaining work to
read on the journey. I read with great interest all through, though the Monte
Carlo parts perhaps are not equal to the Parisian and American. These last
seem to be particularly good. I have just seen a favourable review in the
Telegraph.

I hope you will not now take to writing poetry or editing Manilius.

I am now going to Paris and shall be at the Continental probably till the
16th.

To Edward Marsh[2]

MS. BERG

1 October 1912   *Trinity College*

Dear Mr Marsh,

I well remember meeting you at Gosse's, though I did not then connect
you with the Master of Downing. The lady who sat next me at supper, on
hearing your name, wondered if you were the author of *The Beetle*:[3] I had not
then read that book, so I did not know what a fearful suspicion this was. I
now have a suspicion, less fearful though perhaps equally erroneous, that you
may be the author of a little book Bowes and Bowes[4] have just sent me,
containing a beautiful poem on Good Friday; if so, I thank you for the gift.[5]

If you want to get poetry out of me,[6] you must be either a relative or a
duchess; and you are neither. As a brother and as a snob I am accessible from
two quarters, but from no others. Besides, I do not really belong to your
'new era'; and none even of my few unpublished poems have been written
within the last two years.

I shall be very much interested in your book. One of the names you
mention is new to me, and there are others of whom I have only read a

---

[1] Of *Caviare*, Richards' first novel, just published.

[2] Edward Howard Marsh (1872–1953), son of Professor Howard Marsh, Master of Downing
College, Cambridge; Civil Servant in the Colonial Office, 1896; Private Secretary to Winston
Churchill, 1905; Knighted 1937; friend and editor of Rupert Brooke; collector and patron
of modern art.

[3] Mystery novel, published in 1897, by Richard Marsh (died 1915).

[4] The Cambridge publishers and booksellers.

[5] Possibly *ΧΑΡΙΤΕΣΣΙ*, published anonymously, 1911. There is no evidence that Marsh
contributed.

[6] For *Georgian Poetry*, the annual selection edited by Marsh, 1912–1921. Despite this
refusal Housman later contributed poems to *The Cambridge Review* and *The Times*.

little. You do not mention Chesterton:[1] his 'Ballad of the White Horse' is absurd in its plan and its conception and often cheap and brassy in its ornament, but it contains quite a lot of really magnificent verses, which impressed me more than anything I have read for a long time.

However, literary criticism is not what you were asking me for.

I am yours truly A. E. HOUSMAN

To Mrs Platt

MS. U.C.L.

10 October 1912 *Trinity College*

Dear Mrs Platt,

I shall be coming to town on the 17th to attend a meeting at University College, so I give you notice, as you kindly told me to do, in order that you may ask me to dinner if you feel inclined.

The last winter was so mild that I had no excuse for drinking the sloe gin: it is therefore still maturing, and no doubt will become specially excellent. I gave some to a fellow of the College who has gout, and is consequently a connoisseur, and he admired it very much.

I am yours sincerely A. E. HOUSMAN

To A. S. F. Gow[2]

MS. TRINITY

28 November 1912 *Trinity College*

Dear Gow,

I have taken tickets for *Milestones*[3] for Tuesday 3 December. They are in the front row of the circle, which I hope suits you: it is my favourite part of a theatre.

Yours sincerely A. E. HOUSMAN

[1] Gilbert Keith Chesterton (1874–1936) contributed an extract from his 'Ballad of the White Horse'.

[2] Andrew Sydenham Farrar Gow (born 1886), son of James Gow, Headmaster of Westminster School; Fellow of Trinity College, Cambridge, 1911; assistant master at Eton College, 1914–1925; lecturer at Trinity College and in the University, 1925–1951; author of *A. E. Housman: A Sketch and List of His Writings*, 1936.

[3] Play by Arnold Bennett and Edward Knoblock, first produced at the Royalty Theatre on 5 March 1912, now being performed at the New Theatre, Cambridge.

To Thomas Hardy[1]

MS. DORCHESTER

28 November 1912   *Trinity College*

Dear Mr Hardy,

Let me say how sorry I am to see to-day the news of your bereavement.[2] Several times since I was at Dorchester in 1900 I had met Mrs Hardy at the Gosses' when she was visiting London, and though the last of these occasions was some years ago, I had not heard of any failure of her health. I beg you to accept my sympathy and believe me always yours very truly

A. E. HOUSMAN

To Mrs Platt

MS. U.C.L.

26 December 1912   *Trinity College*

Dear Mrs Platt,

I received yesterday your kind and beautiful present of the Dogana,[3] in its sumptuous frame, which I suppose I must not admire unless I want to be suspected of not having taste enough to admire the picture properly, which I think I do. I am very grateful, and hope that heaven will reward you with a happy new year.

I was much in need of something to divert my mind from the horrors of my situation, for Trinity College is a besieged city. A week ago there came a telegram to say that one of the junior Fellows, Pearse,[4] whom Platt will know by name, had left his home, mad and armed, and would probably make his way here. All entrances to the College have therefore been closed, except the Great Gate, which is guarded by a double force of Porters. Cambridge was perplexed at first, but has now invented the explanation that it is the Master[5] who has gone mad, and has made these arrangements in order that he may shoot at the Fellows from the Lodge as they come through the Great Gate. The Provost of King's[6] gives imitations of the Master thus engaged: 'Ah, there is dear Dr Jackson!' bang!!

What makes matters worse is that the College evidently sets no value on

---

[1] Novelist and poet (1840–1928).
[2] Emma Lavinia (*née* Gifford) was married to Hardy in 1874. She died on 27 November 1912.
[3] The Venice custom-house, the subject of innumerable paintings.
[4] James Pearse; Fellow since 1910.
[5] The Rev. Henry Montagu Butler (1833–1918); Headmaster of Harrow School, 1859–1885; Master of Trinity College, 1886–1918.
[6] Montague Rhodes James (1862–1936), medievalist and author of ghost stories; Director of the Fitzwilliam Museum, 1894; Provost of King's College, Cambridge, 1905–1918; Provost of Eton College, 1918–1936; appointed to the Order of Merit, 1930.

my life or even on that of the Archdeacon of Ely;[1] for Whewell's Court is left quite unprotected and I have to look under the bed every night.

My remembrances therefore to your husband and family: to-morrow I may be no more than a remembrance myself.

Yours sincerely

A. E. HOUSMAN

To Grant Richards

MS. FEINBERG

17 January 1913   *Trinity College*

My dear Richards,

I am exceedingly sorry to hear of your illness. I remember your having some similar trouble, which you bore with great fortitude, once when we were in Paris together.[2] One of my chief objections to the management of the universe is that we suffer so much more from our gentler and more amiable vices than from our darkest crimes.

If the *Daily Sketch* will publish an expression of regret, that is all I want:[3] no fee, on any account. What I object to is that when some people have asked leave to print my poems, and I have refused it, other people go and print them without asking.

Yours sincerely

A. E. HOUSMAN

I shall be in London for a few hours on Tuesday, but only to keep a dinner engagement. I don't know when I am likely to be up for any time.

To Alice Rothenstein

MS. HARVARD

14 February 1913   *Trinity College*

Dear Mrs Rothenstein,

Bertrand Russell[4] said to me yesterday 'Have you seen anything of the Rothensteins lately?' and it went through my heart like a spear of ice that neither had I seen them *nor had they heard from me*, though you wrote to me at the beginning of the year. But if you ever have to examine for University

[1] The Rev. William Cunningham (1849–1914); Fellow of Trinity College, 1891; Professor of Economics at King's College, London, 1891; Archdeacon of Ely, 1907.

[2] In 1907, when Richards was recovering from shingles.

[3] *The Daily Sketch*, 2 January 1913, printed 'Oh, when I was in love with you' (*A Shropshire Lad* XVIII). A brief apology for using the poem without permission appeared on 25 January.

[4] Mathematician and philosopher (1872–1970), second son of Viscount Amberley and grandson of the first Earl Russell; Fellow of Trinity College, 1896; succeeded to Earldom, 1931; appointed to the Order of Merit, 1949; awarded Nobel Prize for Literature, 1950.

128

Scholarships you will find as I do that all one's leisure is fully occupied by wishing that one was dead; and I am only just at the end of this tribulation.

I suppose I am right in directing this letter to your town mansion and not to your place in Gloucestershire. *Iles* is a regular Gloucestershire name.[1] I have not been down there since I saw you last. I was telling Russell that I can remember when his father and mother used to live on the hill just opposite Woodchester. You and William ought to be in the country now to observe the progress of this extraordinary spring, or winter as it calls itself.

I suppose you have seen Mrs Cornford's new book.[2] Her portrait in the frontispiece is pleasing and recognisable, but Cornford's is almost a caricature.

Best wishes to all of you.

Yours sincerely   A. E. HOUSMAN

To Lily Thicknesse

TEXT: MEMOIR

8 March 1913   *[Trinity College]*

Dear Mrs Thicknesse,

. . . The chief excitements of the term here have been an agitation, by a highly undistinguished set of persons, to introduce conscription for undergraduates, as a last effort to frighten the Germans; and an exhibition of post-impressionist undergraduate art, which is calculated to frighten the Germans a good deal more.

My respects to both of you . . .

Yours sincerely   A. E. HOUSMAN

To Katharine Symons

MS. LILLY

22 May 1913   *Trinity College*

My dear Kate,

I must return you your chart,[3] which is a monument of industry and ingenuity, and I cannot add anything to it. My edition of Prince's *Worthies* is 1810, the same as yours. The marginal note you speak of must mean 'Sir W. Pole's *Description of Devon*, chapter on Exmouth'. This book was in manuscript when Prince wrote, but has since been published.[4] Neither this College

---

[1] Rothenstein had decided to move to Iles Farm, Far Oakridge.
[2] *Death and the Princess*, 1912. The frontispiece, by Mrs Bernard Darwin, is an illustration to the poem; it represents the Princess with a vast, horned and cloven-footed woodland god.
[3] Of the Housmans' family tree.
[4] The book was printed in 1791. John Prince's *Worthies of Devon* was first published in 1701.

nor the University Library has a copy, but I may be able to find one somewhere in Cambridge. I don't know anything of the Clevedon lady, except that I have heard mamma speak of her.

Your affectionate brother   A. E. HOUSMAN

To Alice Rothenstein

MS. HARVARD

4 June 1913   *Trinity College*

Dear Mrs Rothenstein,

Alas, no, I cannot come to London on the 10th; though I ought not to say alas, as the obstacle consists in my having been asked to dine at Jesus to meet Thomas Hardy, who is receiving an honorary degree.

If my friends ask me to Woodchester, and you are in your country mansion at the time, I certainly will come and see you. Remember me to William.

Yours sincerely   A. E. HOUSMAN

To Henry Jackson

MS. TRINITY

10 June 1913   *Trinity College*

My dear Jackson,

I cannot express in words how little store I set by the enclosed composition,[1] and how impossible it will be for you to injure my amour propre by any criticisms and corrections. I apprehend that it may be both too short and too stiff, apart from other demerits and defects; but now it is your turn.

I am going abroad on Saturday, and expect to be away rather more than a week.

Yours sincerely   A. E. HOUSMAN

Address to H. M. Butler[2]

[2 July 1913]   *Trinity College*

It would not be fitting that the completion of your eightieth year, an event which evokes congratulations from so many quarters, should be let pass without recognition and celebration by the society which for nearly twenty-seven years has known you as its Master. But ceremony and circumstance

---

[1] Draft of an address, printed below, from the Fellows of Trinity College to congratulate the Master on his eightieth birthday.
[2] Text from *Henry Montagu Butler* by J. R. M. Butler, 1925.

130

are ill suited to the close and domestic tie by which you are bound to those who now address you, and they have chosen the simplest fashion of expressing what they sincerely feel. They remember the distinction of your young life within these walls, your active services during the tenure of your fellowship, your prosperous labours and eminent success at Harrow, and, above all, the years of genial and dignified maturity during which you have presided over Trinity College, your ardent zeal for its common welfare, your considerate kindness towards its individual members, young and old, and the union of charm and authority with which you have represented it within the University and before the world; they recall the wisdom and tact with which you have fulfilled the duties of your office, and the prompt and graceful eloquence, issuing from rich stores of reading and memory, with which you have adorned it; and to their felicitations upon the just contentment which must on this anniversary be afforded you by the retrospect of your career, the happiness of your home, and the promise of your descendants, they add the assurance of their admiring and affectionate regard.

To Grant Richards

MS. FEINBERG

23 September 1913   *Trinity College*

My dear Richards,

Your new encroachment on literature[1] reached me just as I was going abroad, and I found it excellently suited for reading while travelling. I am only just back, or I would have thanked you before. I have seen a review which says it is better than *Caviare*, and I hope the public will take that view, though I found *Caviare* the more continuously entertaining.

I was chiefly in the west of Normandy, riding about in a motor car which I hired very cheap in Paris.

Yours sincerely   A. E. HOUSMAN

To Grant Richards

TEXT: RICHARDS

24 September 1913   *[Trinity College]*

Thanks for the cheque, for which I enclose receipt. It is rather a weight off my mind, as I thought you might have been betting on horses whose names begin with JE.[2]

---

[1] Richards' second novel, *Valentine*.
[2] The plot of *Valentine* hinges on the fact that two horses have names beginning with these letters.

Rothenstein told me that he had given permission to reproduce one of his drawings of me.[1] There are two, one of which is much more repulsive than the other, because the artist touched it up with a lot of imaginary black strokes; and no doubt this is the one selected.[2] It is no good my minding, so I do not mind: if I did mind, I daresay I should mind the letter-press even more.

You will have had a note from me about *Valentine* which crossed yours.

To William Rothenstein

MS. HARVARD

8 October 1913   *Trinity College*

My dear Rothenstein,

Full term begins on Friday, and this is to remind you that when you come here on your mission to our dusky brethren[3] you are going to stay with me. I should like to know as far ahead as possible when you are coming, how long you can stay, and what your engagements are.

I hired a motor in Paris and went for a tour in western Normandy in very good weather.

I suppose you are now back in London having your children educated. My kind regards to Mrs Rothenstein.

Yours sincerely   A. E. HOUSMAN

To Laurence Housman

TEXT: MEMOIR

10 October 1913   [*Trinity College*]

My dear Laurence,

. . . An American ecclesiastic was here the other day, who asked to be presented to me, and from whom I gathered that his favourite work would be *A Shropshire Lad*, but for the existence of that fascinating story, *The Were Wolf*,[4] which, again, would be his favourite work, but for the existence of the most brilliant political satire ever written, *King John of Jingalo*.[5]

Your affectionate brother   A. E. HOUSMAN

[1] In Holbrook Jackson's *The Eighteen Nineties*, 1913.
[2] This drawing, which Rothenstein continued to exhibit for some years, was later bought by Trinity College. Housman then persuaded the College to exchange it for the one presented by Rothenstein to him, and then destroyed it.
[3] Rothenstein was one of the founders of the India Society in 1910.
[4] By Clemence Housman, 1895.
[5] By Laurence Housman, 1912.

To Edmund Gosse

MS. BROTHERTON
11 December 1913   *Trinity College*

My dear Gosse,

I must just write to say how much I enjoyed your dinner and the august and agreeable society which you had got together.

Never before have I seen, and never do I expect to see again, a Prime Minister and a Poet Laureate composing a Missive to a Monarch.[1]

Yours sincerely   A. E. HOUSMAN

To A. S. F. Gow

MS. TRINITY
8 March 1914   *Trinity College*

Dear Gow,

I am sorry for your affliction, and that you could not come to *The Alchemist*,[2] which however would have aggravated the symptoms, as laughing is bad for the mumps. Stuart[3] went in your stead. It was very long, and there was a certain amount of repetition, but a great deal that was very amusing,— more amusing now than it can have been in Ben Jonson's day. The acting too was very good on the whole. I did not think Dennis Robertson[4] really satisfactory as Subtle, and both Birch[5] as Face and Burnaby[6] as Ananias (who was very comic) overacted now and then, and Abel Drugger's voice, which was excellent, was better than his acting: the representative of Sir Epicure Mammon[7] seemed to me to act most evenly and to be most like a real person. The widow is a weak and silly element in the play, and was acted by a young man who succeeded in looking like an underbred young woman.

I heard several ladies in the audience declaring that now they must read the drama, and I daresay I shall.

Fletcher[8] is leaving us and going to London to help Lloyd George[9] manage the panel doctors.

[1] See *Asquith* by Roy Jenkins, 1954, p. 295. Gosse's dinner party on 10 December was probably the first time Housman met Bridges.

[2] By Ben Jonson, performed at Cambridge by the Marlowe Society, 5-10 March 1914.

[3] Charles Erskine Stuart, classical scholar and Fellow of Trinity College.

[4] Dennis Holme Robertson (born 1890). Professor of Political Economy, 1944-1957; knighted, 1953.

[5] Francis Lyall Birch (1889-1956); Fellow of King's College.

[6] The Rev. John Burnaby (born 1891); Fellow of Trinity College, 1915; Regius Professor of Divinity, 1952-1958.

[7] C. E. Harman, later Lord Justice Harman.

[8] Walter Morley Fletcher (1873-1933); Fellow of Trinity College, 1897; Tutor, 1905; Secretary to the Medical Research Committee under the National Insurance Act, 1914; knighted, 1918; Chairman of the Commission on Medical Research in India, 1927.

[9] David Lloyd George (1863-1945); Member of Parliament from 1890; as Chancellor of

I hope you will soon be well; but you see the results of going to live among contagious boys.[1]

Yours sincerely   A. E. HOUSMAN

To Grant Richards

TEXT: RICHARDS

2 May 1914   *[Trinity College]*

I ought to write and give you some account of my doings in the south, about which you gave yourself so much trouble. I took the walk you mapped out from Cassis to La Ciotat on a very beautiful day, and followed your lines I think pretty well. I did not go to Ste Baume however, as it did not happen to square with my other plans. I ate much bouillabaisse, the best at Isnard's, the next best in the suburb of L'Estaque; but in several places it was not so good as at Foyot's in Paris. Brandade I did not think much of, and Aioli at Pascal's was rather nasty, perhaps because lukewarm. *The Gourmet's Guide* on Marseilles is full of blunders: the errors are as bloody as the Dwarf.[2]

I hired a motor with an amiable meridional chauffeur who knew the country, and went to Aix, Arles, Aigues-mortes, Montmajour (which is probably what you meant when you wrote Fontveille), Les Baux, St Remy, Beaucaire, Nîmes, Pont du Gard, Avignon, Villeneuve les Avignon, Vaucluse, Carpentras[3] (where I did not see Dreyfus, nor much else), Vaison, Orange, and I think that is all. Weather good, with a few days of mistral; judas trees in very magnificent bloom. I was in Paris with the King,[4] but he did me no harm except once keeping me waiting half-an-hour to cross the street.

The College library wants as many editions as it can get of the *Shropshire Lad*, so will you send me one specimen of each of those you now have on sale.

the Exchequer he introduced the contributory health insurance scheme in 1911. It aroused opposition from the doctors, who saw the creation of a public health service as a threat to private practice.

[1] As a master at Eton.

[2] *The Gourmet's Guide to Europe* by N. Newnham-Davis. Richards published the third edition in 1911. The author contributed to *The Sporting Times* over the signature 'The Dwarf of Blood'.

[3] A Jewish settlement. Captain Alfred Dreyfus (1859–1935) was the French army officer whose conviction on a charge of treason in 1894, re-trial in 1899, when he was again found guilty, and rehabilitation in 1907, became the *cause célèbre* of the time.

[4] King George V and Queen Mary paid a State Visit to Paris, 21–24 April 1914.

To Sydney Cockerell

9 May 1914   *Trinity College*

Dear Cockerell,

I am very much obliged for the two narratives,[1] which I return. Both are delightfully entertaining, and Blunt's very charming as well.

Yours sincerely   A. E. HOUSMAN

To Grant Richards

MS. FEINBERG

31 May 1914   *Trinity College*

My dear Richards,

The errors in the Marseilles pages of the *Gourmet's Guide* are not such as to lead anyone seriously astray in practice (except the statement that you get Bouillabaisse in perfection at La Réserve), and some of them are only misprints. The really outrageous thing is the fairy-tale on p. 104 about a wine called Pouilly Suisse after the proprietor of a vineyard, both non-existent. The wine is Pouilly-Fuissé, i.e. Pouilly blent with Fuissé, or Fuissey as they sometimes spell it.

You ought not to reprint my immortal poems, as you appear to have done in 1912, without asking me about corrections. The consequence is that two mistakes in punctuation have been carried on.

I observe that the illustrated edition is now bound in black instead of white. It strikes me as ugly, but I don't set up to be a judge, and I am indifferent to the fate of that edition, which was only printed to amuse you. I daresay black is appropriate to the funereal nature of the contents.

Yours sincerely   A. E. HOUSMAN

To Grant Richards

MS. FEINBERG

28 June 1914   *Woodchester*

My dear Richards,

These Riccardi people[2] must needs annoy me when I am away on a week's

---

[1] Accounts, taken from the diaries of Wilfrid Scawen Blunt (1840–1922) and another friend, of a visit paid by Housman to Blunt's house, Newbuildings Place, Sussex, in November 1911. Blunt wrote to Cockerell on 3 December 1911: 'We all liked Housman when he was here a week ago, though anything less like a Shropshire Lad it would be impossible to conceive.'

[2] Philip Lee Warner and the Riccardi Press produced a limited edition of *A Shropshire Lad* in 1914.

holiday. I have made in pencil corrections of all the errors I have found, some of which seem to be deliberate. I go back to Cambridge on Tuesday.

Yours sincerely   A. E. HOUSMAN

To Grant Richards

TEXT: RICHARDS

6 September 1914   *Trinity College*

I have corrected two misprints in the poem, and I have no objection to its being printed, as it was printed, I believe, in a similar connection by Ross in a bibliography.[1]

Do not disturb Frank Harris in his beliefs, which are sincere and characteristic, that I am a professor of Greek and that there are 200 pages in *A Shropshire Lad*.

To Lily Thicknesse

TEXT: MEMOIR

24 November 1914   *[Trinity College]*

Dear Mrs Thicknesse,

. . . The thirst for blood is raging among the youth of England. More than half the undergraduates are away, but mostly not at the front, because they all want to be officers. I am going out when they make me a Field Marshal. Meanwhile I have three nephews being inoculated for typhoid and catching pneumonia on Salisbury Plain and performing other acts of war calculated to make the German Emperor realise that he is a very misguided man . . .

Yours sincerely   A. E. HOUSMAN

To Edmund Gosse

MS. B.M.

27 January 1915   *Trinity College*

My dear Gosse,

You don't realise the situation. It is not your hand that the Censor[2] does

---

[1] The reference is probably to Robert Ross (1869–1918), journalist, writer on art, and literary executor to Oscar Wilde.

[2] A letter from Gosse to Compton Mackenzie (born 1883), who was living in Capri, was delayed by the Censor for a week, and then sent on with a note telling Mackenzie to advise his correspondent to write 'shortly and clearly'. Failing to obtain precise instructions from the Censor's office, Gosse wrote to *The Times*, protesting that his writing was clear and asking how many words he was allowed. His letter appeared on 27 January 1915.

not find clear; it is your vocabulary. One man of letters writing to another naturally writes in English, an ancient and a copious tongue. But nobody in the Censor's office knows 500 words of English: 450 words of English, with 550 of slang, are amply sufficient to express all the ideas which circulate in that studious cloister's pale. And if the Censor finds your letters long, it is not that they are long by measurement, but that they take a long time to read when most of the words have to be looked out in the dictionary. For instance, you may have used the word *tendency*. That is a word which nobody in the Censor's office ever utters, ever hears, or ever sees: when they mean *tendency* they always say *trend*, and so do all the writers whom they have ever read. (What they say when they mean *trend* I don't know: perhaps they never do mean it.) Again, writing to a novelist, you may possibly have made some allusion to 'my uncle Toby'.[1] Imagine the scene in the Censor's office: the perusal of your letter suspended, and piles of other correspondence accumulating, while the Postal Directory is searched for Tobias Gosse, who is not to be found: then the Censor has to knit his brows over the problem whether perchance you have a maternal uncle christened Tobias or whether this is a code-word by which you and Compton Mackenzie have agreed to designate the German Emperor. And considering that one of you writes from Hanover Terrace,[2] while the other resides in Capri, a place of which the Censor never heard except in connexion with Krupp,[3] I think he treats you very handsomely in taking the more lenient and less probable view and allowing your letter to pass.

To add that I wish to be remembered to Mrs Gosse is irrelevant but sincere; and I am yours ever

A. E. HOUSMAN

To Grant Richards

MS. CONGRESS

14 February 1915   *Trinity College*

My dear Richards,

1. I have had a bill from R. and R. Clark for binding 50 copies of Juvenal on 3 December 1914. I daresay it is all right, but I had the impression that these items generally appeared as sets-off in your accounts with me.

2. My holidays begin on 13 March, and I am beginning to consider what

---

[1] In Sterne's *Tristram Shandy*.
[2] Gosse's house in Regents Park, London.
[3] Friedrich Alfred Krupp (1854–1902), head of the German armaments firm. In 1902 a Naples newspaper accused him of homosexual practices in Capri; the charge was repeated in the German Socialist paper *Vorwärts*, and Krupp did nothing to clear his name. He died shortly afterwards as the result of a stroke.

to do with them. What are your present ideas about the Riviera? My own notion is to spend about three weeks abroad, and it would suit me best if those three weeks were either at the beginning or the end of the vacation: i.e. roughly 13 March to 3 April, or else 5–26 April; but these limits I mention as the extremes of earliness, lateness, and narrowness: I need not necessarily go so early nor so late, nor be abroad so short a time.

You probably know that passports will be necessary, and that all old passports ceased to be valid on the first of this month.

Would you come and spend a night here some time before the end of term? All our feasts and also our usual guest-nights are suppressed, and our meals are somewhat simplified; but on Tuesdays and Thursdays we have rather better dinners than on other days. I don't ask you for a Sunday, because we have a Sabbatarian kitchen and I could not give you a proper lunch. The only Tuesday or Thursday ahead which would not suit me is the 25th inst. If you can select a date to come, come for lunch, and I will try to invite a kindred spirit. I have lately invested in some rather good Corton 1898.

You seem to have changed your business address.

Yours sincerely   A. E. HOUSMAN

To Lily Thicknesse

TEXT: MEMOIR

7 March 1915   *[Trinity College]*

Dear Mrs Thicknesse,

   . . . On the 16th I shall be beyond the Channel or beneath it: more probably the former, for steamers seem to ram submarines better than submarines torpedo steamers. Hitherto I have always refused to go to the Riviera, but now is my chance, when the worst classes who infest it are away.

   . . . Here we have 1000 undergraduates and 20,000 soldiers, 500 of them billeted in the building in which I write these lines, and one of them doing a quick-step overhead . . .

Yours sincerely   A. E. HOUSMAN

To Grant Richards

TEXT: RICHARDS

7 April 1915   *Trinity College*

I found here your gift of Dreiser's book,[1] which I have been skimming, and I am glad to see that he recognises some of your many virtues.

[1] *A Traveller at Forty* by Theodore Dreiser, 1913. The book describes Dreiser's first visit to Europe and contains a friendly description of Richards and his family.

138

The mathematician[1] whom you sat next to at our high table, upon hearing that I had been to the Riviera with you, said that he hoped you had not been running after women all the time. Whether this was an inference from your conversation or a generalisation from his own experience of travelling-companions I do not know.

You crowned all your good actions by sending me that note about the permit from the Prefecture, as to which you were right when both Cook and the Consulate were wrong.

To Grant Richards

TEXT: RICHARDS

14 April 1915 *[Trinity College]*

You should not let what the mathematician said worry you. When his mind is not occupied by mathematics or pottery it is apt to run on the relations of the sexes, and I seldom sit next him without that topic arising. He possesses all the editions of *Fanny Hill*,[2] a book with which I daresay you never polluted your mind. The question he asked would probably have been asked about anyone else who had been travelling with me. You told me that Belfort Bax[3] made some such enquiry about me.

To Grant Richards

TEXT: RICHARDS

15 July 1915 *[Trinity College]*

I am sorry that I cannot avail myself of your kind and attractive invitation, as early in August I am going to stay with my sister and brother-in-law at Dulverton, and must finish the text and notes of my third book of Manilius, which, though it will not sell so well as your novel,[4] is really a much more classy work. The printers, if they have not all gone to the wars, may just as well be printing this while I am on my holiday, and I should be grateful if you would begin to make arrangements. The preface is already written in the rough, and will be ready for them when they are ready for it.

[1] James Whitbread Lee Glaisher (1848–1928); Fellow of Trinity College from 1871; President of the University Bicycle Club, 1882–1885.
[2] The eighteenth-century pornographic classic by John Cleland.
[3] Barrister, author and journalist (1854–1926) living on the Riviera, where Housman and Richards paid him a visit.
[4] *Bittersweet*, 1915.

To Grant Richards

MS. LILLY

12 September 1915   *Trinity College*

My dear Richards,
   I have now been back nearly a week, and you probably longer. I am writing now because Walter Raleigh[1] has asked if he may print some poems from *A Shropshire Lad* in one of the *Times Broadsheets* for the trenches, and I have said he may; so don't immediately send him a lawyer's letter when you see them.
   There is someone in your office who sends me proofs addressed to S. E. Homeman. I don't mind opprobrious names, but I am apprehensive that the missives may go astray.

   Yours sincerely   A. E. HOUSMAN

To Grant Richards

TEXT: RICHARDS

3 October 1915   *[Trinity College]*

   I congratulate you very heartily[2] and send you every wish for your happiness; and perhaps you will also convey my respects to Mrs Richards and, I am inclined to add, my congratulations too, because, whatever your other faults may be, there can be few ladies who have a more good-tempered husband.
   It would give me great pleasure to come and see you on the last week-end of the month . . .
   I see in the paper that you are having some bother over Hugh Lane's will, which certainly seems to be ungrammatical.[3]

To Katharine Symons

MS. LILLY

5 October 1915   *Trinity College*

My dear Kate,
   I have been scanning the casualty lists in these last days, and when I saw

---

[1] Literary critic (1861–1922); Professor of English at Oxford, 1904–1922; an enthusiastic admirer of Housman's verse.
[2] Richards had just re-married. His second wife was a Hungarian widow with a daughter.
[3] Sir Hugh Percy Lane (1875–1915) had in 1913 bequeathed his collection of modern paintings to the National Gallery, London. In February 1915, three months before his death, he added a codicil to his will leaving the pictures to the City of Dublin. The codicil however was unwitnessed and despite Irish protests it was impossible to give effect to his wishes, though a later compromise allowed the pictures to be shared between the two cities.

your card this morning I feared what the news must be.[1] Well, my dear, it is little I or anyone else can do to comfort you, or think of anything to say that you will not have thought of. But I remember your telling me at the beginning of the war that he had almost a hope and expectation of dying in battle, and we must be glad that it was a victorious battle in which he died. I do not know that I can do better than send you some verses that I wrote many years ago;[2] because the essential business of poetry, as it has been said, is to harmonise the sadness of the universe, and it is somehow more sustaining and healing than prose. Do assure Edward of my feeling for you all, and also, though I do not know her, the poor young girl.

Your affectionate brother   A. E. HOUSMAN

I send back the copy of his letter, because others will want to see it. I do not know where Jerry[3] is, but never mind that at present.

To Grant Richards

TEXT: RICHARDS

16 October 1915   [*Trinity College*]

I do rather think that the birthday etc. might go off better if no irrelevant visitor were there to spoil the fun; and so, in spite of my affection for children, I should like to postpone my visit. Probably any week-end in November that suited you would suit me.

As to the blind people,[4] they may have what they want.

To Grant Richards

TEXT: RICHARDS

22 December 1915   [*Trinity College*]

I enclose the last pages of Manilius III with two corrections, and the book may now be printed and published without any more tinkering from me.

The compliments of the season.

[1] Katharine Symons' third son, Clement Aubrey Symons (born 1893) was killed in action in France.
[2] 'Illic Jacet', first published in *The Academy*, 24 February 1900. Katharine Symons had it reprinted in *The Edwardian*, December 1915 (the magazine of King Edward VI School, Bath, where C. A. Symons had been educated). Housman included it in *Last Poems*.
[3] Noel Victor Housman Symons, her youngest son (born 1894).
[4] The National Institute for the Blind had asked permission to print *A Shropshire Lad* in Braille.

To Grant Richards

TEXT: RICHARDS

8 January 1916   *[Trinity College]*

I write about Manilius III, and shall probably write again, not out of impatience, but because, when book II was publishing, you and the printers went to sleep in each other's arms for a whole month and then wrote to ask me for corrections though I had said there would be none.

I sent all that I had to send before Christmas. I hope that, as I suggested, the binding is being got ready, so that the rest of the book will not have to wait for it.   `

To Grant Richards

TEXT: RICHARDS

3 February 1916   *[Trinity College]*

When you say you '*would* like to' go to France with me, is that a mere sigh or a serious wish? Because I should be both agreeable to it and desirous of it; only I understood that the difficulties now put in the way of getting a passport were almost insuperable. In any case I should not make the venture without a courier such as you to protect me.

Can I induce you to come and stay with me a night or two some time this term? Oldmeadow[1] is going to be dining in hall on Sunday the 20th with the Roman Catholic Monsignore,[2] if that will attract you, and possibly, though I am not sure, I might get him to dine with me on the Saturday. But any date that would suit you would probably suit me.

I have not been able to see the *Studio*[3] yet.

To Grant Richards

TEXT: RICHARDS

[circa 10 February 1916]   *[Trinity College]*

I am writing to tell you, directly on hearing it myself, that cerebro-spinal meningitis exists among the soldiers quartered in this college, who are supposed to have brought it with them from Ashford. I am not going to stir, and I believe that infection is conveyed only by close association; but consider whether this will make you change your mind about coming here on the 19th, and let me know as soon as is convenient to you.

[1] Ernest James Oldmeadow, author and music critic (1867–1949).
[2] The Rev. Christopher Scott, Provost of Northampton and Rector of the Church of the English Martyrs, Cambridge, since 1890.
[3] Review of the New English Art Club exhibition in the issue for January 1916. Hester Frood's *Countess Weir* is singled out for praise.

142

To Grant Richards

MS. CONGRESS

19 February 1916 *Trinity College*

My dear Richards,

I am very sorry indeed to see in the paper to-day the sudden death of your uncle[1]—though I suppose it was not altogether sudden, as it took place in the Acland Home.[2] When I saw him last, at your house, he seemed full of sturdiness. There are far too few severe and thorough scholars of his sort.

Yours sincerely   A. E. HOUSMAN

To Grant Richards

TEXT: RICHARDS

2 March 1916 *Trinity College*

[W. A. Merrill][3] published in 1907 an edition of Lucretius, containing nothing original, but collecting the work of others with that bibliographical fulness in which Americans excel. He has since changed his opinions on the text and developed originality as a reactionary, and his obtuseness enables him to stick to the reading of the manuscripts in many places where the critics whom he formerly followed abandoned them. I have a very low opinion of his intelligence, and he is bumptious into the bargain . . .

I return [Merrill's] letter.

Probably you will have seen a notice of your uncle in last week's *Oxford Magazine*, written I suppose by the Warden or someone else at Wadham.

To Grant Richards

TEXT: RICHARDS

[*circa 30 March 1916*] [*Trinity College*]

. . . The sinking of the *Sussex*[4] is no deterrent to me; quite the reverse. I argue thus: only a certain number of steamers are destined to sink; one of that number has sunk already without me on board; and that diminishes by one the number of my chances of destruction. But women cannot reason, so I suppose your designs are knocked on the head.[5]

I have pretty well made up my mind to go at least as far as Paris, probably about 20 April.

[1] Herbert Richards.
[2] The Oxford nursing home.
[3] Richards' text omits the name, but Merrill's is the only one that fits.
[4] *S.S. Sussex* was torpedoed by a German submarine off the French coast on 24 March 1916.
[5] Richards' wife objected to the proposed journey.

143

To Arthur Platt[1]

TEXT: MEMOIR

6 April 1916 [*Trinity College*]

Dear Platt,

If you prefer Aeschylus to Manilius you are no true scholar; you must be deeply tainted with literature, as indeed I always suspected you were.

The Bible is supposed to be full of types, and perhaps St Paul—ce type là—prefigures Don Quixote.[2] The resemblances you mention had not struck me, but they will bear thinking on. I wonder if St Paul's experiences in the third heaven are susceptible of the same explanation as Don Quixote's in the moon.

Yours sincerely   A. E. HOUSMAN

To Grant Richards

TEXT: RICHARDS

6 April 1916 [*Trinity College*]

Many thanks for your letter and your wish to preserve my life; but I have just applied for leave to go through Folkestone and Dieppe by the 7.0 p.m. from Charing Cross on Wednesday the 19th. After all, a quick death is better than a slow journey; and as I am only an author and not a publisher I am comparatively well prepared to meet my God. But I shall be sorry if my choice of the shorter route spoils any chance I may have had of crossing in your company. I shall pretty certainly be in London the Monday before I go, and may perhaps see you then.

I shall be interested to read my new volume of poems, but you don't tell me who the publisher is.[3] By the way, when are you going to bring out my edition of Catullus? Clement Shorter[4] announced it on your behalf ten years ago.

---

[1] This is the only surviving letter from Housman to his close friend and colleague at University College. The remainder were destroyed by Mrs Platt after her husband's death as 'too Rabelaisian'.

[2] The reference is to Platt's paper on Cervantes, read to the University College Literary Society in 1916 and published in *Nine Essays*, 1927.

[3] Richards had asked Housman about a rumour that he was about to bring out another volume of poems.

[4] Almost certainly a slip for Robertson Nicoll (see p. 80, note 2). Clement King Shorter (1857–1926) was a prolific literary biographer and editor successively of *The Illustrated London News*, *The Sphere* and *The Tatler*.

To Grant Richards

TEXT: RICHARDS

15 April 1916   *[Trinity College]*

Not on account of mines or torpedoes, which I despise as much as ever, but because the Folkestone route is closed and the voyage by Southampton–Havre, without the solace and protection of your company, is a long and weary subtraction from the short holiday I meant to take, I am not going to France.

Many thanks for the present of Valpy's Manilius[1] from you and your relatives. I had the edition already, but not so neat a copy.

To Grant Richards

MS. CONGRESS

12 June 1916   *Trinity College*

My dear Richards,

The first observation I have to make is that you have not answered my last letter. Your secretary wrote to me on 17 May that she had sent it after you to the continent, and added 'it will be some days before you can hear from him'. And so it was.

I asked you to come here for a week-end during the May term. The term is now over, but there will still be a certain number of people here, and if you like to come I shall be pleased to have you.

I don't know when you go to Cornwall, but I don't think you will carry me off there before the end of July, because this is my chief time for work.

I shall be interested to hear of your experiences of travel, because towards the end of August I think of trying to get to France, if not Italy.

Yours sincerely   A. E. HOUSMAN

To Mrs Platt

MS. U.C.L.

14 June 1916   *Trinity College*

Dear Mrs Platt,

It is very good of you to ask me to the rites of the Bona Dea[2] (as you have married a walking dictionary you can soon find out all about her); and, to be strictly honest, it would be possible for me to come to London on the 19th.

[1] Published in 1819.
[2] A Roman women's gathering at which the presence of men was sacrilege.

But it would not be convenient, and also I should have to cut a meeting and deprive the Vice-Chancellor of my valuable advice; so laziness and conscientiousness combined enable me to master my passion for tea and ladies, and I hope you will not be vindictively wrathful if I say no.

Ladies in Cambridge are getting into closer touch with war: they are to be allowed to paint shells. I greatly fear that patriotism together with feminine unscrupulousness will lead them to poison the paint.

Yours sincerely   A. E. HOUSMAN

To Grant Richards

MS. CONGRESS

26 June 1916   *Trinity College*

My dear Richards,

I ought of course to have answered your letter before now. Your invitation[1] is very attractive, and I should like to come, so far as I can judge at present. I have never been into Cornwall except just across the Tamar.

From what I hear, it seems as if the advance on our front were to begin to-morrow.[2] Civilians are not to cross to France for the next three weeks or so, and all vessels crossing for some time back have been filled with big guns, even to the exclusion, except at fixed dates, of officers on leave.

Yours sincerely   A. E. HOUSMAN

To Grant Richards

MS. CONGRESS

6 July 1916   *Trinity College*

My dear Richards,

I should think the 4th would be better than the 5th of August for travelling, with the double Bank Holiday looming ahead; so if you will make arrangements on that hypothesis it will be very nice of you.

As to how long I should stay, which we have not fixed, the first and great point of course is that my stay falls entirely within your own, and I am not going to be left unprotected among your huge family in a remote corner of England.

Thanks for the newspaper extracts.

Yours sincerely   A. E. HOUSMAN

[1] To spend a holiday at Richards' cottage at Ruan Minor, near The Lizard.
[2] The long awaited British offensive on the Somme began, after several days of heavy bombardment, on 1 July 1916.

To Alice Rothenstein

MS. HARVARD

10 July 1916 *Trinity College*

Dear Mrs Rothenstein,

It is extremely kind of you to ask me to Oakridge, and of course it is attractive; but after Cornwall I shall probably be going to my sister in Somerset, and not long after, if possible, to France, so my holidays will be pretty well filled up.

Your William has behaved quite nicely here, and I have just sent him off all safe and sound, so any breakages will have been caused by the journey and I shall not be responsible.

Yours sincerely   A. E. HOUSMAN

To Lady Ramsay

MS. U.C.L.

27 July 1916 *Trinity College*

Dear Lady Ramsay,

I have heard with great regret of the death of your husband,[1] from whom I always received the utmost kindness and friendliness throughout the many years which we passed as colleagues in London and during which I had the pleasure of watching the growth of his reputation and influence. I had been told indeed of his serious illness, but the loss to science and to his friends, though not unexpected, is none the less grievous; and I beg you to accept my sincere sympathy with yourself and your family in your bereavement.

I am yours sincerely   A. E. HOUSMAN

To Grant Richards

TEXT: RICHARDS

13 September 1916 *[Trinity College]*

I was very much distressed, and not on your account only, to see poor Gerard's death in the *Times*.[2] He was a nice boy, and it is sad that he had not the health and strength of other boys. I hope you and Mrs Richards are well, and not more overcome by sorrow for his loss than must needs be.

---

[1] Sir William Ramsay (1852–1916), celebrated for his discovery of the inert gases; Professor of Chemistry at University College, London, 1887–1916; knighted, 1902; winner of Nobel Prize, 1904.

[2] Richards' eldest son was killed by the collapse of a sand-cave at Poldu.

To Grant Richards

MS. CONGRESS

23 October 1916   *Trinity College*

My dear Richards,

I am grateful though ashamed to receive your present of a new stick. The old one perished nobly in the destruction of a venomous serpent,[1] and I only hope the new one may make as good an end.

1.45 on Thursday the 31st let it be. My kind regards to Mrs Richards and the family.

Yours sincerely   A. E. HOUSMAN

To Grant Richards

TEXT: RICHARDS

7 November 1916   *[Trinity College]*

I hope you and Mrs Richards enjoyed your tour—or are enjoying it, as I don't know if you are back yet.

But what I am writing about is this. A friend of mine (and acquaintance of yours) went to Bowes and Bowes to-day and asked for a 6*d.* copy of *A Shropshire Lad*. They brought it, but charged him 1/– for it, saying it had gone up to this owing to the war. I said I thought probably they were out of 6*d.* copies and offered him a 1/– one instead, but he sticks to his story.

To Grant Richards

TEXT: RICHARDS

5 December 1916   *[Trinity College]*

It would have given me great pleasure to come and see you and Mrs Richards, but I am engaged to spend the week-end in London, if the Government allows me to travel at all.[2]

Your Hunhunter at Clare,[3] from your account, must have troubles enough without adding me; and I for the last three weeks have been having a series of three colds on the top of one another. But if you like to let me know his

---

[1] In Cornwall Housman had killed an adder while walking with Richards and his children.

[2] There were no travel restrictions at this time in England and the reference is probably to the Cabinet crisis. On 4 December *The Times* announced that the Government was to be reconstructed. Mr Asquith resigned the following day and was succeeded as Prime Minister by Mr Lloyd George on 6 December.

[3] Desmond Young, author (with Justin McKenna) of *The Hun Hunters*, recently published by Richards.

name and rank, perhaps I may try to make his acquaintance when I am better. I do not make any particular complaint about your doubling the price of my book, but of course it diminishes the sale and therefore diminishes my chances of the advertisement to which I am always looking forward: a soldier is to receive a bullet in the breast, and it is to be turned aside from his heart by a copy of *A Shropshire Lad* which he is carrying there. Hitherto it is only the Bible which has performed this trick.

To Laurence Housman

TEXT: MEMOIR

10 February 1917 [*Trinity College*]

My dear Laurence,

. . . Thanks for your *Return of Alcestis*,[1] which as a whole I do not very much admire, in spite of a good many good lines. On the other hand the last work of yours that I read, *The Royal Runaway*,[2] I thought even better than *John of Jingalo*, at least till the revolution came, which I did not much believe in.

I was at Eton last Sunday and came across two boys, the sons of suffragists named Harben living somewhere near, to whom on one occasion in a closed carriage you recited reams of poetry which they supposed to be your own; but the only fragment which they could repeat was mine. It says a great deal for your conversational ascendancy that the incident took place, for in any other company those two boys would do the talking and not the listening . . .

Your affectionate brother A. E. HOUSMAN

To Edmund Gosse

MS. B.M.

9 April 1917 *Trinity College*

My dear Gosse,

Naturally I have been reading your life of Swinburne, and naturally also I have been enjoying it. It is a great comfort to have it done by someone who knows chalk from cheese: only I am surprised that you think so much of the second series of *Poems and Ballads*,[3] apart from 'Ave atque Vale'. And by the by it rejoices me to find that the only two things I ever admired in his later

---

[1] Probably the typescript. The play was included in Laurence Housman's trilogy *The Wheel*, 1919.
[2] Published in 1914.
[3] Published in 1878.

volumes—'Ave atque Vale' itself and the prologue to 'Tristram',—are both of them early. I offer you the following as a heading for Chapter VIII:

> The naked hulk alongside came,
>   And the twain were casting dice;
> 'The game is done! I've won, I've won!'
>   Quoth Watts, and Whistler thrice.[1]

It is above my usual standard; and I have composed part of another stanza, equally fine:

> Is that a Death? and are there two?
>   Is Death that Dunton's mate?

Now in prospect of a second edition, I make these remarks.

Pp. 45–7. Swinburne put it out of the power of the judges to award him the Newdigate,[2] by breaking the rules of the competition. In his time, and for years afterwards, the prescribed metre was the heroic couplet.

P. 79. Not *A Winter's Tale* but *The Merry Wives*, revived by Phelps at the Gaiety; and the date would be 1874, for I heard it sung in January 1875.[3]

P. 100. His pocket was either metaphorical or very large, for *Atalanta* was written in a ledger, now in the Fitzwilliam Museum.

P. 155. I have seen "Cleopatra" in a magazine of the sixties, *Cornhill* I think, with an illustration.[4]

P. 168. 'Ave atque Vale' had been published, I think, in the *Fortnightly* in 1875.

P. 200. Whose is the verse in inverted commas, slightly reminiscent of Wordsworth?[5]

P. 229. What you say about the *Persae* is quite wickedly false:[6] 'here lies our good Edmund'[7] in fact.

But what ought to turn the pudic snows of your countenance to scarlet is the bottom of p. 125, where you have taken Swinburne's heavy-handed irony for seriousness. That view of Mary is the view he imputes to his enemies her defenders.

[1] Parody of a verse in Coleridge's 'Ancient Mariner'. Theodore Watts, poet and novelist (1832–1914), who in 1897 assumed the name Watts-Dunton, rescued Swinburne when he was drinking himself to death in 1879 and gave him a home for the next thirty years. Under Watts's influence Swinburne in 1888 wrote a violent attack on his former friend James McNeill Whistler, the American-born painter (1834–1903), and the resulting quarrel was never mended.
[2] The Oxford prize for English verse.
[3] The reference is to a song by Swinburne, 'Love laid his sleepless head'.
[4] On p. 98 Gosse himself mentioned this magazine publication of 'Cleopatra'. On p. 155 he speaks of the later separate publication as a new work.
[5] Gosse had in fact misquoted Wordsworth.
[6] See the second paragraph of the next letter.
[7] A punning reference to Goldsmith's epitaph on Burke.

Perhaps we should both blush if you unfolded the awful inner meaning of 'a way which those who knew him will easily imagine for themselves' on p. 82.[1]
You may possibly be able to say, from your own knowledge or Mr T. J. Wise's,[2] whether Swinburne is the author of two poems signed "Etonensis"[3] in a volume entitled *The Whippingham Papers*,[4] sold in Paris to Anglo-Saxons.
Lord Redesdale misdates Swinburne's death on p. 317.[5]

My kind regards to Mrs Gosse.   Yours sincerely   A. E. HOUSMAN

To Edmund Gosse

MS. B.M.

13 April 1917   *Trinity College*

My dear Gosse,

If you are going to indulge in depression of spirits because I manage to find half a dozen mistakes in 350 pages, you will cut yourself off from my valued corrections in the future. As for my finding 'little to like', you know perfectly well that you write delightfully and that your taste and knowledge made you just the man for the work; and you do not need to hear it from me, especially when all the world is saying it. For my own part I always feel impertinent and embarrassed when I praise people: this is a defect of character, I know; and I suffer for it, like Cordelia. The chief fault of your book is one which I did not mention, that there is too little of it.

There are not, and could not be, any odes in praise of Athenian liberty in the *Persae*, for all the odes are sung by Persian elders. You probably had in your mind a celebrated passage of dialogue where Atossa enquires who is lord and governor of the Athenians and is answered that they are no man's servants or subjects. There is an ode in praise of Athens (though not of its liberty) in Euripides' *Medea*, but I suppose Swinburne would not deign to recite him.

I am sending *The Whippingham Papers* by parcel post. The two poems have some affinity to passages in "Love's Cross Currents" and "The Sisters";[6] the verse seems to me good enough for Swinburne, and in the second poem the stanza is like him; and the names *Reggie* and *Algernon*[7] are observable.

---

[1] Gosse's discreet reference to Swinburne's drunkenness and obsession with flagellation.
[2] Book-collector, bibliographer and forger (1859–1937); owner of the Ashley Library now in the British Museum.
[3] 'Reginald's Flogging', a poem in two parts, was in fact by Swinburne.
[4] An anonymous collection of flagellant writings, first published in 1888.
[5] In a letter printed by Gosse as an appendix.
[6] Respectively a novel (1905) and a tragedy (1892) by Swinburne.
[7] In 'Reginald's Flogging' Algernon is a school friend of the hero, Reggie Fane.

151

You will see that on p. iii the poet is said to be the author of another work, *The Romance of Chastisement*,[1] which I have not come across: my library is sadly incomplete, and not at all worth leaving to the British Museum when I die.

Yours sincerely   A. E. HOUSMAN

To Grant Richards

TEXT: RICHARDS

20 June 1917   [*Trinity College*]

Vaughan Williams did have an interview with me six years or more ago, and induced me by appeals ad misericordiam to let him print words on the programme of a concert for which he had already made arrangements; but the permission applied to that concert only. I knew what the results would be, and told him so.

To Alice Rothenstein

MS. HARVARD

9 August 1917   *Trinity College*

Dear Mrs Rothenstein,

It is very good of you to write and enquire after me, and if I were to be in Gloucestershire I would certainly come and see you, but that is not likely at present, and before long I am hoping to get to France, where I have not been for two years and a half, much to the detriment of my health and spirits. I hope that you and William and all the family are as flourishing as is consistent with being fed on war-bread.

Yours sincerely   A. E. HOUSMAN

To Grant Richards

MS. CONGRESS

22 August 1917   *Trinity College*

My dear Richards,

Symondsbury was the village I spoke of, but I have never been inside it, and have only seen the beauty of its knolls and trees from the top of a neighbouring hill. It is two miles from the sea, and not in sight of it, as the high

---

[1] Sub-titled *Revelations of the School and Bedroom. By an Expert.* It was first published in 1870. The anonymous author was not Swinburne but St George Henry Stock.

hill and cliff of Eype, which you see from Lyme, intervene. When you do get to the beach, I expect it is chiefly pebbles. I know nothing about lodgings, and I don't think there can be much of an inn.

Abbotsbury is not a bad place for downs and open country, but as for bathing—! it is on the Chesil Bank, where death is certain owing to the currents and desirable owing to the stones.

The War Office does not view with favour my proposed escape to France, so I shall start at the beginning of next month on a tour to Rochester, Canterbury, Winchester and Salisbury. When I am turning home I shall write to you, and if you then wish me to come to Bigfrith I shall be very pleased. I hope you are all well.

Yours sincerely   A. E. HOUSMAN

To F. J. H. Jenkinson[1]

MS. CAMBRIDGE

7 November 1917   *Trinity College*

My dear Jenkinson,

I am not quite sure if you are the right person to write to, nor who is chairman of the Library Extension Subsyndicate; but anyhow I shall probably not be coming to the meeting to-morrow, as I am nursing a cold.

Yours   A. E. HOUSMAN

To Wilbur Cross[2]

MS. YALE

18 November 1917   *Trinity College*

Dear Sir,

I am obliged by your letter, but I neither have any poem which I wish to publish nor am likely to write one at any early date.

I am yours very truly   A. E. HOUSMAN

To J. W. Mackail

MS. TRINITY

11 December 1917   *Trinity College*

Dear Mackail,

I am very glad to have your paper on Horace.[3] I thought your chapter on

[1] 1853–1923; University Librarian from 1890.
[2] American author and editor (1862–1948); Professor of English at Yale University, 1902–1921; Governor of Connecticut, 1931–1939; at the time of this letter editor of *The Yale Review*.
[3] Read to the Classical Association and reprinted in Mackail's *Classical Studies*, 1925.

153

him in your *Latin Literature*[1] one of the best, and this is a worthy continuation.

Yours very truly

A. E. HOUSMAN

Postcard to Percy Withers[2]

MS. WITHERS

18 January 1918   *Trinity College*

I will walk with you to the Navarros'[3] door on Sunday: I shall not cross the threshold myself, but I am not going to keep you out of paradise.

Yours

A. E. HOUSMAN

To Mrs Withers

MS. WITHERS

10 March 1918   *Trinity College*

Dear Mrs Withers,

Porters so seldom bring one things on Sundays that I am even more overwhelmed than I otherwise should be by your kindness in enriching me with blackberry jelly from your end of the town, where the grocers still have jams. I have been enjoined this evening not to write you a charming letter, so I will put a firm constraint on myself and abstain from being so; but I am tempted to be very charming indeed.

I am yours sincerely

A. E. HOUSMAN

To Stephen Gaselee[4]

MS. CAMBRIDGE

7 May 1918   *Trinity College*

Dear Gaselee,

I shall be delighted to dine with you on Whit-Sunday. I was just on the

---

[1] Published in 1895.

[2] Doctor and miscellaneous writer (1867–1945). He made Housman's acquaintance while stationed on war service at Cambridge in 1917. Though he never became a close friend, Housman was at ease with him and his family and often stayed with them. He left a sympathetic account of Housman in *A Buried Life*, 1940.

[3] José Maria de Navarro, Fellow of Trinity College; University Lecturer in Archaeology and Anthropology, 1926–1929.

[4] Classical scholar and bibliographer of Petronius (1882–1943); Fellow and Librarian of Magdalene College, Cambridge, 1908–1919; Librarian of the Foreign Office, 1920; knighted, 1935.

154

point of writing to you about the translations of Petronius, which I happen to be wanting to consult, and cannot find many within my reach. Burnaby, Wilson and Co., Lowe [1905], Ryan [1905], Heseltine [1912], Friedlaender [1891] and the French [by Nodot] of 1694 are all I can get at either the University or the College library or on my own shelves, for the University copy of Bohn[1] is out, as I suppose it always is. Jackson possesses a copy, and also one of Addison [1736], but cannot lay hands on either. No doubt you have quite a number, and perhaps sometime you would let me have a look at them. It is only one passage that I am concerned with.

Perhaps you know that we have in the College library a MS translation, 18th century apparently, based on Burnaby and not so good in diction, but more understanding and helpful in the passage I consulted it for.

Yours sincerely   A. E. HOUSMAN

To Alice Rothenstein

MS. HARVARD

6 July 1918   *Trinity College*

Dear Mrs Rothenstein,

It is possible,—do not be agitated,—that I shall be coming to Woodchester or Amberley towards the end of August; and then you may be sure that I shall walk over to see you. Thank you all the same for your kindness in asking me to Oakridge, and also for amiable messages which I have received from our friend Dr Withers.

I have been glad to see in the papers and hear privately of the success of W's exhibition in London.[2]

I am yours sincerely   A. E. HOUSMAN

To Alice Rothenstein

MS. HARVARD

22 August 1918   *Trinity College*

Dear Mrs Rothenstein,

Alas, my plans for coming to Gloucestershire are upset. At the hotel at Amberley, where I had meant to stay, they are full till the end of September, which is too late. For me the cloud has a silver lining, as I escape the horrors which now encompass travelling: for you, of course, the gloom is unmitigated.

---

[1] Edited by W. K. Kelly, 1848.
[2] Of drawings of the fighting in Flanders. The exhibition, at the Goupil Gallery, was opened by H. A. L. Fisher, the President of the Board of Education, on 25 April 1918.

I have met M. André Gide,[1] who had a letter from William, and I shall see him again if he does not shortly go off to France, as he threatens.

I wish William good luck on the lines of communication.[2]

Yours sincerely   A. E. HOUSMAN

To Martin Secker[3]

MS. LILLY

29 September 1918   *Trinity College*

Dear Mr Secker,

Many thanks to you for sending me the anonymous book on Women,[4] which is acute and entertaining to read and flatters some of my own prejudices; though it contains so many general propositions that it must contain a good deal which is not quite true.

I am yours very truly   A. E. HOUSMAN

To Grant Richards

MS. CONGRESS

11 October 1918   *Trinity College*

My dear Richards,

I shall be very pleased to come to you on the 25th, when your woodlands ought to be looking very well. I was in Gloucestershire most of September, and saw the Rothensteins. From the fragment of your autobiography which I see in the weekly press[5] I gather that you have had a holiday or holidays.

My kind regards to Mrs Richards, who owes me a photograph of young pigs.[6]

Yours sincerely   A. E. HOUSMAN

[1] French novelist and playwright (1869–1951), staying at Cambridge in the summer and autumn of 1918.

[2] Rothenstein was called up for military service on 24 July, but before enlistment was appointed Director of Art and Civic Education in the projected Army University. His departure for France was delayed by formalities and he spent the rest of the war lecturing to Australian Education Officers at Cambridge.

[3] English publisher (born 1882).

[4] *Women*, just published by Secker.

[5] His advertisements in *The Times Literary Supplement*.

[6] With Housman among them, taken near Zennor during his Cornish holiday in 1916.

To Grant Richards

TEXT: RICHARDS

25 November 1918 [*Trinity College*]
Yours is a terrible long illness,[1] but I am glad that you seem to be fairly comfortable.

I have sent to your office a list of eight mistakes in the octavo edition of *A Shropshire Lad*, probably all taken over from 1916. The smaller editions (except the cursed *Lesser Classics*) have a purer text, with only one error I think; but this reappears in the last issue (for which by the way I ought to have begun by thanking you): p. 5 (only the 5 is invisible), last line but two, there should be a colon after *town*.

To Edmund Gosse

MS. TRINITY

29 December 1918 *Trinity College*

My dear Gosse,
I send these notes on Swinburne's letters[2] in hopes that they may be of use for the next edition.

Vol. I
p. 162. Read '*as* Knox'.
171. *a* and *w* should be the Greek letters alpha and omega.
209. 'no person, may worship' would be a less puzzling punctuation: whether Swinburne's, I don't know.
212. 'as to *his* dealings of my own': *his* wants altering or removing.
260. 'The Last Oracle' appeared in *Belgravia*, and as early as 1876 if the date of letter CXXXV is right.
282. Read '*m*'est parvenu'.

Vol. II
p. 25. Veuillot's name is misprinted.
36. Read 'En *plein* été' and '*Ton* adorable'.
120. Read '*stray* squibs'.
126. Read 'damning *blot*'.
145. The League cannot have been the Primrose League. Swinburne's verses were against the House of Lords, which was withstanding Gladstone's attempt to lower the franchise without a redistribution of seats.

---

[1] Richards had gone down with influenza during Housman's visit to Bigfrith a month before. The illness had later developed into pleurisy and pneumonia.
[2] Edited by Gosse and T. J. Wise, 1918.

183. Read '*such* pleasure'.
186. Read 'Sandys' '.
214. Read 'Etonie'.

An explanation of Vol. I letter CV would be welcome, if it could be given without causing pain in Buckingham Palace. Does it refer to the French play about Queen Victoria's foster-sister, of which I have heard fragments from you and others?[1]

Thank you for collecting and editing the letters, and best wishes for the New Year to you and Mrs Gosse.

Yours sincerely   A. E. HOUSMAN

To Robert Bridges[2]

MS. BRIDGES

30 December 1918   *Trinity College*

My dear Bridges,

I must send you my thanks for the poems of G. M. Hopkins.[3] I value the book as your gift, and also for some good condensed lines and an engaging attitude of mind which now and again shines through. But the faults which you very fairly and judicially set forth thrust themselves more upon my notice; and also another. Sprung Rhythm, as he calls it in his sober and sensible preface, is just as easy to write as other forms of verse; and many a humble scribbler of words for music-hall songs has written it well. But he does not: he does not make it audible; he puts light syllables in the stress and heavy syllables in the slack, and has to be helped out with typographical signs explaining that things are to be understood as being what in fact they are not. Also the English language is a thing which I respect very much, and I resent even the violence Keats did to it; and here is a lesser than Keats doing much more. Moreover his early poems are the promise of something better, if less original; and originality is not nearly so good as goodness, even when it is good. His manner strikes me as deliberately adopted to compensate

---

[1] 'The rightful Queen of England is at this moment a prisoner in Newgate.' (Swinburne to Thomas Purnell, 20 February 1875). The reference is to Swinburne's pastiche of Hugo, *La Soeur de la Reine*, a play in French about a twin sister of Queen Victoria. The surviving fragments were first printed in 1964.

[2] Robert Seymour Bridges (1844–1930), originally trained as a doctor, had been Poet Laureate since 1913; appointed to the Order of Merit, 1929. Housman greatly admired his early work.

[3] Edited by Bridges and first published in 1918, nearly thirty years after the author's death. At Bridges' request Housman had translated the dedication into Latin.

158

by strangeness for the lack of pure merit, like the manner which Carlyle took up after he was thirty. Well, the paper warns me I must not run on, and perhaps you will not think this a very grateful letter.

I am yours sincerely   A. E. HOUSMAN

To Edmund Gosse

MS. B.M.

20 January 1919   *Trinity College*

My dear Gosse,

I return with gratitude a memoir[1] which I have read with a great deal of pleasure, not only for the interest of the facts, which are pretty much what I had surmised, but also, if it is not impertinent to say so, for the wholesome air of good sense with which you have surrounded them, and the ease with which you have done it.

The Menken interlude[2] I partly knew through Bywater. If that lady had left an account of her various and eminent partners, it would be better reading than 'Infelicia',[3] though I am afraid her tolerance of Swinburne shows that she did not properly appreciate the Benicia Boy.[4]

The Eton anecdote on p. 19 is perplexing, because Etonians tell me that the only person privileged to flog is the headmaster.[5]

It is curious that though Sade is the author who most influenced Swinburne, and though Swinburne's writings are full of sadism properly so called, his own propensities were those of Rousseau and Sacher-Masoch. It is true that these are cheaper to indulge, but that does not seem to have been the reason.

Was *Charenton*[6] published? From the Letters (which are not in my hands

---

[1] A typescript circulated by Gosse among friends, giving an account of Swinburne's addiction to drink and flagellation and explaining why these details had been omitted from the biography. Recipients included Max Beerbohm, A. C. Bradley and Walter Raleigh. It was first printed in 1962 as an appendix to Swinburne's *Letters*, edited by Cecil Lang.

[2] Adah Isaacs Menken, an American circus performer and courtesan (1835–1868), went to live with Swinburne in December 1867. The arrangement was made by Rossetti in the hope of turning Swinburne's interests away from whipping, but it did not succeed, and she left after six weeks, having found Swinburne completely impotent.

[3] A volume of her poems, 1868.

[4] Professional name of John Carmel Heenan, a young Irish-American prize-fighter, married to Adah Menken, 1859–1861.

[5] Account by Swinburne of being allowed to bathe his face in eau de cologne before being beaten by his housemaster. The use of the birch (which Etonians call flogging) is confined to the Headmaster.

[6] A poem in French written by Swinburne in 1861. It was not published until 1951. In Letter XVI Gosse unaccountably prints 'Charenton' in place of the correct reading, 'Antitheism'.

at this moment) it seemed that Lord Houghton[1] had mentioned it in his review of *Atalanta in Calydon*,[2] which however is not the case. Judging from dates, drink had a great deal to do with his best poetry, though the poetry declined before the drinking stopped. The history of the Mohammedan world confirms Horace's opinion of the connexion between the two;[3] and if American poetry were worth anything I should weep, as now I do not, at the sight of America going bone-dry.

Can you tell me anything about *Quagg* and *Grace Walkers*[4] mentioned in connexion with Sala[5] on p. 16 of vol. I of the Letters? If, as I gather, they occur in some book which appealed to Swinburne's sense of humour, it might be worth looking up. If on the other hand they belong to the 'Mysteries of Verbena Lodge',[6] mysteries let them remain.

I am yours sincerely   A. E. HOUSMAN

To Grant Richards

MS. CONGRESS

1 March 1919   *Trinity College*

My dear Richards,

It is exceedingly good of you to interest yourself in my behalf and write to me in such detail, but I don't much think that I shall take advantage of it at present, or before June, as I hear appalling accounts of the prices of everything in Paris, and even accommodation seems to be scarce. I hope you and Mrs Richards are having good weather at Nice and enjoying yourselves as much as I did when I was there with you. Please remember me to Belfort Bax.

Yours sincerely   A. E. HOUSMAN

[1] Richard Monckton Milnes (1809–1885; created Baron Houghton, 1863), politician, writer and collector of erotica, had introduced Swinburne to the works of Sade.

[2] In *The Edinburgh Review*, July 1865.

[3] e.g. *Epistles* I. xix. 2–3.

[4] The reference is to 'Colonel Quagg's Conversion', in *Household Words*, 1855. Swinburne was fascinated by this story, in which Colonel Quagg terrorizes a Massachussetts sect called the Grace-Walking Brethren, flogging any member he catches passing his smithy; he is then flogged himself and converted to the sect.

[5] George Augustus Sala (1828–1896), a journalist liked and admired by Swinburne.

[6] The 'mysterious house in St John's Wood, where two golden-haired and rouge-cheeked ladies received, in luxuriously furnished rooms, gentlemen whom they consented to chastise for large sums', described by Gosse in the memoir. Swinburne became a regular visitor in the mid-eighteen-sixties.

To Grant Richards

MS. CONGRESS

5 May 1919   *Trinity College*

My dear Richards,

I think that in writing to Mrs Richards I mentioned the first week of June as one in which you might find it pleasant to be here. I must now warn you against it, for there will not be a bed to be had in the place. The rowing authorities have stupidly put the races earlier than usual, at a time in the term when men have not finished their examinations and begun to go down; so there is much trouble ahead for this already congested town and university.

Yours sincerely   A. E. HOUSMAN

To Grant Richards

MS. CONGRESS

15 May 1919   *Trinity College*

My dear Richards,

The dinner of the inter-University club 'The Arcades' is to take place at Oxford on the 31st, so I shall then be there, but I hope you will not be much put out by coming here on the 24th instead. I hope you will both lunch in my rooms on the Saturday and Sunday, and of course I should like you to dine in hall on Saturday, if Mrs Richards will not cry her eyes out at being deserted. I do not admire that demoralising animal the horse as much as you do, so I shall let you do your gloating at Newmarket alone. Will you let me know exactly what time to expect you on Saturday? Perhaps I could get Quiller-Couch to meet you at lunch.

The best inn here on the whole is the University Arms, and the most pleasantly situated: its drawback is that it is more than half-a-mile from the College, nearly half-way to the station. The Bull is nearly central and stands on the best street in the town, but it is dingy, and the food not very good, at least when I tried it last. The best for food is the Lion, which also is central, but stands on a narrow and busy street. A smaller inn, the Blue Boar, close to Trinity, is well spoken of.

The place is looking beautiful at present, and I hope this weather will hold. I am reading Wilfrid Blunt with a good deal of interest.[1]

With kind regards to Mrs Richards, I am yours sincerely

A. E. HOUSMAN

---

[1] *My Diaries*, 1919. The index confuses A.E.H. with Laurence Housman, who is named as the author of *A Shropshire Lad*.

161

To J. W. Mackail

MS. FITZWILLIAM

23 May 1919   *Trinity College*

Dear Mackail,

I cannot help being touched and flattered by your anxiety to make me publish, and I am grateful to you for sending me Mrs Meynell's volume,[1] though I had already seen it. But my unwillingness remains, because it is not due to any doubt of the possibility of deluding the public, by printing and binding and so on, into the belief that it is getting its money's worth, but to my own notions of what is proper. However, I shall be contributing a new piece shortly to a MS anthology[2] which is being got up, and in due season I will send you this drop of water to moisten your parched tongue.

Yours sincerely   A. E. HOUSMAN

To Henry Jackson[3]

MS. TRINITY

14 July 1919   *Trinity College*

Dear Jackson,

The present year, in which your eightieth birthday was been followed by your retirement from the office of Vice-Master, affords the Fellows of your College a suitable opportunity of expressing in symbol their affection for yourself and their sense of your services to the foundation which received you more than sixty years ago.

We therefore ask you to accept from us, as some token of these feelings, a copy of a vessel from which your most illustrious predecessor[4] in the Chair of Greek is thought to have derived a solace not unknown or unwelcome to its present occupant; and we trust that the figure of Porson's tobacco-jar may often meet your eyes, and bring us before your mind, in moments tranquillised by its contents.

Our tribute carries with it the personal affection of friends and the grati-

---

[1] *A Father of Women and Other Poems*, 1917.

[2] Forty representative writers were asked to contribute an autograph poem each for a volume to be presented to Thomas Hardy on his 79th birthday, 2 June 1919. The paper and binding were supervised by Cockerell, Bridges wrote the foreword, the organisation was done by Walter de la Mare, Gosse, Henry Newbolt and Siegfried Sassoon. The last, who had originally proposed the scheme, made the presentation at Hardy's home, Max Gate, Dorchester.

[3] Drafted by Housman for signature by the Master and Fellows of Trinity College. The address, date, salutation and subscription are added in another hand. The letter was privately printed by The Cambridge University Press.

[4] Richard Porson (1759–1808), Regius Professor of Greek from 1792 until his death.

162

tude of a community. From the day when first you were elected a Fellow of the College, no measure has been undertaken for the promotion of its welfare or the increase of its efficiency which has not been furthered by your zeal or due to your initiative. In Trinity, in Cambridge, in the whole academic world and far beyond it, you have earned a name on the lips of men and a place in their hearts to which few or none in the present or the past can make pretension. And this eminence you owe not only or chiefly to the fame of your learning and the influence of your teaching, nor even to that abounding and proverbial hospitality which for many a long year has made your rooms the hearthstone of the Society and a guesthouse in Cambridge for pilgrims from the ends of the earth, but to the broad and true humanity of your nature, endearing you alike to old and young, responsive to all varieties of character or pursuit, and remote from nothing that concerns mankind. The College which you have served and adorned so long, proud as it is of your intellect and attainments, and grateful for your devotion, is happy above all that in possessing you it possesses one of the great English worthies.

We are

Your affectionate friends

To Mrs Richards

TEXT: RICHARDS

15 July 1919 [*Trinity College*]

On returning here after a month's holiday I found awaiting me the screens which you have been kind enough to make for my reading–lamp and candles. They beautify my surroundings very much, and I am very grateful to you for your skill and amiability.

To Grant Richards

TEXT: RICHARDS

21 July 1919 [*Trinity College*]

. . . I am afraid we are not likely to travel together nor even to meet. I took a month's change at midsummer, which I was much in need of, and now I have settled down to work: and also I rather think that August heat in France might put my health out of order again. So I am thinking of starting on 28 August or perhaps 2 September.

As it appears that a military permit is still required for Paris I should be glad if you could tell me whether your friend is still in power and prepared to make things easy for me. Moreover I am not clear whether, after leaving Paris for the South, one can re-enter it without further trouble.

163

Most likely I shall not stay long at Brive or any other place, but motor about. After my sacrifices for my country during the war[1] I am beginning to spend money on myself instead of saving it up for the Welsh miners.[2]

Please keep me informed of your plans, and let me know when you come back, as I ought to have the text and notes of Manilius IV ready before I go, and they may as well be printing while I am away.

I hope you will all enjoy yourselves.

To Grant Richards

TEXT: RICHARDS

24 August 1919 [*Trinity College*]

Your office has very kindly and dexterously secured me the French visa, but unluckily it is for Boulogne, whereas I am going by Dieppe. I ought to have mentioned this particular, but I did not think of it. I do not know if the Consulate is like Pontius Pilate and refuses to alter what it has written; but in the hope that this is not so I am again enclosing the passport, if I can ask you to get it amended. As this is Sunday and there are no postal orders about, I enclose a 10/– note, in case it is wanted.

I shall have to come to town some day this week; and if there is any day (other than Saturday) on which you could lunch with me at the Café Royal, I wish you would let me know what day it is, and would also engage a table there in my name.

To Grant Richards

MS. CONGRESS

29 August 1919 *Trinity College*

My dear Richards,

I have sent Manilius IV to your Office. I leave here on Monday morning, and down to the next Sunday I expect to be at Hôtel Terminus St Lazare; after that letters addressed to me at Cambridge will be forwarded from time to time.

I am going by Dieppe because the hotel is at the Paris station of that line. Besides I crossed with you from Folkestone to Dieppe without discomfort,— though that may have been due to your magic presence. The visa has been put right.

---

[1] At the outbreak of the war Housman had sent the Chancellor of the Exchequer a donation of several hundred pounds, the bulk of his savings.

[2] Who were threatening to strike against new income tax regulations.

164

It would certainly be very agreeable to stay a couple of nights at Bigfrith on my way home, if nothing intervenes. I expect to come back about the 25th.

Yours sincerely   A. E. HOUSMAN

This volume of Manilius, apart from the rise in prices, is likely to be more expensive than I or II (let alone III, which was short), because it contains a larger proportion of notes, which I suppose are the most expensive part.

To Grant Richards

TEXT: RICHARDS

14 September 1919   *Brive*

If you do not intervene to prevent it, what will happen is this. On Wednesday the 24th I shall arrive at Bigfrith some time in the afternoon, in a motor which will deposit me with a small bag, containing little except a clean shirt, and will take my larger luggage on to Cambridge, and there you will have me for two nights.

I am returning to Paris, Hôtel Terminus St Lazare, on Thursday the 18th. There I shall be till Tuesday the 23rd, when I shall cross, and sleep at Newhaven. I should like to hear from you as soon as I reach Paris, because I shall have to write to Cambridge about the motor.

The passage of the Channel was as good as could be.

To Grant Richards

MS. CONGRESS

19 September 1919   *Hôtel Terminus*

My dear Richards,

This is a great pleasure, apart from its unexpectedness. It will be no good looking for me here this evening, and I am also engaged to-morrow evening and Monday evening: otherwise I have no tie. Usually I leave the hotel not long after 9 a.m., and to-morrow I will look you up at the Normandy soon after that time, unless I hear from you to the contrary.

Yours sincerely   A. E. HOUSMAN

To Grant Richards

MS. CONGRESS

27 September 1919   *Trinity College*

My dear Richards,

I enclose cheque for £100. Whether I shall post this letter to-day is

165

uncertain, as I had better wait to see what effect the strike has on the post.[1] My *New Statesman* arrived this morning as usual.

I began to read *Antonio*[2] in the train and found it quite interesting.

I hope neither you nor Mrs Richards are suffering much from the cold you caught from me, which lies heavy on my conscience, as I do not like to return evil for so much kindness.

Yours sincerely   A. E. HOUSMAN

To Grant Richards

TEXT: RICHARDS

[October 1919]   *[Trinity College]*

I have not finished Proust's book,[3] but I have read enough to form the opinion that an English translation would not sell, and, apart from that, could not be really satisfactory, as the merit of the French is in great part a matter of diction and vocabulary. Moreover, the second section of the book, in which I am now rather stuck, is not at all equal to the first. The second volume, I am told, is not good.

To Grant Richards

MS. CONGRESS

7 November 1919   *Trinity College*

My dear Richards,

If you give me Simon's book[4] it will be very good of you. I enclose the poem. The poems were not supposed to be *addressed* to Hardy, only specimens of our stuff, published or unpublished.

Yours sincerely   A. E. HOUSMAN

---

[1] A railway strike from 26 September to 5 October caused the suspension of the parcel post.

[2] By Ernest Oldmeadow, 1914.

[3] *A la recherche du temps perdu*, 1913–1927. The first section, *Du Côté de chez Swann*, was re-issued in 1917 in one volume; and in 1919 in two; the second section, *A l'ombre des jeunes filles en fleurs*, was published in one volume, 1918. Housman's advice on an English edition lost Richards a title which would have brought him profit. The translation by C. K. Scott-Moncrieff and Stephen Hudson, 1922–1931, published by Chatto and Windus, proved immensely successful.

[4] *Wine and Spirits. The connoisseur's textbook* by André Simon, 1919.

To H. W. Garrod

MS. SPARROW

26 November 1919 *Trinity College*

Dear Mr Garrod,

I am grateful for the gift of your interesting and spirited book of poems,[1] and I am glad that the locust and the rest of the Lord's great army have not eaten all the last four years. I hope too that you will not perish untimely by the fury of undergraduates.[2]

Yours very truly A. E. HOUSMAN

To Grant Richards

TEXT: RICHARDS

30 November 1919 *[Trinity College]*

I had thought of 6/- net as the price for Manilius IV. Of course the increase in the cost of production is greater than that, but I have always sold at less than cost price, so it does not make the difference between profit and loss.

This reminds me that it is just three months since I sent you the manuscript, and I wonder when the printers are going to start upon it.

Thanks for the book on wines: but mortal passions have invaded the sacred precincts of the cellar to such an extent that he knows of no German or Hungarian wine and does know of stuff from Australia and California.

To J. S. Phillimore[3]

MS. TRINITY

30 November 1919 *Trinity College*

Dear Phillimore,

I am very much in your debt for the gift of your address,[4] and am glad that I did not miss it by not hearing it delivered. It contains a great deal of truth well and tellingly said, together with some things which I do not assent to. Your strictures on German scholarship have something of the intemperate zeal of the convert, like attacks on the Church of Rome by runaway monks.

---

[1] *Worms and Epitaphs*, 1919.

[2] 'Intruders', a poem in the book, is a bitter attack on the Oxford undergraduates who had come up straight from school and taken the places of men killed in the war.

[3] John Swinnerton Phillimore (1873–1926); Lecturer at Christ Church, Oxford, 1895; Professor of Greek at Glasgow, 1899; Professor of Humanity, 1906.

[4] 'The Revival of Criticism', delivered to the Classical Association at Oxford, 17 May 1919.

I should say that for the last hundred years individual German scholars have been the superiors in genius as well as learning of all scholars outside Germany except Madvig and Cobet;[1] and that the herd or group vices of the German school which you particularly reprehend took their rise from Sedan and may be expected to decline after this second and greater Jena: though indeed they have already been declining since the early years of the century. There are some of your examples which do not at all convince me: for instance on p. 19 the required jingle is not procured unless the locative *Romai* was a trisyllable. I thought pp. 7–8 very good and salutary.

Yours sincerely   A. E. HOUSMAN

To Laurence Housman

TEXT: MEMOIR

4 December 1919   *[Trinity College]*

My dear Laurence,

. . . I have not thanked you as I should for the trilogy[2] you sent me on 17 November, but I have not been able to read it through at leisure till lately. You do not need to be told that there is a good deal to admire in it; and there are passages, such as the last four lines, which I like very much. But as to the style in general I cannot do better than copy out a couple of sentences from a review of mine:[3] 'In the sixties it seemed indeed as if there had arisen a band of writers to launch poetry on a new career; but time showed that they were cruising in a backwater, not finding a channel for the main stream, and in twenty years all heart had gone out of the enterprise. The fashions of that interlude are already so antique that Mr Gilbert Murray can adapt them for his rendering of Euripides; and they now receive academic approbation, which is the second death.' As to the moral rules incumbent on gods and men, they alter as time goes on, but do not improve, though each age in succession thinks its own rules right. My own sense of propriety however is not so much offended by anything you have taken from the ancient story as by your scuttling Alcestis at Scapa Flow on p. 74.[4]

I hear from Kate that you are leaving for America on the 30th, and I wish you a pleasant and prosperous tour. If they pay you in dollars you ought to come back rich . . .

Your affectionate brother   A. E. HOUSMAN

[1] Dutch editor and grammarian (1813–1889).
[2] *The Wheel*, 1919.
[3] Of *The Cambridge History of English Literature*, volumes XIII and XIV, in *The Cambridge Review*, 23 May 1917.
[4] In *The Doom of Admetus* (Part III of *The Wheel*). The German battleships and cruisers interned at Scapa Flow were sunk and abandoned by their crews on 21 June 1919, a week before the signature of the Treaty of Versailles.

168

To an Unnamed Correspondent[1]

MS. PRINCETON

8 December 1919 *Trinity College*

My dear Sir,

I take it very kindly of you that you should write to me about my books, especially as there are not many who find pleasure, as you do, both in my poems and in my editions of the classics. If you are good enough to send me the work on Horace[2] of which you speak, I shall be glad and grateful.

I am yours very truly A. E. HOUSMAN

To Grant Richards

TEXT: RICHARDS

16 December 1919 *[Trinity College]*

This is molestation and persecution. You sent me the proofs to correct when the edition[3] was preparing, and when you do that there are practically no errors. I am too full at this moment of more interesting work to waste my time trying to find mistakes where none are likely to be. Besides I have a copy of the edition, probably more than one.

If you do not like illustrations, why did you print this edition? It was all your doing, none of mine; and I thought the public quite right in not buying it.

To Mrs Richards

TEXT: RICHARDS

[December 1919] *[Trinity College]*

Many thanks for your gift of walnuts and deliciously scented apples. I am glad to see that your garden has prospered and that the children of the neighbourhood have not taken all the fruit. We are looking forward to the winter without much fear, as the Government has just allowed the College a good coal ration. Tell Grant that I am eating and drinking a great deal, as there are many Feasts of one sort and another.

[1] Probably Louis Untermeyer (born 1885), American author and editor.
[2] Untermeyer's *Including Horace*, 1919.
[3] The illustrated edition of 1908, which Richards was reprinting.

To R. St J. Parry[1]

MS. TRINITY

3 January 1920   *Trinity College*

My dear Parry,

I must begin with grateful acknowledgment to you and my other friends, because I could not read your letter without feelings which had some pure pleasure in them; but this was swallowed up in surprise, and surprise itself was engulfed in horror.

Not if the stipend were £150,000 instead of £150 would I be Public Orator.[2] I could not discharge the duties of the office without abandoning all other duties and bidding farewell to such peace of mind as I possess. You none of you have any notion what a slow and barren mind I have, nor what a trouble composition is to me (in prose, I mean: poetry is either easy or impossible). When the job is done, it may have a certain amount of form and finish and perhaps a false air of ease; but there is an awful history behind it. The letter to Jackson last year laid waste three whole mornings: the first, I sat staring in front of me and wishing for death; the second, I wrote down disjointed phrases and sentences which looked loathsome; the third, after a night in which I suppose my subliminal self had been busy, I had some relief in fitting them together and finding they could be improved into something respectable. I can stand this once in a way; but to be doing it often, and have it always hanging over one, and in connexion with subjects much less congenial than Jackson, I could not bear.

The University has been very good to me, and has given me a post in which I have duties which are not disagreeable, and opportunity for studies which I enjoy and in which I can hope to do the University credit; and I should not really be doing it a good turn if I sacrificed that work, as I must, to the performance, even if more efficient than mine would be, of the duties of the Orator.

Do not think this an unkind reply to a kind letter. I have also written to Jackson, as an interview would be useless, and distressing to both of us.

Yours sincerely   A. E. HOUSMAN

To Percy Withers

MS. WITHERS

18 January 1920   *Trinity College*

My dear Withers,

I was very glad to hear from you at Christmas and had intended to reply

---

[1] 1858–1935; Fellow of Trinity College, 1881; Vice-Master, 1919.
[2] The post fell vacant on the retirement of Sir John Sandys in 1919. T. R. Glover, Fellow of St John's College, was elected in his place and retained the office until 1939.

at the New Year, but I suppose the free luncheon of boar's head etc. which prevails in this College from Yule to Epiphany made me sleepy. Perhaps the new University Commission[1] will put a stop to it. I was in the Cotswolds for a fortnight at midsummer, but no nearer to you than Stroud. September I spent in France, partly in Paris but mostly at Brive in the Limousin, a very beautiful neighbourhood, with some nice though not large Romanesque churches about. I found a proprietor of a garage who was a great connoisseur of the local scenery and delighted to take me by the best routes to the best spots, and the weather was just right for motoring and too hot for anything else.

I am glad to hear we may expect to see you here again some day. At present in term-time the place is very crowded, and in college the undergraduates are packed two or three in a box.

Last year I think I wrote two poems,[2] which is more than the average, but not much towards a new volume.

My kind regards to Mrs Withers. I hope you will both enjoy yourselves in Italy; but as there is said to be no coal in that country you had better not start too soon.

Yours sincerely

A. E. HOUSMAN

To Grant Richards

TEXT: RICHARDS

21 January 1920   [*Trinity College*]

The translation is literal,[3] as he claims for it, except where it is a mistranslation, as it now and then is; and it is not affected or pretentious. But it is a very commonplace affair, and both the diction and the verse are poor.

To Alice Rothenstein

MS. HARVARD

21 February 1920   *Trinity College*

Dear Mrs Rothenstein,

The celestial globe arrived yesterday, and seems to have stood the journey pretty well. I am very grateful for it, and I am now completely equipped for dealing with the fifth book of Manilius, for which I required it: I am now just finishing the fourth.

---

[1] Set up in 1919 to consider the organization of the Universities and their allocation of public funds. The report, published in 1922, brought no substantial change.

[2] It is not known which these are.

[3] A French translation, not published, of poems from *A Shropshire Lad*.

If you are going to settle at another spot, I hope you will let me know where it is, and I will try not to miss you if I find myself near it.

I daresay you have been as much amused as I was by the life-like portrait of William in Max Beerbohm's last book.[1] He is more successful with the pen than with the pencil in depicting this model.

With the kindest regards to both of you, I am yours sincerely

A. E. HOUSMAN

To Grant Richards

19 March 1920   *Trinity College*

My dear Richards,

Thanks for sending me Mr Armstrong's music,[2] and his civil letter, which I return.

I am sorry you found Italy so bad: some one, I forget who, told me the passport was the only trouble and things were all right when you got there.

I hope you were not too early for the celebrated plenty of rare flowers in Capri. When I was there it was autumn and they were all gone to seed. I stayed at the Hotel Eden at Anacapri, and found it quite satisfactory; but you probably stuck to the lower town at this season.

In a day or two I will send the corrected proofs of the text and notes of Manilius IV, and those of the preface shortly after.

Yours sincerely   A. E. HOUSMAN

To A. S. F. Gow

29 March 1920   *Trinity College*

Dear Gow,

I suppose you would not like to be Professor of Latin at Liverpool?[3] because I think it possible you might be. They have so bad a field that they are making enquiries everywhere: Postgate wrote to me; Harold Butler has also been asked if he can recommend anyone. Although it is not the ideal

---

[1] *Seven Men*, 1919. Rothenstein, who was a close friend of Beerbohm's and frequently drawn by him, is a prominent character in the story 'Enoch Soames'.

[2] 'Into my heart an air that kills' (*A Shropshire Lad* XL), one of the *Five Short Songs* by Thomas H. W. Armstrong, 1920.

[3] The Professorship became vacant on Postgate's retirement later in the year. He was succeeded by D. A. Slater.

172

situation for you, I would rather see you that than a schoolmaster; but you may not agree.

Yours sincerely

A. E. HOUSMAN

To Robert Bridges

MS. BRIDGES

9 April 1920   *Trinity College*

My dear Bridges,

It is good of you to send me your new volume,[1] and of course I am glad to have it, though I do not expect to be always reading it and carrying it in my head like the first four books of the *Shorter Poems*.[2] You have been spinning down the ringing grooves of change while I have been standing at gaze like Joshua's moon in Ajalon,[3] and the pieces I like best are those which remind me of old times, 'Poor Child' and 'Fortunatus nimium'.

I am yours sincerely

A. E. HOUSMAN

To William Rothenstein

MS. HARVARD

13 April 1920   *Trinity College*

My dear Rothenstein,

I am sorry if it upsets your arrangements, but I am not going to write literary criticism for you or anyone else; and moreover I should feel awkward and embarrassed in writing about Hardy under his nose.[4] I do not mean that it would violate any principles or general notions which I may happen to have, but it would distress my sensations, which I believe are in some respects morbid.

I sympathise with your feelings about leaving Oakridge, but Campden Hill, I always used to think, must be the best spot inside London to live in.

Give my kindest regards to Mrs Rothenstein. I hope I shall see you when you are in Cambridge. I suppose, as your stay is so short, it is no use asking you to any meal here?

Yours sincerely

A. E. HOUSMAN

[1] *October and Other Poems.*
[2] Published in 1873, 1879, 1884 and 1890.
[3] See Tennyson, *Locksley Hall*, and *Joshua*. 10, 12.
[4] Rothenstein had asked for a short piece on Hardy to accompany the drawing of him in *Twenty-Four Portraits*, 1920.

173

To Percy Withers

MS. WITHERS

4 May 1920   *Trinity College*

My dear Withers,

I have decorated your infatuated purchase with my signature and the shortest of my unpublished poems:[1] unpublished, though I also wrote it for Meynell[2] in a book belonging to one of his daughters. I should have thought, though, that this would detract from the value of the book for a true bibliophile; but no doubt this is already a spoilt copy, the leaves having been cut.

I think you have found a house in a good part of the world. I motored through Aynho last year, but I do not remember it distinctly, though I remember Deddington. My Oxford walks did not bring me nearer than Bicester. One great charm of all the parts of Oxfordshire I know is the wide horizon you command even from a slight elevation.

Sciatica is one of the few ailments I sympathise with, as I used to have it myself, no doubt in a mild form, twenty years ago, till I learnt to change my things when I had got into a sweat. Cancer is worse, they say, and being shot through the palm of the hand makes one scream louder.

No doubt you know that Rothenstein also has deserted Gloucestershire, owing, he says, to the ambitions of his children.

I spent three weeks of last September in France, most of it in beautiful country in the Limousin, where I had not been before. Things were cheap, and they were yearning for the return of the English tourist.

My kind regards to Mrs Withers.

Yours sincerely   A. E. HOUSMAN

To Grant Richards

MS. CONGRESS

24 May 1920   *Trinity College*

My dear Richards,

I enclose the MS of the Index to Manilius IV and of a page to be inserted before it. This completes the book.

But I am perplexed and disquieted by certain phenomena in the paged proofs of the text and notes. New errors have been introduced in places which were previously correct. Two of these (p. 3 l. 4 of notes and p. 113 l. 18 of

---

[1] Withers, about to leave Cambridge, had bought a first edition of *A Shropshire Lad* and asked Housman to copy out a verse from one of the poems as a memento. Housman wrote out *Last Poems* XXVII.
[2] Wilfrid Meynell (1852–1948); journalist, editor and biographer; husband of Alice Meynell and, with her, patron of Francis Thompson.

notes) have been put right by the proof-reader; but I have noticed others (p. 114 line 5 from bottom, *61* for *861*; line 2 from bottom, Vrigo for Virgo), and I do not know how many more there may be. As for preventing letters at the beginning and end of lines from getting out of their place, it seems a hopeless business: as fast as they are put straight in one place they fly crooked in another.

Yours sincerely   A. E. HOUSMAN

To Grant Richards

MS. LILLY

1 July 1920   *Trinity College*

My dear Richards,

Your rather immoral but very readable novel[1] reached me at a crisis which made me particularly grateful, for there was a great dearth of literature around me and I had been reduced to *Agatha's Husband*[2] by the authoress of *John Halifax, Gentleman*. Both Agatha's and Olivia's husbands had rather odious wives, and your heroine would have incurred the ruin she deserved if God had been her creator instead of you. I did not think the Monte Carlo part so good as the rest. Your knowledge of the turf and everything connected with it fills me with admiration and horror. I believe however that you have confused the persons of Mr Backhouse and Mr Eaton. The latter (p. 85) 'was the racecourse member of the firm', so I do not see why the firm should tell the lie you make them tell on p. 113, and I think it was probably Mr Eaton whom Olivia met at Kempton Park on p. 127. How did Mr Eaton on p. 249 form an opinion on Brockley's possibilities at Liverpool, a city to which you never sent the horse? That both Mr Eaton and his clerk were christened Alfred may be a compliment to me or merely a coincidence. I cannot square Olivia's arithmetic on p. 91 with the facts (if facts they are) recounted on p. 90.

I enclose the final proofs of Manilius IV, in which there are three corrections to be made. These have been held up for a fortnight because they were sent to Cambridge and not to me in Gloucestershire, whence I returned yesterday. Now will begin the delays of binding, on which you are always descanting in the *Times Literary Supplement*.[3]

I may attempt Paris by the aeroplane route in September, so any information about it which you may possess or acquire would be welcome; also about passports.

Yours sincerely   A. E. HOUSMAN

[1] *Double Life*, 1920
[2] Published in 1853. The anonymous writer was Dinah Maria Mulock.
[3] In his weekly advertisements.

175

To Katharine Symons

26 July 1920 *Trinity College*

My dear Kate,

Christ Church seems to have been the name conferred on the cathedral when it became a cathedral in 1546. To this day Christ Church is not strictly a college: its official description is 'The Dean and Chapter of the Cathedral Church of Christ in Oxford of the foundation of King Henry the Eighth'. They call themselves 'the House'.

I forgot to say that where Magdalene now stands in Cambridge there was formerly a Benedictine Hostel, with separate buildings or staircases for the various monasteries,—Crowland etc.

I am glad that Denis[1] is D.P.H., but I rejoice on trust, as I don't know what it means,—Devastator of Public Health, or Dispenser of Pharmaceutical Horrors.

Your affectionate brother   A. E. HOUSMAN

To Grant Richards

MS. CONGRESS

12 August 1920 *Trinity College*

My dear Richards,

Thanks; if you would answer such letters for me it would save some little trouble. But I seem to remember that on one occasion in the past you mixed up my benevolence to composers with my hard-heartedness to anthologists, so that a poem of mine was published in one collection on your permission when I had refused mine to the editors of others, who had applied to me.

Yours sincerely   A. E. HOUSMAN

To Grant Richards

MS. CONGRESS

15 August 1920 *Trinity College*

My dear Richards,

I am very grateful for the leaflets. I am most attracted by the Aircraft Transport people because theirs is more explicit, and by mentioning a charge for 'Passengers' Excess Baggage' they give me hope of disappointing your

[1] Katharine Symons' second son, Arthur Denis Symons (1891–1951).

176

malevolent expectations about difficulty arising from the weight of my bag. You should not always insist on carrying it.

Do you still possess backstairs influence at the French consulate? Last year you relieved me of the trouble of having to appear in person to get my visa, and I don't yet know if Cook and Son[1] can.

Yours sincerely

A. E. HOUSMAN

To Grant Richards

MS. CONGRESS

17 August 1920   ·   *Trinity College*

My dear Richards,

Cook professes himself able to get me a Visa, so I will not trespass on your kindness. The Visa of last year was for two months.

My inclination to go by the Air Express is confirmed by the crash they had yesterday, which will make them careful in the immediate future. Their cars start from your neighbourhood, the Victory Hotel, Leicester Square; so I shall try to get a bed there for the night, unless you warn me against it.

Yours sincerely

A. E. HOUSMAN

To Grant Richards

MS. CONGRESS

21 August 1920   *Trinity College*

My dear Richards,

Revenge is a valuable passion, and the only sure pillar on which justice rests, so I do not want to hinder your pursuit of Constable if it can be conducted without making me seem to be the pursuer. But have you also a vendetta against James Agate?[2] From reading your serial in the *Literary Supplement* I supposed that he was one of your pets.[3]

I shall stay at the Victory Hotel on the night of Wednesday 8 September, and I shall be delighted if you will dine with me that evening. As I shall have no dress clothes, but only a dark grey or brown suit, you had better select, from your superior knowledge of London, the best restaurant where that

[1] The travel agents.

[2] Messrs Constable and Company had in 1917 published *L. of C.* (*Lines of Communication*) by James Agate (1877–1946), in which 'On the idle hill of summer' (*A Shropshire Lad* XXV) was printed without permission.

[3] The advertisement on 19th August 1920 gave special prominence to Agate's *Responsibility*.

costume would not be conspicuous. Not that I really much mind public reprobation if you do not.

Yours sincerely   A. E. HOUSMAN

To Katharine Symons

MS. TRINITY

3 September 1920   *Trinity College*

My dear Kate,

I return the document with my signature. I made you a present of the two dishes, and I have no business to take any credit with R.E. and M. Symons for your thoughtfulness on their behalf.

The two books arrived in time. The Library now closes for three weeks or so, but after that there is no reason why you should not have again the book which is not at Bath.

They tell me here that the right thing to do with railway stock and shares is to stick to them; but I shiver when I look forward to the additional trouble in filling up my Income Tax return.

I shall leave here on the 8th and return not later than the 18th.

When I was at Monmouth I did not succeed in finding all the beauty you speak of; but I was there less than a week, and was walking to distant places like Raglan and Chepstow and Speech House.

I am glad for the sake of both of you to hear about the school. Do you remember Mr J. C. Whall who was an assistant master at Bromsgrove?[1] I see he died the other day.

Your affectionate brother   A. E. HOUSMAN

To Grant Richards

MS. CONGRESS

5 September 1920   *Trinity College*

My dear Richards,

7.30 at the Café Royal on Wednesday. Perhaps you and Charles[2] would come and find me about five minutes earlier in the lounge of the Victory Hotel (are you sleeping there?).

About the probable date of publication of Manilius IV, the probable strike in the binding trade, the inevitable shipwreck of the vessel which

[1] From 1874; later Rector of Montgomery.
[2] Richards' son, at this time working in his firm. He delighted Housman by producing a graph to show annual sales of *A Shropshire Lad* since 1898.

178

conveys it from Glasgow to London, we can talk when we meet; but I want to put in writing for your convenience that on its publication I think it ought to be advertised once at least both in the *Classical Review* and the *Classical Quarterly*, as the other day I discovered that a scholar here, and a friend of mine, did not know that book III had yet appeared.

Suppose I produced a new volume of poetry, in what part of the year ought it to be published, and how long would it take after the MS left my hands?

Yours sincerely   A. E. HOUSMAN

Postcard to Grant Richards[1]

MS. CONGRESS

9 September 1920   *[Paris]*

All right.   A. E. HOUSMAN

Postcard to Grant Richards

MS. CONGRESS

22 September 1920   *[Trinity College]*

No copy of Manilius IV is to be sent to the *Classical Quarterly*, which does not review books.

Again the label on the back has been stuck on upside-down, as in the first copies of book III four years ago.

A. E. HOUSMAN

To Grant Richards

TEXT: RICHARDS

28 September 1920   *[Trinity College]*

Oh, damn the *Bookman*.[2] The author wrote to me some months ago asking for private particulars and I thought that my reply had chilled him off. I have not been photographed, I think, since 1894: that was the year when I was beginning to write *A Shropshire Lad*, and if for that reason they would care to have it, I could send you one, as I do not want to seem churlish. As to Rothenstein, his portraits are of 15 years ago, and one of them, the

---

[1] Sent to announce his safe arrival by air.

[2] *The Bookman*, November 1920, printed an article on Housman by John Freeman. It was illustrated with photographs by van der Weyde (1894), Hoppé and Grant Richards.

one he shows in exhibitions, is a venomous libel, to which he adds fresh strokes whenever he feels nasty. This is full face; the other one, more side face, he reserves for his private delectation.

Now I think of it, I was photographed by Hoppé, also about 15 years ago, and I think I rather lately received a copy for the first time; but I do not know what I have done with it.

To Katharine Symons

MS. LILLY

3 October 1920 *Trinity College*

My dear Kate,

Well, I flew there, and am never going by any other route in future. Surrey from overhead is delightful, Kent and France less interesting, the Channel disappointing, because on both days there was too much mist to let both shores be seen at once. It was rather windy, and the machine sometimes imitated a ship at sea (though that is due to differing densities of atmosphere and not to wind) but not in a very life-like manner. Members of your unhappy sex were sick, however. The noise is great, and I alighted rather deaf, not having stuffed my ears with the cotton-wool provided. Nor did I put on the life-belt which they oblige one to take. To avoid crossing the 60 miles of sea which a straight flight would involve, they go from Croydon to Hythe, Hythe to Boulogne, Boulogne to Paris. You are in the air $2\frac{1}{2}$ hours: from Leicester Square to your hotel in Paris you take little more than four; though on the return journey we were two hours late in starting because the machine required repairs, having been damaged on the previous day by a passenger who butted his head through the window to be sick. My chief trouble is that what I now want is no longer a motor and a chauffeur but an aeroplane and a tame pilot, which I suppose are more expensive. The weather in France was beautiful, though I read of storms in London. Unfortunately I got poisoned at a restaurant and was out of action for the best part of two days. Pray why should the manager of W. H. Smith's establishment in Paris want to know if you are my sister? It was not me he asked, but Grant Richards; and twice.

Love to all.

Your affectionate brother A. E. HOUSMAN

To A. F. Scholfield[1]

MS. TRINITY

6 November 1920   *Trinity College*

Dear Scholfield,

I have the Lucretius,[2] and it is not worth having: the Persius,[3] from what I know of Cartault, would be much the same; and no edition of a Greek author produced in France can be fit for exportation. The editions of Cicero,[4] when they appear, might be worth getting; and also any book, if there were any, edited by Havet[5] or Lejay.[6]

Yours sincerely   A. E. HOUSMAN

To Grant Richards

MS. BUFFALO

20 December 1920   *Trinity College*

My dear Richards,

I return Lovat Fraser's[7] designs, most of which I do not like at all, though the landscapes are generally pleasing. The trouble with book-illustrators, as with composers who set poems to music, is not merely that they are completely wrapped up in their own art and their precious selves, and regard the author merely as a peg to hang things on, but that they seem to have less than the ordinary human allowance of sense and feeling. To transpose into the 18th century a book which begins with Queen Victoria's jubilee is the act of a rhinoceros. I should look a fool if I allowed the book to appear with these decorations.

This reminds me. I am told that composers in some cases have mutilated my poems,—that Vaughan Williams cut two verses out of "Is my team ploughing"[8] (I wonder how he would like me to cut two bars out of his music), and that a lady whose name I forget has set one verse of "The new mistress", omitting the others. So I am afraid I must ask you, when giving consent to composers, to exact the condition that these pranks are not to be played.

---

[1] Alwyn Faber Scholfield (1884-1969); Librarian of Trinity College, 1919-1923; University Librarian, 1923-1949. He had asked for advice on books for the College Library.
[2] Edited by Alfred Ernout (born 1879), 1920.
[3] Edited by Augustin Cartault (1847-1922), 1920.
[4] In the *Collections des Universités de France*, beginning in 1921.
[5] Louis Havet (1849-1925) produced an edition of Phaedrus, 1895, and *Notes Critiques sur Properce*, 1916.
[6] Paul Lejay (1861-1920) edited Horace, 1903, and a series of single books of Virgil, 1921.
[7] Claud Lovat Fraser (1890-1921) made a set of illustrations to *A Shropshire Lad*. They were published posthumously as *Sixty-three Unpublished Designs*, 1924. Housman's comments on the drawings are printed in Richards, pp. 181-3.
[8] In his song cycle *On Wenlock Edge*, 1909.

181

Mr Cecil Roberts[1] must be an angelic character, if he persists in being civil to you after a quarrel. I was not annoyed by the paragraph,[2] for undeserved renown is what I chiefly prize. I am much more celebrated in Cambridge for having flown to France and back last September than for anything else I have done.

I don't think Machen[3] ought to drink port on the top of burgundy.

Yours sincerely   A. E. HOUSMAN

To Mrs Platt

MS. U.C.L.

23 December 1920   *Trinity College*

Dear Mrs Platt,

I shall be delighted to dine and stay the night on Monday 3 January. 31 December is excluded because I and other choice spirits here always see the New Year in on oysters and stout, to do what we can for the cause of human progress and the improvement of the world.

I congratulate you on having managed to live with Platt so long.[4] This is a compliment of the season.

Yours sincerely   A. E. HOUSMAN

To William Rothenstein

MS. HARVARD

28 December 1920   *Trinity College*

My dear Rothenstein,

I am very grateful for the proof,[5] especially as the portrait is not in the eminent artist's most virulent vein. I very seldom find myself in London, but when next I do I will try to find you out in your eligible quarter of the town.

---

[1] Cecil Edric Mornington Roberts, poet, novelist and miscellaneous writer (born 1892), at this time editor of *The Nottingham Journal and Express*.

[2] In *The Nottingham Journal and Express*, 2 December 1920, under the heading 'Books and Bookmen': 'Mr Housman has just published, with his friend Grant Richards, another book of his edition of Manilius. The Professor is less known than the poet of "The Shropshire Lad", and still less known is the Mr Housman the gourmet, to whom I believe such a skilled epicure as Mr Grant Richards gives first place.'

[3] Arthur Machen, novelist, essayist and translator (1863–1947); a friend of Richards', who published several of his books.

[4] They had been married for nearly thirty-five years.

[5] Of his portrait, drawn in 1916, now reproduced in Rothenstein's *Twenty-Four Portraits*, 1920.

182

My kindest regards to Mrs Rothenstein, and a happy new year to all of you, not even excluding the ambitious children who have uprooted you from Oakridge.

Yours sincerely   A. E. HOUSMAN

To Percy Withers

MS. WITHERS

28 December 1920   *Trinity College*

My dear Withers,

You certainly have had plenty of troubles, but I hope you are now happily at the end of them,—except that the shocking convulsion in your cellar must be permanent in its effects. Yours must be a pleasant part of the country, though in my Oxford days I never walked nearer it than Bicester. I am here for Christmas as usual, my own family having an aversion for Christmas gatherings and Trinity College very much the reverse. I am afraid we shall not have our new and much superior Combination Room ready for you by the spring, as a builders' strike and other things have delayed operations. The wall at the dais end of the Hall was found to have stood 300 years on no foundation supporting a weight of sixty tons: it might have fallen on us any day as we sat at meat, but contented itself with merely cracking.

A happy new year to both of you, and many of them.

Yours sincerely   A. E. HOUSMAN

To Grant Richards

TEXT: RICHARDS

5 January 1921   *Trinity College*

My dear Richards,

'My new book' does not exist, and possibly never may. Neither your traveller nor anybody else must be told that it is even contemplated. What I asked you[1] was a question inspired by an unusually bright and sanguine mood, which has not at present been justified.

I saw E. B. Osborn's remarks,[2] but they did not alter my opinion of him.

Yours sincerely   A. E. HOUSMAN

[1] In the letter of 5 September 1920.
[2] Edward Bolland Osborn, author and journalist (1867–1938). In an article on Georgian poetry in *The Morning Post*, 17 December 1920, he wrote of Housman's 'smooth, shining tabloids of sentimentality' prescribed as 'an antidote to the bulky pomposity of late Victorianism.'

To Grant Richards

TEXT: RICHARDS
20 March 1921 [*Trinity College*]

I do not want revenue from gramophone and mechanical rights, and Mr Ireland[1] is welcome to as much of it as his publisher will let him have. I hope it may be sufficient to console him for not being allowed to print the poem he wants.

Address to Sir James George Frazer[2]
[*April 1921*]

The friends and admirers who have united to found in your honour an annual lectureship in Social Anthropology, a science requiring no such link to connect it with your name, are not altogether content to set up their monument and withdraw in silence. They feel, and they hope that you will understand, the wish to approach more nearly an author whose works have bound to him in familiarity and affection even those to whom he is not personally known, and to indulge, by this short address, an emotion warmer than mere intellectual gratitude.

The Golden Bough, compared by Virgil to the mistletoe but now revealing some affinity to the banyan, has not only waxed a great tree but has spread to a spacious and hospitable forest, whose king receives homage in many tongues from a multitude resorting thither for its fruit or timber or refreshing shade. There they find learning mated with literature, labour disguised in ease, and a museum of dark and uncouth superstitions invested with the charm of a truly sympathetic magic. There you have gathered together, for the admonition of a proud and oblivious race, the scattered and fading relics of its foolish childhood, whether withdrawn from our view among savage folk and in different countries, or lying unnoticed at our doors. The forgotten milestones of the road which man has travelled, the mazes and blind alleys of his appointed progress through time, are illuminated by your art and genius, and the strangest of remote and ancient things are brought near to the minds and hearts of your contemporaries.

They return you thanks for all that they have received at your hands, and they wish you years of life and continuance of strength to crown with new sheaves that rich and various harvest of discoveries which has already rewarded your untiring industry and your single-hearted quest of truth.

---

[1] John Ireland (1879–1962) composed a setting of 'Hawthorn Time' (*A Shropshire Lad* XXXIX), which was published and recorded in 1921.

[2] Privately printed, 1921, for the sponsors of the Frazer Lectureship in Social Anthropology. Frazer (1854–1941) was elected Fellow of Trinity College, 1879; knighted, 1914; appointed to the Order of Merit, 1925. *The Golden Bough* was published in 1890, but this volume later proved to be only the first of a long series. Frazer's reply, 30 April 1921, was printed with this address, and published with it in *The Frazer Lectures*, 1932.

To D. A. Winstanley[1]

MS. TRINITY

29 April 1921   *Trinity College*

Dear Winstanley,
    I enclose my essays at inscriptions for Prior[2] and Sedley Taylor.[3] Their form is dictated by the necessity of putting the names in the nominative case; for neither Sedley nor Taylor is declinable, and the question of the declinability of Prior would excite acrimonious controversy.
    To prevent the engraver from introducing J or U I have copied them out in proper script; but I know that my labour will be lost, as it was in the case of the late Master's inscription.[4]

    Yours sincerely   A. E. HOUSMAN

To Percy Withers

MS. WITHERS

1 June 1921   *Trinity College*

My dear Withers,
    Next Tuesday, the 7th, I am motoring to Stroud; and as you lie on my way I was wondering if I might drop in on you for lunch and renew acquaintance with you and Mrs Withers after what seems a rather long interval. I should arrive some time between 12 and 1. I suppose there is some place near where the chauffeur could stable his steed. I hope you are both well and still contented with your home.

    Yours sincerely   A. E. HOUSMAN

To Grant Richards

MS. CONGRESS

28 June 1921   *Trinity College*

My dear Richards,
    I am motoring to Eton on Saturday, and as you are, so to speak, in the neighbourhood, and spend that day at home, I was wondering if I might drop in for lunch, as I am not wanted at Eton before tea-time.

---

[1] Denys Arthur Winstanley (1877–1947), Tutor of Trinity College, 1919; Senior Tutor 1925; Vice-Master, 1935.
[2] Joseph Prior (1834–1918), Fellow of Trinity College from 1860 until his death.
[3] 1834–1920; Fellow of Trinity College, 1861–1869; lived in the College for the rest of his life.
[4] These later inscriptions for memorials in Trinity College Chapel were correctly engraved.

I wrote you a letter more than a month ago, with questions about foreign reviews of my Manilius, to which you have not condescended to reply. My kind regards to Mrs Richards.

Yours sincerely   A. E. HOUSMAN

To Grant Richards

MS. CONGRESS

21 July 1921   *Trinity College*

My dear Richards,

I am very sorry to hear the tale of all your unmerited troubles; though 'lassitude and inertia' are my normal condition, especially in this weather. I hope you will not worry yourself about anything connected with me.

I have been away from Cambridge a great deal since the beginning of June, and I now am settling down to work. I am obliged to be here at the beginning of August for a meeting of the Classical Association, damn it: I am not a member, but they have chosen to meet here, and Americans are coming, and I am the only classical professor of Cambridge who is able to deliver an address.[1] If I go away later in the month it will be to meet some of my family at Monmouth. I intend to go to Paris for a week about 10 September, and if that is about the time when you will be going to fetch Mrs Richards back, of course I should like to go with you. I would not insist on your flying, as I could face land and sea with you for courier.

Yours sincerely   A. E. HOUSMAN

Thanks for the information about *Museum*.[2]

To Grant Richards

TEXT: RICHARDS

16 September 1921   *Trinity College*

I suppose you are back from Jersey. In the first place I must thank you for *Tahiti*,[3] which in my postcard I forgot to do. Secondly, Winstanley, whom you have met here, and I are coming to London some day next week, *not Friday*, to see Max Beerbohm's things at the Leicester Gallery[4] and lunch at the Café Royal at 1 o'clock; and I wish you would join us, at least at lunch, and let me know in good time what day would suit you best.

[1] Housman's paper, read on 4 August 1921, was 'The Application of Thought to Textual Criticism'. It was printed in the *Proceedings of the Classical Association*, 1922.
[2] A Dutch classical periodical, which had just printed a review of Manilius IV.
[3] By George Calderon, 1921.
[4] The exhibition of his caricatures opened on 11 May 1921.

To Grant Richards

TEXT: RICHARDS

27 September 1921   *[Trinity College]*

Tell him that the wish to include a glimpse of my personality in a literary article is low, unworthy, and American. Tell him that some men are more interesting than their books but my book is more interesting than its man. Tell him that Frank Harris found me rude and Wilfrid Blunt found me dull. Tell him anything else that you think will put him off. Of course if he did nevertheless persist in coming to see me I should not turn him out, as I only do that to newspaper reporters.

To Percy Withers

MS. WITHERS

30 October 1921   *Trinity College*

My dear Withers,

It is very kind of you to ask me, and I know that if I came I should enjoy myself; but I do not see the chance of getting away this term, which is full of continuous engagements to an extent which I cannot remember the like of. These engagements, I ought in honesty to confess, are many of them convivial, but not all: for instance next week is full of prelections by candidates (ten in number) for the professorship of Greek, some of which I want to hear and one of which I must.[1]

This extraordinary autumn is at last beginning to put on colour, about a month late.

Coming back from Stroud I was arrested by the beauty of the church at Bloxham, and so made the acquaintance of the Vicar (or Rector), who directed me to Adderbury and King's Sutton. It was a great treasure-trove, as I had never heard of this group, though it appears that they are celebrated.

My kind regards to Mrs Withers. I am really sorry not to be able to take advantage of your invitation.

Yours sincerely   A. E. HOUSMAN

[1] The Regius Professorship was left vacant by the death of Henry Jackson. After first declining to stand, Arthur Platt was persuaded to become a candidate, but the appointment went to A. C. Pearson.

To Charles Sayle[1]

MS. LILLY

9 November 1921 *Trinity College*

My dear Sayle,

It may be vanity, but I believe myself to be more capable of uttering one word and adding nothing than either the late Mr Gladstone or the present Sir John Sandys.[2] But I rather gather that 'Oxford' is to be prefaced by other words, which is not so much in my true vein: still, I suppose I could say something.

Yours sincerely   A. E. HOUSMAN

To Grant Richards

MS. CONGRESS

11 November 1921 *Trinity College*

My dear Richards,

I will not under any circumstances allow a portrait of me to appear in an 'authorised edition'. Mrs Asquith[3] and Lord Alfred Douglas[4] can do such things if they like.

The municipal hospitality of Ventimiglia must have made me very drunk, for I forget the whole affair.[5] My recollection is that you and I climbed in mist or drizzle a hill with a castle on it, that we lunched at a restaurant where you after much palaver induced the proprietor to furnish us with a viand which I did not much admire, small envelopes of paste enclosing mincemeat, and that we walked through the town and under some trees by the shore to a rough stone breakwater. But I suppose I dreamt all this while I was under the table.

Yours sincerely   A. E. HOUSMAN

[1] Charles Edward Sayle (1864–1924), poet and bibliographer, on the staff of the University Library; secretary of the club of Oxford men at Cambridge. He had invited Housman to propose the toast of Oxford at the annual dinner.
[2] 1844–1922; Public Orator at Cambridge, 1876–1919; author of *A History of Classical Scholarship*, 1903–1908; knighted, 1911.
[3] Margot (*née* Tennant) Asquith (1864–1945), second wife of H. H. Asquith, published her *Autobiography* in 1922.
[4] Lord Alfred Bruce Douglas (1870–1945) habitually included portraits of himself in his books. His *Collected Poems* appeared in 1919.
[5] A mythical official reception for Housman on his visit in 1915. The story came from Belfort Bax, who insisted that he had had it from Housman and Richards themselves on their return from an outing to Ventimiglia, and had now asked Richards for confirmation from Housman that it was unfounded.

To A. C. Pearson[1]

MS. KING'S

16 November 1921   *Trinity College*

Dear Professor Pearson,

I congratulate you very sincerely on your election. As Platt was after all a candidate, my sentiments were divided, and my joy is not unalloyed; but I told the electors who consulted me that I was glad it was they and not I who had to choose between you, and that they would be very wrong if they chose any of the other eight. The chief danger was that some of them had a passion for youth, or comparative youth; but merit has gained the day against it.

Yours very truly   A. E. HOUSMAN

To Harriet Monroe[2]

MS. CHICAGO

30 November 1921   *Trinity College*

Dear Madam,

I do not think I have ever sent unpublished poems to Mr Witter Bynner: I have sent him a few which have appeared in English papers or journals, and one or more of these have reappeared in American publications.

I am flattered by your request, but I have no poems by me which I wish to see in print. I thank you very much for the two numbers of *Poetry* which you have been kind enough to send me.

I am yours sincerely   A. E. HOUSMAN

To Grant Richards

MS. CONGRESS

16 December 1921   *Trinity College*

My dear Richards,

It is very kind of you to ask me to stay longer, and I should not be averse from meeting Robert Lynd;[3] but it would upset arrangements which I have made, and would consequently interfere with my comfort, to which I am much attached; so I will pray you to have me excused.

On Friday I would travel with you to Cookham, if that would suit you.

Yours sincerely   A. E. HOUSMAN

[1] Alfred Chilton Pearson (1861–1935), Professor of Greek at Liverpool since 1919; previously an undergraduate at Christ's College, Cambridge, schoolmaster and business-man; Regius Professor of Greek at Cambridge, 1921–1928.
[2] American poet (1860–1936); editor of *Poetry* (*Chicago*) since 1912.
[3] Essayist (1879–1949).

To Sydney Cockerell

MS. PRINCETON

16 December 1921   *Trinity College*

My dear Cockerell,

This is so very precious that I return it instantly, after showing it to Winstanley, who shared my curiosity about Miss Cornforth.[1] I am very grateful for the sight of it. It will often flash upon that inward eye which is the bliss of solitude.

Yours very truly   A. E. HOUSMAN

To A. S. F. Gow

MS. TRINITY

7 January 1922   *Trinity College*

Dear Gow,

There is a short and rather good book on Rossetti by Joseph Knight,[2] who knew him well, and I suppose the diffuse and solemn William Michael[3] would yield you something; but lives of Meredith are no use. W. B. Scott[4] is more promising; but most of the amusing tales about the menagerie[5] probably do not exist in print.

Yours sincerely   A. E. HOUSMAN

To A. F. Scholfield

MS. TRINITY

25 February 1922   *Trinity College*

Dear Scholfield,

This gentleman is hoping to pay his railway fare to Italy by selling some of the few copies remaining of his book; he has also bought a copy of my Manilius and presumably thereby impaired his fortune: therefore I am to

---

[1] Probably one of Rossetti's drawings of Fanny Cornforth (*circa* 1824–*circa* 1906). Her real name was Sarah Cox; she became Rossetti's model in about 1856, and in 1862 installed herself as his housekeeper. She antagonized his family and friends by her coarse manners (she was known among them as The Elephant) and quarrelled with them after his death. Almost all reference to her was suppressed in memoirs of Rossetti for over sixty years after his death.

[2] Published in 1887.

[3] W. M. Rossetti edited the *Rossetti Papers* in 1903 and published numerous reminiscences of his brother.

[4] In *Autobiographical Notes*, 1903.

[5] The eccentrics in Rossetti's circle.

suggest to the College Library that it shall purchase a copy of his work. He will send one on approval if you should wish it.

Yours sincerely   A. E. HOUSMAN

To an Unnamed Correspondent

MS. COLUMBIA

8 March 1922   *Trinity College*

Dear Sir,

The Press of this University proposed to Jackson in the last year of his life that his scattered papers should be collected and reprinted. He was pleased by the proposal, but he wished to make changes and additions, which were prevented first by the state of his health and then by his death. The Press, after consulting those members of the University who are most interested in Greek philosophy, has decided not to proceed with the design. The reasons given are that the collection would not possess unity or completeness, and that the papers themselves are readily accessible. This of course is truer of England than of Norway; and I am sorry that your wish is not likely to be gratified. It is possible that a memoir may some day be published,[1] but I do not think it has yet been taken in hand. I thank you for the interest which you take in the matter, and it would have given pleasure to Jackson.

I am yours very truly   A. E. HOUSMAN

To Grant Richards

MS. LILLY

3 April 1922   *Trinity College*

My dear Richards,

Thanks to you, I believe I possess Machen's complete works. He is always interesting (except in the *Evening News*) and to some extent good. Mixing up religion and sexuality is not a thing I am fond of, and in this book[2] the Welsh element rather annoys me. The imitation of Rabelais is very clever.

I knew already, having been told, that it is wrong to have one's wine brought in a cradle, and now I know further that it is wrong to decant it; so in future I shall just have the cork drawn, and suck the liquid out of the bottle through a tube.

Yours sincerely   A. E. HOUSMAN

[1] *Henry Jackson O.M.* by R. St J. Parry, 1926, contained a selection of letters and short comments, but none of Jackson's substantial papers.
[2] *The Secret Glory*, 1922.

To Sydney Cockerell

MS. FITZWILLIAM

3 April 1922   *Trinity College*

Dear Cockerell,

Heffer[1] sent Hardy's poems all right, and at odd times I have been reading and marking them.[2] When you require them I can finish the job with little delay. At this moment I am rather full of my own affairs.

Yours sincerely   A. E. HOUSMAN

To Grant Richards

MS. LILLY

9 April 1922   *Trinity College*

My dear Richards,

It is now practically certain that I shall have a volume of poems ready for the autumn;[3] so I wish you would take what steps are necessary as soon as they are necessary. But do not mention it to anyone until you are obliged to mention it.

Perhaps you can tell me what my legal position is as regards a poem which I contributed in 1899 to the *Academy*.[4] They sent me a cheque, but I returned it: I don't know if that makes any difference.

Yours sincerely   A. E. HOUSMAN

To Grant Richards

MS. LILLY

18 April 1922   *Trinity College*

My dear Richards,

Thanks for your reply. The book will probably be rather shorter than *A Shropshire Lad*; and it had better have a wider page, or smaller print, or both, as there are more poems in it which have long lines.

I desire particularly that the price should be moderate.

[1] The Cambridge bookshop.
[2] Apparently for a projected selection (which was not published) from Hardy's *Collected Poems*, 1919.
[3] *Last Poems*, published on 19 October 1922.
[4] 'Illic Jaeet', in the issue for 24 February 1900.

192

As to America, I much prefer that they should wait.
What is the *latest* date for sending you the complete manuscript?

Yours sincerely   A. E. HOUSMAN

To J. B. Priestley[1]

MS. TEXAS

19 April 1922   *Trinity College*

Dear Mr Priestley,
I am much obliged by your kindness in sending me your *Brief Diversions*.[2]
Some of the parodies and other verses I had read with interest and pleasure
in the *Cambridge Review*.

I am yours very truly   A. E. HOUSMAN

To Grant Richards

MS. LILLY

22 April 1922   *Trinity College*

My dear Richards,
The end of September, as far as I can judge, would suit me quite well for
publication. The size of page should at any rate not be more than in the
Riccardi edition, if so much. The poems should not be run on, as originally
in *A Shropshire Lad*, but each should start on a fresh page.
If, as I rather gather from what you say, printers no longer print from MS,
then I should be obliged if you did the type-writing, though it will not be
more legible than the hand I write literature in.
The Oxford dictionary defines *reach* as 'to stretch out continuously, to
extend', and quotes 'how high reacheth the house' (1526) and 'the portico
reaches along the whole front' (1687). Perhaps your friends are baffled by the
subjunctive mood, and think it ought to be *reaches*;[3] but see Psalm 138.6
'*Though* the Lord *be* high, yet hath he respect unto the lowly.'
When you next print *A Shropshire Lad* I want to make two alterations.[4]

Yours sincerely   A. E. HOUSMAN

---

[1] John Boynton Priestley (born 1894), novelist, essayist and playwright.
[2] Published in 1922. It contains a parody of Housman entitled 'To all the Gravediggers
between Ludlow Town and Hughley'.
[3] In *A Shropshire Lad* XXXVI, line 11.
[4] In XXXVIII and LII. Housman intended the changes to be made in a reprint to be
issued at the same time as the first edition of *Last Poems*, but his instructions were overlooked and the alterations did not appear until 1923.

To John Drinkwater[1]

MS. MARQUETTE

26 April 1922   *Trinity College*

Dear Mr Drinkwater,
   A silly review[2] in to-day's *Times* reminds me that I never thanked you—or
at least I think I did not, and indeed I usually put off writing letters till they
do not get written at all—for giving me your *Seeds of Time*[3] when you were
last in Cambridge. I particularly admired the third poem.[4]

   I am yours very truly   A. E. HOUSMAN

To Sydney Cockerell

MS. PRINCETON

1 May 1922   *Trinity College*

Dear Cockerell,
   I return Hardy's poems, and in the table of contents I have marked those
I like best. Longer lines mean that I feel sure those poems ought to be in-
cluded in a selection.

   Yours sincerely   A. E. HOUSMAN

To Grant Richards

MS. LILLY

9 May 1922   *Trinity College*

My dear Richards,
   There is no leakage:[5] what has happened is merely that *John o' London*
wrote a paragraph,[6] completely false, about the early adventures of *A Shropshire Lad*, and this reminded a man whom I knew here as Lieut. Lee, and who

---

[1] Poet, playwright and miscellaneous writer (1882–1937).
[2] Of Drinkwater's *Selected Poems*, denouncing him, with extensive quotation, as a mere
imitator of Housman.
[3] Published in 1921.
[4] 'A Lesson to my Ghost'.
[5] In *The Weekly Dispatch*, 7 May 1922, in the column 'Books and their Writers', 'Argo-
naut' recalls printing 'As I gird on for fighting' in *The Blunderbuss*, a magazine for cadets at
Trinity College, and reprints it.
[6] In the issue for 6 May 1922: 'When, in 1896, Mr A. E. Housman sent the manuscript
of *A Shropshire Lad* to a London publisher, it was accepted forthwith. In the letter of
acceptance was a query as to when a second book of verse might be expected. Mr Housman
replied: "As it has taken me twenty years to write this volume, maybe after twenty years
more I'll send you another."'

now seems to have a job on the *Weekly Despatch*, that I had let him have a poem for the *Blunderbuss* which he was editing.[1]

The only person besides you whom I have told is sure to be equally trustworthy, and is not in touch with journalists.

The photograph is Hoppé's, about 15 years ago I should think. It appeared in the *British Weekly* in an article which you had more to do with than I.

Yours sincerely   A. E. HOUSMAN

To Katharine Symons

MS. BATH

12 May 1922   *Trinity College*

My dear Kate,

I do not think that the rules of the London Library are to be taken very seriously. I never paid a fine in my life, and once when I kept a book three years it provoked no more than a mild remonstrance.

I fell into conversation the other day with a great though very Protestant medievalist,[2] and I enclose his rather illegible letter, which probably is not much to your purpose. Gasquet's book[3] is said to be rather dishonest in its suppressions. If one of your authorities is a book on Bath Abbey by one Hunt,[4] be warned that his preface betrays great ignorance, or what specialists regard as such.

To prefer Sussex to Monmouth is a sign of some refinement of taste. I think that very likely in late July or August I might come down your way. I think of going to Paris for a week at the beginning of June, and then staying here.

Thanks for the learned *Edwardian*,[5] which I return, as I seem to remember you are not rich in copies. I also return Jerry's letter, interesting as usual. His present companion is a new character to me.

Another book by Laurence, rather well reviewed.[6] I hope Edward is quite recovered from his illness.

Your affectionate brother   A. E. HOUSMAN

[1] In the issue for March 1917.
[2] George Gordon Coulton (1858–1947), lecturer in Mediaeval History, whose views involved him in bitter controversy with Roman Catholics.
[3] *Monastic Life in the Middle Ages* by Cardinal Gasquet, 1922.
[4] *An Account of the Priory of St Peter and St Paul, Bath* by William Hunt, 1893.
[5] School Magazine of King Edward VI School, Bath.
[6] *Little Plays of St Francis*.

To Grant Richards

MS. CONGRESS

22 May 1922 *Trinity College*

My dear Richards,

I am very much touched by your solicitude for the corruption of my mind, and I eagerly expect the new Proust.[1] I rather gather from your epistle to the world last Thursday[2] that your Mr Ronald Firbank[3] is a bit in the same line. I never heard of Jean Cocteau,[4] but I do know something of the Paris *bains de vapeur* (or *vapeurs* as Mr van Vechten[5] says).

I am flying to Paris (though not necessarily to these haunts of vice) on 1 June and I shall sleep in London the night before, Hotel Victoria, Northumberland Avenue; so perhaps we might manage to dine together.

Yours sincerely   A. E. HOUSMAN

To Percy Withers

MS. WITHERS

23 May 1922 *Trinity College*

My dear Withers,

The marmalade has just arrived quite safe, and two pots when I only hoped for one; and I am very grateful both to you and Mrs Withers for your respective shares in the gift. It is a great pity that you should be laid up, and very nice of you to lay it on Bridges and not on your entertainment of me.

Yours sincerely   A. E. HOUSMAN

To Percy Withers

MS. WITHERS

12 June 1922 *Trinity College*

My dear Withers,

I am concerned to hear about your health,[6] and I hope you will soon find relief, whichever way the doctors may decide. The photograph is not quite true to my own notion of my gentleness and sweetness of nature, but neither perhaps is my external appearance.

---

[1] Probably the second volume of *Le Côté des Guermantes*, 1921.
[2] His advertisement in *The Times Literary Supplement*.
[3] Novelist (1886–1926). Richards published his *Flower Beneath the Foot* in 1923.
[4] French poet, novelist, playwright, black-and-white artist and film director (1889–1963).
[5] American author (1880–1964).
[6] Withers began to suffer from diabetes at this time.

I am just back from France and have broached the first jar of marmalade, which inspires me with respect as well as gratitude towards Mrs Withers.

Yours sincerely   A. E. HOUSMAN

To Grant Richards

TEXT: RICHARDS

15 June 1922   *[Trinity College]*

I cannot arrange the order of the poems satisfactorily until I know for certain which I shall include and which omit; and on that point, as I told you, I want to consult one or two people.[1] Therefore I want the poems printed first simply according to the various metres they are written in, not at all as they will afterwards stand. Will the transposition which will then have to be made before the book arrives at its proper form be very expensive? If so, perhaps type-writing had better be used, but I do not like it, as it makes things look repulsive.

To Grant Richards

TEXT: RICHARDS

19 June 1922   *[Trinity College]*

Herewith the manuscript, 50 pages. Please acknowledge receipt. After all, I do not think much transposition will be required.

You must not do what you spoke of doing, preserve a copy of the book in its present state, as I value the opinion of posterity too much.[2] When it is printed let *two* copies be sent to me at first, for correction. It will save the printers trouble if you tell them that they had better not try to improve my spelling and punctuation.

To A. S. F. Gow

MS. TRINITY

20 June 1922   *Trinity College*

Dear Gow,

Many thanks: these Persons of Quality drink from a Hippocrene or Onocrene of their own.[3]

[1] Mackail and W. P. Ker. Housman also took the advice of a third friend, probably Pollard.
[2] The manuscript was returned to Housman, who later presented it to the Fitzwilliam Museum. The typescript, made by Richards' secretary for the printer, seems not to have survived.
[3] Hippocrene (fountain of the horse) was the Muses' spring on Mount Helicon. Onocrene is a fountain for asses.

I shall be here till the end of July, I expect. I hope we shall see you as usual when your term is over.

Yours   A. E. HOUSMAN

To J. W. Mackail

MS. FITZWILLIAM

26 June 1922   *Trinity College*

Secret as the grave.

Dear Mackail,

I am bringing out a volume of poems this autumn: will you do me the kindness to look through them first? They are neither long nor many.

Yours sincerely   A. E. HOUSMAN

To Grant Richards

MS. LILLY

8 July 1922   *Trinity College*

My dear Richards,

I do not know what penalty the *Tatler* people have laid themselves open to,[1] and anyhow I should think they had better be left alone. I am told that Vaughan Williams has mutilated another poem just as badly, to suit his precious music. Probably the sort of people who read the *Tatler* would not realise that anything was missing, or prefer the full text if they had it.

The poem in italics is to stand facing p. 1, so I do not think the print is too small.

Yours sincerely   A. E. HOUSMAN

To Grant Richards

MS. LILLY

12 July 1922   *Trinity College*

My dear Richards,

I am no judge of this sort of thing, but there is nothing in the design[2] which I much object to, except the portrait of a tramp sucking a stick.

Yours sincerely   A. E. HOUSMAN

---

[1] By the unauthorised printing of part of 'Bredon Hill' (*A Shropshire Lad* XXI), with illustrations by Percy Home, in the issue for 5 July.
[2] For the wrapper.

To Theodore Spicer-Simson[1]

MS. PRINCETON

17 July 1922   *Trinity College*

Dear Sir,

I am not qualified to judge your medallions as works of art, but they please me, and Mr Hardy's portrait is certainly a good likeness. As you are kind enough to propose a portrait of me, I shall be very willing to sit to you, if it can be arranged; only it unfortunately happens that I shall be away from Cambridge from the 21st to the 24th.

I am yours very truly   A. E. HOUSMAN

To J. W. Mackail

MS. FITZWILLIAM

18 July 1922   *Trinity College*

Dear Mackail,

Thanks for *The Dead Sanctuary*,[2] which I have read with mild pleasure and disapproval. It is quite a wrong sort of thing, as wrong as *The Revolt of Islam*,[3] and there is something of silliness in expending so much adornment on a quite arbitrary fiction, which does not seem to have even the bad excuse of allegory; and it very seldom rises, as it does at the end of the 56th stanza, into anything really poetical. And yet it is somehow winning and likeable, and it is quite free from vice and sham.

Thanks also for consenting to look through my proofs, which I enclose. I want you to note anything which strikes you as falling below my average, or as open to exception for any other reason. The piece I myself am most in doubt about is the longest;[4] and I fear that is not its worst fault. You need not be afraid of stifling a masterpiece through a temporary aberration of judgment, as I am consulting one or two other people, and shall not give effect to a single opinion unless it coincides with my own private suspicions.

Yours sincerely   A. E. HOUSMAN

[1] American sculptor (1871–1959), whose portrait medallions of English writers were reproduced in his *Men of Letters of the British Isles*, 1924.
[2] By J. B. Trinick, with an introductory note by Mackail, 1922.
[3] By Shelley, 1818.
[4] 'Hell Gate' (*Last Poems* XXXI).

To J. W. Mackail

MS. FITZWILLIAM

25 July 1922   *Trinity College*

Dear Mackail,

I thought that p. 27 and 50 and perhaps 33 were rather thin, and I shall probably take them out, though another counsellor is very strong for 27. 15 is not much in itself, and I only put it in for variety, as I did no. XX in *A Shropshire Lad*. 57 I have no particular admiration for, though I like bits of it. 39 I think good, and 10 does not dissatisfy me; but I believe I am too fond of the Laura Matilda stanza,[1] which I think the most beautiful and the most difficult in English.

On p. 5 'home' and 'native land' signify 'the sea where they fished for you and me'.

25 dissatisfies me too, but not quite in the same way. The first and last stanzas came into my head; the middle ones are composed. I think the last stanza really requires that the poem should have five stanzas.

36. 'you do lie' is not really for metre's sake, but an imitation, false I daresay, of the ballads which I do imitate.

About "Hell gate" my troubles were, first, that the whole thing is on the edge of the absurd: if it does not topple over, that is well so far. Secondly, as you perceive, the texture of the diction, especially in the parts which I had to compose, is not what it should be, and I rather despair of mending it. It would not do simply to omit the passages you mention: I should have to put something in their place, and it probably would be nothing better. As to three consecutive initial *and*'s, that occurs in the "L'Allegro" of my great exemplar; and Shelley in "The Invitation" and again in "Ariel to Miranda" has five. On p. 43 I think the repetition has a certain value; on p. 42 it is mitigated by the intervention of a full stop, and offends the eye more than the ear.

46. I must confess I do not know what lines 3 and 4 mean. I find that I originally wrote 'forest hut', which may be better.

I wish you would turn an unfriendly eye on p. 29. I stuck it in to keep apart two poems which should not come together. The first two lines are as good as need be; but is not the idea of the poem trite and banal, and the execution too neat and too near to smartness?

Please keep the proofs for the present, if you will allow me to worry you again, as perhaps I may want to when W. P. Ker[2] comes back from the Alps,

---

[1] The metre of *Last Poems* VIII, previously used by Housman in *A Shropshire Lad* IV and XXXV; so called after the fictitious author of 'Drury's Dirge' in *Rejected Addresses* by Horace and James Smith, 1812.

[2] William Paton Ker (1855–1923), Professor of English at University College, London, 1889–1922; Professor of Poetry at Oxford, 1920–1923; the leading English scholar of the day and one of Housman's best-liked and trusted colleagues in London.

on whose summits he is now pirouetting. Meanwhile thanks for what you have already done.

Yours sincerely   A. E. HOUSMAN

Exception is taken, as I foresaw it would be, to 'spruce' on p. 44. I think it is the right word, and helps, like 'finery of fire', to keep the piece from being too solemn; and moreover Milton talks about 'the spruce and jocund Spring'. The alternative is 'brave', which I like less, partly because it has the same vowel-sound as 'failed' in the next line. What do you think?

To Grant Richards

MS. LILLY

26 July 1922   *Trinity College*

My dear Richards,
  The correction of proofs will be held up for three weeks or so by the absence of W. P. Ker in Switzerland; so I write on details which I want to be clear about.
  What is the exact height of page available for containing printed matter? The p. 22 which I enclose is a specimen of the largest number of verses, composing one poem, which now stand on one page. Would the addition of the vine-leaf at the end exceed the measure, or involve diminishing the spaces between verse and verse? Would the further prefixing of a number or title do so?
  The p. 2 which I enclose will probably be p. 1. That being so, does the poem begin too high up, and will one verse or more have to go over the page?
  I ask these questions because I want to be able to map out exactly what page each poem or part of a poem will stand on.
  What is the proper procedure about the agreement? Does your solicitor draw it up and send it to my solicitor; or do you draw it up and I submit it to some Society for the Protection of Authors against Publishers?
  Thanks for Story's book on Paris restaurants,[1] which I have not yet had time to look at properly: I see a fair sprinkling of names unknown to me.

Yours sincerely   A. E. HOUSMAN

To Grant Richards

MS. LILLY

24 August 1922   *Angel Hotel, Midhurst*

My dear Richards,
  I enclose corrected proofs, which can now be put into book form, as there will be little further change.

---

[1] *Paris à la Carte* by Sommerville Story, 1922.

Silence may now be broken, as I am safely away from Cambridge and out of humanity's reach. When you make the announcement in print I shall have to censure your fanfares. I should think that the first had better be something quite short, such as—'I shall publish on ―――― the only book of poetry written by Mr A. E. Housman since the appearance of *A Shropshire Lad* twenty-six years ago'
or perhaps better simply—
— 'Mr A. E. Housman's second volume of poetry'.[1]
I shall be here, as I told you, till 5 September, and then I shall be going into Gloucestershire for a week, not returning through London; so I shall be glad if you can pay me a day's visit here as you say.

> Yours sincerely
>
> A. E. HOUSMAN

The printers, as usual, when making corrections, seize the opportunity of introducing new errors.

To Theodore Spicer-Simson

MS. PRINCETON

14 September 1922   *Trinity College*

Dear Mr Spicer-Simson,
  I am very grateful for your gift of the medallion which I find awaiting me here on my return from a month's absence.
  Neither Thomson[2] nor Rutherford[3] seems to be in residence here at present, but when they come back I will not fail to show them the portrait and excite their envy.

> I am yours sincerely
>
> A. E. HOUSMAN

To L. W. Payne[4]

MS. TEXAS

14 September 1922   *Trinity College*

Dear Mr Payne,
  I have so long made it a rule to refuse English anthologists permission to

[1] The announcement appeared as: 'Early in October I shall publish a new book by A. E. Housman. It will be entitled *Last Poems*.'
[2] Joseph John Thomson (1856–1940), discoverer of the electron, 1897; winner of the Nobel Prize for Physics, 1906; knighted, 1908; appointed to the Order of Merit, 1912; Master of Trinity College, Cambridge, 1918–1940.
[3] Ernest Rutherford (1871–1937), winner of the Nobel Prize for Chemistry, 1908; knighted, 1914; Cavendish Professor of Experimental Physics at Cambridge, 1919–1937; appointed to the Order of Merit, 1925; created baron, 1931; celebrated for his work on atomic structure.
[4] Leonidas Warren Payne (1873–1945), Professor of English in the University of Texas since 1919. He had asked for permission to include poems by Housman in *Selections from English Literature*, edited by himself and Nina Hill, 1922.

January 9th
1875

My dear Mamma

I have now seen Oxford St, Regent St, Holborn, Cheapside, Cornhill, Piccadilly &c, but not much of the Strand. On Wednesday we went to Waterloo Place, Pall Mall & St James' park where I saw the band of the Grenadier Guards, & some of the 1st Life Guards. We went to the Chapel Royal for service, — the queen's present was given by an attenuated person with gorgeous trimming, who Cousin Mary thinks is an earl, as there was one of those coronets on his carriage. Then we went to Trafalgar square, which is quite magical & to Westminster. I explored the north transept where the statesmen are, I looked at Pitt's & Fox's monuments & went into Poet's corner. Service was at 3, with an anthem by Greene which was like a boa constrictor — very long & very ugly. We had a beautiful one by Goss at the Chapel Royal in the morning.

On Thursday we went by Omnibus to Holborn Viaduct got out & walked about the city

Letter to Lucy Housman, 9 January 1875

1 Gascorough Villas
Woodridings, Pinner
28 June 1911

Dear Butler,

I did not see at the time the announcement, which I understand has been made, of your appointment as my successor, so that I am rather belated in sending my best wishes for your success

Letter to H. E. Butler, 28 June 1911

A.E.H. at 18

. . . at 35

. . . in his fifties

... at 70

Trinity College
17 July 1926

Dear Roberts

(for members of the Family need not throw one another's titles in their teeth) : if you were able to come to tea on Tuesday the 20th, th.t would suit me well.

Yours sincerely

A. E. Housman.

Letter to S. C. Roberts, 17 July 1926

Postcard to Katherine Symons (his last correspondence)

reprint poems of mine that I cannot now give permission to anyone. But my permission is not required in America, where the poems are not copyright.

I am yours sincerely

A. E. HOUSMAN

To Percy Withers

MS. WITHERS

30 September 1922   *Trinity College*

My dear Withers,

I enclose the reply I got from the *custos hortorum* at St John's[1] when I wrote about the alleged distribution of surplus Alpines at this season; and I hope that, operation or no operation, you will be in case to do as he proposes in the spring. I wish you had a better account to give of yourself, and I am sorry there seems to be no chance of seeing you here this term. As to seeing you at Souldern, I am afraid there is not much chance of that either, and, considering the effect I have on your health, it is better so. The book of poems is even smaller than *A.S.L.*, so do not promise yourself repletion. My kind regards to Mrs Withers.

Yours sincerely

A. E. HOUSMAN

To Grant Richards

TEXT: RICHARDS

3 October 1922   *[Trinity College]*

You must not print editions of *A Shropshire Lad* without letting me see the proofs. I have just been looking through the editions of 1918 and 1921, and in both I find the same set of blunders in punctuation and ordering of lines, some of which I have corrected again and again, and the filthy beasts of printers for ever introduce them anew.

To Grant Richards

MS. CONGRESS

11 October 1922   *Trinity College*

My dear Richards,

No, don't send Mr Bert Thomas[2] a photograph.

One or two of his caricatures which I have seen I thought not bad.

Yours sincerely

A. E. HOUSMAN

[1] Oxford.

[2] Cartoonist (1883–1966) well-known for his cartoons of the First World War and a regular contributor to *Punch*, where his caricature of Housman appeared on 25 October 1922 to mark the publication of *Last Poems*. It is reproduced in Richards.

To Grant Richards

MS. LILLY

12 October 1922   *Trinity College*

My dear Richards,

1. I knew the printers would do something, and I only wondered what it would be. On p. 52 they have removed a comma from the end of the first line and a semi-colon from the end of the second.

2. Remember that I am not S. P. B. Mais,[1] and do not quote reviews in your weekly epistle, when reviews begin to appear. Brag about the sale as much as you like.

3. Please add to the list of those who are to have copies from the author sent to them:

W. T. Vesey Esq.,[2] Caius College, Cambridge.

Yours sincerely   A. E. HOUSMAN

Postcard to Grant Richards

MS. LILLY

14 October 1922   *Trinity College*

No, don't put in an errata slip. The blunder will probably enhance the value of the first edition in the eyes of bibliophiles, an idiotic class.

Yours   A. E. HOUSMAN

To Grant Richards

MS. LILLY

18 October 1922   *Trinity College*

My dear Richards,

I return the printers' letter. Printers seem to regard this sort of error as the act of God: I remember the same thing in several places in the Juvenal.

I do not require any copies beyond the six I have.

What the *Times* has done[3] is what the *Standard* did in the case of Lord Beaconsfield's *Endymion*;[4] and in some way which I do not understand it was supposed to have injured the sale.

Yours sincerely   A. E. HOUSMAN

[1] Novelist, lecturer, journalist and writer on the countryside (born 1885).

[2] William Trevor Lendrum, who assumed the name Vesey in 1917 (1854–1935); Fellow of Gonville and Caius College since 1890; an authority on Pindar and a keen horseman; hunted with the Cottesmore. Housman wrote his obituary in *The Caian*, xliii (1935).

[3] *The Times* prematurely reviewed *Last Poems* on 17 October.   [4] Published in 1880.

To John Drinkwater

MS. MARQUETTE

22 October 1922   *Trinity College*

My dear Mr Drinkwater,
  I have written your name and mine in the book[1] with great pleasure, and I thank you for the gift of your own volume of poems,[2] among which I think perhaps I like the two sonnets best.

  I am yours very truly   A. E. HOUSMAN

I have corrected errors of the press on p. 52.

To Gilbert Murray

MS. BODLEY

25 October 1922   *Trinity College*

My dear Murray,
  I seem to be esteemed on Boar's Hill,[3] which is satisfactory. I am not conscious of having been influenced by writing verse in Greek and Latin, and I think we have models enough in English. The new-fangled verse you speak of hardly comes to my ears (I suppose you move in the midst of some of its authors); but I have been admiring Blunden[4] for some time. He describes too much; but when one can describe so well, the temptation must be great.

  Yours sincerely   A. E. HOUSMAN

To Edmund Gosse

MS. B.M.

25 October 1922   *Trinity College*

My dear Gosse,
  I thought you were very nice about me in the *Sunday Times*,[5] and I have copied out a poem for you as you wish.[6] It is one of those which I did not put

---

[1] *Last Poems.*
[2] *Preludes*, 1922.
[3] Where Bridges and Masefield as well as Murray lived, just outside Oxford.
[4] Edmund Charles Blunden (born 1896) had published at this time *The Waggoner and other poems*, 1920, and *The Shepherd*, 1922.
[5] Review of *Last Poems* in the 22 October issue; reprinted in *More Books on the Table*, 1923.
[6] 'Tarry, delight' (*More Poems* XV).

into the book; for I know you bibliophiles and your passion for *l'inédit* irrespective of merit.

Please thank Mrs Gosse for her kind regards, which are reciprocal.

Yours sincerely   A. E. HOUSMAN

Postcard to Grant Richards

MS. CONGRESS

26 October 1922   *Trinity College*

Thanks. The press-cutting agency sends me, with due delay, more notices than I want to see.

What guarantee have I that all these editions of yours are being printed correctly?

A. E. HOUSMAN

To P. P. Stevens[1]

27 October 1922   *Trinity College*

Dear Stevens,

Certainly not. I have only two spare copies, and they are for the good and pure. The most shocking things about you 'devotees of editions' are the shamelessness with which you avow your vice and the calm stupidity with which you stab the vanity of authors. How do you suppose we feel when we hear all this fuss about the difference between a first edition and a tenth? The only merits of any edition are correctness and legibility. This astounds you; and when I tell you that the first edition contained an error which is corrected in the second, you will be ready to tear your hair.

I told the publishers to send a copy on publication to one of your fellow devotees, who insincerely pretends, like you, to be interested in my poetry. When he got it, he could not wait to read it, he despatched it to me by the next post for my autograph. I am really glad when I hear that knavish booksellers are practising extortion on fellows of your sort, and demanding sums which range from 7/6 to a guinea, according as the customer looks a lesser or a greater fool.

However, in consideration of the Tankard,[2] and your share in my educa-

---

[1] Text from a typescript made by Mr John Carter from the original, which was sold at Sotheby's on 17 December 1946. Paul Pearman Stevens was one of Housman's pupils at University College, London, where he took a degree in 1911.

[2] Presented to Housman by his colleagues and pupils when he left University College in 1911; the inscription on it reads: 'Malt does more than Milton can to justify God's ways to man' (*A Shropshire Lad* LXII).

tion, I am prepared to autograph a copy of the second edition, if you like to buy one; but as it has the proper number of stops on p. 52, you may think 5/- too high a price.[1]

How are you earning your bread? Honestly, I hope.

Yours sincerely   A. E. HOUSMAN

To Sydney Cockerell

MS. FITZWILLIAM

1 November 1922   *Trinity College*

Dear Cockerell,

As I still cannot lay my hands on the *Shropshire Lad* MS., and as you are more ardent for possession than the College Library, I send the MS. of *Last Poems*. Half-a-dozen pieces are missing. The MS., as you will see, did not go to the printers but a typewritten copy was made in the publisher's office.

Yours sincerely   A. E. HOUSMAN

To Laurence Housman

MS. LILLY

5 December 1922   *Trinity College*

My dear Laurence,

Thanks for *Dethronements*,[2] though I do not think it one of your good books, nothing like so good as *Angels and Ministers*.[3] I do not believe that any of the people resembled or resemble your figures; and in the second dialogue the falsification of history is quite awful.

On p. 48 there is a misprint, *make* for *may*, and on p. 61, *Collins*. I gather from p. 19 that you are one of the many people who think that Morley wrote a book in favour of compromise:[4] else I don't understand "And yet".

I liked the remark about America on p. 71.[5]

Your affectionate brother   A. E. HOUSMAN

[1] Housman in fact relented and sent Stevens an inscribed first edition on 3 November.
[2] Published in 1922.
[3] Published in 1921.
[4] *On Compromise*, 1874, by John Morley (1838–1923) attacks the principle of compromise throughout.
[5] 'The blaring of brass and the beating of drums . . . is the kind of noise which America knows how to make; a sound of triumph insistent and strained, having in it no beauty and no joy.'

To Laurence Housman[1]

TEXT: MEMOIR

[circa *7 December 1922*]   [*Trinity College*]

My dear Laurence,

. . . To represent Chamberlain as an injured man, and Balfour as the man who injured him, is like saying that Christ crucified Pontius Pilate. 'The downfall of the man of business' (p. 6) was caused by eating, drinking, and smoking immoderately, and taking aperients instead of exercise. From the election of 1905 he came back in much better plight than Balfour, and was in a position to patronise him by finding him a seat. What Balfour did in his premiership was to prevent Chamberlain from quite ruining the party. Outside Parliament, Chamberlain was much the stronger of the two: everything in Unionism which was vulgar and sordid and greedy looked to him as its leader. When he started his precious tariff-reform, a thing which he had not intellect enough to comprehend, Balfour could not oppose him, especially as Free Trade was not the fetish to him that it is to Liberals: what he did was to temporise, and hold together, at the cost of much humiliation to himself and damage to his position, the party which Chamberlain would have torn asunder and led two thirds of it down a blind alley into a pit. His reward was to be driven from the leadership a few years later by those two thirds.

Page 64. The only occasion when Churchill came down to fight in the Central division of Birmingham was in 1885, before a Unionist party existed. In 1889, when Bright died, he did not come down, and the reason was Chamberlain, who was not going to have another cock crowing on his dunghill. On 2 April, when the writ was moved, Hartington came to Churchill and said that Chamberlain was furious and in a state of extreme irritation. The question was decided straight away by a meeting of Chamberlain, Hartington, and Hicks Beach, Churchill having declared that he would accept their decision. That Balfour, who was then Chief Secretary for Ireland, had even an opportunity of hearing about it before it was settled is hardly possible. He was afterwards sent down to Birmingham to pacify the Conservatives there and persuade them to vote for Chamberlain's nominee; so I think your report of Chamberlain's remarks on the subject makes him out a very impudent dog.

Your affectionate brother (though I have received a press-cutting which authoritatively states that we are not brothers)   A. E. HOUSMAN

---

[1] Laurence Housman printed this letter as a continuation of the preceding one. The references are to *Dethronements*.

To Percy Withers

MS. WITHERS

22 December 1922   *Trinity College*

My dear Withers,

Your generous enthusiasm is very nice, but I have not myself felt more than a faint pleasure in the success of the book, which is not really a matter of much importance. I was pleased by letters I had from Masefield and others.

Lewis,[1] as perhaps you know, had a long and severe illness this year; and although he is now quite chirpy, I think he is rather shaken. His pronunciation is less distinct, and he is less regular in coming to Combination Room.

You do not say anything about your own health, nor whether you have had or are going to have an operation. I hope silence means that things are not going badly.

With kind regards to Mrs Withers

     I am yours sincerely   A. E. HOUSMAN

I met the Rector (or Vicar) of Croughton[2] at Eton some months ago.

To John Drinkwater

MS. MARQUETTE

25 December 1922   *Trinity College*

My dear Mr Drinkwater,

There are only two complete translations of Horace's odes which I have done more than glance at, and of those I think Conington's [1863] better, though less showy, than Theodore Martin's [1860]: closer to the sense, and nearer, though of course not near enough, to Horace's manner. The most poetical versions of Horace which I have come across are Calverley's in his *Verses and Translations* [1862], and they are as close as Conington's; but they are too Tennysonian to be very Horatian.

     I am yours sincerely   A. E. HOUSMAN

Conington's translations of Horace's satires and epistles [1870] are among the best verse translations in English.

---

[1] William James Lewis (1847–1926), Professor of Mineralogy at Cambridge since 1881.
[2] The Rev. John Willis Price (1872–1940), novelist and writer of verse; Vicar of Croughton, 1912–1940.

To Grant Richards

TEXT: RICHARDS

28 December 1922   *[Trinity College]*

The wine has arrived, and I am very grateful. There is a great amateur of sherry in this college, with whom I must sample it.

I am prepared to receive royalty from America for the sale of *A Shropshire Lad*. I suppose it will be the same as for *Last Poems*.

In the copies of the small *Shropshire Lad* which you sent me a few weeks ago the corrections I gave you have not been made. Is that the case with all the 5000 (or whatever it was) which you had printed lately?

A happy new year to you and yours.

Postcard to Grant Richards

MS. LILLY

10 January 1923   *Trinity College*

I suppose the Braille[1] people may do *Last Poems* as they did the other book. The blind want cheering up.

Yours   A. E. HOUSMAN

Postcard to F. W. Hall[2]

MS. LILLY

15 January 1923   *Trinity College*

I have told Arnold[3] that I can send him six or eight pages about the middle of February.   A.E.H.

---

[1] i.e. the National Institute for the Blind.

[2] Frederick William Hall (1868–1933); Fellow of St John's College, Oxford since 1897; President, 1931; Joint Editor of *The Classical Quarterly*, 1911–1930.

[3] Edward Vernon Arnold (1857–1926), Professor of Latin in the University College of North Wales and co-Editor with Hall of *The Classical Quarterly*. It is not known which paper by Housman is here in question, though it is possibly 'Notes on the *Thebais* of Statius', published in *The Classical Quarterly*, January and April 1933. For the subsequent history of this affair see the letters to Hall (p. 242) and to Reginald Hackforth (p. 309).

To Witter Bynner

MS. HARVARD

6 February 1923   *Trinity College*

Dear Witter Bynner,

You sent me your *Canticle of Pan*,[1] and I ought to have thanked you for it if I did not; but I am afraid you are not the only person who has reason to complain of my ungracious silence. The fact is that I have a strong tendency to postpone writing all letters; and so it often happens that they do not get written at all, because I have gradually come to fancy that I have written them because I ought to have written them.

Thanks for what you say about my last volume. The sale is larger than I expected, though I expected a larger sale than the publisher and booksellers did.

      I am yours sincerely   A. E. HOUSMAN

Postcard to Grant Richards

MS. CONGRESS

14 February 1923   *Trinity College*

If I did lay it down (which I do not remember) that composers were not to give titles of their own to my poems, they have broken the rule often before now, and it is no good adhering to it.

      A. E. HOUSMAN

To Katharine Symons

MS. LILLY

26 March 1923   *Trinity College*

My dear Kate,

Thanks for your letter on my birthday with its enclosures. I may as well sit down at once and answer it, not being much good for anything else. For the last three weeks I have been about as ill as I ever have been in the course of a fairly healthy life with boils on the neck and a carbuncle on the back; though I daresay poor Basil has often been worse. The doctor says I am better to-day, and I think perhaps I am.

It is very pleasant to see how happy and active Jerry is: he seems to have found his vocation. I don't exactly know what his office is, nor whereabouts he is in the large province of Bengal: not far from Calcutta apparently.

---

[1] Published in 1920.

I had meant to spend this vacation in interesting work: now, as soon as I can get out, I shall probably have to waste the rest of it at the seaside.

I receive, though I do not wish to, the *Weekly Westminster* in which my verses are translated. The prize copy of Greek elegiacs had a false quantity in the second line: I did not read on to see if there were more.

Your affectionate brother   A. E. HOUSMAN

To Grant Richards

TEXT: RICHARDS

4 May 1923   [*Trinity College*]

I wish, if you can, you would stop the *Westminster* (Saturday) setting poems of mine to be turned into Greek and Latin. They will soon have reprinted the whole volume. What makes it worse is that they award prizes to copies containing false quantities.

My old, dear, and intimate friend Princess Marie Louise,[1] who is furnishing the Queen's doll's-house,[2] asked me some months ago to let 12 poems of mine be copied small to form one volume in the library; and I selected the 12 shortest and simplest and least likely to fatigue the attention of dolls or members of the illustrious House of Hanover. Now she says that there is to be printed a book describing or reproducing the contents of this library, and asks me to allow these poems to be included in it: and I have consented. So do not send a solicitor's letter to the Queen (for the book is to be hers) when it appears. The issue is to be 2000 copies in this country and 500 for America, and the Queen is to do what she likes with the proceeds. As I say, the poems are my shortest, and the 12 together are 96 lines.

I have to thank you for sending me several things, including Mrs Taylor's book on the renascence,[3] which I find I can read . . .

I have been ill for two months, worse than I ever was in my life (though that may not be saying much), with carbuncles, which I never had before and do not want to have again. At last I am better, but it has ruined my Easter holiday.

---

[1] 1872–1956; second daughter of Princess Helena and granddaughter of Queen Victoria; published *My Memories of Six Reigns*, 1956.

[2] An ambitious scheme designed to show posterity an English Queen's way of life in the twentieth century and to incorporate the work of leading artists and craftsmen. The house itself was designed by Sir Edwin Lutyens. E. V. Lucas advised on the choice of books for the library. Apart from Housman's, each book contained an original story written for the occasion. The only author who refused was Bernard Shaw. It is exhibited at Windsor Castle.

[3] *Aspects of the Italian Renaissance* by Rachel Annand Taylor, 1923.

To Percy Withers

MS. WITHERS

16 May 1923   *Trinity College*

My dear Withers

For nearly three months I have been ill, not on a scale which would inspire your respect, but enough to make me very angry and disgusted, and in fact worse than I ever was in my life. It has been a succession of carbuncles, which I thought had ended a week ago, but it had not. At present I am not in a case to accept hospitality, and, in particular, your cellar would be almost as bad for me as for you. I had thought of proposing to call on you when I motor into Gloucestershire on 4 June, but it is now settled that I shall go by another route. When I come back, about 20 June, it appears that you will not be at home; so I cannot hope for anything nearer than July, as I don't want to leave Cambridge again till the vacation term begins.

When I saw the invention of Insulin[1] I thought of you, and I expected to hear that you were cured already: I hope you will be soon; and then we will try if our Audit ale can make you ill again. I doubt its power, for it is not as good as it was before the war.

How about your book?[2]

My kind regards to Mrs Withers and many thanks to both of you for the kindness of your invitation.

Yours sincerely   A. E. HOUSMAN

To Robert Bridges

MS. BRIDGES

2 July 1923   *Trinity College*

My dear Bridges,

Thanks for your enquiries, and also for what you say of my poems. The title of the next volume will be *Posthumous Poems* or *Chansons d' Outre-tombe.*

Before the end of the month I hope to go abroad: till then I am here, as I do not yet think myself quite well enough to stay with people, and I am taking periodical inoculations; but I should be quite able to look after you properly if you could find time to stay as my guest in Trinity, and we should all be pleased and honoured. I expect to be back again before the end of August, and by then I ought to be quite well. There is nothing now to

---

[1] Discovered as a remedy for diabetes in 1922 by Sir Frederick Banting and C. H. Best.
[2] *Friends in Solitude*, 1923.

prevent me from running over to Oxford for the day, except on a Thursday, if you could not find time to come here.

Yours sincerely   A. E. HOUSMAN

To Robert Bridges

MS. BRIDGES

5 July 1923   *Trinity College*

My dear Bridges,

I am not likely to go abroad before the 31st,—if then; for they are making such a fuss about my passport that I apprehend war with France is imminent; so there would be plenty of time for you to favour me with a visit here. If you have not yet slept in our Guest Room, emblazoned by Sir William Harcourt with the emblems of his descent from the Plantagenets,[1] I think you ought. But if not, I certainly should be pleased to pay you a visit in September.

Yours sincerely   A. E. HOUSMAN

To Grant Richards

TEXT: RICHARDS

24 July 1923   *[Trinity College]*

This proceeding of the *Weekly Scotsman*, with its mutilation and misprint, is intolerable.[2]

As to the *Westminster*, it did, to my surprise, set a piece from *A Shropshire Lad* for translation a few weeks ago; and I thought perhaps your embargo had been confined to the other book. But I am told by those who read the paper that the translations have never appeared; so I suppose you have terrorised it somehow.

I shall cross to Paris on the 31st by the Handley Page from Croydon at 4.30. I shall stay at the Continental for about three days, and then, I think, go by train to Le Mans and engage a car there, which will be cheaper than in Paris. My idea is to follow the south coast[3] and come back by the north. Thanks for all your maps, books and other aids.

If we are in Paris together, I probably should not be free in the evenings but should be during the day. I am afraid I cannot come up to town this week. The Poet Laureate is paying me a visit on Thursday.

I suppose I gave Christabel Marillier[4] permission, but I forget, and it does

---

[1] Harcourt was proud of his descent from the twelfth-century Robert de Harcourt, whose wife was a cousin of Queen Adeliza, second wife of King Henry I.
[2] The 21 July issue printed 'The Deserter' (*Last Poems* XIII). There was no apology.
[3] Of Brittany.
[4] Composer of 'Loveliest of Trees' (setting of *A Shropshire Lad* II), 1923.

214

not matter. Boosey[1] have suddenly enriched me with £6 for gramophone rights, Vaughan Williams I think . . .

I read through the *Bookman* you sent me a week or two ago, and it may have improved my mind, but I did not make out why you sent it.[2] I hope you will keep your end up with Frank Harris.

To Katharine Symons

MS. TRINITY

18 August 1923   *Hôtel Continental, Paris*

My dear Kate,

Your letter reached me here yesterday on my return from a motor tour of a fortnight in Brittany. The weather has been most obsequious; blazing hot all the time while motor-travel could temper it, and turning cool now that heat would be a nuisance. Brittany is much less wild than I supposed, and much like parts of England, the neighbourhood of Midhurst for instance, though not so hilly. The churches and cathedrals are better than I had any idea of, and extraordinarily numerous. You would be more interested in the varieties of the female head-dress, which is different for every district. Finisterre is an impressive headland, and provided a fine sunset, and also a Scotch mist. The coast scenery in general is extraordinarily superior to the English in its mixture of land and water, and the islands and rocks. Carnac is almost as unimpressive as Stonehenge.

Together with your letter I have one from some photographers, who say that they are taking, 'for press purposes', photographs of ladies and gentlemen who are in the habit of flying between London and Paris, and they want to take mine, as they 'understand that I have also had that distinction'. I was delayed a day because the weather of 31 July was too dangerous for the aeroplane to start; but on 1 August I had the best voyage I have ever had. We crossed the Channel 7000 feet high, higher than the piles of clouds which lay over both shores, and both coasts were visible at once, which I have not found before.

I am better, but not well. I spent the first half of June at Woodchester, and went over to Cheltenham to see J. R. Polson,[3] whom I had not met for 30 years, and who seems very well and flourishing. I expect to return to Cambridge on the 28th. Love to all on the premises.

Your affectionate brother   A. E. HOUSMAN

[1] Messrs Boosey and Hawkes, music publishers.
[2] The number for June 1923 reviewed settings of four poems from *A Shropshire Lad* by C. W. Orr.
[3] James Ronald Polson (born 1859) was Housman's contemporary at Bromsgrove School. He became a doctor and practised in Worcester.

To Grant Richards

TEXT: RICHARDS

[Postmark 23 September 1923]   *Trinity College*

I have seen a reply which your firm sent to Longman when they asked if they might include two pieces from *Last Poems* in Bridges' selection of poetry for schools.[1] It is quite the sort of answer which I should wish you to write, though in point of fact I do not unconditionally prohibit the use of *Last Poems* as I do of *A Shropshire Lad*; but I have given Bridges permission to include the two pieces in question.

I had better also tell you that I believe that he (being Poet Laureate, and an unscrupulous character, and apparently such an admirer of my verse that he thinks its presence or absence will make all the difference to the book) intends to include three poems from *A Shropshire Lad*, though I have not given him my permission, because he thinks he has reason to think that I shall not prosecute him. Well, I shall not; and you will please turn a blind eye too.

To E. V. Lucas

MS. BERG

3 November 1923   *Trinity College*

Dear Lucas,

Thanks for your letter, which is the second I owe to the poet in *The Times*, whom I judge from his versification to be a very gallant soldier.[2]

Yours sincerely   A. E. HOUSMAN

To Percy Withers

MS. WITHERS

28 December 1923   *Trinity College*

My dear Withers,

I am glad that Insulin has behaved well and not failed as these new infallible remedies do fail on occasion. I am sorry that it has not yet brought you to the level of drinking Audit ale, because this year's brew is quite good: last

---

[1] *The Chilswell Book of English Poetry*, 1924.

[2] The only poem printed in *The Times* near this date is 'An Armistice Day Anthem' by the Master of the Temple (the Rev. W. H. Draper) on 1 November 1923. It begins:

'What say the dead who are at rest,
    The heroes true and brave?
We fought our fight, we gave our best
    The cause of man to save.'

year's was a powerful explosive, and filled our cellars with the shards of bottles till we sent it back to its brewer, for use in case Yarmouth were bombarded again;[1] but there its strength ended, and you could probably have drunk it with impunity.

I return you all good wishes for the new year, and I hope there may be nothing to prevent me from availing myself of your kind invitation in the warm months.

I was pleased to see a very favourable review of your book long ago in one of the weeklies.

There is nothing the matter with me except too much alcohol and too little exercise, as usual in the winter.

With kind regards to Mrs Withers

I am yours sincerely   A. E. HOUSMAN

To Katharine Symons

MS. TRINITY

3 January 1924   *Trinity College*

My dear Kate,

This post-card comes in the nick of time to make me answer your letter. I am quite well now, except for a slight goutiness; but that is chronic, my friends, so do not grieve for me.[2] I have been here since I came back from Brittany at the end of August, except that a month ago I went to Oxford to read a paper and stayed a week-end with the Poet Laureate on the top of Boar's Hill there. He is an amazing old man: at 79 he gets up at five in the morning, lights his own fire and makes his coffee, and does a lot of work before breakfast. He has a large number of correct opinions, and is delighted when he finds that I have them too, and shakes hands with me when I say that the Nun's Priest's Tale is Chaucer's best poem, and that civilisation without slavery is impossible.

I am very sorry to hear of the break in Jerry's career, which seemed to be proceeding so famously; and it is a pity that the wretched country of India should be deprived of his services. I do not yet know how much Denis was fined at Cambridge over the motor-car affair.

I am glad you and Edward are so comfortable. I like the notion of coming to Bath some time this year. I believe the Pump-room hotel, which used to be a good one, is opened again; and that, I suppose, is not so very far from you.

Your affectionate brother   A. E. HOUSMAN

[1] Trinity Audit ale was supplied by E. Lacon and Company. Yarmouth was bombarded by German cruisers in 1916. It had also been bombed by a Zeppelin in January 1915, when two people were killed.
[2] Quoted from Mr Pecksniff in Dickens' *Martin Chuzzlewit*, chapter 9.

To A. S. F. Gow

MS. TRINITY

9 January 1924   *Trinity College*

Dear Gow,

I am glad you are to be here at the end of next week. I am writing because you are lodged in the inner Guest Room, and I want to entertain the Family[1] at dinner in the outer room on Friday 18 January, which I cannot do without your permission, for which I hereby sue. Will you yourself make one of the party? unless you prefer to dine in Hall. It is at eight o'clock.

Yours sincerely   A. E. HOUSMAN

I am writing with a sprained wrist.

To Lily Thicknesse

TEXT: MEMOIR

10 March 1924   *[Trinity College]*

Dear Mrs Thicknesse,

. . . Last year a French school-ma'm wrote to me wanting to translate *A Shropshire Lad* and asking what share of the proceeds I should expect. I replied that I should take nothing; but then mine is a character of unusual and almost disagreeable nobility . . .

Yours sincerely   A. E. HOUSMAN

To Messrs Grant Richards

MS. CONGRESS

14 March 1924   *Trinity College*

Dear Sirs,

I have never laid down any general rule against the inclusion of poems from *Last Poems* in anthologies. The rule regarding *A Shropshire Lad* still holds good. It is true that the Poet Laureate has printed three poems from it in his recent anthology, but he does not pretend that I gave him permission to do so.

I am yours faithfully   A. E. HOUSMAN

---

[1] A dining club, limited to twelve members, each of whom entertained the others once a year.

To F. C. Owlett[1]

Dear Mr Owlett,
   Gilbert Murray introduced me some twelve years ago to Mrs Taylor's poems,[2] and I admired the beauty and richness of their ornament. I do not put her first among living woman poets in this country: I will not provoke your wrath and scorn by saying whom I do; especially as you have on your side "names from which there would be no appeal". But there are no such names really: contemporary criticism is always fallible: think of Lamb and Shelley. It is very unreasonable for people to be depressed by unfavourable reviews: they should say to themselves "do I write better than Wordsworth and Shelley and Keats? am I worse treated than they were?"

   I am yours very truly   A. E. HOUSMAN

To the Editor of The Times[3]

[Early May 1924]   *[Trinity College]*

KEATS, THE FALL OF HYPERION, l. 97.

Sir,
   This poem was not printed in Keats's lifetime, and his manuscript has been lost; but in the copy made under the direction of Woodhouse lines 97–101 of the first canto run as follows:—

> When in mid-way the sickening east wind
> Shifts sudden to the south, the small warm rain
> Melts out the frozen incense from all flowers,
> And fills the air with so much pleasant health
> That even the dying man forgets his shroud.

When an east wind shifts to the south, whether "in mid-way", whatever that may be taken to mean, or "in mid-day", as Lord Houghton printed, the result which is here described does not necessarily nor even usually follow. In order that rain may melt out incense from flowers, both flowers and incense must be there; and this condition is not fulfilled in any month between the autumnal and the vernal equinox. Such flowers as bloom in that half of the year are mostly scentless.
   Keats wrote "in mid-May", as in the Ode to a Nightingale he wrote

---

[1] Text from *The Dalhousie Review* XXIX, 1950. Frederick Charles Owlett was a literary journalist and contributor to *The Spectator*. His poems, *Kultur and Anarchy*, were published in 1917, and a book on Francis Thompson in 1936.
[2] See p. 106.
[2] Text from *The Times Literary Supplement*, 8 May 1924.

"mid-May's eldest child"; and for confirmation the next lines are these:—
> Even so that lofty sacrificial fire,
> Sending forth Maian incense, spread around
> Forgetfulness of everything but bliss.

A.E.H.

To the Headmaster of Eton College[1]

MS. TRINITY

24 July 1924   *Trinity College*

My dear Headmaster,

In consequence of your flattering request I have been looking at my verses, and I think them so much inferior to the *Loves of the Triangles*[2] that I am not willing to have them published. Do not tell me that there is much more vanity than modesty in this, because I know it already.

I am yours sincerely   A. E. HOUSMAN

To Edmund Gosse

MS. B.M.

24 July 1924   *Trinity College*

My dear Gosse,

It would be kind of you if in some odd moment you would look through these translations and say what you think of them. They are by a Dane in America, H. Troller Steenstrŭp, who wants to translate my poems and says that perhaps I am acquainted with Mr Edmund Gosse who is excellently well versed in Danish, and might induce him to compare the original with the translations to decide if he is qualified for the work.[3]

I assure you that my request is not prompted by rancour at receiving this morning a circular from you asking for a contribution to the W. P. Ker Memorial, when I had sent one more than a week ago. I daresay you thought it insufficient, or perhaps it was embezzled by Gregory Foster,[4] who signed the receipt.

---

[1] Cyril Argentine Alington (1872–1955), formerly Headmaster of Shrewsbury School; Headmaster of Eton College, 1916–1933; Dean of Durham, 1933–1955.

[2] At the conclusion of Housman's paper on Erasmus Darwin, which he had recently read to an Eton society, stood his parody of Darwin, 'Fragments of a Didactic Poem on Latin Grammar'. *The Loves of the Triangles* is a parody of Darwin's *The Loves of the Plants* and was published in *The Anti-Jacobin*, April 1798. Housman's parody had already appeared in *The University College Gazette*, 1899. It is reprinted in *Memoir*.

[3] This translation was not published.

[4] (Thomas) Gregory Foster (1866–1931), Provost of University College, London, 1904–1929; knighted, 1917; created baronet, 1930.

Please give my kind regards to Mrs Gosse. I see that Philip has been writing a successful book.[1]   Yours sincerely   A. E. HOUSMAN

To Katharine Symons

MS. TRINITY

30 July 1924   *Trinity College*

My dear Kate,
Thanks for your letter. I think of coming to Bath on Monday 18 August and staying for three weeks. As you kindly offer to see about rooms, I shall be glad if you will. I think you said that the hotel made out of the old Bath College would be the nearest to you, and the situation at any rate is pleasant. But I shall want a sitting room as well as a bed-room, and it must depend on whether they can furnish that. I am not sure if lodgings might not be better than an hotel, and I suppose they might be got even nearer to you. I do not limit you to any particular price, and I am prepared to go even to the Empire (or Imperial) if necessary.
I hope by now you are both, or all, safe home from Wales, and the better for your holiday. I have managed to get sciatica, but it is passing away.

Your affectionate brother   A. E. HOUSMAN

To Witter Bynner

MS. HARVARD

6 August 1924   *Trinity College*

Dear Witter Bynner,
Many thanks for your friendly letter and flattering poem.[2] I cannot write sonnets myself, but I suppose the next best thing is to be the cause of sonnets.

Yours very truly   A. E. HOUSMAN

To Robert Bridges

MS. BRIDGES

27 August 1924   *The Spa Hotel, Bath*

My dear Bridges,
I am glad you are safe home from America,[3] where I hope you have lit a

---

[1] Philip Gosse (1879–1959), naturalist, doctor and author. He published *The Pirates' Who's Who* in 1924.
[2] Sonnet 'To A. E. Housman', published in *The New Republic*, 2 July 1924.
[3] Where he had been a visiting lecturer at Ann Arbor University, Michigan.

candle or sown seed. They are terribly docile, but have not much earth, so it is apt to wither away.

I am here till 8 September, when I shall greedily be returning to urgent and agreeable work. But as you are kind enough to ask me, will you put me up for the night? It is half way home and will be a pleasant halt. I could get to you before one o'clock, and should be moving on about two o'clock on the next day. Do not get up a dinner party for me, because I have no proper clothes.

My kind regards to Mrs Bridges.

Yours sincerely   A. E. HOUSMAN

To J. B. Priestley

MS. TEXAS

18 September 1924   *Trinity College*

Dear Sir,

I am much obliged by your kindness in sending me your book, parts of which I had read with pleasure in periodicals.[1]

I can easily swallow all the flattery brewed by you and F. L. Lucas;[2] but I wish people would not call me a Stoic. I am a Cyrenaic; and for the Stoics, except as systematisers of knowledge in succession to the Peripatetics, I have a great dislike and contempt.

I am yours faithfully   A. E. HOUSMAN

To Robert Bridges

MS. BRIDGES

25 September 1924   *Trinity College*

My dear Bridges,

I adjure you not to waste your time on Manilius. He writes on astronomy and astrology without knowing either. My interest in him is purely technical. His best poetry you will find in I 483–531, where he appeals to the regularity of the heavenly motions as evidence of the divinity and eternity of the universe. He has nothing else so good, and little that is nearly so good.

Yours sincerely   A. E. HOUSMAN

[1] *Figures in Modern Literature*, 1924, which contained essays on nine authors, including Housman, reprinted from *The London Mercury*.

[2] Essayist and critic (1894–1967); Fellow of King's College, Cambridge, 1920–1967. His essay on Housman, 'Few, but Roses', originally published in the *New Statesman*, 20 October 1923, was reprinted in his collection *Authors Dead and Living*, 1926. See also p. 441, item 23.

To John Sparrow[1]

MS. SPARROW

3 October 1924   *Trinity College*

Dear Sir,

Judging from the context[2] I should say that seeing the record cut is one of the unpleasant things which the athlete escapes by dying young; and this may help to determine the meaning.

I am yours very truly   A. E. HOUSMAN

To Grant Richards

MS. CONGRESS

5 October 1924   *Trinity College*

My dear Richards,

Certainly I will not have the two books published in one volume; and as this is what the Florence Press asks, the answer is simply no.

Yours sincerely   A. E. HOUSMAN

To Messrs Macmillan and Company

MS. MACMILLAN

16 November 1924   *Trinity College*

Dear Sirs,

In the last twenty years I have produced several editions of Latin classics, which are printed at my expense, offered to the public at less than cost price, and sold for me by a publisher on commission.

I am just completing an edition of Lucan, which I wish to produce in the same way. The printers of my last three books, Messrs Robert Maclehose and Co. of the Glasgow University Press, are prepared to undertake the work; and Mr Charles Whibley[3] has suggested to me that you may be willing to act as publishers for me on the usual terms, and to be the channel of my communications with the printers. As in 1895 you refused to publish another book of mine, *A Shropshire Lad*, under similar conditions, I did not think this likely; but he assures me you are now less haughty.

---

[1] John Hanbury Angus Sparrow (born 1906), barrister, essayist and critic; Warden of All Souls College, Oxford since 1952; author of the introduction to the Penguin edition of Housman's *Collected Poems*, 1956, and an authority on Housman's manuscripts. At the time of this letter he was still at school at Winchester.

[2] In 'To an Athlete Dying Young' (*A Shropshire Lad* XIX).

[3] Journalist and critic (1859–1930).

If so, I will send you the text and notes, which are already complete and constitute the bulk of the work, that you may transmit them to Messrs Maclehose and obtain an estimate of the cost.

I am yours faithfully   A. E. HOUSMAN[1]

To Percy Withers

MS. WITHERS

31 December 1924   *Trinity College*

My dear Withers,

I am glad to hear what I suppose is tolerably good news of your health, and to receive your Christmas reproaches. It is true that I do not write to you, but then there are few people to whom I do, and never willingly. You write with ease, elegance and evident enjoyment, whereas I hate it. Like Miss Squeers, I am screaming out loud all the time I write,[2] which takes off my attention rather and I hope will excuse mistakes.

I will remember you at midnight, when I shall be drinking to absent friends in stout and oysters, which are very salubrious, and which I take medicinally to neutralise the excesses of Christmas. When you give Mrs Winslow's soothing syrup to a baby, 'the little darling wakes up as bright as a button';[3] and so do I on New Year's day.

The Poet Laureate's joke was made subsequently but independently by a scholar here in the form 'all my eye and Beatus Martinus'.[4]

I was in Paris in June at the Presidential Election, when the French Revolution which I hoped to witness was spoilt by the rain,[5] and at Bath in August, where the rain would have spoilt an English Revolution had Bath been never so Bolshevik. George Saintsbury[6] lives there now, and is to be recognised, I hear, by the shabbiness of his clothes and especially of his top-hat, which nevertheless, when rain comes on, he protects with oil-cloth.

My kind regards to Mrs Withers, and a happy New Year to both of you.

Yours sincerely   A. E. HOUSMAN

---

[1] The firm replied on 19 November that commission publishing was out of their line and that there was not sufficient ground for making an exception. The book was published instead by Blackwell. See also p. 245.

[2] See Dickens' *Nicholas Nickleby*, chapter 15.

[3] Quoted from the advertisement for a popular Victorian remedy.

[4] See pp. 418–19. The pun is on the slang expression (meaning 'nonsense') 'all my eye and Betty Martin'.

[5] The parliamentary elections of May 1924 had produced a Chamber dominated by Radicals and Socialists. These refused to take office so long as Alexandre Millerand remained President of the Republic. Deadlock was broken after a month by his resignation, and on 13 June the National Assembly, at Versailles, elected Gaston Doumergue in his place.

[6] Literary critic and authority on wine (1845–1933).

To an Unnamed Correspondent[1]

Do not ever read books about versification: no poet ever learnt it that way. If you are going to be a poet, it will come to you naturally and you will pick up all you need from reading poetry.

To Grant Richards

TEXT: RICHARDS

4 January 1925 [*Trinity College*]

I am obliged to write to you about the following matter, because I do not know how I stand.

I have received a press-cutting from America which says that Henry Holt and Co have published *A Shropshire Lad* and *Last Poems* together in one volume.[2] I have written to ask them if this is true: if it is, I shall take *Last Poems* away from them, supposing that I can. But I find that in my agreement with them there is no clause empowering me to withdraw from them my licence to publish, as there is in my agreement with you. Before I go to a solicitor, perhaps you can give me a notion of what my rights are.

Thanks for your novel,[3] though neither it nor any of them are as good as *Caviare*.

I enclose the *menus régionales* which you wished to have returned, and I do not wonder, as they make one's mouth water.

P.S. Can I make them destroy the combined book?

To Herbert Thring[4]

MS. SOCIETY OF AUTHORS

12 January 1925 *Trinity College*

Dear Sir,

My subscription to the Society of Authors does not, I presume, entitle me to ask for your official assistance in the following matter; but if you would consent to act as my solicitor, or recommend to me some other solicitor competent to deal with the case, I should be grateful.

My book *Last Poems* is copyrighted in the United States and published there by Messrs Henry Holt and Co. of 19 West 44th Street, New York. I learn that they have lately issued, in a single volume, these poems together

---

[1] Text from *Notes and Queries*, 28 April 1928. This letter cannot be dated, and I have placed it here arbitrarily.
[2] He was misled. The two books were bound separately and merely put in a box together.
[3] *Every Wife*, 1925. [4] 1859–1941; Secretary of the Society of Authors since 1892.

225

with the contents of another book of mine, which is not copyrighted in the United States, *A Shropshire Lad*. This they have done without asking my leave, and against my desire. I wish therefore, if I can, to do two things: to make them withdraw this volume, and to transfer *Last Poems* to another American publisher.

I do not send you my agreement with Messrs Holt (which does not seem to contain anything exactly bearing on the case) till I have your reply.

I am yours faithfully   A. E. HOUSMAN

To Herbert Thring

MS. SOCIETY OF AUTHORS

16 January 1925   *Trinity College*

Dear Sir,

I beg to acknowledge the return of the publisher's agreement which I sent you; and beyond that I have only to thank you for your opinion and excuse myself for troubling you.

I am yours truly   A. E. HOUSMAN

To F. W. Hall

MS. LILLY

3 February 1925   *Trinity College*

Dear Hall,

I am quite willing that my name should appear in the appeal for subscriptions towards Cave's[1] portrait, and I enclose cheque for five guineas. I am to meet him next week for the first time.

I am busy finishing off my Lucan, and also writing a review,[2] a job which I always regret undertaking, as it always absorbs a disproportionate amount of time, because I am so fearfully conscientious. When it is completed, if it ever is, I ought to turn to at Manilius V, or the unfinished windows in Aladdin's tower unfinished will remain.[3]

Yours sincerely   A. E. HOUSMAN

[1] George Cave (1856–1928), lawyer and politician; Member of Parliament, 1906–1918; Home Secretary, 1916–1919; created Viscount, 1918; Lord Chancellor, 1922–1924 and 1924–1928; Chancellor of Oxford University, 1925–1928. The appeal was for a portrait of St John's College, of which Cave was a member.

[2] Of A. C. Pearson's edition of Sophocles in *The Classical Review*, 1925.

[3] See *The Arabian Nights*. Aladdin's tower was built by the genie of the lamp. The windows were set in frames of jewels. The last was left for the sultan to complete, but after exhausting all his treasures he had to abandon the attempt.

To W. E. Rudge[1]

MS. LILLY

9 February 1925   *Trinity College*

Dear Sir,

I am obliged and flattered by your letter of 22 January.

I am personally willing that you should publish, as you wish, an edition of *A Shropshire Lad* or *Last Poems* or both, provided that the two are not included in one volume.

As to *A Shropshire Lad* you do not need my consent, as it is not copyright in America.

As to *Last Poems*, I suppose it would be proper to consult my American publishers, Messrs Henry Holt and Co.

I must make it a condition, in the case of *Last Poems*, that the proofs are sent to me for correction; and though I have no right to make conditions in the case of *A Shropshire Lad*, I shall be obliged if you will follow the same course, as the last American edition I saw was full of errors.

I am yours very truly   A. E. HOUSMAN

As you are good enough to offer me a copy of Mr Spicer-Simson's book, I should be very glad to have it.

To J. J. Thomson

TYPESCRIPT: TRINITY

22 February 1925   *Trinity College*

My dear Master,

I take up my pen in a rather sorrowful mood, because I recognise the compliment implied in the Council's offer of the Clark Lectureship, and am grateful for their friendliness and for yours, and therefore I cannot help feeling ungracious in making the answer which nevertheless is the only answer possible.

I do regard myself as a connoisseur; I think I can tell good from bad in literature. But literary criticism, referring opinions to principles and setting them forth so as to command assent, is a high and rare accomplishment and quite beyond me. I remember Walter Raleigh's Clark lecture on Landor:[2] it was unpretending, and not adorned or even polished, but I was thinking all the while that I could never have hit the nail on the head like that. And not only have I no talent for producing the genuine article, but no taste or

---

[1] American printer and typographer (1876–1931).
[2] On 3 June 1911, the last in his series *Prose Writers of the Romantic Revival*.

inclination for producing a substitute. If I devoted a whole year (and it would not take less) to the composition of six lectures on literature, the result would be nothing which could give me, I do not say satisfaction, but consolation for the wasted time; and the year would be one of anxiety and depression, the more vexatious because it would be subtracted from those minute and pedantic studies in which I am fitted to excel and which give me pleasure.

I am sorry if this explanation is tedious, but I would rather be tedious than seem thankless and churlish.

I am yours sincerely   A. E. HOUSMAN

To Grant Richards

MS. CONGRESS

3 March 1925   *Trinity College*

My dear Richards,

I have not read this through, but I have dipped into it, and it will not do. It is sometimes surprisingly close to the original, but at other times the formal French phrases crop up; and my verse really will not go into French verse. The worst is that he sometimes does not understand the English: for instance in VIII 'a love to keep you clean' is translated 'amour, qui garde propre ta maison'.[1]

Yours sincerely   A. E. HOUSMAN

To Katharine Symons

MS. LILLY

14 March 1925   *Trinity College*

My dear Kate,

I was very sorry to hear your news of Jerry's misfortunes. I suppose he is now back, and you have seen him, and I hope that the voyage and absence from India has already done him good. I should have written to you before, but I am so languid with a month of bronchitis that I neglect most things, correspondence especially. I have gone on lecturing, which I daresay did me no good; and now that term is over matters may mend.

The Eton Librarian I suppose was Mr Broadbent,[2] whom I have often met. When he and the Earl of Oxford and Asquith were undergraduates together they were supposed to be about equally able; but it was a great

[1] No French translation was published.
[2] Henry Broadbent (1852–1935); Fellow of Exeter College, Oxford, 1874; assistant master at Eton College, 1876; Librarian, 1920.

mistake. He is rather a figure of fun, with the largest and most bloodshot eyes I ever saw, and produces Greek and Latin verses which should be pointed but are not.

Love to all.

Your affectionate brother
A. E. HOUSMAN

To Witter Bynner

MS. HARVARD

15 April 1925   *Trinity College*

My dear Witter Bynner,

There is no need for you to apologize, but writing an introduction[1] is what I would not do for anyone, or rather, it would be more accurate to say, I could not. I am sorry that the publishers attach so much weight to such a thing.

I hope you are well and flourishing. New Mexico must be one of the more romantic of the States.

I am yours sincerely
A. E. HOUSMAN

To Percy Withers

MS. WITHERS

29 May 1925   *Trinity College*

My dear Withers,

I am sorry to hear no better account of your health, though glad that your tour was a success. As to your kind invitation, June I am spending in Gloucestershire; but if you could have me to lunch on my way there, on Tuesday the 2nd, that would be very delightful.

Death and marriage are raging through this College with such fury that I ought to be grateful for having escaped both.

My kind regards to Mrs Withers.

Yours sincerely
A. E. HOUSMAN

To A. S. F. Gow

MS. TRINITY

27 June 1925   *Trinity College*

Dear Gow,

I understand that the Council will shortly invite you to return to the

[1] To Bynner's *Caravan*, 1925.

College and offer you a post on the teaching staff, and I earnestly hope that you will accept it. I have always gone about saying that you ought never to have been allowed to leave Cambridge, and I am delighted at the chance of getting you back. I know of course that you have been successful in your present profession, and I suppose that you are on the eve of having a house, which means what may be called opulence; but it will never allow you the leisure which you ought to have if you are to lay out your talents properly and enter into the joy of the Lord. Eton no doubt is a very pleasant society, but Cambridge is not bad, even after our lamentable loss of Benson.[1] If you resent all this as impertinent interference, I am quite prepared to support that.

Yours sincerely   A. E. HOUSMAN

To Grant Richards

TEXT: RICHARDS

7 August 1925   [*Trinity College*]

It[2] was not "originally published at 5*s*." but at 2/6; even the second edition, though much inferior, was only 3/6.

I have just been stopped in the street by an American lady who was yearning for the last work of your Mr Mais in the window of a shop whose door was locked. She seemed to want me to break the glass for her, but I persuaded her that there were other shops in the town.

To Laurence Housman

TEXT: MEMOIR

18 August 1925   [*Trinity College*]

My dear Laurence,

. . . On the 27th I am going abroad for about a month, leaving behind me a nearly completed and in great part printed edition of Lucan with Basil Blackwell of Oxford. If the French kill me with one of these lethal railways of theirs, J. D. Duff[3] of this college is to be asked to finish it and see it through the press . . .

Your affectionate brother   A. E. HOUSMAN

[1] Arthur Christopher Benson (1862–1925), poet and novelist; assistant master at Eton College, 1885; Fellow of Magdalene College, Cambridge, 1904; Master, 1915–1925.
[2] *A Shropshire Lad*.
[3] See p. 405, note 3.

To H. E. Butler

MS. ST JOHN'S

2 October 1925   *Trinity College*

My dear Butler,

I cannot possibly decline the kind and flattering invitation of the Professors' Dining Club, and the 16th will suit me quite well.

I am yours very truly   A. E. HOUSMAN

To Mrs H. E. Butler

MS. ST JOHN'S

17 October 1925   *Trinity College*

Dear Mrs Butler,

Enfeebled though I am by the jolting of the Great Eastern Railway, I must write a line to thank you for your hospitality and say how much I enjoyed my stay.

I hope your youngest son brought the first day of his second year to a happy close.

Yours sincerely   A. E. HOUSMAN

To Robert Bridges

MS. BRIDGES

18 December 1925   *Trinity College*

My dear Bridges,

I am very grateful for your kindness in sending me your new book of poems[1] to cheer my Christmas. Though some of them were not new to me, or not quite; and I was amused to read in verse on pp. 69–72 what I had heard from your lips in prose.

Along with your novelties I am glad to see you using the old and beautiful stanza, now unjustly despised because so often ill managed, of XVIII, which ought not to be left to Laura Matilda.[2] You will probably condemn my judgment if I say that what most affects me is the last verse on p. 63.[3]

My kind regards to Mrs Bridges, and all wishes for a happy Christmas.

Yours sincerely   A. E. HOUSMAN

[1] *New Verse*, 1925.
[2] See p. 200, note 1.
[3]   'But I long since had left it;
            what fortune now befals
            finds me on other meadows
            by other trees and walls.' (from 'The Sleeping Mansion')

To Percy Withers

25 December 1925   *Trinity College*

My dear Withers,

I am very sorry to hear of your breaking down after you had been enjoying yourself so much in Italy, and I hope the gradual improvement you report will go steadily on. Lewis lately got pleurisy and was carried off by his doctor to the nursing home, but there is quite good news of him, and he may manage to beat, as he is determined, the longevity of his predecessor in the Chair.[1] I am well enough: I believe I answered your letter in September and told you I had been in the Pyrenees. I have a book just coming out, but it is one of my serious works, and you will not want to read it; nor will any mad American millionaire pay £80 for it, as one did the other day for an auto-graphed first edition of *A Shropshire Lad*. My brother, who has commercial talents, had bought the last six copies in 1898 and got me to sign them. I hope you will be consoled for the stiff price which, I gathered, you paid for your own copy.

I close this letter in order to go and dress for our domestic Feast, and as I guzzle and guttle I shall wish that you were here and had not taken leave of these agreeable vices.

With kind regards to Mrs Withers

I am yours sincerely   A. E. HOUSMAN

To Laurence Housman

MS. STREET

29 December 1925   [*Trinity College*]

My dear Laurence,

Thanks for your Christmas present.[2] I like "Blind Man's Buff" the best of the stories. "Farvingdon" I read when it came out, perhaps in Quilter's magazine.[3]

At our last Feast I had the new Dean of Westminster[4] next me, and he said he had long been wishing to thank me for the amusement he had derived from my writings, especially about Queen Victoria and her Ministers. So if I bring you money, you bring me fame.

[1] William Hallowes Miller (1801–1880) was Professor of Mineralogy for forty-eight years.
[2] His new book, *Odd Pairs: a Book of Tales*.
[3] I have not traced the first publication of 'The Defence of Farvingdon'. By Quilter's magazine Housman means *The Universal Review* (1888–1890) edited by Harry Quilter, which contained three contributions by Laurence Housman in 1890, but not this story, which was written in 1895.
[4] The Very Rev. William Foxley Norris (1859–1937).

232

Now that Hughley is burnt down it is curious to think that I never saw it; though it cannot have been much to see. A happy new year to both of you.

Your affectionate brother A. E. HOUSMAN

To Katharine Symons

MS. TRINITY

15 January 1926 *Trinity College*

My dear Kate,

I am obliged to write to you, as otherwise you may be perplexed by communications from the London Library. I am taking steps to have you made a life member; but as you cannot be elected before 8 February (if then), the Librarian suggests sending you a receipt 'subject to the Committee's Approval' which will entitle you to full privileges and enable you to make use of the Library at once in your own right. Finally you will have to sign a form. Make hay while the sun shines, for perhaps the Committee will not approve of you.

Your affectionate brother A. E. HOUSMAN

To R. St J. Parry

MS. C.U.P.

17 January 1926 *Trinity College*

My dear Parry,

There is at least one address of Platt's, beside the Prelection, which well deserves to be published:[1] a most interesting and entertaining discourse on Aristotle, delivered on some public occasion at University College.[2] If Mrs Platt has not the manuscript, it is probably in the possession of the secretarial department or the Union Society.

His other remains are likely to be papers read to the students' Literary Society, some of which I heard, and they were very good to listen to. How they would look in print I do not feel quite sure; but they were full of good stuff, apart from the fun.

I should not enjoy writing an introduction, but I would do it for his sake, and in the interests of scholarship and literature.

Yours sincerely A. E. HOUSMAN

[1] In *Nine Essays*, the projected volume of his posthumous papers. The Prelection, delivered in Cambridge in 1921, when he was a candidate for the Professorship of Greek, was on chapters 45–48 of Plato's *Phaedo*.
[2] 'Science and Arts among the Ancients', delivered at the Opening of Session in University College, London, October 1899.

233

To S. C. Roberts[1]

MS. C.U.P.

22 January 1926   *Trinity College*

Dear Mr Roberts,

About a week ago I heard from the Vice-Master of this college that the Press was thinking of printing Platt's prelection and perhaps some more of his remains; and he asked me some questions, which I answered. Yesterday I had a letter from Mrs Platt to say that she was having some of his MSS typed and proposed to send them (in that form) to me; and I told her that they should go to you. But this morning Edward Platt sends me the MS of the prelection, which I now hold at your disposal. It has not been typed.[2]

Yours very truly   A. E. HOUSMAN

To Grant Richards

MS. CONGRESS

28 January 1926   *Trinity College*

My dear Richards,

The Headmaster of Winchester[3] can have XXXVI from *Last Poems*,[4] and if he wants a title he can call it "Revolution",[5] which may be of use, as most readers do not seem to see that it is a parable.

I hope your negotiations may turn out as you hope, but you are apt to be sanguine.[6]

Yours sincerely   A. E. HOUSMAN

To Lady Frazer[7]

26 February 1926   *Trinity College*

I am told that if I show myself at the Queens' Society they will worry me to read them a paper myself. They must be quite impudent enough, for I do

---

[1] Sydney Castle Roberts (1887–1966); Secretary of the Cambridge University Press, 1922–1948; Master of Pembroke College, Cambridge, 1948–1958; knighted, 1958.

[2] Housman, having agreed to write the preface, was now being treated as editor of the volume.

[3] The Rev. Alwyn Terrell Petre Williams (born 1888); later Dean of Christ Church, Oxford, Bishop of Durham and Bishop of Winchester.

[4] For *The Winchester College Lines Book* (second edition), 1926.

[5] This title was adopted in subsequent editions of *Last Poems*.

[6] Richards, again facing bankruptcy, was trying to raise further capital in order to stay in business.

[7] Text from Messrs Maggs' catalogue No. 798, 1950.

not suppose that Sir James volunteered his. Besides an undergraduate went into Heffer's the other day and asked when my Posthumous Poems would be published; so, as I am a *sexagenarius*, I am afraid of becoming an *Argeus*, and I especially avoid Queens' because they have a *pons sublicius*.[1]

To H. M. Adams[2]

MS. TRINITY

3 March 1926   *Trinity College*

Dear Adams,

I enclose the MS of *A Shropshire Lad*. XXXV is missing, and after XXXVI the numeration differs a good deal from the final order, because while the book was printing I took out five pieces and put in the three now numbered XXXIV, XXXVII, and XLI, which are together at the end.

Yours sincerely

A. E. HOUSMAN

To T. S. Eliot[3]

MS. ELIOT

2 April 1926   *Trinity College*

Dear Mr Eliot,

I am much flattered, but my knowledge of Wilkie Collins[4] is not what you have been led to suppose it, and for literary criticism I have no talent and fortunately no inclination either. I am glad that you take an interest in him, and I should like to see him revived as they are reviving Anthony Trollope, whose merit, whatever may be thought of their comparative value, was of a much less singular and original sort.

I am yours sincerely

A. E. HOUSMAN

---

[1] Frazer gives an account of the Argei in his edition of Ovid's *Fasti*, volume 4, p. 74. They were effigies of men made from rushes thrown annually from the Pons Sublicius in Rome into the Tiber.

[2] Librarian of Trinity College, Cambridge, 1924–1957.

[3] Thomas Stearns Eliot (1888–1965), the American-born poet and critic; editor of *The Criterion* and a director of the publishing firm of Faber and Gwyer (later Faber and Faber); awarded the Nobel Prize for Literature and appointed to the Order of Merit, 1948.

[4] Eliot wrote an introduction for the Oxford University Press edition of *The Moonstone*, 1928. He seems to have asked Housman to do the same for another of Collins' books.

To the Earl of Oxford and Asquith[1]

MS. BODLEY

22 April 1926   Trinity College

Dear Lord Oxford,

I am much obliged by your kindness in sending me your address on Scaliger,[2] a short report of which I had been interested to read in the papers. One statement which both you and Sandys[3] have made in reliance on Mark Pattison,[4] that Scaliger in the Manilius of 1579 passed from textual criticism to chronology, is not true. There is hardly a word about chronology in the book, which is in fact his greatest work in textual criticism; and this study continued to occupy him long after the *Emendatio temporum* of 1583, for the second edition of Manilius in 1600, when he had at last got hold of a good manuscript, was much enlarged and in great part rewritten. Pattison had never read the book: he was a spectator of all time and all existence, and the contemplation of that repulsive scene is fatal to accurate learning.[5]

I am yours very truly   A. E. HOUSMAN

To Percy Withers

MS. WITHERS

23 April 1926   Trinity College

My dear Withers,

I was just thinking of writing to you about Lewis's death. He left Cambridge only about a fortnight or three weeks before, and seemed in his usual health, but for the last twelvemonth he had been aging, and his articulation had grown very indistinct. At Godalming, where he was staying with his sister, he had an attack of what the doctors called false angina pectoris, but he had got better, and on the morning of the day when he died he wrote a letter; in the afternoon he went to his bedroom to sleep, and was found dead. The cause of death was given as a clot in the lungs. He was buried from Oriel, and

---

[1] Herbert Henry Asquith (1852–1928); Member of Parliament, 1886–1918 and 1920–1924; Home Secretary, 1892–1895; Chancellor of the Exchequer, 1905–1908; Prime Minister, 1908–1916; created Earl of Oxford and Asquith, 1925.

[2] Presidential address to the Scottish Classical Association delivered in Edinburgh on 20 March 1926.

[3] In *A History of Classical Scholarship*, 1903–1908, volume 2, p. 202. His essay on Scaliger was first published in *The Quarterly Review*, 1860.

[4] 1813–1884; Rector of Lincoln College, Oxford, 1861–1884.

[5] An echo of Scaliger's remark on Pliny (quoted by Asquith): 'Fere omnia tractavit: nil exacte.'

our Vice-Master went over to represent the College: the other Lewis[1] and Hicks[2] were also there.

You do not give definite information about your own health, but I hope no news is good news. I expect to be away for the first half of June, and again for about a month from 26 July; but outside those periods I know of nothing to keep me from your arms. I remember no spring so early as this, not even 1893.

With kind regards to Mrs Withers I am yours sincerely

A. E. HOUSMAN

To A. F. Scholfield

MS. TRINITY

8 May 1926   *Trinity College*

Dear Scholfield,

Maittaire's *Opera et fragmenta poetarum Latinorum*, 1713, though obsolete, is a book which a University Library ought to have, and I have sometimes wanted to consult it.

The editio princeps of Manilius (Regiomontanus') is interesting to scholars as well as bibliophiles, for its merit and authorship, and Jenkinson, when I was trying to buy a copy for myself, offered to buy one for the Library out of some fund which he said was available; but I did not feel justified in taking advantage of that, and the copy I was after sold for £60.

Yours sincerely   A. E. HOUSMAN

To Katharine Symons

MS. TRINITY

2 June 1926   *Trinity College*

My dear Kate,

I should write to tell you that I am going abroad on Saturday for a fortnight or three weeks: first on a short visit to Venice, where my poor gondolier says he is dying[3] and wants to see me again, and then to Paris.

Laurence was here a month ago and seemed well and thriving, as I hope are you and Edward.

Your affectionate brother   A. E. HOUSMAN

---

[1] Thomas Crompton Lewis (1851–1929); Fellow of Trinity College, 1877; employed in the Indian Education Service, 1881–1906; thereafter lived in Cambridge and served on the Board of Indian Civil Service Studies.

[2] Robert Drew Hicks (1850–1929), Fellow of Trinity College.

[3] Housman gave him money during this illness, but was infuriated to receive begging letters from the family after the man's death in 1930.

To A. S. F. Gow

MS. TRINITY

4 June 1926   *Trinity College*

Dear Gow,

I am very much taken aback, and my feelings are mixed; but, however deeply I may deplore the misdirection of so much industry, it is impossible not to be touched and pleased by the proof of so much kindness and friendliness, and I thank you for it.[1]

Yours sincerely   A. E. HOUSMAN

To A. F. Scholfield

MS. TRINITY

5 June 1926   *Trinity College*

Dear Scholfield,

I take a double pleasure in the gift I received yesterday from you and Gow and others, because it evinces both friendly feelings and a scholarly interest in the infinitely little.

Yours   A. E. HOUSMAN

To Katharine Symons

MS. TRINITY

23 June 1926   *Trinity College*

My dear Kate,

I got back safe yesterday, after three days' beautiful weather in Venice and a very dull time in Paris till just the last. My gondolier was looking pretty well, as warmth suits him, but he is quite unable to row and gets out of breath if he goes up many stairs. He is being sent by the municipal authorities for another three months' treatment in hospital, as they still find bacilli in his blood, and I suppose he will go steadily down hill. I was surprised to find what pleasure it gave me to be in Venice again. It was like coming home, when sounds and smells which one had forgotten stole upon one's senses; and certainly there is no place like it in the world: everything there is better in reality than in memory. I first saw it on a romantic evening after sunset in 1900, and I left it on a sunshiny morning, and I shall not go there again.

---

[1] Gow had compiled and arranged the printing of a complete list of Housman's articles and other contributions to periodicals. It is reprinted in a revised form in his *A. E. Housman: A Sketch*, 1936.

I enclose a notice about the Woodchester pavement,[1] which you may wish to see. I shall be there from 31 July to 7 August.

I did not know of our grandfather's christening feat. It must have been just when he was leaving Stroud for Woodchester, and I suppose he wanted to clear things up.

Your affectionate brother   A. E. HOUSMAN

To Percy Withers

MS. WITHERS

7 July 1926   *Trinity College*

My dear Withers,

I am very much grieved to hear that you are laid up, and I suffer on both sides of my nature, the altruistic and the egotistic. I hope it is not very serious and will not last long. My gondolier, who had summoned me to his death-bed, was quite revived by the summer weather: pray follow his example.

Yours sincerely   A. E. HOUSMAN

To A. F. Scholfield

MS. TRINITY

21 July 1926   *Trinity College*

Dear Scholfield,

It appears that the Library has a rule by which not more than five books can be had out for a person in statu pupillari. I do not know if this is ever widened, but, if so, it might properly be done for W. H. Semple,[2] a research student in St John's College, who is studying Apollinaris Sidonius under my direction and finds that five books are not enough to work with and that the books he wants are not to be found elsewhere than in the Library. He is a graduate of Belfast, and has acted for three years as assistant to the Professors of Latin and of English there.

Yours sincerely   A. E. HOUSMAN

---

[1] A Roman pavement discovered in the churchyard.
[2] William Hugh Semple (born 1900), Hulme Professor of Latin at Manchester, 1935–1967.

To an Unnamed Correspondent

MS. NEWCASTLE

25 July 1926   *Trinity College*

Dear Sir,

I do not feel able to refuse your request, and I have copied and signed two poems. If I do not say that I hope this will do the good you expect, it is because I have one thing in common with Keats and am incapable of hope.[1]

Yours very truly   A. E. HOUSMAN

To F. W. Hall

MS. SPARROW

21 September 1926   *Trinity College*

My dear Hall,

Many thanks for the photographs. I much prefer Dodd[2] to Rothenstein, who never gets a likeness of anyone, being presumably too great an artist.

I enclose the list of Adversaria. Some years ago your Librarian, Stevenson[3] I think it was, asked me for copies of the Adversaria themselves. The offprints were then in packages on a top shelf, and I had not the courage to tackle them; but Gow has sorted them out, and I now have a set, not complete however, which I mean to send when I have found time to correct misprints and such things.

Yours sincerely   A. E. HOUSMAN

To Percy Withers

MS. WITHERS

21 September 1926   *Trinity College*

My dear Withers,

This is very good and delightful news about your health, and apparently the consequence of shingles!

Ye fearful saints, fresh courage take:
The clouds ye so much dread

---

[1] See Keats's letter to Mrs Brawne, 24 October 1820: 'If ever there was a person born without the faculty of hope, I am he.'

[2] Francis Dodd (1874–1949) was in 1926 commissioned by St John's College, Oxford, to make a portrait drawing of Housman. It is reproduced in *A. E. Housman* by A. S. F. Gow, 1936.

[3] William Henry Stevenson (1858–1924); Fellow and Librarian of St John's College, 1904–1924.

240

Are big with mercy, and shall break
In blessings on your head.[1]

I hope Sussex and Kent will give the finishing touches. Do not miss Box-grove, four miles from Chichester, with its black marble.

I have seen some good ones too: Coventry for the first time, Southwell, Newark and Tideswell. I have been spending a month in Gloucestershire and Worcestershire, winding up with a motor-tour through Derbyshire, which was new to me. Consequently I have had my full allowance of running about, and am now settled down to work in this quietest of the Cambridge months; so that I shall put off availing myself of your kind invitation. The peaches on the bowling-green are ripe, and a good crop, as they generally are; and the younger fellows of the College, in spite of their aversion from port, stay after dinner to eat them in the Combination Room.

Now that Lewis is gone, I don't know whom to send you news of. I think that the Master of Magdalene,[2] though his home is in Croughton and I believe he is there now, is not an acquaintance of yours, though quite a desirable one. My kind regards to Mrs Withers.

Yours sincerely   A. E. HOUSMAN

To F. W. Hall

MS. TEXAS

12 October 1926   *Trinity College*

Dear Hall,

Very many thanks for the new photograph,[3] which is even better than the old.

We have just elected two Fellows, a classic and a mathematician,[4] as in the good old days.

Yours sincerely   A. E. HOUSMAN

To S. C. Roberts

MS. PRIVATE

14 October 1926   *Trinity College*

Dear Roberts,

A report of mine, some twenty years ago, decided the Syndics not to accept a treatise of Richmond's on the pagination of the archetype of Catullus'

---

[1] The third verse of Cowper's hymn, 'God moves in a mysterious way'.
[2] Allen Beville Ramsay (1872–1955), assistant master at Eton College, 1895–1925; Master of Magdalene College, 1925–1947.
[3] Of the portrait by Dodd.
[4] R. M. Rattenbury and L. H. Thomas.

MSS;[1] and, as A. W. Ward,[2] who was his grandmother or some such relation, had gone and told him that I was the referee, he knew to whom he was indebted. He bore me no ill will, and has an almost embarrassing respect for me; and I am not willing to risk the chance of doing him another ill turn. He is an active and competent chaser and collator of MSS, but I seldom agree with his criticism or interpretation. That should not count against him, as I should have to say the same of several scholars whose works are printed by University Presses, and they would naturally say the same of me.

If it is not impertinent, I suggest that H. E. Butler might be asked for his opinion. I daresay the Syndics, or some of them, know enough about the passions which seethe in the world of classical scholarship to understand that there is one person to whom the work should not be submitted.[3]

I asked the Syndics through their Secretary that my former report, which was very elaborate, might be returned to me, if that were legitimate: as it did not come, I suppose it was not.

Yours sincerely   A. E. HOUSMAN

To F. W. Hall

MS. LILLY

20 October 1926   *Trinity College*

Dear Hall,

I still have by me the famous bone of contention.[4] When the Board of Management offered to have it inserted, I declined, because I thought it would be humiliating to Arnold; but that obstacle no longer exists. Its length, 20 foolscap pages of my handwriting, may be greater than what you are in want of.

Yours sincerely   A. E. HOUSMAN

To Grant Richards

TEXT: RICHARDS

21 October 1926   *[Trinity College]*

I do not want to take the books away from your firm.[5] The *vis inertiae*, no longer regarded as a true cause in the physical world, governs me all the same.

---

[1] Oliffe Leigh Richmond (born 1881); Fellow of King's College, Cambridge, 1905; Professor of Humanity at Edinburgh University, 1919–1948. The treatise on Catullus remained unpublished. He had now produced an edition of Propertius, which was issued by the Cambridge University Press in 1928.

[2] Adolphus William Ward (1837–1924); Master of Peterhouse, Cambridge, 1900–1924; editor-in-chief of *The Cambridge Modern History*, 1901–1912; knighted, 1913.

[3] J. S. Phillimore.

[4] See the letter of 15 January 1923.

[5] Richards' firm was sold and reorganized as the Richards Press.

242

To S. C. Roberts

MS. C.U.P.

29 October 1926   *Trinity College*

Dear Roberts,

Your order for Platt's *Essays* is logical in itself, but in some cases it visibly conflicts with the order in which they were composed. In particular, "Fitz-Gerald", which is the earliest of all, ought not to come after "Cervantes" nor near "Cervantes", because in "FitzGerald" he speaks of himself as knowing hardly any Spanish, whereas when he wrote "Cervantes" he knew it quite well.

"Plato on the Immortality of the Soul" (a title which will have to be altered) rightly stands last, and I should like to put first "Arts and Science among the Ancients", which is the most carefully written and was delivered before a large public; then between them the Literary Society essays, whose chronology I roughly know, in an order nearly that of their date, which can best be managed by sandwiching ancient and modern subjects. I give the list over the page.

Yours sincerely   A. E. HOUSMAN

1. Arts and Science among the Ancients.
2. FitzGerald.
3. Lucian.
4. La Rochefoucauld.
5. Aristophanes.
6. Cervantes.
7. Julian.
8. Poetry and Science.
9. Plato on the Immortality of the Soul.[1]

To Katharine Symons

MS. TRINITY

14 November 1926   *Trinity College*

My dear Kate,

I knew it was a long time since I had written to you, but did not realise how long, and fancied that I wrote when I came back here at the end of August. The week at Woodchester was fine: the pavement, which I had seen the last time it was opened, 35 years ago, attracted great numbers and was kept open for a second week. I was dragged in to make speeches explaining it, as there were few local orators to do so, and the visitors were very ignorant

---

[1] This, with one small exception (3 and 5 reversed), was the order adopted. See p. 248.

and very grateful. I had pleasant motor journeys from Bromsgrove and back by different routes. Basil was not well enough to come with me. The two stays at Tardebigge were quiet and agreeable. Then I spent the inside of a week motoring about Derbyshire, which was new to me, and in parts very picturesque indeed, especially Dovedale, of which I walked the best ten miles. September I passed here in pleasant and peaceful work.

Your house looks nice, and I am glad that you are so content with it. Laurence was here in the summer,[1] to arrange for performing his plays here this term; but as I have heard no more about it I suppose it fell through. We have good store of coal in the college, which we eke out with wood, and I am not stinted.[2]

I am glad your sons are going on well, and I hope your husband is. Send the *Shropshire Lad* for signature by all means: I am used to it.

Your affectionate brother   A. E. HOUSMAN

To H. E. Butler

MS. ST JOHN'S

21 November 1926   *Trinity College*

Dear Butler,

The University Press here is bringing out a collection of Platt's papers, and I have undertaken to write a preface; and, for the purposes of plagiarism, I want to get hold of your obituary in *The Times*[3] and Chambers' in the College Magazine.[4] If you have these and will lend them to me, I will return them faithfully. I feel sure that I really have them myself, but if so I cannot lay my hands on them. If you have not the *Times* notice, could you give me the date? That wretched publication Whitaker's *Almanack* does not.

Yours sincerely   A. E. HOUSMAN

To S. C. Roberts

MS. C.U.P.

12 December 1926   *Trinity College*

Dear Roberts,

I enclose the preface I promised for Platt's book, and also, what is more valuable, a list which I have compiled of his writings.

---

[1] On 30 April Laurence Housman gave a reading from his *Little Plays of St Francis* to the English Association.

[2] The coal shortage resulted from the miners' strike, which began on 30 April and went on for most of the year.

[3] For 17 March 1925.   [4] *The University College Magazine*, June 1925.

Is there to be a portrait? It would be a great addition, and there is an excellent photograph.

I feel sure that it will be necessary for me to see the proofs of Platt's essays.

Yours sincerely   A. E. HOUSMAN

To Grant Richards

TEXT: RICHARDS

17 December 1926   [*Trinity College*]

I suppose the new arrangement is satisfactory to you, and if so I am glad of it; and for my own part it is a relief not to have the bother of making new arrangements. But when the arrangements are complete I am going to exact royalties on *A Shropshire Lad* for the future as well as on the other book.

To Sir Frederick Macmillan[1]

MS. MACMILLAN

27 December 1926   *Trinity College*

Dear Sir Frederick Macmillan,

I am much obliged by your amiable letter. The Lucan however was published last January, and is now nearly sold out, which testifies to such efficiency in the publisher as even you could hardly surpass.

I am yours sincerely   A. E. HOUSMAN

To Charles Wilson[2]

MS. NEWCASTLE

7 January 1927   *Trinity College*

Dear Mr Wilson,

Many thanks for your photograph of Keats's grave. When I was in Rome I failed to find it, though I found Shelley's.

[1] Frederick Orridge Macmillan (1851–1936); chairman of Messrs Macmillan and Company, 1896–1936; knighted, 1909. See p. 223. On 22 December 1926 he wrote to Housman asking if the firm might publish his edition of Lucan after all. 'I remember thinking at the time that this was possibly a case in which it would be wise to relax our rule but I expect that what decided us not to do so was a phrase in your letter describing us as "haughty". . . . It may be that it is too late, but this letter will at all events convince you that the quality of humility has not been omitted from our composition.'

[2] Charles Wilson, the 'pitman poet' of Willington, Co. Durham (1891–1967), published a number of poems in pamphlet form, 1915–1916. In later years he dealt in books and autographs, and appears to have corresponded with Housman chiefly in order to acquire his answers. His *Collected Poems* appeared in 1915.

245

As to your enquiry about my lectures, none of them have been published, and they are all very dry.

I am yours very truly   A. E. HOUSMAN

To Alice Rothenstein

MS. HARVARD

16 January 1927   *Trinity College*

Dear Mrs Rothenstein,

The evening before I got your letter I had been at the Cornfords'[1] and we had been talking about you and your family, and I was glad to hear from them that William was much better and also your eldest daughter. I congratulate you also on your second daughter's scholarship,[2] and hope you will enjoy yourselves in Italy. Your story about the sycamores is just like what has happened in the Woodchester valley. On the east side there used to be a belt of beeches half way up the hill, dividing the downs from the fields, and making a piece of scenery which in its way was as beautiful as anything anywhere; and now the greater part of them are down and the whole look of the place changed. You might tell William that he has lost his monopoly in my features, as I have been drawn this last year for my two Colleges by two artists named Dodd and Gleadowe.[3] The two drawings are very unlike, but neither of them makes me look so nasty as the portrait which this College bought from William, and so prevented him, to my great relief, from exhibiting it any more in public and from adding malignant touches from time to time, as he used to do when he was out of temper. But I have a beautiful and forgiving nature, and I wish him as well as you a happy new year in response to your wishes for me.

Yours sincerely   A. E. HOUSMAN

To Cyril Clemens[4]

2 February 1927   *Trinity College*

Dear Mr Clemens,

Although the office of honorary Vice-President of the Mark Twain Society

[1] Francis Macdonald Cornford (1874–1943); Fellow of Trinity College, Cambridge since 1899; Professor of Ancient Philosophy, 1931; husband of Frances Cornford.

[2] Betty Rothenstein (later Mrs Ensor Holiday) had won a scholarship to the Royal College of Art.

[3] Reginald Morier York Gleadowe (1888–1944), Slade Professor of Fine Art at Oxford, 1928–1933, made a drawing of Housman for Trinity College, Cambridge.

[4] American author (born 1902), biographer of President Truman and Lord Attlee, nephew of Samuel Langhorne Clemens (Mark Twain) and President of the International Mark Twain Society. This letter is printed in facsimile in his *An Evening with A. E. Housman*, 1937.

246

is a reward beyond the merits of any efforts which I may have made to write poetry, it is a token of kindness on your part, and one for which I offer the Society my thanks.

The elegy on Stephen Dowling Botts in *Huckleberry Finn*[1] is one of the poems I know by heart.

I am yours very truly   A. E. HOUSMAN

To Grant Richards

TEXT: RICHARDS

9 February 1927   *[Trinity College]*

I don't allow the wireless people to recite my poems, but as I allow the poems to be sung to music there is no reason why the songs should not be broadcast. I daresay the music is spoilt, but that is the composer's look out; and the words are mostly inaudible.

To Martin Secker

MS. BROWN

15 February 1927   *Trinity College*

Dear Mr Secker,

From time to time I receive from you kind presents of books, which perhaps I do not always acknowledge; but I certainly must thank you for *Jew Süss*,[2] a work much spoken of and one which I have been meaning to read.

Yours sincerely   A. E. HOUSMAN

To H. E. Butler

MS. ST JOHN'S

26 February 1927   *Trinity College*

Dear Butler,

I am very much obliged to you and the Librarian, and I am ashamed to trouble you further. But the date of 1917 for the La Rochefoucauld[3] can only be the date of a second reading, for I heard it read myself; it must therefore have been before 1911, and my impression is that it was a good many years before.

[1] *The Adventures of Huckleberry Finn* by Mark Twain, 1884.
[2] By Lion Feuchtwanger, 1925; first English edition, 1926.
[3] In Platt's *Nine Essays*. The correct date was 1902.

The whole thing is not of great importance, but if I cannot get all the dates I must omit all.

Yours sincerely A. E. HOUSMAN

To S. C. Roberts

MS. C.U.P.

1 March 1927 *Trinity College*

Dear Roberts,

Herewith the proofs of Platt's *Nine Essays* corrected *for revise*, and manuscript of three extracts for insertion.

The Preface and Bibliography will not need to pass through the stage of revise, so I am keeping the proofs of them for the present.

Would it be a troublous matter to make "Lucian" and "Aristophanes" change places? That would agree better with what I now find to be the chronological order.

Yours sincerely A. E. HOUSMAN

You may notice that I have not added the date of "Julian", but I hope to get it.

Postcard to Grant Richards

TEXT: RICHARDS

1 March 1927 [*Trinity College*]

I have just seen an edition of *A Shropshire Lad*, 1925, with a disgusting misprint, souls' for soul's, on p. 99:[1] how many more I don't know. I have said again and again that new editions must be sent to me for correction.

To Mrs Withers

MS. WITHERS

11 March 1927 *Trinity College*

Dear Mrs Withers,

It will relieve your kind heart to know that I did not at all feel the need of a rug, and got home without any alloyment of the pleasure of my stay with you.

Your attentive handmaids however seem to have retained two pairs of boots as a souvenir, and perhaps you will notice them wearing them for earrings.

With kind regards to both of you I am yours sincerely A. E. HOUSMAN

[1] In LXII line 56.

To Percy Withers

MS. WITHERS

26 March 1927   *Trinity College*

My dear Withers,

I am shocked to find that yours is among the rather numerous letters which I have left unanswered in the last fortnight, which has been rather busy. Yours is indeed a vexatious experience. That seizure of pain on making a sudden motion is the sort of thing I sometimes had thirty years ago, before I learnt to keep sciatica at bay; but God forbid that I should compare my puny ailments with yours. I hope you are now making up for the backsliding. I am quite well: last week I thought I had a gouty toe, but that was mere conceit, like Bloody Mary's pregnancy,[1] and the doctor said it was a corn, and cut it there and then.

As for the visit you kindly propose, any week-end in May except the last would probably suit me. Our crocuses too have been magnificent: two years ago we planted thousands at the near end of our avenue, where there used to be none, and they now eclipse the rest.

Bridges does not send me much of his new-fangled stuff,[2] because he has given up hopes of converting me to it. He will be sorry for the death of his friend and almost neighbour Wicksteed.[3]

My kind regards to Mrs Withers.

Yours sincerely   A. E. HOUSMAN

To Mrs Platt

MS. U.C.L.

8 April 1927   *Trinity College*

Dear Mrs Platt,

About the Daddy Wordsworth passage[4] I felt just as you do, but the only thing I ventured to cut out on the ground that I disapproved was an uncalled for reference to a living person. When I get the revise (I hope it is the revise which you have got, not the first proof, which was full of blunders) I will consult the Secretary of the Press and see what can be done.

---

[1] Mary Tudor's confinement was expected at the end of April 1555. She declared that she could feel the child; but though she remained swollen the pains passed without result.

[2] Bridges' last volume at this date was *New Verse*, 1925. *The Testament of Beauty* was privately printed and issued in parts from 1927. His later poems contained many metrical experiments, and he adopted a reformed spelling in both verse and prose.

[3] Philip Henry Wicksteed (1844–1927), Unitarian Minister, theologian, political economist, lecturer, prolific writer and translator.

[4] In *Nine Essays*, p. 181, in 'Poetry and Science': 'I am really sorry to knock up so often against Daddy Wordsworth, as FitzGerald called him; he was a most respectable old gentleman and he wrote some magnificent poetry, but it is hard to keep from laughing at him.'

I am sorry to hear that Dorothy[1] has been so unwell: she used to look the picture of health. I hope you enjoyed Italy.

Yours sincerely   A. E. HOUSMAN

To Mrs Platt

MS. U.C.L.

19 April 1927   *Trinity College*

Dear Mrs Platt,

I will try what can be done about sparing the feelings of the relations of liars.[2] I will see that you get back the manuscripts and the Quarto when there is no longer any chance of their being required for verification.

The people at University College let me see the little book of sonnets:[3] the one which Professor Collie[4] speaks of is I suppose that which was written in the spring of the last year of his life, and it is very touching.

I am yours sincerely   A. E. HOUSMAN

To S. C. Roberts

MS. C.U.P.

22 April 1927   *Trinity College*

Dear Roberts,

Mrs Platt writes to me desiring, I think rightly, to have two sentences of Platt's modified; so we shall have to see what can be done. I have not yet received the revise, though I suppose that the revise was what was sent to Edward Platt a few weeks ago.

Yours sincerely   A. E. HOUSMAN

To S. C. Roberts

MS. PRIVATE

27 April 1927   *Trinity College*

Dear Roberts,

I enclose the whole of the Platt volume corrected for press, except that I do not know how to correct the portrait, which is spotty.

---

[1] Platt's daughter.

[2] A reference to the essay on Lucian in *Nine Essays*, p. 111: 'Also those who had told lies and written them in books were hung up by their tongues, Ctesias the historian and Herodotus and Marco Polo and Sir John Mandeville and many others.' The manuscript evidently mentioned other more recent liars.

[3] By Platt; privately printed by University College, London.

[4] 1859–1942; Professor of Organic Chemistry at University College, London, 1902–1928.

You will see that most of your queries are negatived, which is because we think that Platt meant to write as he did.

As to the necessity of the note on p. 2, one of my two partners did not know the meaning of 'declared', and queried it.[1] At p. 66 Roger Fry's 'average' will be a great puzzle.[2] You are old enough to know who Gunn and Shrewsbury[3] were, but the number of those who do is always lessening, and they are on their way to join 'the celebrated Mrs Rudd', who was a subject of conversation at General Paoli's on 28 April 1778,[4] and is not in the *Dictionary of National Biography*. But my true object in adding the notes was to win a smile from Platt's beatified spirit and mitigate the tedium of Paradise.

Mrs Platt is Mildred, Miss Platt is Dorothy.

Yours sincerely   A. E. HOUSMAN

To S. C. Roberts

MS. PRIVATE

4 May 1927   *Trinity College*

Dear Roberts,

I have made a very necessary correction on the title-page. The essays are not edited by me but by three persons of whom I am one: if I had been sole editor I could not have allowed p. 178 to appear.[5]

The portrait in its present condition makes Platt look much more battered than he was.

Yours sincerely   A. E. HOUSMAN

To S. C. Roberts

MS. PRIVATE

22 May 1927   *Trinity College*

Dear Roberts,

I shrink from looking through a work on English Prosody; but Sir George

---

[1] 'They said that science was the one thing needful, that arts had had an unconscionably long innings and it was time they declared.' Housman's note reads: *Terms borrowed from the game of cricket.*

[2] 'The world is too much with us, and we think the average of Mr Fry or the colour of a riband to be more important to us.' Housman noted: *A cricketer of the day.* The cricketer meant was C. B. Fry (1872–1956), the celebrated batsman; Roger Fry (1866–1934), painter and writer on art, was Slade Professor of Fine Art at Cambridge, 1933–1934.

[3] Housman here also noted that they were cricketers.

[4] In Boswell's *Life of Johnson.* Mrs Rudd was a forger who was sensationally acquitted when her two accomplices were found guilty.

[5] The two others were presumably Parry and Butler. Page 178 reads, in part: 'Professor Housman has now left us so long that we may be permitted to speak of him in this Society as what he is, the most exquisite poet of our own times.'

Young[1] has talked to me on the subject, and is a competent observer who has really thought about it, and would not give you such shallow and ignorant stuff as Saintsbury's three volumes.[2]

The Poet Laureate, who takes a fierce interest in the matter, might possibly consent to read the work, but might not write you a very judicial report. Lascelles Abercrombie[3] is perhaps qualified.

Yours sincerely   A. E. HOUSMAN

To Wilbur Cross

MS. YALE

25 May 1927   *Trinity College*

Dear Sir,

My 'Fragment of a Greek Tragedy' was written in 1883 and printed in a school magazine. It has since appeared in two college magazines and also, with more publicity, in the *Cornhill* of 1901. If you think it worth while to print it a fifth time, I can make no objection.[4] I have no copy, but the *Cornhill* is probably accessible to you at Yale. In the circumstances I cannot accept the honorarium you are kind enough to offer, but I should like to see and correct the proofs, as on the last occasion when it was printed[5] I made a few changes which I think are improvements.

I am yours very truly   A. E. HOUSMAN

To Katharine Symons

MS. TRINITY

19 August 1927   *Trinity College*

My dear Kate,

It occurs to me that I have not written to you for a long while and that I had better let you know I am going to London to-day and to Paris to-morrow, where my address till the 24th will be Royal Monceau Hotel, Avenue Hoche, and thence probably into Burgundy.[6] I expect to be away about a month.

---

[1] Third baronet; barrister and magistrate (1837–1930). His book, *An English Prosody on Inductive Lines*, was published by the Cambridge University Press in 1928.

[2] *History of English Prosody*, 1906–1910.

[3] Poet and critic (1881–1938); Professor of English at Leeds, 1922–1929; in London University, 1929–1935.

[4] It was printed in *The Yale Review*, 1928.

[5] In *The Trinity Magazine*, 1921. Housman probably did not yet know of a privately printed version produced in America at the Snail's Pace Press, Amherst, 1925.

[6] On a motor tour with Richards.

You most likely are not at Bath, but I don't think you gave me a sketch of how you meant to spend the summer. You probably heard that I was prevented from going on from Woodchester to Tardebigge[1] in June because one of their maids fell off a bicycle. I hope you and all of yours are well.

Your affectionate brother   A. E. HOUSMAN

To Mr Leippert[2]

MS. BRITTON

19 September 1927   *Trinity College*

Dear Mr Leippert,
    I am just returned from travelling on the Continent. I am quite willing to write my name in your book, which I have often done even for people who have not been christened after me.

Yours very truly   A. E. HOUSMAN

To Katharine Symons

MS. LILLY

20 September 1927   *Trinity College*

My dear Kate,
    What I wrote to you from Paris was nothing but an egotistical note to inform you of my doings and intentions. I received your letter all right, but could not lay my hand on it at the time. I am very glad that your anxieties about Denis and Jerry are happily at an end. At Woodchester I saw Mr Aynsley and his daughters, but not his wife. They are quite new-comers there, having the house just above the Wises, which belonged to the youngest sister of Miss Dorothea Beale, who died last year.
    I flew home by the new 'Silver Wing' aeroplane, which is more roomy and steadier, and contains an attendant to supply you with cheese and biscuits and various liquors, and to point out objects of interest on the route: also an emergency door in the roof, which ought to be very tranquillising. But I did not enjoy it, as I had got ptomaine poisoning in Paris from stale fish, for the third time in my experience, and I am still rather out of sorts. The weather had been very dull, but we struck sunshine in the Channel.
    Love to all.

Your affectionate brother   A. E. HOUSMAN

---

[1] To stay with his brother Basil.
[2] Not identified.

253

To John Drinkwater

MS. MARQUETTE

3 October 1927   *Trinity College*

Dear Mr Drinkwater,

A *Shropshire Lad* is not copyright in the United States, and consequently my consent is not required; but if the book[1] were to be published in England, I should object, in fairness to the many anthologists to whom I have said no in the past.

Extracts from *Last Poems* I have sometimes allowed; but I am not anxious to draw down upon myself the fate which Horace dreaded,[2] and suffer recitation in schools.

I shall hope to see you when you are in Cambridge.

Yours sincerely   A. E. HOUSMAN

To Grant Richards

TEXT: RICHARDS

17 October 1927   *Trinity College*

Many thanks for your list of wines in Burgundy, and also for the reminiscences[3] appended. Your memory is better than mine in most respects; but I think that at Feurs what we had was two bottles of white wine (the first probably *Pouilly-Fuissé*) and then half a bottle of *Moulin-à-vent*. The Ballottine de pigeonneau at Chablis, as I remember it, was slices of cold pâté. Do not forget the onion-cheese soup at the Chateaubriant.

Montrachet Ainé cannot owe its origin to Saintsbury,[4] for I find it in a much older book by Vizetelly.[5]

> Aequam memento rebus in arduis
> Servare mentem (Horace *Odes* III. 3. 1–2)

means "be sure to preserve a tranquil mind amidst difficulties".

I have read and noted what you say about starting business again, and the proposals as regards my poems seem to be satisfactory; only I should object to the two books being issued in the same form at the same price, as the one is less than two-thirds of the other in length.

I had not heard that Manilius I was out of print, but I expect it is true; and the Juvenal must be very nearly so.

---

[1] *Twentieth-Century Poetry*, edited by John Drinkwater, Henry Seidel Canby and William Rose Benét, New York, 1929. No English edition appeared.
[2] See *Epistles* I. xx.
[3] Of their tour in August and September.
[4] *Notes on a Cellar-Book*, 1920.
[5] *Wines of the World* by Henry Vizetelly, 1875.

To John Drinkwater

MS. MARQUETTE

20 October 1927   *Trinity College*

Dear Mr Drinkwater,

I shall be very glad if you will come to tea at four o'clock to-morrow. I put it as early as 4, because I want to go to Valéry's lecture at 5.[1]

Yours sincerely   A. E. HOUSMAN

Postcard to Stephen Gaselee

MS. CAMBRIDGE

9 November 1927   *Trinity College*

Thanks; I have plodded through De Vreese.[2] He has mugged up a lot of astrology; but what a goose, trying to make Trimalchio an expert and Petronius a fool.

A.E.H.

To the Richards Press

MS. B.M.

14 November 1927   *Trinity College*

Dear Sirs,

I shall insist on any right I may possess to have the quotation removed from p. ii of this book;[3] and the book will be improved by its removal. It is dragged in, and has nothing to do with the authors' argument; in eight lines they have made seven alterations (and one in Macaulay over the page); and it was not the German Emperor but the German people which called ours a mercenary army, as in fact it was and is.

I am yours faithfully   A. E. HOUSMAN

To Edward Symons[4]

MS. LILLY

21 November 1927   *Trinity College*

My dear Symons,

I enclose what I suppose to be a translation of the verses. I am glad to hear

---

[1] Paul Valéry, French poet (1871–1945), lectured on *L'Inspiration Poétique*.
[2] *Petron und die Astrologie* by J. G. W. M. de Vreese, 1927.
[3] I have failed to discover which book is meant.
[4] His brother-in-law.

255

of your success in banting:[1] I could give up most of the things your doctor denies you without much difficulty, even pastry as made in this College kitchen. Love to Kate, who may like to know that the other day I had a second visit from a Mr Palmer,[2] an official in Nigeria, who is a descendant of our great-great-grandfather through his daughter Mary and the Higgins.

Yours sincerely   A. E. HOUSMAN

To Percy Withers

MS. WITHERS

29 November 1927   *Trinity College*

My dear Withers,
    I suppose you have long ago trodden the Italian winepress to the skins and stalks and are now at home again, feeling as well, I hope, as you seemed to be feeling when you wrote to me from Siena. I spent a month in France in August–September, half of it on a motor-tour through Burgundy, Franche Comté, the Jura, Lyons and Clermont-Ferrand, in company with Grant Richards, eating much trout and écrevisse and drinking wine which was not as old as one ought to find in its land of origin. All this fortnight was fine weather where I was, though in Paris and generally north of the Alps it was as wretched as most of the summer. I have never seen so much of France at one time before.
    With kind regards to Mrs Withers I am

Yours sincerely   A. E. HOUSMAN

John Drinkwater called on me about a month ago; he was delivering addresses to the male and female young.

To Grant Richards

TEXT: RICHARDS

13 December 1927   *[Trinity College]*

Miss Hemmerde[3] has sent me Corvo's book,[4] which I have read and will shortly return. When he depicts Italians or describes Venice it is delightful; the talk about himself I skip; the quarrels with other people show them in a

---

[1] Dieting.
[2] (Herbert) Richmond Palmer (1877–1958); Governor of the Gambia, 1930–1933; Governor of Cyprus, 1933–1939; knighted, 1933.
[3] Richards' secretary.
[4] Typescript of *The Desire and Pursuit of the Whole*, published in 1934.

256

better light than him. I am obliged to Mr A. J. A. Symons[1] for presenting me with his biography.[2] I don't know whether the *Dialogus*[3] also sent is a present from him or from you or whether I should return it. It is in decent Latin, and the matter is mildly interesting, though it leaves me calm. I don't know if it is Corvo's: my passions would probably be more inflamed by his letters,[4] which are what I thought you were going to send me.

I am thinking that it is time for a cheaper edition of *Last Poems*. I have not said so to the publishers yet.

To Basil Housman

MS. LILLY

29 December 1927   *Trinity College*

My dear Basil,

I have had a terrible shock from a telegram to-day from a London fishmonger. All the native oysters have been torn from their beds by tempest, and I shall have to eat the New Year in on Dutch. For me it therefore opens gloomily, but I hope that you and Jeannie will not find it saddened by any such calamity.

I spent four weeks of August and September in France; and the fortnight during which I was motoring about Burgundy and the east with Grant Richards was very successful, for we were followed about by fine weather and able to see a great deal. The present cold finds me prepared, as I have just got two new gas stoves, 'Sunbeam', recommended by an expert, which give much more heat and burn much less gas than those which I inherited from my predecessor in these rooms.

I had a visit not long ago from Clarence Darrow, the great American barrister for defending murderers.[5] He had only a few days in England, but he could not return home without seeing me, because he had so often used my poems to rescue his clients from the electric chair. Loeb and Leopold owe their life sentence partly to me; and he gave me a copy of his speech, in which, sure enough, two of my pieces are misquoted.

Don't trouble to acknowledge what my banker sends to yours at the New Year,—unless he doesn't, as the Irishman would say. Love to Jeannie.

Your affectionate brother   A. E. HOUSMAN

[1] 1900–1941; book collector, bibliographer and authority on Baron Corvo.

[2] *Frederick Baron Corvo*, 1927.

[3] *Jocundus Robertus*, privately printed, 1926. The anonymous author was Philip G. Bainbrigge.

[4] An unpublished set of pornographic letters on the homosexual underworld of Venice.

[5] 1857–1938; in 1924 he came out of retirement to defend Loeb and Leopold, the Chicago youths who had kidnapped and murdered a boy to show that they could commit a 'perfect' crime.

To Robert Bridges

MS. BRIDGES

31 December 1927   *Trinity College*

My dear Bridges,

It is very good of you to write to me for the New Year, and I hope my answer may wade through the snow to the top of Boar's Hill and carry you my good wishes in return. I am afraid I am not likely to follow it to Oxford myself at this season. I am glad that the philosophical poem[1] progresses: at present I am occupied with your rival Lucretius, on whom I have to lecture next term; which I do in the spirit of the true pedant, ignoring philosophy as much as possible and poetry altogether. The man to whose essays I wrote a preface was Arthur Platt, my Greek colleague at University College, a dear and wonderful creature.

My kind regards to Mrs Bridges.

Yours sincerely   A. E. HOUSMAN

To an Unnamed Society

MS. BERG

7 January 1928   *Trinity College*

Dear Sirs,

I am obliged by your letter, but I do not give any lectures except those which are part of my duty here.

I am yours faithfully   A. E. HOUSMAN

To Grant Richards

MS. CONGRESS

17 January 1928   *Trinity College*

My dear Richards,

I hope I have not kept you waiting for the return of the proofs now enclosed, but in these last few days I have been rather occupied.

I shall be very glad to be one of the dedicatees.[2] But it was not only the fresh trout but the fresh truffles of the Gorge du Loup which dwell in my memory.

I am not sure that I have seen any of the books about wine which you mention. The menu of Sorret is very appetising.

---

[1] *The Testament of Beauty*, published in 1929.
[2] Of Richards' *The Coasts of Pleasure*, 1928.

'Hans Tiransil' may be a Dane in America who wrote to me about translating *Last Poems* and produced some versions which Gosse said were good. Kind regards to Mrs Richards (also Hélène),[1] and thanks for her New Year letter.

Yours sincerely   A. E. HOUSMAN

To an Unnamed Correspondent[2]

MS. LILLY

18 January 1928   *Trinity College*

Dear Sir,
You are at liberty to publish the two versions,—the more so, as Welsh translations of my poems are said to be better than the original. I am obliged to you for sending them to me, but I have forgotten all my Welsh except *cwrw da.*[3]

I am yours faithfully   A. E. HOUSMAN

To Grant Richards

MS. CONGRESS

19 January 1928   *Trinity College*

My dear Richards,
You did enclose two notes from Symons, which I have not kept, though the handwriting was very magnificent.
You may cite me as a witness to the onion-cheese soup.
As to *Last Poems* and your new business, I am not so confident as you seem to be about the latter. When I last heard, the arrangements were due to take place in November, and here is January. I don't know who your capitalists are, but I do know that if I were a capitalist I should not set you up as a publisher but engage you as a courier, salary unlimited. Not hearing from you before the end of the year I had drafted a letter to the Richards Press about *Last Poems*, and it would have gone if your letter had not just now arrived. They have behaved quite properly to me as far as I have observed, and I will not do anything uncivil to them.

Yours sincerely   A. E. HOUSMAN

[1] Richards' step-daughter.
[2] The headmaster of Llanwrst County School, Wales.
[3] Good beer.

To A. S. F. Gow

MS. TRINITY

20 January 1928   *Trinity College*

Dear Gow,

I enclose what I have written for Taylor.[1] I have put it with labour into capital script in the vain hope of excluding J's and U's, which the executant will nevertheless introduce wherever he thinks proper, and only half of which will be removed.

Yours sincerely   A. E. HOUSMAN

To an Unnamed Correspondent[2]

MS. LILLY

23 January 1928   *Trinity College*

Dear Sir,

French is the only tongue of which I know enough to keep my translators in order; in other languages I generally give permission and hope for the best, and I have no reason to hope for less than the best from you.

I am yours faithfully   A. E. HOUSMAN

To William Rothenstein

MS. HARVARD

24 January 1928   *Trinity College*

My dear Rothenstein,

If you get the consent of all the nine others, I will not stick out.[3] But you are much too great an artist to catch a likeness. Of course I do not know what I look like myself, but my acquaintances do not recognise me, so much are my traits ennobled by your pencil. Also I am much exhausted by having sat for two drawings for my two colleges in the last year, mutually much disapproved by the two artists. Also the languor of extreme senility makes me more and more averse to locomotion. Also a journalist present in the

---

[1] The memorial inscription in Trinity College Chapel to Henry Martyn Taylor (1842–1927), Senior Fellow of the College.

[2] See p. 259, note 2.

[3] Rothenstein had proposed to make a painting of the party of pall-bearers at Hardy's funeral in Westminster Abbey on 15 January 1928. The others were Stanley Baldwin, Ramsay MacDonald, J. M. Barrie, John Galsworthy, Edmund Gosse, Rudyard Kipling, A. B. Ramsay, Bernard Shaw and E. M. Walker, Pro-Provost of Queen's College, Oxford.

Abbey says that my person proved as polished as my verse, after which I desire to be for ever invisible.

I had heard, and was sorry to hear, that you had not been at all well. Please give my kind regards to Mrs Rothenstein. I shall hope to see you here in March. I met your younger son[1] at our High Table a year or two ago.

    Yours sincerely   A. E. HOUSMAN

To Grant Richards

MS. CONGRESS

30 January 1928   *Trinity College*

My dear Richards,

2000 copies of the 3/6 edition of *A Shropshire Lad* were prepared for the public on 15 June last year, and 5000 of the small edition some time later, as the stock was running low. I have written to the Richards Press asking about the stock of *Last Poems*, as that is a subject about which I am curious myself. But I have not unsettled their minds by foreshadowing transfer, and I am not inclined to do so till your prospects are clearer. They send me royalties and accounts fairly regularly.

Last term we reformed the College kitchen and engaged a new chef, who was at one time employed at the Café Royal. He is an improvement on the old one, who had grown up from scullery-boy under this venerable roof; but his variety and inventiveness are ahead of his execution.

    Yours sincerely   A. E. HOUSMAN

To William Rothenstein

MS. HARVARD

17 February 1928   *Trinity College*

My dear Rothenstein,

I have some slight reason to think that you will not capture all your ten, and I feel a suspicion that you want to use me as a decoy: 'the churlish recluse A. E. Housman has consented, how then can you or anyone refuse?'[2] It is just possible that I might be in London one day before the end of term, and if so I would let you know.

    Yours sincerely   A. E. HOUSMAN

[1] Michael Rothenstein (born 1908), painter and writer on art.
[2] All the other pall-bearers except Barrie had already agreed to sit for the painting.

To Sir James Barrie[1]

TEXT: RICHARDS

20 February 1928   [*Trinity College*]

I hear you are coy to Rothenstein. I also do not want to sit (the more so because I have suffered enough from his pencil for one lifetime), and if you will stand firm, so will I. . . .

Though Rothenstein cannot draw a likeness, he has a pretty wit, and told Shaw that the secret of his health at his age must be that he has been able to extract ultra-violet rays from lime-light.

To William Rothenstein

MS. HARVARD

25 February 1928   *Trinity College*

My dear Rothenstein,

It is very nice and honest of you to tell me that Barrie has refused to sit, because I now shall also refuse, as I warned you. I am also grateful for your *mot* about Shaw.

Yours sincerely   A. E. HOUSMAN

To T. S. Eliot

MS. HARVARD

12 March 1928   *Trinity College*

Dear Mr Eliot,

It is very kind of you to send me your edition of *The Moonstone*, and I have enjoyed reading your preface. I still incline to think *The Woman in White*[2] the best, chiefly on account of the two characters you mention; and I put *No Name* very high, for the art with which trivial incidents are made to cause intense and painful excitement. I am glad you have a good word for *Poor Miss Finch. Armadale* I never took to; he cannot manage the supernatural; and I was not young enough when I read it.

Yours sincerely   A. E. HOUSMAN

---

[1] Scottish playwright (1860–1937); knighted, 1913; appointed to the Order of Merit, 1922. A frequently repeated story, which cannot be substantiated, describes Housman's first meeting with him. They were placed next to each other at dinner in Trinity in 1922 and did not exchange a word all evening. The next day Barrie wrote to apologise and explain that he was a very shy man, but made matters worse by misspelling Housman's name. Housman replied in the identical words, with only the spelling correction added.

[2] See p. 235, note 4.

To Mr Leippert[1]

27 March 1928   *Trinity College*

Dear Mr Leippert,

I cannot forbid you to write to me but you must not expect replies. I hate writing and my relatives and friends very seldom get letters from me.

Lucan would do you no good. He has rhetoric and epigram but no true poetry. My edition (Blackwell, 1926) is for advanced scholars and is scientific —not literary.

The authorised publishers of the *Shropshire Lad* in the United States are Messrs. Holt.

I am yours sincerely   A. E. HOUSMAN

To Percy Withers

MS. WITHERS

23 April 1928   *Trinity College*

My dear Withers,

If you wanted a letter at Christmas you did not go about the right way to get it, for you told me that my letter in the autumn was the only one I had ever written you except in answer to one of your own; and this so filled me with the consciousness of virtue that I have been resting in contemplation of my merit ever since.

It is very good of you nevertheless to ask me to pay you a visit, and I should be delighted to come for three nights in either of the week-ends surrounding the 13th and the 20th of May. In June I am going abroad.

This is not a late spring. Till the cold set in after Easter it was quite an early one; but there have been so many early springs in the last fifteen years that people have forgotten the proper time for leaves and flowers to come out. For twenty years or so from 1887 onward I noted these things in a diary, on the strength of which I inform you that the lilac usually comes into blossom on 7 May; and it is opening now by Magdalene Bridge, though I admit that it is always early there.

I am glad that your report of your health is as good as can reasonably be expected. My kind regards to Mrs Withers. I myself am well, and yours sincerely

A. E. HOUSMAN

[1] Text from *The Dalhousie Review* XXIX, 1950.

To Grant Richards

MS. CONGRESS

24 April 1928   *Trinity College*

My dear Richards,

I return with thanks M. des Ombiaux' book,[1] which is readable enough, but, like so many books on wine, too literary and not scientific enough.

I will also send back Corvo's letters in a day or two. That sort of thing is not really improved by literary elegances, and I have been more amused with things written in urinals.

Yours sincerely   A. E. HOUSMAN

To the Richards Press

MS. B.M.

24 April 1928   *Trinity College*

Dear Sirs,

I am sorry to have left your letter of 2 March, with its enclosures, so long without a reply, but I was first ill and then busy.

I do not so very much admire the special bindings, and, apart from that, the notion does not appeal to me. My idea has always been to let the public have my poems as cheap as possible.

This leads me to a matter on which I have been meaning to write to you for some time. As *Last Poems* has now been out for more than five years, I think it is time to have a cheaper edition, uniform in external appearance with the 3/6 *Shropshire Lad*, but lower in price, because the contents are so much smaller. My own preference would be 2/6.

I am yours faithfully   A. E. HOUSMAN

To Seymour Adelman[2]

TEXT: MEMOIR

6 May 1928   *Trinity College*

Dear Mr Adelman,

... The words of mine which have reached your ears may be something like this. I can no more define poetry than a terrier can define a rat; but he knows a rat when he comes across one, and I recognise poetry by definite

---

[1] *Le Vin* by Maurice des Ombiaux, 1928.
[2] American collector.

264

physical sensations, either down the spine, or at the back of the throat, or in the pit of the stomach.[1]

The influence of Heine is evident in *A Shropshire Lad*. For Keats I have the greatest admiration, but I should not have thought that my writing had any affinity to his.

An illustrated edition was produced to please the publisher: the illustrations were Shropshire landscapes by William Hyde. They were in colour, which always looks vulgar, and the edition is now withdrawn. The late Lovat Fraser made drawings which he called illustrations, and I suppose that they had artistic merit, but illustrations they were not. All the figures, when there were figures, were put into eighteenth-century costume, and No. XXX was represented by a fat old man asleep on a chair. . .

Neither illustrators nor composers care twopence about words, and generally do not understand them.

Yours sincerely   A. E. HOUSMAN

To the Registrar to the University of Oxford[2]

MS. OXFORD

10 May 1928   *Trinity College*

Dear Mr Registrar,

I beg to thank you for your communication, received to-day, of the kind and flattering intention of the Hebdomadal Council to propose that the Degree of Doctor of Letters in the University of Oxford should be conferred upon me. My obligation to them, and my sense of the honour proposed, are not less because it is one which I am not able to accept. In pursuance of a resolution taken long ago, and for reasons which it would be tedious to enumerate and perhaps not quite easy to formulate, I have declined similar distinctions offered me by the generosity of other Universities; and the case is not altered even when the University which designs to bestow its favour on me is my own. I only ask that neither ingratitude nor lack of appreciation may be inferred from my action, as they are far indeed from my mind.

I am yours faithfully   A. E. HOUSMAN

[1] This account of Housman's response to poetry was later used in his Leslie Stephen Lecture, *The Name and Nature of Poetry*, 1933. It was first made public by Laurence Housman in a newspaper interview in America in 1921.

[2] Edwin Stuart Craig (1865–1939), Fellow of Magdalen College, Oxford; University Registrar, 1926–1930.

To the Richards Press[1]

Dear Sirs,

Judging from the correctness of the proofs of *Last Poems* which you send me, and the promptitude with which they appeared, I infer that the first edition has been kept in type, and that you propose printing the cheaper edition from the same. But if this edition were to be uniform with that of *A Shropshire Lad*, the title would appear at the top of each page; and I doubt if there is room for it. The lines of the poems would certainly on some pages want squeezing together: you are better able to judge than I am if they could could be squeezed enough.

The only change I should be making myself is to add a title to XXXVI on p. 70.[2]

Yours faithfully   A. E. HOUSMAN

To Lady Gosse

MS. CAMBRIDGE

17 May 1928   *Trinity College*

Dear Lady Gosse,

Though the bulletins of the last few days had prepared me for this morning's news, the national and personal loss is none the less a pain.[3] I am glad to remember that after the long separation due to my residence in Cambridge I met your husband last January at Hardy's funeral, when he seemed as young as ever. In common with all the friends who will miss his delightful conversation and companionship, I know and feel what the sorrow of your bereavement must be; and I am sure you will understand how sincere is my sympathy.

Always yours very truly   A. E. HOUSMAN

To Mrs Withers

MS. WITHERS

23 May 1928   *Trinity College*

Dear Mrs Withers,

At the feast last night I was complimented on my appearance of good health,

---

[1] Text from a typescript made by Mr John Carter from the original, which was sold at Sotheby's on 19 June 1962.
[2] See p. 234.
[3] Sir Edmund Gosse died on 16 May 1928.

which I hope you will take as a deserved tribute to the benefit of a stay under your hospitable roof. My internal sensations quite correspond, and with kind regards to both of you I am yours sincerely   A. E. HOUSMAN

To Grant Richards

MS. CONGRESS

4 June 1928   *Trinity College*

My dear Richards,
    If it were convenient to you to stay at St Germain as my guest I should be delighted; and Louis[1] should be able to take you in and out of Paris, unless your business interviews there were too numerous or inconveniently fixed.
    I see you are crossing on Friday: is it still only two nights you mean to stay?
    I would send the car to meet you at the Rue Caumartin on your arrival, as you and Louis might easily miss one another at the Gare du Nord.
    I am leaving Cambridge to-day, though I do not cross till to-morrow.

Yours sincerely   A. E. HOUSMAN

To Seymour Adelman

TEXT: MEMOIR

21 June 1928   *[Trinity College]*

Dear Mr Adelman,
    ... *A Shropshire Lad* was published while Mr Wilde was in prison, and when he came out I sent him a copy myself. Robert Ross told me that when he visited his friend in jail[2] he learnt some of the poems by heart and recited them to him; so that was his first acquaintance with them. I do not think I ever heard of Reginald Turner.[3] Parts of *The Ballad of Reading Gaol*[4] are above Wilde's average, but I suspect they were written by Lord Alfred Douglas. ...

Yours sincerely   A. E. HOUSMAN

[1] The chauffeur who had driven Housman and Richards on their tour of Burgundy the year before.
[2] At Reading, in May 1896.
[3] Novelist, journalist and friend of Wilde and Max Beerbohm (1869–1938). Adelman had bought a copy of *A Shropshire Lad* formerly owned by him.
[4] First published in 1898. There is no evidence that Douglas composed any part of the poem, though he was living with Wilde at the time it was completed and revised.

To Grant Richards

TEXT: RICHARDS

22 June 1928   *Trinity College*

... At the present moment a cheaper edition of *Last Poems* is preparing for the autumn as I thought it high time: 5000 copies, as it is said that no lower number would be remunerative. . .

I enclose *Irish Wine*.[1] Many thanks for the map of the French provinces, which arrived soon after you left. You will be amused to hear that the careful Louis knocked down a small girl.

I forget the exact circumstances under which I have just received, at your request, a signed and numbered copy of Shane Leslie's poems,[2] though I remember you saying something about them. Am I to keep it? and should I acknowledge it to anyone else?

To the Richards Press

MS. B.M.

24 June 1928   *Trinity College*

Dear Sirs,

I thank you for the two books. I have gone through them and find that the text contains fifteen errors of one sort or another, which I have enumerated inside the cover of the copy which I return.

Most are cases of stops omitted or obliterated; but p. 57 *climbing* for *chiming* is atrocious, and p. 70 *steafast* for *stedfast*, p. 76 *fathers'* for *father's*, and p. 84 *slept* for *stept* are as bad as p. 66 *the all* for *all the*, and must equally be corrected. It is clear that the text was not submitted to me when stereotyped. A correction-slip as enclosed should be printed and sent out with every copy already bound.[3]

Yours faithfully   A. E. HOUSMAN

To Grant Richards

TEXT: RICHARDS

25 June 1928   *Trinity College*

At the present moment my feelings towards you are much embittered by the discovery that your last small edition of *A Shropshire Lad* contains 15 errors, some of them filthy.

---

[1] By Maurice Healy, 1928.
[2] *The Poems of Shane Leslie*, 1928.
[3] This was done.

To Katharine Symons

MS. TRINITY

1 July 1928 *Trinity College*

My dear Kate,

I have been staying a fortnight at St Germain, which is to Paris something what Richmond is to London, in a luxurious hotel with a magnificent view and just on the edge of the forest, which, by the way, harbours ferocious insects, both of the mosquito and the horse-fly breed. Also I had a motor-car and saw a great deal of places within a moderate distance of Paris. The country is pretty in many parts, and the roads often run through forests.

Edwin Grey[1] died in May at at the age of 72: I thought he was about two years younger. I learn with pain that he was a Congregationalist, and, what is worse, an earnest one, and a Deacon.

Probably many things have happened to your numerous and active family since I heard last, but I hope nothing bad. I have not heard how Denis' candidature turned out. I hope you and Edward are well, as this leaves me at present. Edie Wise seems to be in a poor way, with her digestion out of order.

Your affectionate brother   A. E. HOUSMAN

To the Richards Press

MS. B.M.

1 July 1928 *Trinity College*

Dear Sirs,

I am obliged by your letter of 28 June, but before I answer it in detail I had better say what follows.

I have been approached by another firm of publishers, indeed by more than one, who want me to transfer my books to them. My relations with you have always been quite satisfactory, and I have no cause whatever for discontent; and although I am offered certain monetary inducements, and prospects of pushing the sale of the books are held out, these do not weigh with me, and I should not on that account do anything which I thought likely to injure you or your feelings. Still, the present bother about correcting and reprinting, which has been brought upon you by no fault of your own, must be rather unwelcome to you, and therefore at this juncture I present the proposal for your consideration. The idea is that the cost of the production of the stock in your possession should be paid to you, and the plates taken over at an agreed price.

I should like to have a dozen copies of the correction-slip when it is printed.

Yours faithfully   A. E. HOUSMAN

[1] The son of a Bromsgrove carpenter and a friend of Housman's in boyhood.

269

To the Richards Press

MS. B.M.

3 July 1928 *Trinity College*

Dear Sirs,

I thank you for your letter of yesterday. I have no wish to transfer my books elsewhere, nor do I desire an increase of royalty: a poet, says Horace,[1] is seldom avaricious. We will therefore go on as heretofore.

I am yours faithfully   A. E. HOUSMAN

To Grant Richards

MS. CONGRESS

4 July 1928 *Trinity College*

My dear Richards,

The Richards Press fear that my departure would definitely affect the prestige of the house; and as I have no complaint whatever against them I do not see that I can well detach myself.

Yours sincerely   A. E. HOUSMAN

Thanks for Bramah's book,[2] which I am reading after dinner with amusement. I would send Shane Leslie back to you if you thought you could find a more appreciative recipient.

No! it has disappeared. You told me to give it to my bedmaker: I did not, but I left your letter lying about, and I suppose this is the consequence.

To Grant Richards

MS. CONGRESS

14 July 1928 *Trinity College*

My dear Richards,

If I did not know how easily composition comes to you, I should be sorry to have caused you to write so much. It has interested me to read it, but the utmost that I can say is that if the Richards Press change their title to Grant Richards Limited I shall regard that as a shabby act and take the books away.

Yours sincerely   A. E. HOUSMAN

---

[1] 'Vatis avarus non temere est animus.' (*Epistles* II. i. 119).
[2] *Kai Lung Unrolls his Mat* by Ernest Bramah, 1928.

To Grant Richards

MS. LILLY

9 October 1928   *Trinity College*

My dear Richards,

If Mr Symons will consider, he will see that to do as he wishes would be a shabby act towards the generations of anthologists whom I have repelled by saying that I have an invariable rule.[1] He may be consoled, and also amused, if you tell him that to include me in an anthology of the Nineties would be just as technically correct, and just as essentially inappropriate, as to include Lot in a book on Sodomites; in saying which I am not saying a word against sodomy, nor implying that intoxication and incest are in any way preferable.

Thanks for the handbook on hanging,[2] though the author seems to be rather a buffoon.

Yours sincerely   A. E. HOUSMAN

If Mr Symons ever feels sad, he ought to be able to cheer himself up by contemplating his handwriting.[3]

To the Editor of The Times[4]

[circa *13 December 1928*]   [*Trinity College*]

SHELLEY'S SKYLARK

Sir,

Although this ode is not one of Shelley's best poems and enjoys more fame than it deserves, it is good enough to be worth interpreting. Quintilian says that you will never understand the poets unless you learn astronomy;[5] and as this subject is not now much studied in girls' schools it was only to be expected that Mr Moore's "Egeria"[6] should darken with misinformation the ignorance of Mr Eliot. In the stanza

Keen as are the arrows
Of that silver sphere

[1] A. J. A. Symons had asked permission to include poems by Housman in *A Book of Nineties Verse*, 1928.
[2] *A Handbook on Hanging* by Charles Duff, 1928.
[3] Symons was an expert calligrapher.
[4] Text from *The Times Literary Supplement*, 20 December 1928.
[5] *Institutio Oratoria* I. iv. 4.
[6] In *For Lancelot Andrewes*, 1928, T. S. Eliot wrote à propos Shelley's 'Ode to a Skylark': 'I am still ignorant to what Sphere Shelley refers, or why it should have silver arrows, or what the devil he means by an intense lamp narrowing in the white dawn.' The book was reviewed in *The Times Literary Supplement* on 6 December 1928. The following week T. Sturge Moore contributed a letter to say that 'a schoolgirl would know that the "silver sphere" is the moon.'

Whose intense lamp narrows
In the white dawn clear
Until we hardly see—we feel that it is there,

the silver sphere is the Morning Star, the planet Venus; and Shelley is giving a true description of her disappearance and using an apt comparison. The moon, when her intense lamp narrows in the white dawn clear, is not a sphere but a sickle: when she is a sphere at sunrise she is near the western horizon, visible in broad daylight and disappearing only when she sets; so that nothing could be less like the vanishing of the skylark.

                                                                    A.E.H.

To the Richards Press

MS. B.M.

14 December 1928   *Trinity College*

Dear Sirs,
    I refuse the request of the Teesdale Musical Tournament to print the poem. If I had the power, which I suppose I have not, I would prohibit them from using it for elocution.

        Yours faithfully   A. E. HOUSMAN

To Robert Bridges

MS. BRIDGES

28 December 1928   *Trinity College*

My dear Bridges,
    You were so civil and amiable in writing to me about this time last year that I cannot better employ the feast of the Holy Innocents than in writing to you. I wish you a happy new year, and there is really no reason why I should not wish you many, as you would agree if you had seen Sir George Young the other day at 92. He comes here every Christmas, and singles me out for conversation on English metre; and fortunately he is one of the few persons whom I can hear talk upon that subject without visibly losing my temper. He probably sent you the book which he published on his 90th birthday; and he is now engaged in a short essay to dissuade mankind from writing Greek with accents.[1]
    I am myself engaged on one of my serious works, the fifth and last volume of Manilius. It ought to be out in a year's time, and then I shall have done what I came on earth to do, and can devote the rest of my days to religious

[1] *Homer and the Greek Accents*, 1930.

272

meditation. I hope that your *De rerum natura* is progressing smoothly; but I was sorry to hear from H. F. Stewart[1] that you were having some trouble with your eyes.

With kind regards to Mrs Bridges I am yours sincerely

A. E. HOUSMAN

To Percy Withers

MS. WITHERS

28 December 1928 *Trinity College*

My dear Withers,

Christmas generally brings me a certain amount of abuse for being a bad letter-writer, but nobody else makes such a moan as you do; so I suppose your feelings towards me are especially tender. In June I did what I had often thought of doing before, spent a fortnight at St Germain-en-Laye just outside Paris, in the luxurious Pavillon Henri Quatre, on the edge of the forest and commanding the famous view. I had a motor, and so saw a good deal within a fifty-mile radius which I had not seen before. In August and September I passed a month of the best of the summer with relations and friends in Worcestershire, Gloucestershire and Hampshire, and, in motoring, saw many fine churches or abbeys, most of which were new to me. The use and abuse of the ball-moulding in the Decorated period in the district between Gloucester and Hereford is remarkable.

I wish your news of your health made a more equable story. A sacral plexus is a new monster to me: I knew that I had a solar plexus, because it makes my poetry for me; but the other has not hitherto molested me. I hope your son is through with his trouble. A happy new year to you and Mrs Withers and all your family.

Yours sincerely A. E. HOUSMAN

To A. C. Pearson

MS. KING'S

30 December 1928 *Trinity College*

My dear Pearson,

I made several attempts during term to find you in your rooms, but, though I found a fire in the grate and papers on the table, that was all. I cannot let the year run out without wishing you a happy one to follow, and hoping that your sense of well-being will be as much increased by relief from duties as

---

[1] The Rev. Hugh Fraser Stewart (1863–1948), Fellow of Trinity College and Praelector in French since 1918.

mine would be. I am glad that Cambridge has seen you, though for too few years, in the chair of Porson and Dobree.[1] I hope that you approve of the successor we have given you:[2] I suppose he is what would be called a safe choice.

My kind regards to Mrs Pearson.

Yours sincerely   A. E. HOUSMAN

To the Richards Press

MS. B.M.

1 January 1929   *Trinity College*

Dear Sirs,

I am much obliged by your letter of yesterday, but I have a dislike of limited editions. I know that there is money in them, but I cannot stop.

But I was just about to write to you on another matter. I have been working at the fifth and last volume of my Manilius, and the text and notes (that is much the greater part of it) should be ready for printing two months hence. It would be natural to publish it in the same way as the other four, but it occurs to me that this sort of book is very much out of your line, and that you may very well have no particular wish to undertake it. If so, I can without difficulty put it into other hands; and I beg that you will tell me just how you feel about it, which you can do with perfect freedom.[3]

I am yours faithfully   A. E. HOUSMAN

To Grant Richards

TEXT: RICHARDS

15 January 1929   *[Trinity College]*

The poem on R.L.S. appeared at his death in the *Academy* in 1894.[4] I know nothing of the reprint.

I have a second cousin whose name is Arthur, but I do not know that he is also W.; and he is a clergyman, I think in Sussex.

In the 17th century one of the Colonna family, hearing that there were sunken ships in the lake of Nemi, did some dredging and brought up a pipe or something inscribed with the name of Tiberius—though one account does

---

[1] Peter Paul Dobree (1782–1825), Regius Professor of Greek at Cambridge, 1823–1825.
[2] The new Professor was Donald Struan Robertson (born 1885), Fellow of Trinity College since 1909; Vice-Master, 1947–1951.
[3] The book was published by the Richards Press in December 1930.
[4] The poem was privately reprinted in America *circa* 1928 in an edition of 50 copies.

not go quite so far as that. There is not a word about them in Suetonius, nor so far as I know in any classic, and it was not likely that there would be. There is a treatise by one V. Malfatti, *Le navi romane nel lago di Nemi*, 1905, which Mr Buhrer[1] probably knows.

Thanks for his book, but I would rather you did not send me books out of mere bounty, because I have hardly anywhere to put them.

To Percy Withers

MS. WITHERS

15 January 1929   *Trinity College*

My dear Withers,

I am very sorry that you are again laid up with one of your unduly large assortment of the troubles which th' inabstinence of Eve[2] has brought on men. I have been rather lucky myself.

I have the greatest admiration, which is worth nothing, for Mr Griggs's[3] etchings; and, though I despise limited editions and will not let my own publishers produce one, I did let the Riccardi Press do one of *A Shropshire Lad* in 1914,—a fact which may perhaps quell Mr Griggs's desire. If not, he is at liberty to produce another. But I must warn you that I resist any alteration in the interest of what is supposed to be typographical beauty. I remember that the Riccardi Press transferred to the ends of lines dashes which I had put at the beginning, and I made them put them back. It is absolutely necessary that I should correct the proofs.

No collected edition is likely to appear in my lifetime.

Yours sincerely   A. E. HOUSMAN

To Philip Gosse

MS. CAMBRIDGE

[Postmark *31 January 1929*]   *Trinity College*

Dear Philip,

I probably have a few of your father's letters, if I knew where to lay my hands upon them, but they would be of no use for the book. We did not

---

[1] Albert Buhrer, a friend of Richards'. His new book was *Rosetta, a sequence of sonnets and other poems*, 1929.

[2] See Milton, *Paradise Lost* XI. 476.

[3] Frederick Landseer Maur Griggs (1876–1938). Thanks to Withers' intercession his illustrations to *A Shropshire Lad* and *Last Poems* were published in limited editions of the two books issued by the Alcuin Press, 1929.

275

correspond regularly or often, and they are all questions or answers about small points.

I am very glad that the *Life and Letters*[1] are preparing, and I hope that full and not excessively discreet use will be made of his diary, which must be priceless, and ought finally to be in the British Museum.[2]

Please give my kind regards to your mother when you see her.

Yours sincerely   A. E. HOUSMAN

To Laurence Housman

TEXT: MEMOIR

16 February 1929   *Trinity College*

My dear Laurence,

Only the archangel Raphael could recite my poetry properly, but I have no doubt you would do it quite nicely, and I shall try not to set up interfering wave-lengths. But understand that I incur no obligation to do the same for you on your 70th birthday.[3]

You had better select with care. The financial expert who reorganised Grant Richards's business for his creditors thought that he would like to read *A Shropshire Lad*. He did, or as much as he could; then, in his own words, 'I put it behind the fire. Filthiest book I ever read: all about—'[4]

> Now all day long the horned herds
> Dance to the piping of the birds;
> Now the bumble-bee is rife,
> And other forms of insect life;
> The skylark in the sky so blue
> Now makes noise enough for two,
> And lovers on the grass so green
> —Muse, oh Muse, eschew th' obscene.

Your affectionate brother   A. E. HOUSMAN

[1] *The Life and Letters of Sir Edmund Gosse* by Evan Charteris was published in 1931.
[2] His appointments diaries are now in the Brotherton Collection, University of Leeds. *The Book of Gosse*, recording the guests entertained in his house, is in the University Library, Cambridge.
[3] This was the first time Housman allowed his poems to be broadcast. Laurence Housman read a selection on A.E.H's 70th birthday, 26 March, 1929.
[4] The remainder of the sentence is omitted by Laurence Housman as 'unprintable'.

To Cyril Clemens

MS. CLEMENS

19 February 1929   *Trinity College*

Dear Mr Clemens,
I do not remember what I wrote about *Huckleberry Finn*, and I cannot suppose that it is worth reprinting; but no doubt it was sincere, and I do not forbid you to use it.

I am yours sincerely   A. E. HOUSMAN

To Lord Stamfordham[1]

MS. WINDSOR

23 February 1929   *Trinity College*

Dear Lord Stamfordham,
With all gratitude for His Majesty's most kind and flattering wish to confer upon me the Order of Merit I humbly beg permission to decline this high honour.[2] I hope to escape the reproach of thanklessness or churlish behaviour by borrowing the words in which an equally loyal subject, Admiral Cornwallis,[3] declined a similar mark of the Royal favour: 'I am, unhappily, of a turn of mind that would make my receiving that honour the most unpleasant thing imaginable.'

I am yours very truly   A. E. HOUSMAN

To Laurence Housman

TEXT: MEMOIR

25 February 1929   *[Trinity College]*

My dear Laurence,
I have no quarrel with your selection. I shall not attend your Sunday afternoon service[4]. The Richards Press are punctual and so far as I know honest in their payments, and I am not so many hundred pounds to the bad, in my capacity of author, as I once was. . . .

Your affectionate brother   A. E. HOUSMAN

[1] The text of this letter is taken from the draft (MS Lilly) corrected from the original by Mr Robert Mackworth-Young. Arthur John Bigge (1849–1931) was Private Secretary to Queen Victoria, 1895–1901; to Prince George (later King George V), 1901–1931; knighted, 1895; created Lord Stamfordham, 1911.
[2] The only other person known to have refused the Order of Merit is Bernard Shaw. The vacancy left by Housman's refusal was filled by the appointment of Bridges in June 1929.
[3] Sir William Cornwallis (1744–1819); Admiral, 1799; knighted, 1815.
[4] The broadcast.

To Grant Richards

MS. HARVARD

27 February 1929   *Trinity College*

My dear Richards,

No, I will not have anything to do with Mr Adam[1] nor with illustrations by Véra Willoughby[2] or anyone else. I once sacrificed myself to your craving for such things, but never again.

Owing to my admiration of Griggs's etchings I have reluctantly acceded to his wish to bring out a limited edition of both books at the Alcuin Press, which supposes itself to be very first class.

In the interesting menu of a Paris restaurant which you sent me there are *praires*. These may be among the shell-fish which I have eaten at Marseilles, but I do not remember them: can you describe them?

On the afternoon Laurence is to broadcast some of my poems.

Yours sincerely   A. E. HOUSMAN

To Katharine Symons

MS. LILLY

1 March 1929   *Trinity College*

My dear Kate,

Shirts had better be included;[3] and do not stint yourself for a few shillings or indeed for more than a few. I keep my benevolence for cases that I know about: as for distressed miners, who have twice tried to starve me, let them starve. My fear is that the suits may prove too tight. He must be restrained from writing me a nice letter.

The only name that I can find on the back of the Holden portrait[4] is my own. But I have now laid my hands on the Magdalen papers, and that was Henry.

Your affectionate brother   A. E. HOUSMAN

[1] Not identified.
[2] Illustrator whose work was published between 1925 and 1929.
[3] Katharine Symons had asked Housman for an old suit and underclothes to give to an unemployed gardener in Bath. He responded by sending two good suits and money for other clothes.
[4] Portrait of a seventeenth-century ancestor, Fellow of Magdalen College, Oxford.

To Katharine Symons

MS. LILLY

6 March 1929   *Trinity College*

My dear Kate,

I enclose cheque for £2 and thanks for the trouble you have taken. I hope the vests don't tickle him as most vests do me.

Our grandfather must have become incumbent of Catshill (he was not Vicar, as it was not separated from Bromsgrove, I believe) about 1840 or earlier, but at first he lived at Lydiat Ash. I suppose he moved to Fockbury in 1847 when the old Brettell died. *Alumni Cantabrigienses*[1] is no good for subsequent careers.

I had no trouble from the cold except the gas going wrong for a day and a half. Mine was the only tap in this Court of the College which did not freeze. Thanks for the photographs, which look pleasant.

Your affectionate brother   A. E. HOUSMAN

To A. F. Scholfield

MS. TRINITY

12 March 1929   *Trinity College*

Dear Scholfield,

I molested you some time ago with enquiries about having photographs taken from facsimiles in the Library, but I am sorry to say that as often happens my memory is not clear about your reply.

I want twenty photographs, life size, on stiff paper, of fol. 48ᵛ of 899. bb. 14, taken in deadly secrecy for use in an Examination. The cost will ultimately be paid by the University. If you think it among your proper functions to give orders to have this done, I shall be grateful; but probably it is not, and it may do me good to have to do something for myself.

Yours sincerely   A. E. HOUSMAN

To the Richards Press

MS. B.M.

21 March 1929   *Trinity College*

Dear Sirs,

Early next month I shall be sending you the text and notes,—that is 3/4 of the whole,—of my fifth volume of Manilius; so you had better be preparing the minds of Messrs Robert Maclehose and Co.

[1] By John Venn and J. A. Venn, 1922–1954.

On former occasions I have sent them a deposit of £100, and this will be forthcoming if required.

Yours faithfully   A. E. HOUSMAN

To Percy Withers

MS. WITHERS

29 March 1929   *Trinity College*

My dear Withers,

Many thanks to you and Mrs Withers for your congratulations, or disguised condolences, on the fact that King David thinks I ought to be dead.[1] I am I suppose very much younger and heartier than most men at seventy, but any gratitude to the Most High on that account is tempered by the reflection that it may mean living to ninety. I wish you had a better account to give of yourself. If you saw the crocuses in Cambridge just now it might do you good.

You are kind enough to speak of a visit. I have let myself in for examination next term, and so I do not yet know how far I shall be master of my time in May and the first half of June. If present engagements hold, I am going to Worcestershire on 8 July, and perhaps it might suit you if I took you on the way and came to you two or three days before. I think I have not seen your garden at that season. I understand that Laurence did not read me very well, dropping his voice too much at impressive points.

Yours sincerely   A. E. HOUSMAN

Postcard to Laurence Housman

TEXT: MEMOIR

[circa *1 April 1929*]   [*Trinity College*]

I received from you or C.[2] a cheering exhortation to shoulder the steg;[3] and the Postmaster General reinforced it by repeating this word on the back of the telegram. I find that it means a male bird, especially a gander . . . I am in quest of one. . .

[1] See Psalm 90.
[2] Clemence Housman.
[3] 'Shoulder the sky, my lad, and drink your ale.' (*Last Poems* IX).

To A. F. Scholfield

MS. TRINITY

16 April 1929   *Trinity College*

Dear Scholfield,

Many thanks for the twenty photographs from the MS of Lucretius received this morning.

I must also thank both you and Gow for a telegram on my birthday from a place called Morea,[1] which I had ignorantly supposed to be in Greece.

Yours sincerely   A. E. HOUSMAN

To Arthur Quiller-Couch[2]

9 May 1929   *Trinity College*

My dear Q,

I am annoyed to find that Tuesday the 14th is a date when I am engaged to dine at Christ's. I wish that colleges would show more concern for gluttons and drunkards in arranging their Feasts.

Yours   A. E. HOUSMAN

To John Drinkwater

MS. MARQUETTE

18 May 1929   *Trinity College*

My dear Mr Drinkwater,

I do not remember exactly what reply I made to you on the former occasion, but I suppose it was this: that I had no right, and therefore no desire, to prevent the inclusion of poems from *A Shropshire Lad* in an anthology published in America; that, as regards *Last Poems*, I had no inexorable rule of refusing anthologists, though selections from so small a book ought to be few. If the book were to be published in England, I should not allow poems from *A Shropshire Lad* to be included; but this, it appears, is not the case. I do not care about the remuneration.

I am yours very truly   A. E. HOUSMAN

[1] The P. & O. liner, then sailing to Gibraltar.
[2] Text from *Arthur Quiller-Couch* by F. Brittain, 1947.

To S. C. Roberts

MS. PRIVATE

22 May 1929   *Trinity College*

Dear Roberts,

I thank the Syndics of the Press for their offer to reprint my edition of Juvenal[1] and gladly accept it on the terms proposed.

They will not be able to offer the book to the public at 4/6 net as I did, but the price had better be moderate, as even the pleasure of buying copies for less than they cost to print did not entice mankind to take more than eighteen per annum.

Although the amount of correction and addition which I should make is small, I should not wish to tackle it till after the vacation, in which I shall be occupied with my last volume of Manilius.

I am yours sincerely   A. E. HOUSMAN

To an Unnamed Correspondent

MS. LILLY

13 June 1929   *Trinity College*

Dear Sir,

When I get hold of a first issue of *Last Poems* I insert the missing stops on p. 52. I believe that this destroys the value of the book for bibliophiles, so you can bring an action against me if you like.

Yours faithfully   A. E. HOUSMAN

To Robert Bridges

MS. BRIDGES

23 June 1929   *Trinity College*

My dear Bridges,

If the Order of Merit gives you pleasure, I shall share it; and no one can dispute your title to it. I hope you do not mind having Galsworthy for a yoke-fellow as much as I should.[2] If ever there was a man without a spark of genius, that man is he.

I cannot conclude without bewailing the untoward and very sudden attack of old age which forbids us to expect you here to-morrow. My kind regards to Mrs Bridges.

Yours sincerely   A. E. HOUSMAN

---

[1] It was published in October 1931 at 10s. 6d.

[2] Galsworthy was appointed to the Order of Merit on 3 June 1929—the same day as Bridges.

To S. C. Roberts

MS. C.U.P.

3 July 1929   *Trinity College*

Dear Roberts,

The Registrary[1] tells me that he thinks I shall be right in sending this bill to the Press. It is the cost of the photographs of a Latin MS provided for the candidates in the Second Part of the Classical Tripos, Group A. The only reason why it is made out to the Librarian is that he was kind enough to arrange for the taking of the photographs.

But, as I ordered 20 copies, and there were only 11 candidates, I am personally responsible for the excess, whatever it may be.

Yours sincerely   A. E. HOUSMAN

To Katharine Symons

MS. TRINITY

16 August 1929   *Trinity College*

My dear Kate,

I am leaving here next Thursday for France, and expect to return on 13 September. For part of the time I shall have no fixed address, but letters will be forwarded at intervals. I am not flying, as I am taking great care of my life till the book I am now engaged on is finished.

After leaving Tardebigge I spent four days on a motor tour, in which I got as near to you as Honiton. I had always wanted to go there, as the neighbourhood looks so beautiful from the railway,—and Defoe in his tour of England admired it equally,[2]—but for walking out from the town it is not satisfactory. Two other beauty-spots which I visited were Chipping Campden and Bourton-on-the-water; also Sherborne, where I found the interior of the Minster much finer than I had any idea of.

I thought Basil looking older,—his hair whiter. He seemed to get a good deal better during the fortnight I was there.

I hope you and Edward are flourishing: I daresay you are now in Hampshire.

Your affectionate brother   A. E. HOUSMAN

[1] Ernest Harrison (1877–1943), Fellow of Trinity College from 1900; University Registrary since 1925.

[2] See *A Tour thro' the Whole Island of Great Britain*, 1724–1727.

To Grant Richards

TEXT: RICHARDS

14 September 1929   *[Trinity College]*

Your lumbago caused me much selfish annoyance, and I hope (altruistically) that you are now rid of it. Morgan and Pope[1] have Frank Harris's book[2] for you. They provided me with a car less liable to sudden illness than the one we had two years ago, and a chauffeur whose strong point, like Louis', was smiling, not finding his way nor knowing north from south. Much fine scenery after Périgueux, and a fine cathedral at Rodez. Food not varied or inventive, especially soup: I do not mind Santé twice in ten days, but Parmentier I do. I was however agreeably surprised by a Palestine soup which had not the faintest trace of artichoke. The best meal was at the Gastronome at Clermont-Ferrand. In Paris I was not best pleased with the Belle Aurore, where they made me ill, perhaps with the very poor caviar: when I ordered fraises des bois, of which they had run short, they offered me a mixture of raspberries with what they had left, thinking apparently that I should not know the difference. But the place is thoroughly and pleasantly French, and the hors d'oeuvres look as if one could lunch entirely on them. The Grand Veneur is good though its plats régionaux are not an exciting selection. At the place in the Place St Michel I was disgusted with a pretended Sole Normande smothered with *mushrooms*, of all things in the world, and tasting exactly like the usual sole de la maison of a Parisian restaurant. The best cooking that I found was at the Escargot. Avoid Clos Vougeot 1915: for some reason it has turned out badly, as did Lafite 1900.

My kind regards to Mrs Richards.

To Harris Rackham[3]

16 September 1929   *Trinity College*

Dear Rackham,

I am just back from abroad, and I am rejoiced to see from to-day's *Times* that you have been recovering.[4]

We ought no doubt to say Mílan, as Shakespeare did; but when you ask for

---

[1] An Anglo-American car-hire firm in Paris.

[2] The second volume of *My Life and Loves*, 1925–1929.

[3] Copy, written in another hand, at Trinity College, Cambridge. Harris Rackham (1868–1934), Fellow of Christ's College, Cambridge, was University Lecturer in Classics, 1926–1934.

[4] *The Times*, 16 September 1929, printed a letter from Rackham objecting to the B.B.C.'s adoption of the pronunciation Milán.

284

Milán from an English poet, Shelley in 'Hellas' has 'Its unwearied wings could fan The quenchless ashes of Milan', and Sydney Dobell in 'The Roman' 'the proud banners that wave for Milan'. Both these are for the rhyme, a thing for which poets will do anything consistent with honour, as Miss Fotheringay would for lobster and champagne.[1]

Yours sincerely   A. E. HOUSMAN

To Charles Williams[2]

MS. O.U.P.

21 September 1929   *Trinity College*

Dear Mr Williams,

I well remember you (not personally I am sorry to say) and your poetry, and I am obliged by your interest in the Introductory Lecture.[3] I should never republish it by itself, but I have sometimes thought of including it (as it has been printed) in a volume with my inaugural lecture at Cambridge (which has not)[4] and an address which I delivered several years ago before the Classical Association and which appeared in their journal.[5] The great obstacle to this scheme is one which prevented me from letting the Cambridge press publish the inaugural lecture in 1911: that it contains a statement which I cannot verify. Not far from the beginning of this century I saw, in some literary journal I suppose, an account of an autograph, or some early impression, of Shelley's 'O world, O life, O time', in which the eighth line ran 'Fresh spring and autumn, summer and winter hoar'; and this I now cannot trace. It is not in Forman's second edition.[6] If the erudition of you people

---

[1] See Thackeray, *The History of Pendennis*, chapter xiii.

[2] Charles Walter Stansby Williams (1886–1945), poet and religious writer; at the time of this letter a reader for the Oxford University Press.

[3] Delivered at University College, London, on 3 October 1892 and printed for distribution in the College at the time, but not published until 1937.

[4] Delivered on 9 May 1911; published as *The Confines of Criticism*, 1969. See p. 286, note.

[5] 'The Application of Thought to Textual Criticism', in *Proceedings of the Classical Association*, 1922.

[6] The accepted form of this line from Shelley's posthumously published poem is 'Fresh Spring, and Summer, and Winter hoar'. In his annotated edition of 1870, W. M. Rossetti corrected the metre by inserting 'Autumn' after 'Summer'. This emendation was savagely attacked by Swinburne who praised the rhythm of the traditional reading. In his 1911 lecture Housman used Swinburne's comments as an example of the danger of basing textual criticism on aesthetic principles, declaring that Swinburne was admiring a misprint. The problem is discussed, and largely solved, in 'Shelley, Swinburne and Housman', by John Carter and John Sparrow (*The Times Literary Supplement*, 21 November 1968).

at the Oxford Press could discover it, that would put a new face on things; though I am not sure that even then a Cambridge inaugural would properly appear under your auspices.

Many thanks for the Keats.[1]

I am yours sincerely

A. E. HOUSMAN

To Katharine Symons

MS. TRINITY

26 September 1929   *Trinity College*

My dear Kate,

You will have heard from Jeannie about Basil's state of health and approaching retirement. I remember your telling me last year that you had offered to share with him what you inherited from Uncle Joe, and I suppose there is room for hope that the County Council will award him something of a pension. But as you know more of that household's affairs than I do, I wish you would tell me how much you think I ought to add in future to the £50 per annum I now send them.

Looking at your letter of 20 August it is amusing to see that you despaired of any more hot weather. I had rather more of it than I wanted in the south of France and even in Paris; but after two holidays of absolutely uninterrupted fine days one must not complain of trifles. I spent eleven days on my motor tour: after Périgueux the country became very picturesque, first limestone, then red earth in the Rouergue, then limestone again in the Cevennes, and so round again to Burgundy where I was two years ago. The cathedrals are not so fine in the south as in the north, but there is a very good one which I did not know of at Rodez; le Puy en Vélay, as I did know, is the most extraordinary place in the world, and Angoulême has a magnificent situation.

You kindly asked me to come and see you before the end of the vacation, but I have had my full dose of holiday and am now settled down to work again. Perhaps I had better tell you that the doctor, whom I made overhaul me when I turned 70, says that my heart is not as stout as it was and ought to be; and I found this out when climbing the Puy de Parioux, about the height of Snowdon, on a hot afternoon.

Your grandchildren must have had plenty of fun at Exmouth and Exeter, and I hope Michael is well again. Love to Edward and anyone else.

Your affectionate brother

A. E. HOUSMAN

[1] Bridges' *A Critical Introduction to Keats*, published by the Oxford University Press, 1929; sent to Housman as a specimen format of the Introductory Lecture.

286

To Charles Williams

MS. O.U.P.

1 October 1929   *Trinity College*

Dear Mr Williams,

Thanks for your note; but no doubt you see that Rossetti's reading (which he did not alter in deference to Swinburne)[1] is not the reading I am in search of.

Yours very truly   A. E. HOUSMAN

To A. Hudson-Williams[2]

MS. HUDSON-WILLIAMS

18 October 1929   *Trinity College*

Dear Mr Hudson-Williams,

At the request of the Classical Board I have undertaken to fill in as well as I can the office of Mr Nock[3] in directing your research during his absence.

I propose therefore that during this term you should come and see me once a fortnight. The hour most convenient to me would be 6 p.m., the day Thursday; but if this would not suit you it would be possible to arrange otherwise.

Yours very truly   A. E. HOUSMAN

To Robert Bridges

MS. BRIDGES

27 November 1929   *Trinity College*

My dear Bridges,

I thank you for your friendly gift.[4] As you will have surmised, it comes too late to save my pocket; but I shall now be able to keep it uncut and so enlarge the fortune of my heirs. I had meant to put off writing to you till the end of the year, by which time I might have matured some valuable criticism, or again I might not: now I will only say that I took most pleasure, and it was great, in passages such as III 354–84 or lines like I 295–6, admiring more,

---

[1] See p. 285, note 6. In deference to Swinburne's criticism Rossetti withdrew the emendation from his second edition, 1878; but it was retained in his frequently reprinted one-volume unannotated edition in Moxon's *Popular Poets* series, of which Housman had a copy.

[2] Born 1907; graduate student at Cambridge, 1928–1930; now Senior Lecturer in Classics, University College of Wales, Aberystwyth.

[3] Arthur Darby Nock (1902–1963); Fellow of Clare College, Cambridge, 1923; University Lecturer in Classics, 1926; Professor of the History of Religion at Harvard, 1930–1963.

[4] Of *The Testament of Beauty*.

you may think, the riches of heaven's pavement than aught divine or holy else enjoyed in vision beatific.[1]

The boom, though boom it be, gives one a sort of satisfaction, probably shared by Mrs Bridges, to whom my kind regards.

Yours sincerely   A. E. HOUSMAN

To Percy Withers

MS. WITHERS

4 December 1929   *Trinity College*

My dear Withers,

I am glad you like the new edition,[2] from which I have stood as much aloof as possible. I do not envy people who appreciate that sort of thing, because they suffer so terribly from books which do not come up to their standard; and I am amazed at the bitterness with which they speak about the ordinary editions of *A Shropshire Lad*, which, being legible, are all that I could desire.

I too am pleased with the noise about the *Testament of Beauty*, excessive though it is and in its nature contemptible. He himself rates it at its true value and calls it 'this blatant and incontinent boom'. I tell him that at any rate it probably makes Mrs Bridges happy, as wives are like that. Before I leave the subject, my kind regards to yours.

I spent three weeks of September in France, mostly touring in a motor-car: Poitiers, Angoulême, Périgueux (pâté de Périgord not nearly so good as, for instance, at Toulouse), Cahors, Rodez, Mende, Le Puy en Vélay, and thence back to Paris through places where I had been before in Auvergne and Burgundy. The cathedral at Rodez, quite unknown to me, very fine, and the surrounding country, the Romergue, remarkable, very red soil, between the limestone of the Dordogne and the Cevennes. I hope the rheumatism keeps off.

Yours sincerely   A. E. HOUSMAN

To the Richards Press

MS. B.M.

9 December 1929   *Trinity College*

Dear Sirs,

I enclose corrected proofs of *Last Poems*.[3]

[1] See Milton, *Paradise Lost* I. 678.
[2] The Alcuin edition.
[3] Housman had authorised the printing of 5,000 copies of a smaller edition uniform with that of *A Shropshire Lad*.

288

Comparing the small edition of *A Shropshire Lad* I am sure that most of the over-runnings which I have marked are unnecessary. Printers seem to love it for its own sake.

Yours faithfully   A. E. HOUSMAN

To J. W. Mackail

MS. TRINITY

26 December 1929   *Trinity College*

Dear Mackail,
 It was very unlucky that I was out when you called. If you, or you and the Lord Lieutenant,[1] happen to be in Cambridge one of these days about one o'clock, we could lunch off our cold Christmas sideboard: boar's head, game pie, beef, ham, tongue, plum pudding, mince pies.

Yours sincerely   A. E. HOUSMAN

To Mrs Platt

MS. U.C.L.

31 December 1929   *Trinity College*

Dear Mrs Platt,
 It is very good of you to brew me some of your sloe-gin, but I do not think I have any friend trustworthy enough to convey it to me without taking a swig. I suppose I shall be coming to London some time to see the Italian pictures,[2] though I shall not appreciate them, and I had better come and fetch it away myself.
 A happy New Year to you and yours.

Yours sincerely   A. E. HOUSMAN

To Percy Withers

MS. WITHERS

31 December 1929   *Trinity College*

My dear Withers,
 This is to wish a happy New Year to you and Mrs Withers and your family, now I suppose under your roof. I hope you will enjoy the weeks you mean to

---

[1] Presumably the Lord Lieutenant of Cambridgeshire, C. R. W. Adeane.
[2] The Royal Academy Winter Exhibition at Burlington House, January to March 1930. It attracted more visitors than any show since the Watts exhibition in 1905.

spend abroad, though I suppose that Burlington House at this moment contains more of value than the galleries either of Dresden or of Munich. Not that I should be able to tell. Stout and oysters are more on my level, and till midnight comes and brings them I can think of little else. If ever I am inclined to repine, I think of the lot of a friend of mine[1] to whom I have just been writing, who was born with a distaste for beer. You say nothing of your health, and I suppose no news is good news.

Yours sincerely   A. E. HOUSMAN

To A. Allen Brockington[2]

[circa *1930*]

... I have a great admiration for some of the poetry which Browning wrote between 1835 and 1869, especially in the period of *Bells and Pomegranates*; but on my own writing he has had no influence at all, except that the phrase "to rest or roam" in one of my poems is probably a reminiscence of "to roam or rest" in one of his.

To The Richards Press

MS. B.M.

14 January 1930   *Trinity College*

Dear Sirs,
    I enclose 22 more pages of Manilius V to satisfy the cravings of the printers.

Yours faithfully   A. E. HOUSMAN

To John Carter[3]

MS. LILLY

4 February 1930   *Trinity College*

Dear Mr Carter,
    I do not know of any copies of the Introductory Lecture except my own and that in the British Museum. It was not published, but two or three

---

[1] Possibly Richards, though no letter to him of this date has come to light.
[2] 1872–1938; religious and miscellaneous writer and lecturer on English Literature for the Cambridge University Board of Extra-mural Studies. This letter is quoted in his *Browning and the Twentieth Century*, 1932, as Housman's answer to an enquiry.
[3] John Waynflete Carter (born 1905), bibliographer, who in 1933, together with Mr John Sparrow, arranged the private reprint of Housman's Introductory Lecture of 1892; editor of Housman's *Collected Poems*, 1939, and *Selected Prose*, 1961.

290

hundred were printed by the College Council and distributed to members of the College.

I am yours very truly   A. E. HOUSMAN

To Mrs Platt

MS. U.C.L.

4 February 1930   *Trinity College*

Dear Mrs Platt,
    The intoxicant has arrived. As you advised me to keep it till March, I have not opened the bottle, and am therefore in a condition to express my gratitude legibly and grammatically.

Yours sincerely   A. E. HOUSMAN

To the Richards Press

MS. B.M.

4 February 1930   *Trinity College*

Dear Sirs,
    The printers have now had a large batch of the MS of Manilius V for more than two months without doing anything to it; though I suppose I ought not to count the first week of January, during which they were doubtless drunk.

Yours faithfully   A. E. HOUSMAN

To Grant Richards

MS. CONGRESS

5 February 1930   *Trinity College*

My dear Richards,
    I return D. H. Lawrence,[1] with thanks for your perilous enterprise on my behalf. It did not inflame my passions to any great extent, but it is much more wholesome than Frank Harris or James Joyce.[2]
    I hope you and yours are well. I have not seen any news of Hélène.

Yours sincerely   A. E. HOUSMAN

[1] *Lady Chatterley's Lover*, 1928, banned in Great Britain as an obscene book until 1960
[2] Joyce's *Ulysses*, 1922, was banned in Great Britain until 1936.

To Katharine Symons

MS. LILLY

11 February 1930   *Trinity College*

My dear Kate,

I am quite willing to inscribe the copy of *A Shropshire Lad*, but I have always refused to copy out verses and sign them. There is a bookseller here who the other day offered £120 for a copy with my autograph possessed by a friend of mine, but that was probably in good condition. I suppose there was a maniac millionaire in the background.

I can hear nothing of any portrait of A. J. Macleane,[1] and it is extremely unlikely that we should have one. He was neither eminent or resident; and it is only of late years that the college has cared to secure portraits even of those who are.

At the end of the holidays I spent a few days near Oakham and saw a number of fine churches in south Lincolnshire. Boston must be the largest and finest parish church in England: Yarmouth and St Michael's Coventry are said to cover more ground, but they have less bulk and grandeur.

I did not know that Jerry was to be in England this year, and I am glad to hear such a good report of him. I expect however that you told me he was coming and that it passed out of my senile memory.

Love to all.

Your affectionate brother   A. E. HOUSMAN

To the Richards Press

MS. B.M.

14 February 1930   *Trinity College*

Dear Sirs,

The amount of manuscript still to come is much less than a quarter of the whole and will pretty certainly be finished before the end of April: instalments of it could be sent earlier. As it will not contain much of the small print and intricate matter, it should not give much trouble to the printers' readers. The index of course cannot be constructed before the book is in pages. I do not think that the printers at any stage have been held up by a lack of manuscript; so that they could hitherto have 'proceeded without interruption' so far as I am concerned.

When I sent you the first manuscript I offered to pay a deposit of £100 (I think), but you said that it did not seem expected. I can pay it now, or more, if you think it advisable.

Yours faithfully   A. E. HOUSMAN

---

[1] Arthur John Macleane (1813–1858), who was an undergraduate of Trinity College, 1841–1845, was Headmaster of King Edward VI School, Bath, for the last four years of his life.

To Charles Williams

MS. O.U.P.

21 March 1930   *Trinity College*

Dear Mr Williams,
   On the one hand I must thank and congratulate you, but on the other you have cooked your own goose, for Mr Ingpen's[1] report contradicts that on which I relied.

   Yours sincerely   A. E. HOUSMAN

To Grant Richards

MS. CONGRESS

29 March 1930   *Trinity College*

My dear Richards,
   Yes, I should like to see the book,[2] the more so as I thought that Willy had drunk himself to death long ago and that this was the reason why Colette was going on without him. You gave me some of your father's copies of their books.

   Yours sincerely   A. E. HOUSMAN

To Grant Richards

TEXT: RICHARDS

16 April 1930   *[Trinity College]*

Boulestin's[3] noble invitation is just the thing to draw me to London, which the Italian pictures did not. Of course lunch would suit me better than dinner,

---

[1] See p. 285, note 6. Roger Ingpen, the leading Shelley expert (died 1936), had reported that Shelley's manuscript contains the disputed line in its traditional form. In their article Carter and Sparrow show that Ingpen's report was inaccurate, and that Shelley, recognising that the line was incomplete, had left a blank space after 'Summer'. They conclude that Housman was right, even though he could never find the evidence to prove it and therefore never published his argument.

[2] *Le Troisième Sexe*, 1927. Willy was the pseudonym of Henri Gauthier Villars (1859–1931), husband of the French novelist Colette (1873–1954) with whom he collaborated in several books.

[3] Xavier Marcel Boulestin (died 1943), French music critic, novelist, theatrical designer and culinary expert, opened his London restaurant in 1925. His dinner in honour of Housman was given on 7 May 1930. The only other guests were Richards and A. H. Adair.

and I suppose you too; and no Wednesday nor Friday would be possible. I did not know of the white Haut Brion, and I see from Cassagnac's book[1] that it is a recent invention.

To Monica Bridges[2]

MS. BRIDGES

22 April 1930   *Trinity College*

Dear Mrs Bridges,

I write to offer you my sympathy in your loss, which indeed we all share in a measure;[3] but of your husband's departure it may be said, if of anyone's, that nothing is here for tears, nothing to wail or knock the breast.[4] A fortunate and honoured existence is ended in the fulness of time; life did not long outstay strength; and his poetry, though the vulgar could never admire it rightly, did at last win him fame even among the vulgar. For myself, I do not suppose that there is anything which I have read oftener than the first four books of *Shorter Poems*.

       I am yours sincerely   A. E. HOUSMAN

To the Richards Press

MS. B.M.

24 April 1930   *Trinity College*

Dear Sirs,

All the volumes of Manilius have been published at much less than cost price; and six shillings net, the same as book IV, is the price I should put on book V, which I think will not be much larger.

       Yours faithfully   A. E. HOUSMAN

[1] *Les Vins de France*, 1927.
[2] Mary Monica Waterhouse (died 1940), daughter of Alfred Waterhouse, R.A., married Bridges in 1884.
[3] Bridges died on 21 April 1930.
[4] Milton, *Samson Agonistes*, l. 1721.

To G. H. Wiggins[1]

MS. B.M.

10 May 1930   *Trinity College*

Dear Sir,

I do not want an advertisement of my book from the *Daily Mail*.[2] They ought simply to publish their regret that the poem was reprinted without my permission.

Yours faithfully   A. E. HOUSMAN

To Percy Withers

MS. WITHERS

11 May 1930   *Trinity College*

My dear Withers,

Although you are not to be home till the 17th from the tour which I hope you are enjoying, I had better write to you while I am at leisure and thank you for your invitation. So far as I can judge, I shall be travelling to Worcestershire about 8 August, and could take you on my way, as I did once before. Next month I expect to be going to France.

I am rejoiced to hear of your return to wine-bibbing. Laurence of this College[3] (I forget if you have met him) has been suffering from gouty eczema, well earned: his doctor limited him to whisky, and he made no progress. So he called in another doctor, who ordered him a bottle of Burgundy a day: he mended rapidly and is now well.

I think Masefield is the right Laureate.[4] The other poets in the same class were out of the question for one reason or another; and Newbolt,[5] who would do the job best, is too little of a poet.

My kind regards to Mrs Withers.

Yours sincerely   A. E. HOUSMAN

---

[1] Of the Richards Press.

[2] On 3 May 1930 *The Daily Mail* printed Housman's 'Epitaph on an Army of Mercenaries' without permission. Four days later the editor offered to print an acknowledgment that the poem came from *Last Poems*. In the end a simple apology appeared on 15 May.

[3] Reginald Vere Laurence (1876–1934), Fellow of Trinity College since 1901; one of Housman's few close friends at Cambridge.

[4] The appointment was announced on 9 May.

[5] Henry John Newbolt (1862–1938); knighted, 1915; Companion of Honour, 1922. His name was widely canvassed. The King wished to appoint Kipling and the Prime Minister (Ramsay MacDonald) favoured Housman; but both were expected to decline, and no offer was made to them.

To John Masefield

MS. BODLEY

11 May 1930   *Trinity College*

Dear Masefield,

My purpose in writing is not chiefly to congratulate you that the King has made the choice which I should have made myself, but rather to warn you, if you need the warning, that you will now become the target for a good deal of spite, and to exhort you not to worry about it.

You do not need to be consoled, as some Laureates might, for the vanished butt of Canary sack.

In sporting circles here they are asking the question: if Boar's Hill get it three times, do they keep it?

Yours sincerely   A. E. HOUSMAN

To Laurence Housman

TEXT: MEMOIR

12 May 1930   *[Trinity College]*

My dear Laurence,

. . . No, I was not given the chance of being Laureate. I thought Masefield the right choice, as all the other good poets are too obviously unsuited for the official duties . . .

Your affectionate brother   A. E. HOUSMAN

To S. C. Roberts

MS. C.U.P.

20 May 1930   *Trinity College*

Dear Roberts,

I enclose a copy of Juvenal with the necessary corrections. I shall also have to write a preface for the second edition; but this should keep you busy and happy for the present.

Yours sincerely   A. E. HOUSMAN

To Katharine Symons

MS. TRINITY

30 May 1930   *Trinity College*

My dear Kate,

I shall leave here on Monday, sleep at Croydon, and fly to Paris on Tuesday for about a fortnight.

If I do not come home alive, my book V of Manilius, all written and mostly printed, will be seen through the press by a Fellow of this college named Andrew Gow.

Your affectionate brother   A. E. HOUSMAN

To Henry Tonks[1]

MS. TEXAS

29 June 1930   *Trinity College*

Dear Tonks,
Ages though it is since we last met, I feel that on the occasion of your retirement I must write to congratulate you on the successful tenure of the Slade chair which you have brought to a close and to wish you contentment and happiness in your leisure.

Yours sincerely   A. E. HOUSMAN

To the Richards Press

MS. B.M.

29 June 1930   *Trinity*

Dear Sirs,
In the paged proofs of Manilius V which I received last week I find that the printers have inserted in p. 4 line 5 from the bottom a comma which was not previously there, and have altered *strepitus* to strepticus in p. 17 line 3 from the bottom. I shall therefore have to read these 94 pages through with minute care to find out what other pranks they have played.

Yours faithfully   A. E. HOUSMAN

To the Richards Press

MS. B.M.

3 July 1930   *Trinity College*

Dear Sirs,
Messrs Maclehose offer a vague general explanation which does not touch the peculiar mysteries to which I called attention. I can understand that *strepitus* on p. 17 may accidentally have been altered by the transposition of

---

[1] Painter (1862–1937); one of the founders of the New English Art Club; Slade Professor of Fine Art in London University, 1917–1930.

two of its nine letters to *streptius*; but what I do not understand is what happened next. I should have thought that the compositor, if he suspected that something had gone wrong, would have looked at the proof, which must have been somewhere on the premises, and put it right; instead of which he seems to have gone to the case of type, picked out a tenth letter, *c*, and stuck it in. And, similarly, whence came the intrusive comma on p. 4? It did not fall from the sky.

Yours faithfully   A. E. HOUSMAN

To the Richards Press

MS. B.M.

11 July 1930   *Trinity College*

Dear Sirs,

1. The table on slip 11 must not be shifted to any other place in the preceding or following type matter: if it is shifted at all it must have a place to itself. But I have been measuring, and I calculate that if the first page of the preface is made to contain only 18 or 20 lines, that will bring the table to the top of a later page. This will be very nearly what was done in book IV: I dare say the look of the first page will horrify you and the printers, but I do not mind. The blank space after line 14 could be widened.

2. Some time ago you wrote to me about the paper for this new volume, suggesting that it should be better and more durable. I in my ignorance had supposed that the paper of the others was rather good, and in I–III I thought it pleasing: the paper of IV is too thick, and I acquiesced in it because I was told that the other had ceased to be manufactured. Perhaps you would let me know your ideas. The new paper ought not to be too unlike the old.

Yours faithfully   A. E. HOUSMAN

To F. C. Owlett

MS. SPARROW

30 July 1930   *Trinity College*

Dear Mr Owlett,

Many thanks to you for sending me your *Chatterton*[1] in its finished form, which certainly is very finished.

Yours sincerely   A. E. HOUSMAN

[1] *Chatterton's Apology*, 1930.

298

To the Richards Press

MS. B.M.

10 September 1930   *Trinity College*

Dear Sirs,

I enclose for second corrections, which I hope will be final, the entire paged proofs of Manilius V, and also manuscript matter to be printed on p. xlvii. I shall now be able to send the MS of the Index within a week. I have made alterations in the title-page. I am afraid I do not know the Latin for 'Ltd.', and if you value that term it must be added, as you suggest, in English elsewhere.[1]

Yours faithfully   A. E. HOUSMAN

To Joseph Ishill[2]

MS. HARVARD

17 September 1930   *Trinity College*

Dear Mr Ishill,

I am naturally flattered by your proposal; but I am averse to limited editions. It is true that I have lately allowed one to be printed in England, but that was because I felt an obligation to one of the persons concerned.

But, as *A Shropshire Lad* is not copyright in America, you are of course at liberty to do whatever you like with it and snap your fingers at me.[3]

I am yours very truly   A. E. HOUSMAN

To Charles Wilson

MS. LILLY

27 September 1930   *Trinity College*

Dear Mr Wilson,

Thank you for sending me your pamphlet,[4] which I have read with great interest; and I admire your spirited action. But in spite of all your merits you will not see me at Willington.

Yours very truly   A. E. HOUSMAN

[1] The publisher's imprint on the title-page reads 'apud Societatem The Richards Press'.
[2] American printer and publisher, running the Oriole Press since 1926.
[3] Ishill did not reprint *A Shropshire Lad*.
[4] I have not succeeded in tracing this pamphlet.

To the Richards Press

MS. B.M.

30 September 1930   *Trinity College*

Dear Sirs,
  Here is the last day of September, and I begin to wonder whether the book
will be out before Christmas. The printers have had the MS of the Index for
a fortnight, and the corrected proofs of the rest for three weeks.

          Yours faithfully   A. E. HOUSMAN

To F. C. Owlett

MS. YALE

8 October 1930   *Trinity College*

Dear Mr Owlett,
  I am not prepared to sign your letter;[1] and though Kipling and Masefield
might be more goodnatured, I feel sure that they would not like signing it.
  In style it is not sedate and business-like prose; and its expressions of
opinion, even supposing that they are entirely just, are inopportune, provoca-
tive, and likely to injure your cause; for you know that Watson's work does
not now stand high in general esteem among literary people. In my opinion
he has chiefly brought this on himself by contentedly writing rhetoric instead
of poetry for the last 40 years or so. 'Wordsworth's Grave' is one of the
glories of English literature, and a few more poems of about the same date
had the same quality; but the best things he has written since 1890 have the
merits of epigram rather than of poetry.
  I should advise you to get a poet to write the letter for you, because poets'
prose is generally prosaic, as it should be. The obvious person to ask is the
Poet Laureate; the person whom I should expect to do it best is Mr Laurence
Binyon,[2] who is probably more in sympathy with Watson's manner than
most others now are. Or Sir Henry Newbolt.

          Yours sincerely   A. E. HOUSMAN

To S. C. Roberts

MS. C.U.P.

27 October 1930   *Trinity College*

My dear Roberts,
  You postponed the second edition of my Juvenal to suit my convenience,

---

[1] An appeal on behalf of Sir William Watson. See p. 302.
[2] Poet and art historian (1869–1943); Companion of Honour, 1922.

and, though I have now finished the new and additional preface, I am not in the least impatient to see the book appear: the only reason why I now write is this. In the new preface there are many references to the pages of the old. It would therefore be most convenient if that could be reprinted page for page as it stands; but this I suppose would be difficult, and rendered slightly more difficult by the few small changes I have made. The next best thing therefore would be that the numbering of the old pages should be given in the margin, and, consequentially, that the pages should have no numbering at the top, since it would confuse the reader; and for the same reason, the arabic numbering of pages should begin, not, as usual, with the text, but with the second preface.

Yours sincerely   A. E. HOUSMAN

To the Richards Press

MS. B.M.

4 November 1930   *Trinity College*

Dear Sirs,
    The corrected proofs which I sent you on 22 October must now have been in the printers' hands about twelve days, and as the corrections could easily be made in one hour I suppose they will only take about twelve days more. In the mean time I write to say that I wish the book to be advertised on its appearance both in the *Classical Review* and the *Classical Quarterly*; and it will be necessary for me to see the advertisement in proof, as the advertisement of vol. IV ten years ago was incorrect.

Yours faithfully   A. E. HOUSMAN

To the Richards Press

MS. B.M.

13 November 1930   *Trinity College*

Dear Sirs,
    I thought that you would by now have been able to assure me that my last lot of corrections was actually inserted before the printing began. If not, it must stop. It was begun without my permission, and therefore I cannot feel as sure as I should like that the corrections were carried out.

Yours faithfully   A. E. HOUSMAN

To E. H. Blakeney[1]

25 November 1930   *Trinity College*

My dear Sir,

I am naturally flattered by your solicitude for my miscellaneous writings, but I so little share your desire that when I next make a will I intend to forbid their republication.[2] A list of them down to 1926 was privately printed here by A. S. F. Gow, and after my death it can easily be brought up to date and issued to the public.

Thanks for your stanza on Watson. The appeal published the other day[3] seemed to me so injudicious in its terms that I could not bring myself to sign it, nor, I suppose, could Masefield; and I know that others signed it with great reluctance, fearing that it would defeat its purpose, which they thoroughly approved.

I am glad to hear that the fund is prospering.

I am yours very truly   A. E. HOUSMAN

To the Richards Press

MS. B.M.

26 November 1930   *Trinity College*

Dear Sirs,

I agree that the proofs of the advertisement are unsatisfactory. For one thing, 'accedunt addenda libris I II III IV' should be one line, as I made it; and the insertion of full-stops and commas after the numerals is particularly silly. The advertisement of book IV filled half a page (I enclose a copy, which please return), and so should the present one if possible. Time does not press: the *Classical Review* will not appear before the middle of December, and the *Classical Quarterly* not till January.

Yours faithfully   A. E. HOUSMAN

---

[1] Edward Henry Blakeney (1869–1955), classical scholar and amateur printer; Headmaster of King Henry VIII's School, Ely, 1904–1918; assistant master at Winchester College, 1918–1930. The text of this letter is taken from a copy made by Messrs Blackwell (typescript B.M.), corrected and amplified by the version printed in Blakeney's *Letters from A. E. Housman*, (privately printed) 1941.

[2] This was done.

[3] In *The Times*, 3 November 1930. The appeal describes Watson as 'a lord of language . . . in the Miltonic tradition'. It was signed, among others, by Lascelles Abercrombie, Barrie, Binyon, Blunden, de la Mare, Drinkwater, Elgar, Galsworthy, Lloyd George, Kipling, Mackail and Shaw. Housman contributed twenty guineas to the fund.

To Monica Bridges

MS. BRIDGES

26 November 1930   *Trinity College*

Dear Mrs Bridges,

The inscription[1] was composed in Latin by Dr Bridges himself, who only asked me to trim it for him, and I made as little change as possible. The form of the proper names is his own, and I approve it. *Roberti* and *Harrietta* would be sham Latin, as the names of course were not known to the ancients, and *Elizabetha* would be positively wrong, for *Elizabeth* in the Latin Bible, as in the Greek, is not inflected.

The Latin does mean that the widow spent 19 years of widowhood at Yattendon; and if that is not true it will want altering as you say.

I hope that you and yours are well; but your son must not hope for heaven if he writes MCMXXX for MDCCCXXX.

Yours sincerely   A. E. HOUSMAN

To E. F. Collingwood[2]

MS. TRINITY

28 November 1930   *Trinity College*

Dear Collingwood,

1. At the Audit Feast the sherry started on its rounds only from the Master's left (his less honourable side), and if I had not made a row, most of those on his right would have finished their soup long before it reached them.

2. I am tired of writing in the suggestion book about Irish Stew and saying that it ought to have lots of potato and lots of onion. On the last occasion it not only had neither but was strangely and shockingly garnished with dumplings.

3. Which reminds me that it must be three years since I have eaten boiled beef in Hall. Now that you have moderated the chef's passion for boiled mutton, he might consent to cook it now and then.

4. I was sitting last night next the Professor of Agriculture,[3] to whom I related my success in introducing leeks to the High Table and my failure to introduce salsify. He was much surprised: at St John's they have both frequently as a matter of course.

---

[1] For Bridges' mother's grave in Yattendon.

[2] Edward Foyle Collingwood (born 1900); University Lecturer and Steward of Trinity College, 1930; Chairman of the Council of Durham University, 1963; knighted, 1962.

[3] F. L. Engledow, Fellow of St John's College, Cambridge; Professor of Agriculture, 1930.

I write to you because I am told that when the world is out of joint you are the only means to set it right.

Yours very truly   A. E. HOUSMAN

To S. C. Roberts

MS. C.U.P.

13 December 1930   *Trinity College*

My dear Roberts,

As the copy[1] in which I made the corrections has not been returned to me I cannot certify that they have all been inserted, but I am willing to assume that they have, and I do not suppose that I need see a revise. But the list of MSS will have to disappear from p. xxxviii, because the second preface will begin on p. xxxvii.

The manuscript of the second preface I will send you by hand on Monday morning. It must first be set up in what I believe you call galley proofs, not in pages.

Yours sincerely   A. E. HOUSMAN

Corrected proofs enclosed.

To A. F. Scholfield

MS. TRINITY

15 December 1930   *Trinity College*

Dear Scholfield,

I shall now be bringing out an *editio minor*, and even after that I shall keep the photographs[2] as long as I live. I had thought of bequeathing them to the Trinity Library: you ought to be able to give me impartial advice.

Yours sincerely   A. E. HOUSMAN

To J. W. Mackail

MS. TRINITY

18 December 1930   *Trinity College*

Dear Mackail,

I am glad of your approbation and grateful for your condolence and congratulation;[3] though the condolence is not needed, for I am always glad when

[1] Of the second edition of his Juvenal.

[2] Of the manuscripts of Manilius. Scholfield had suggested that Housman give them to the University Library. Housman's will made no direction for the disposal of these photographs but they were given to Trinity College Library by Laurence Housman.

[3] On the Publication of Manilius V.

a job is finished. I shall now be bringing out an *editio minor*, just text and apparatus in one volume; but it will be a thin octavo, not suitable for your genteel pocket, as I want a roomy page. I do not mean to impoverish myself any more for the public weal, and I have no doubt that either of the University presses would undertake it. The Cambridge Press has volunteered to produce a new edition of the Juvenal, which is now printing.

Yours sincerely   A. E. HOUSMAN

To S. C. Roberts

MS. C.U.P.

19 December 1930   *Trinity College*

Dear Roberts,
   I am not revising the text and notes of Juvenal till they are complete and till I get back the copy of the book; but I notice some stupidities. I do not know why they should desert (as at I 44) the system by which in the first edition (as at I 98) a note on one verse is separated from a note on another, for it is lucid and an aid to the reader; but when in similar circumstances the space separating two notes on different words in the same verse is abolished (as at III 37 and still worse in the last line of p. 49) the damage is serious.

Yours sincerely   A. E. HOUSMAN

To the Richards Press

MS. B.M.

22 December 1930   *Trinity College*

Dear Sirs,
   The proofs of covers and labels of books II and III which I return herewith are correct.
   You have not yet answered, as you said on the 8th inst. that you would, my question about the number of unsold copies of books II III IV; and in the meanwhile I am perplexed by the conduct of booksellers. Deighton Bell and Co in this town, when selling copies of II and IV to a friend of mine the other day, told him that they were the last and that there were no more to be had; and Basil Blackwell at Oxford has been stating for a year or more that II is out of print.

Yours faithfully   A. E. HOUSMAN

To A. F. Scholfield

MS. TRINITY

26 December 1930   *Trinity College*

Dear Scholfield,

What Deighton Bell and Co. tell you is merely part of the conspiracy among book-sellers to restrict the sale of my graver works. Of vol. III, though the binders have lost or mislaid some 40 copies, there remain about 80, and of vol. IV about 180.

Yours sincerely   A. E. HOUSMAN

To Joseph Ishill

MS. HARVARD

26 December 1930   *Trinity College*

Dear Mr Ishill,

Pray accept my thanks for your kind gift of *The Soul of Japan*[1] from the Oriole Press. It is really too good for me, because I am not educated to appreciate beauty of typography.

The pompous edition of *A Shropshire Lad* and *Last Poems* was printed at the Alcuin Press, Chipping Campden, Gloucestershire, and published by The Richards Press Ltd., 90 Newman Street, London W1, in 1929; but I believe that all the 300 copies were sold before publication.

I am yours sincerely   A. E. HOUSMAN

To Percy Withers

MS. WITHERS

26 December 1930   *Trinity College*

My dear Withers,

Between a Feast last night and a dinner-party this evening, I sit me down to thank you and your wife and family for their Christmas greetings and wish you all a happy New Year. Rutherford's daughter, married to another Fellow of Trinity, died suddenly a day or two ago;[2] the wife of the Emeritus Professor of Greek,[3] who himself is paralysed, has cut her throat with a razor which she had bought to give her son-in-law; I have a brother and a brother-in-law both seriously ill and liable to drop dead any moment; and in short

---

[1] By Elie Faure, translated by Rose Freeman Ishill, 1930.
[2] Eileen Fowler, wife of R. H. Fowler, F.R.S., died in childbirth on 23 December 1930.
[3] A. C. Pearson.

Providence has given itself up to the festivities of the season. A more cheerful piece of news is that I have just published the last book I shall ever write, and that I now mean to do nothing for ever and ever. It is one of my more serious works, so you will not read it. I am glad that there is a chance of seeing you again in Cambridge before so very long. I hope and believe that the 1908 port will last out till then. Trusting that you are in rude health I remain yours sincerely

A. E. HOUSMAN

To Alice Rothenstein

MS. HARVARD

1 January 1931   *Trinity College*

Dear Lady Rothenstein,[1]
   When anything of this sort happens to a friend of mine, I always write to his wife, if he has one, and if I have the honour of her acquaintance, because she is the person who is chiefly concerned and who takes most pleasure in it. I therefore send you my warm congratulations (from which I do not altogether exclude Sir William), and my earnest hope that you will not be stuck up.

   Yours sincerely   A. E. HOUSMAN

To Grant Richards

TEXT: RICHARDS

12 January 1931   *[Trinity College]*

   Blette (that is how to spell it) is also called *Poirée*, and in English is *Leaf-beet, Sea-kale-beet, Swiss-chard-beet*, in botany *Beta Cicla*. It belongs to the genus *Chenopodium* or *Goose-foot*, as your newspaper said. The leaves can be cooked like spinach.

To the Richards Press

MS. B.M.

3 February 1931   *Trinity College*

Dear Sirs,
   It would be absurd to send a copy[2] to *The Listener*.

   Yours faithfully   A. E. HOUSMAN

---

[1] A knighthood was conferred on Rothenstein in the New Year Honours list.
[2] Of Manilius V.

To I. R. Brussel[1]

MS. LILLY

16 February 1931   *Trinity College*

Dear Mr Brussel,
    I find it a trouble to invent titles for poems, and do not think it worth while.
I am not alone in this: for instance many of Bridges' *Shorter Poems* have no
titles.

    Yours very truly   A. E. HOUSMAN

To Walter Makin[2]

MS. B.M.

26 February 1931   *Trinity College*

Dear Sir,
    The Richards Press has always treated me very well and I have no inclina-
tion to see another publisher; but if it is made over to, or merged in, another
firm, I shall prefer to transfer the books to their former publisher Mr Grant
Richards.

    Yours very truly   A. E. HOUSMAN

To R. W. Chambers

MS. CARTER

26 February 1931   *Trinity College*

Dear Chambers,
    Many thanks to you and Grattan[3] for your learned and scientific enquiry.
Did you ever hear of the newspaper which reported an address of mine 'On
the application of thought to sexual criticism'?

    Yours sincerely   A. E. HOUSMAN

---

[1] American bookseller.

[2] Manager of the Richards Press.

[3] John Henry Grafton Grattan (1878–1951) was lecturer in English at University College,
London, 1912–1930; Professor of English at Liverpool, 1930–1943. He collaborated with
Chambers on several books.

To L. W. Payne

MS. TEXAS

1 March 1931   *Trinity College*

Dear Mr Payne,

In spite of your courteous and amiable letter I will not assist or encourage young men to write theses on 'The art of A. E. Housman'.[1] All that need be known of my life and books is contained in about a dozen lines of the publication *Who's Who* (A. & C. Black Ltd., 4 Soho Square, London w. 1), which probably circulates in America. I have received a good many similar enquiries and have answered them much in the same way; so do not feel hurt.

Yours very truly   A. E. HOUSMAN

To Reginald Hackforth[2]

12 March 1931   *Trinity College*

Dear Hackforth,

The average Englishman is a sexual monomaniac; and if you and I have escaped the taint we may be thankful.

I am quite accustomed to having my contributions rejected,[3] and I may say with Mr Pecksniff "Do not weep for me: it is chronic." The last occasion was when one editor of the *Classical Quarterly*, having heard me read a paper, asked me to let them have it, and his colleague declined it without consulting him.

You seem to have behaved with strict propriety.

Yours sincerely   A. E. HOUSMAN

To Grant Richards

TEXT: RICHARDS

15 April 1931   *[Trinity College]*

I was interested in your account of the Rothenstein dinner.[4] Mackail, of whom you speak so disparagingly, is a remarkably handsome man.

[1] This thesis by Ouida Mary Valliant, a pupil of Payne's, was completed in 1931. It has not been published.

[2] 1887–1957; Fellow of Sidney Sussex College, Cambridge, 1912; University Lecturer in Classics, 1926; Laurence Professor of Ancient Philosophy, 1939–1952; Editor of *The Classical Quarterly*, 1927–1934. Text from a copy, in another hand, at Trinity College.

[3] 'Praefanda', a note on obscene phrases in the Latin poets, had already been accepted by *The Classical Quarterly* and was in proof when the Board of Management objected to its inclusion. Housman published the paper instead in the German periodical *Hermes*, 1931.

[4] To celebrate his knighthood.

I have just come back from nearly a month in the South of France, Pyrenees and Bordeaux; at which last place I ate for the first time in my life garlic soup, called *tourin blanchie* or *tourin Bordelaise*: very good, though it contained an egg, which I thought irrelevant. Never go to Narbonne: I don't add Quillan, because no one would think of going there, unless mad like me.

To Monica Bridges

MS. BRIDGES

15 April 1931   *Trinity College*

Dear Mrs Bridges,

The letter J did not exist in ancient times, and when I write inscriptions myself I never use it, and try, sometimes in vain, to prevent the stone cutter from inserting it. But in such a detail I probably followed, in my copy, the original in Dr Bridges' handwriting. If *ejus* and *jacet juxta* are used, consistency would require *hujus* and *cujus*.

The phrase which I took for *te decet hymnis* was not familiar to me, and I supposed that the construction was elliptical (for *te decet hymnis celebrare* or the like.) But as you seem to know it, and to know that *hymnus* is the regular form, it is probable that I miscopied what Dr Bridges wrote.

I am yours sincerely   A. E. HOUSMAN

I have been abroad and only came home yesterday.

To Charles Wilson

MS. SPARROW

4 June 1931   *Trinity College*

Dear Mr Wilson,

My feelings are much the same as Huxley's;[1] but in my case school is not the cause, for I was quite uninfluenced by my school, which was a small one. I think the cause is in the home. Class is a real thing: we may wish that it were not, and we may pretend that it is not, but I find that it is.

Thanks for your kind enquiries: I had a month's fine weather abroad. I am sorry to hear of your mother's state of health.

Yours very truly   A. E. HOUSMAN

[1] Aldous Huxley (1894–1963) novelist and essayist. Wilson seems to have made the enquiry of him privately.

To Grant Richards

TEXT: RICHARDS

24 June 1931   *[Trinity College]*

I shall be passing the night of 10 July (Friday) in London. You were kind enough to say that you had a bed in your bijou residence, and if it is empty and you are there I should much like to occupy it. I should also like to take you and Mrs Richards to dine with me somewhere; and if you will come I should be obliged if you would select the restaurant and order the dinner, for which I give you carte blanche. I shall not have evening dress with me.

To the Richards Press

MS. B.M.

23 July 1931   *Trinity College*

Dear Sirs,

Mrs A. M. Henderson must be told that I do not allow poems from *A Shropshire Lad* to be reprinted.[1]

It so happens that I have received this morning a Tauchnitz edition (vol. 5000 of their series) of a book called *Anthology of Modern English Poetry* by Levin L. Schücking which contains two poems, Nos. IV and XLVIII, from *A Shropshire Lad*, without consent from me. I presume the Anthology was originally an American book, and Mr Schücking was of course quite entitled to include the poems, as *A Shropshire Lad* is not copyright in America; but I thought that British copyright holds good on the Continent, and that Tauchnitz would have no right to print the poems without my consent, although the book is 'not to be introduced into the British Empire'.

Yours faithfully   A. E. HOUSMAN

To an Unnamed Correspondent

MS. FEINBERG

23 July 1931   *Trinity College*

Dear Madam,

I am grateful to you for sending me the interview with Mr Yeats,[2] but not even gratitude will induce me to be interviewed myself.

I am yours faithfully   A. E. HOUSMAN

---

[1] Permission had been asked to include poems by Housman in *Attractive Readings in Prose and Verse*; it was published in 1932 but contained nothing by him.

[2] William Butler Yeats (1865–1939), Irish poet, winner of the Nobel Prize for Literature, 1923.

To George Barnes[1]

MS. C.U.P.

30 August 1931   Trinity College

Dear Sir,

I have been away from Cambridge for a month. I now return the book
with lettering corrected. The division IVVE-NALIS is the practice in Latin
inscriptions and ancient manuscripts. SATVRAE I have struck out as being
superfluous; and also to conform with my other books.

Yours faithfully

A. E. HOUSMAN

Please look at p. xl, mutilated since I saw it last.

To Katharine Symons

MS. TRINITY

11 September 1931   Trinity College

My dear Kate,

Well, I came back here at the end of last month, after eight days in Argyll-
shire and in the only good weather I got while away. The scenery was exactly
what I had supposed it would be, and quite good of course, though not my
favourite sort: an artist there[2] whom I knew was however much delighted,
especially with the atmospheric conditions and haziness.

One of my fellow guests was an immensely distant relation of ours, Richmond Palmer, now governor of the Gambia, who has called on me several
times at Cambridge. He knew the Housmans at Lancaster, and told me that
Fanny Ellwood, née Housman, died some weeks or months ago. She must
have been a great age, for when I was six she seemed to me over twenty.

The only new flower that I came across was Grass of Parnassus, which I
had only seen in illustrations to books of botany: a simple green-veined white
flower at the top of a slender stalk.

I hope that Edward is going on well and that Denis's finger is healed. I
heard that you had got a house at Exmouth and were meaning to spend the
holidays there. Basil had two sharp attacks of pain the fortnight I was there,
but was fairly easy most of the time. He did not look worse than last year, but
is feebler on his legs.

Your affectionate brother

A. E. HOUSMAN

[1] 1904–1960; Assistant Secretary of the Cambridge University Press, 1930–1935; later
Head of the B.B.C. Third Programme and Director of Television; Principal of the University College of North Staffordshire, 1956–1960.
[2] Henry Tonks.

To the Richards Press

MS. B.M.

17 September 1931   *Trinity College*

Dear Sirs,

I am charmed to hear that I possess the copyright of Sir William Rothenstein's drawing,[1] and I certainly shall not allow it to be reproduced.

Yours faithfully   A. E. HOUSMAN

To Cyril Clemens[2]

22 October 1931   *Trinity College*

Dear Mr Clemens,

I am naturally flattered that you should entertain the idea of writing a biography of me, but neither you nor anyone else could possibly write one and I certainly would give no assistance. I have sometimes thought of depositing in the British Museum a few pages to be published fifty years after my death.[3] For the present, however, *Who's Who* gives all the external facts.

I am very truly yours   A. E. HOUSMAN

To Grant Richards

TEXT: RICHARDS

13 November 1931   [*Trinity College*]

I have no recollection whatever of having given my consent to Tauchnitz; but when the Richards Press took them to task they said that they had a letter from me giving consent, and they gave its date; and I suppose they would not be brazen enough to tell an utter lie.

But I did not give them consent to omit a comma, nor to alter the English word *Reveille* into *Réveille*,[4] which is not even French. Moreover it is a wretched selection containing, for instance, six pieces of Sassoon's;[5] and I will not give my consent to Heinemann.[6]

---

[1] Presumably the one given to him by Rothenstein in 1907.
[2] Text from *Poet Lore* LIII, 1947.
[3] Housman never carried out this idea. All there is in the British Museum is a small diary containing a few trifling but telling entries about Moses Jackson. It was presented by Laurence Housman in 1942. See p. 440, item 21.
[4] In the title of *A Shropshire Lad* IV.
[5] Siegfried Sassoon (1888–1967). His *Selected Poems* appeared in 1925.
[6] For an English edition.

To Grant Richards

TEXT: RICHARDS

14 December 1931 [*Trinity College*]

I once met Ford Madox Hueffer,[1] as he then was, at Rothenstein's, but I am sure I neither did nor said anything which would take even one page to tell. I hear that I appear also (as doubtless you do) in the reminiscences of Fothergill of Thame;[2] and I am invited to buy the *Private Papers of a bank-rupt bookseller*[3] because on p. 216 there is something about *A Shropshire Lad.*

I have bought for use *The Hungry Traveller in France* by Norman Davey (Jonathan Cape).

To Percy Withers

MS. WITHERS

20 December 1931 *Trinity College*

My dear Withers,

You are the most acrimonious of my correspondents, and insist on making a grievance of what you ought to regard as a natural phenomenon, like the voice of the peacock or the smell of the goat. However, on this occasion I have more to say than usual, because in August I went to Scotland for the first time in my life and was rewarded by finding the only fine weather of my summer. It was Atornish (in Scott's *Lord of the Isles*, now spelt Ard-tornish) on the Sound of Mull; the landscape exactly as I had imagined it. I enjoyed walking about among the red-deer and so forth, but ten days exhausted the neighbourhood, and I shall not go again.

Some of our feasts are suppressed for the sake of economy[4] (i.e. that waiters may suffer from lack of employment and our champagne may go bad in the cellar) but not the Christmas one. I have had my annual milk punch at Jesus and am expecting my annual stout and oysters on St Sylvester's day, after which I shall be able to face another year of life. Also I have lately had a blow-out at the Fishmongers' Hall.[5] Whether you are in palace or cottage, I

---

[1] English novelist (1873–1939) who during the First World War changed his surname to Ford. In writing his reminiscences, he drew heavily on his imagination.

[2] *An Innkeeper's Diary*, 1931. The author, John Rowland Fothergill (1876–1957) studied at the Slade School and was a friend of Rothenstein and other artists. He later became land-lord of The Spread Eagle at Thame, Oxfordshire, where Housman met him in June 1927 when driving back from Gloucestershire to Cambridge.

[3] By W. Y. Darling, published anonymously in 1931.

[4] The severe economic crisis of August 1931 led to the formation of a National Govern-ment. Public expenditure was cut sharply and a general economy drive instituted. Housman at the time gave a substantial portion of his savings as a voluntary donation to the Treasury.

[5] On 12 November.

shall be very glad to come and see you in the summer. My kind regards to Mrs Withers.

Yours sincerely   A. E. HOUSMAN

To Sydney Cockerell

MS. LILLY

15 January 1932   *Trinity College*

My dear Cockerell,
Some things of Edna St Vincent Millay[1] which I have seen make me think her the best living American poet, but as she is said to be profuse and unequal I have never tackled a work of hers; so I shall be grateful for a sight of the sonnets, though I could wish that they were not sonnets.

Yours very truly   A. E. HOUSMAN

To Grant Richards

TEXT: RICHARDS

16 January 1932   *[Trinity College]*

You correctly suppose that I will have no more editions de luxe.[2] Talking of pornography, you have been remiss about promising me a sight of Frank Harris's last two volumes, for I understand there are four in all, and I have only seen two.

To S. C. Roberts

MS. C.U.P.

16 January 1932   *Trinity College*

My dear Roberts,
We had some conversation last year about my *editio minor* of Manilius.[3] This is now complete, text, apparatus, and index, all except the preface, which will be quite short; so I shall be obliged if you will propose it to the Syndics.

I have ideas of my own about size of page and print, and I also want it to be fairly cheap, though I do not suppose you can emulate the Oxford classical texts in that respect.

Yours sincerely   A. E. HOUSMAN

[1] American poet (1892–1950). The sonnets were published in *Fatal Interview*, 1931, which Housman later called 'mighty good'.
[2] Jack Kahane of the Obelisk Press, Paris, had asked for permission to print a de luxe edition of *A Shropshire Lad*.
[3] Published by the Cambridge University Press, 1932.

To S. C. Roberts

MS. C.U.P.

20 January 1932 *Trinity College*

Dear Roberts,

I am sending herewith in two envelopes the text, apparatus criticus, and index of the *ed. minor* of Manilius. It may spare you some calculation to know that the text is about 4270 hexameters.

The point on which I am chiefly set is not anything absolute, but relative: that the page should be wide enough, *or* the print small enough, to let the longest line be printed without running over. Some of the lines are very long: for instance in the neighbourhood of II 935. It might be well to have an interview, which we could arrange when we meet on Friday.

Yours sincerely   A. E. HOUSMAN

To Charles Wilson

MS. SPARROW

6 February 1932 *Trinity College*

Dear Mr Wilson,

Although it is only your fun, just to keep your pen in exercise, I must thank you for your repeated invitation, but need not repeat my answer.

Yours very truly   A. E. HOUSMAN

To S. C. Roberts

MS. PRIVATE

15 February 1932 *Trinity College*

My dear Roberts,

The specimen of printing is now altogether satisfactory; but as to the agreement, I mentioned in one of our conversations that I wished to keep the copyright and to receive as royalty anything that I might receive, and you offered no objection. I therefore return herewith the two copies of the form.

Yours sincerely   A. E. HOUSMAN

To S. C. Roberts

16 February 1932   *Trinity College*

My dear Roberts,

Formally to retain the copyright myself, as you say, and to have it stated in the agreement, is what I desire, and I am indifferent to the mode in which riches will accrue to me.

Yours sincerely   A. E. HOUSMAN

To S. C. Roberts

18 February 1932   *Trinity College*

My dear Roberts,

I enclose the two copies of the agreement signed. I have put down the date 31 March rather at random: in essentials the preface will be finished long before that, but I cannot complete it properly till I have the text and notes in type.

I want text and notes to be first printed separately in galley (I think you call it) before they are combined into pages. I made this petition in the case of the Juvenal also, and you said it should be done; but diabolis aliter visum.[1]

Yours sincerely   A. E. HOUSMAN

To Grant Richards

28 February 1932   *[Trinity College]*

Good. I enclose your ticket.[2] I have accepted in your name as well as my own. We shall be placed side by side, and there is no reason why we should meet beforehand, but I am intending to stay as usual at the Great Eastern hotel in Liverpool Street, which is convenient for getting back to Cambridge next morning. I shall not wear a white waistcoat, partly because I have not got one, partly because I am told on high authority that, though now so common, it is incorrect unless dancing is to follow. The invitation is from the Master of the Company, who sent the second ticket because he will not be able to pay attention to a private guest.

---

[1] The devils decided otherwise. Cf. Virgil *Aeneid* II. 428: *Dis aliter visum*; the gods decided otherwise.

[2] For the dinner of the Girdlers' Company on 17 March 1932.

To L. W. Payne

MS. TEXAS

28 February 1932   *Trinity College*

Dear Mr Payne,

I am obliged by your letter, but I rather avoid reading things written about me and will not trouble you to send me the essay.

I shall be pleased to write my name in your copy of *Last Poems* if you care for it, but for many years I have refused to copy out verses, though I did it once or twice long ago.

One good result of the present financial stringency is that the absurd prices which used to be asked for the first edition of *A Shropshire Lad* are abating.

I am yours sincerely   A. E. HOUSMAN

To Laurence Housman

TEXT: MEMOIR

1 March 1932   *[Trinity College]*

My dear Laurence,

... Your generous offer to pass on Coventry Patmore[1] to me has its allurements, for I have often idly thought of writing an essay on him and have even been inclined sometimes to regard it, as you say, in the light of a duty, because nobody admires his best poetry enough, though the stupid papists may fancy they do. But it would give me more trouble than you can imagine, whereas I want peace in my declining years; and the result would not be good enough to yield me pride or even satisfaction. I should say as little as possible about his nasty mixture of piety and concupiscence; but his essay on English metre is the best thing ever written on the subject, though spoilt by one great mistake...

Your affectionate brother   A. E. HOUSMAN

To Cyril Clemens

MS. COLUMBIA

4 March 1932   *Trinity College*

Dear Mr Clemens,

I have corrected or marked the most inaccurate of your inaccuracies.[2] I do not know why Americans are so fond of writing—and apparently of reading—

---

[1] The essay on Patmore to be included in *The Great Victorians* edited by H. J. Massingham, 1932. It was eventually written by Herbert Read (1893–1968). Laurence Housman contributed one on Florence Nightingale.

[2] In 'Housman as a Conversationalist', intended as a chapter of a full biography but published separately in *The Mark Twain Quarterly*, Winter 1936.

about personal matters; but it seems to be a national characteristic, and it makes me unwilling to meet them, though they are always so kindly and friendly.

Yours very truly   A. E. HOUSMAN

To Joseph Ishill

MS. HARVARD

10 April 1932   *Trinity College*

Dear Mr Ishill,
If you do not mind, I would rather that you did not reprint 'Eight o'clock' in your annual.[1] I always give permission rather reluctantly, and there seems to be no particular fitness in its appearance.

I do not know the laws of the United States, but the 'Copyright 1919 by the Four Seas Company' which you bring to my notice must surely be mere nonsense. I did not copyright the book in America when I published it in England in 1896, and I cannot imagine how anyone else could do it.

I am yours very truly   A. E. HOUSMAN

To E. H. Blakeney

MS. B.M.

22 April 1932   *Trinity College*

Dear Mr Blakeney,
If a postcard dated April 19 but with neither signature nor postmark legible is yours, as I think it may be, I will say in reply that I do not think an edition of Persius is very much needed, and certainly I might be better employed. About Manilius I am not going to take any more trouble, when I have brought out the *editio minor*, just text and apparatus, now printing at the University Press.

Yours sincerely   A. E. HOUSMAN

To William Rothenstein

MS. HARVARD

4 May 1932   *Trinity College*

My dear Rothenstein,
I am afraid I cannot get heavy damages out of you for stealing three words,

[1] *Free Vistas, an Anthology of Life and Letters*, 1933. It contained nothing by Housman.

319

all the rest being Mrs Cornford's.[1] I am told there is another version in circulation with 'small brown woman'. I am reading and enjoying your book. I suppose it is being a painter that makes you able to retain your experiences so distinctly and reproduce them with so much life. Haydon, Fromentin, and Frith[2] are a mixed but respectable society for you.

On p. 138 there is something very wrong with Webb's first sentence.

225–6. To 'tell the truth' about 'a million million stars', there are never more than two thousand separately visible.

253. They have stuck in a comma between Lockwood and Kipling, as of course they would.

273. The place you call Longdon is Longfords.

I should be very glad to see you here again. In this month I might not be able to get you a bedroom without longish notice. I am going away probably on the 27th, but shall be here for the last week of June, and again continuously after 25 July or thereabouts.

My kind regards to Lady Rothenstein, who seems to have a number of nicknames.

Yours sincerely   A. E. HOUSMAN

To Grant Richards

TEXT: RICHARDS

18 May 1932   *[Trinity College]*

Certainly Beerbohm has given you a very nice puff,[3] and I hope it will work.

I am very sorry to hear about Mrs Grant Allen,[4] who always struck me as most interesting and clever.

I shall be in Paris at the Continental from 29 May to 14 June. I cannot offer you anything of an invitation, for I shall have a friend with me who would not mix with you nor you with him; but if by chance you should be there I hope you would come to dine or lunch with me one day. I have several menus of restaurants which you have sent me from time to time, and I should be grateful for any up-to-date information.

If the last two volumes of Frank Harris can be sent to me, as you suggested, I shall be grateful to your friend for taking the trouble; but my wish to read them is not at all intense, and I hope he will not in any way put himself out.

My kind regards to Mrs Richards.

[1] Rothenstein printed Housman's parody (see p. 109) in *Men and Memories*, volume II, 1932.

[2] The autobiographies of these painters were published in 1853, 1909 and 1887 respectively.

[3] Introduction by Max Beerbohm to Richards' *Memories of a Misspent Youth*, 1932.

[4] Richards' aunt, widow of the novelist Grant Allen (1848–1899), had recently died. Housman had been her fellow-guest at Bigfrith and Ruan Minor.

To Grant Richards

TEXT: RICHARDS

31 May 1932   *Hôtel Continental, Paris*

I have been to the Écu de France, which is good and evidently very success-ful, rather uncomfortably crowded after eight. I ate the two things given most prominence in the menu and praised by the patron or chef d'hôtel or whoever he was: they were regional, which meant Norman. One was a sole with mushrooms, certainly very good, though it is not a mixture I approve of; the other was deadly dull, boiled or stewed fowl with mushrooms again, though not the same sort, and the hard uneatable parts of artichoke leaves. The patron stands over the waiters while they serve one, in a menacing manner, so that it is clear their heads will be cut off if they fall short in anything. When I started to order Burgundy the Sommelier insisted on Chambolle-Musigny 1921, which was most excellent. Though Bouillabaisse was not on the menu, the restaurant was faintly pervaded by that agreeable smell or something very like it.

To Katharine Symons

MS. TRINITY

15 June 1932   *Trinity College*

My dear Kate,

I did not know anything of your varicose trouble, which you treated as the Spartan boy did the fox,[1] but I am very glad that you are rid of it, as it seems you are; and it must have been serious, if the treatment took so long. It is also satisfactory that you are able to dispose of your numerous residential seats, and I hope you are now set free from all business worries. Your letter in the *Birmingham Post* is very interesting and puts things (some of which I did not know) into a clear and condensed form. I suppose that I did once hear of the awful fate of the books at Fockbury in our father's youth, but I had quite forgotten it. Our grandmother of course had no brains at all that I could discover; but our grandfather ought to have been ashamed of himself. I am glad however that you have given Catshill his photograph. I return you the cuttings, as I have no proper place to put anything.

In this last fortnight I did not spend any night outside Paris, and did not see many places or things which I had not seen before. The chief novelty was the great improvement which has been made in the aeroplanes in the last twelvemonth, in size, steadiness, freedom from noise, and even to some extent in speed. The science also seems to have progressed: when I began, pilots had to fly below the clouds, because if they flew above them they lost their way; but now they fly *through* them and keep their bearings all right. In leaving

[1] Heroically concealing it.

321

England we could see nothing but mist for the first quarter of an hour or more: then, at the coast, this cleared, and there was the blue channel under a blue sky: on the opposite side, instead of the land of France, a huge forest of white trees towering to all sorts of heights, over which, being then at 6000 feet, we proceeded to fly. Neither cotton wool for the ears, nor things to be sick in, are now provided or needed any more than in railway trains; and (on the 'silver wing', the most expensive machine—though the fare is only £5. 10. 0) you can have a large lunch served if you want it. The first five days were proper June weather, the next five cold and showery; the last five stifling hot, and when I stepped into the aeroplane at Paris, which had been standing in the sun, I wondered how we were going to support the journey; but they kept up a thorough-draught, and England was almost chilly.

At the beginning of July I am going into Oxfordshire for a few days, then for a fortnight to Tardebigge, then for a week to Street.[1]

Your affectionate brother   A. E. HOUSMAN

To S. C. Roberts

MS. C.U.P.

19 June 1932   *Trinity College*

My dear Roberts,

In the paged proofs of Manilius which reached me yesterday I have noticed, what I might easily have missed, a change made on p. 94, wrongly, and without my authority: 549^a and 549^b substituted for 549^A and 549^B. This is very improper, and very disquieting; for there is no record of the change in the galley proof accompanying. Can you ascertain whether there has been more of this sort of thing, and in what places? or shall I have to go through the whole book letter by letter to find out?

On p. 32 the proof-corrector has again given directions for making a change which ought not to be made; but there it has not yet been carried out, so I can frustrate it.

Yours sincerely   A. E. HOUSMAN

To the Richards Press

MS. B.M.

15 July 1932   *Trinity College*

Dear Sirs,

This good lady has actually printed more of me than of her own twaddle; two entire poems, besides bits.[2]

Yours faithfully   A. E. HOUSMAN

[1] In Somerset, where Laurence and Clemence Housman lived.
[2] In an article on Housman in *Great Thoughts*, July 1932, by Irene L. Watts.

To the Richards Press

MS. B.M.

29 July 1932   *Trinity College*

Dear Sirs,

I do not want the money of the editor of *Great Thoughts*. I only hope that being rapped over the knuckles will recall him to propriety.

Yours faithfully   A. E. HOUSMAN

To Grant Richards

TEXT: RICHARDS

16 September 1932   *[Trinity College]*

If you could come and stay a night or two to carry out your benevolent labour,[1] this next week would be the best to choose, as the college is still quite empty, and I could easily find you a room to take the place of the guest-rooms, both of which are permanently occupied. But the week-end would be impossible because of the Annual Gathering on the 26th: on the other hand 1 October would be all right.

To A. F. Scholfield

MS. TRINITY

3 October 1932   *Trinity College*

Dear Scholfield,

Some years ago I asked you if the Library would care to have, when the series was completed, a 'bibliotheca Germanorum erotica et curiosa' which I had ill-advisedly subscribed for,—an index of such literature.[2] When the final volume arrived, I had mislaid the others, and they have only just turned up. If you are still, as you were, disposed to receive them, will you send a stout fellow to fetch them? They are nine volumes, of the shape and size of Pauly-Wissowa,[3] but much thicker.

Yours sincerely   A. E. HOUSMAN

[1] Richards had offered to sort out and rearrange Housman's books.
[2] By Hayn and Gotendorf, first edition 1875; Housman had the third and greatly enlarged edition in nine volumes, 1912–1914, with the final volume, published in 1929.
[3] The great *Real-Encyclopädie der Classischen Altertumswissenschaft*, which began publication in 1893.

To Katharine Symons

MS. TRINITY

13 October 1932   *Trinity College*

My dear Kate,

As term has begun, I suppose it is time that I wrote you a letter. The alarm about Basil, I am glad to see, has died down, though I am afraid he must still be suffering a great deal. When I last heard from you, two of Denis' children were ill, but I hope that also has passed over, and that you had plenty of grandchildren to play with in August and September. I have been here ever since I came back from Street, working quietly. September is a month when I always feel industrious, and a pleasant month in Cambridge. The chief event in this college is that we have a new chef in the kitchen, who is a great improvement on the last one. The last one however was not dismissed for his cookery but for his quarrelsomeness. The new one had an English mother and was born in England, which causes him to pronounce his French name *Bongers* as if it meant persons who bong, to rhyme with congers.

With love,

    Your affectionate brother   A. E. HOUSMAN

Postcard to Virginia Rice[1]

15 October 1932   *Trinity College*

Not necessarily the last, but the last volume which will appear in my lifetime.

                                                    A.E.H.

To the Richards Press

MS. B.M.

19 November 1932   *Trinity College*

Dear Sirs,

If your interpretation of Messrs Curtis Brown's[2] letter is correct—that the Albatross Press have published in the United States an anthology containing poems from *A Shropshire Lad* and now wish to publish it in Europe,—I refuse to allow my poems to appear in it, as I refused in a similar case a few months ago.[3]

Your interpretation is countenanced by the remark that 'should Mr

---

[1] Text from *The Saturday Review of Literature*, 18 July 1936. This postcard was written in answer to a query whether Housman had any more verse for publication after *Last Poems*.

[2] The London literary agents.

[3] *The Albatross Book of Living Verse* edited by Louis Untermeyer. The English edition, 1933, omitted the poems by Housman. The publishers inserted a note explaining that Housman had refused permission.

324

Housman refuse permission . . . it will not be possible to proceed etc.', which seems to imply photographic reproduction of an already published book. But what they actually ask for is permission to include the poems in an anthology which they are 'planning'. However, it makes no difference to my refusal. I do not know why they cannot print other matter and photograph that.

Yours faithfully   A. E. HOUSMAN

To S. C. Roberts

MS. PRIVATE

20 November 1932   *Trinity College*

Dear Roberts,
    Hospitality will protect you from violence, so do not be afraid to come on Friday; but what you make me say in your advertisement[1] in the *Classical Review* is the exact opposite of what I said, and intrinsically idiotic. 'Some of *these* changes, the editor thinks, may be for the worse', when I expressly said that *these* changes proceeded from a change of opinion, and excepted them from the 'much greater number' which did not.

Yours sincerely   A. E. HOUSMAN

To the Editor of The Times[2]

24 November 1932   *Trinity College*

CHAMBERLAIN'S MAIDEN SPEECH

Sir,
    On page 14 of your issue of to-day it is said that Joseph Chamberlain wore an eye-glass when he made his first speech in the House of Commons.[3] He wore a pair of spectacles with black and rather thick rims. Disraeli is described as "frail and cadaverous." His complexion was a pale olive, but did not look cadaverous from the Strangers' Gallery; and of frailty there was not a sign. Sitting as he did with one knee crossed over the other, he showed a very good pair of legs; he walked in and out of the House with a long, easy stride; and after answering a speech of Hartington's, a few days earlier or later, about the Suez Canal shares, he threw himself back into his seat almost with violence.
    Chamberlain's speech was very rapid, and at first too loud for the size of the Chamber. He showed no trace of nervousness except that once, after saying "I protest, Mr Speaker," he rather hurriedly changed the phrase to "I humbly protest."

Yours faithfully   A. E. HOUSMAN

[1] Of the *editio minor* of Manilius.   [2] Text from *The Times*, 25 November 1932.
[3] On 4 August 1876.

To Delos O'Brian[1]

3 December 1932   *Trinity College*

Dear Mr O'Brian,

I have had no photograph taken for many years, but in the ambition of decorating your vestry I enclose one which belongs to the time when I was writing *A Shropshire Lad*.

I am yours very truly   A. E. HOUSMAN

To Percy Withers

MS. WITHERS

4 December 1932   *Trinity College*

My dear Withers,

It is exceedingly kind and thoughtful of you to offer me lodging, but I am not going to my brother's funeral,[2] as it would be difficult and they do not press me to come.

He was my favourite among my brothers and sisters, and the most normal member of the family. He suffered so much pain, especially towards the end, that his death is a release.

My kind regards to Mrs Withers.

Yours sincerely   A. E. HOUSMAN

To E. H. W. Meyerstein[3]

MS. SPARROW

23 December 1932   *Trinity College*

Dear Sir,

I am obliged by your gift and flattered by your request for my comments, but I ought not to give an encouraging response. Your translation, however faithful, is prevented from being a 'poetic counterpart' of the original by insensitiveness in the choice of words. The verse too has not that accomplishment which would be required for an adequate version of Propertius. But I am notoriously a morose critic, and you should not let this answer spoil your Christmas.

I am yours very truly   A. E. HOUSMAN

[1] American minister of religion, not otherwise identified. Text from *The Dalhousie Review* XXIX, 1950.

[2] Basil Housman died on 1 December 1932.

[3] Edward Harry William Meyerstein, poet and novelist (1889–1952), published *Four Elegies of Propertius*, 1932.

To Laurence Housman

TEXT: MEMOIR

28 December 1932   [*Trinity College*]

My dear Laurence,

... I am glad to have the report of your comparatively edifying end, which ought to go well on the stage;[1] for I suppose by this time you are quite an accomplished actor. I observe that in order to make yourself more precious in the eyes of your redeemer you have blackened yourself with Basil's diabolism; and the exact phrase was 'I'm very fond of the devil'. The passage from *The Chinese Lantern* seems to me a judicious selection.

Love and a happy new year to both of you. . . .

    Your affectionate brother   A. E. HOUSMAN

To Laurence Housman

MS. MCGILL

25 January 1933   *Trinity College*

My dear Laurence,

I have signed no end of copies for the most undeserving people, including a lot of my own students at University College, so I never make any difficulty about it. But your friend has come in for a slump in these fancy goods, I am afraid.

I saw from the papers that your death was attracting notice. I should like to hear you on the gramophone some day, but do not send me a record, which would be wasting it.

    Your affectionate brother   A. E. HOUSMAN

To Grant Richards

TEXT: RICHARDS

29 January 1933   [*Trinity College*]

I am touched by your concern for my health and disapproval of my habits, but your picture is darker than the truth. The fire does not usually go out, nor is the bed to which I retire a cold one, as I keep my bedroom so warm with a gas fire that I do not even need to use my hot-water bottle.

---

[1] Laurence Housman wrote, and performed in University College, London, *Nunc Dimittis*, an epilogue to his *Little Plays of St Francis*, in which the author is represented on his deathbed.

327

To Maurice Pollet[1]

MS. LILLY

5 February 1933   *Trinity College*

Dear M. Pollet,

As some of the questions which you ask in your flattering curiosity may be asked by future generations, and as many of them can only be answered by me, I make this reply.

I was born in Worcestershire, not Shropshire, where I have never spent much time. My father's family was Lancashire and my mother's Cornish. I had a sentimental feeling for Shropshire because its hills were our western horizon. I know Ludlow and Wenlock, but my topographical details— Hughley, Abdon under Clee—are sometimes quite wrong. Remember that Tyrtaeus[2] was not a Spartan.

I took an interest in astronomy almost as early as I can remember; the cause, I think, was a little book we had in the house.

I was brought up in the Church of England and in the High Church party, which is much the best religion I have ever come across. But Lemprière's Classical Dictionary, which fell into my hands when I was eight, attached my affections to paganism. I became a deist at thirteen and an atheist at twenty-one.

I never had any scientific education.

I wrote verse at eight or earlier, but very little until I was thirty-five.

Oxford had not much effect on me, except that I there met my greatest friend.

While I was at the Patent Office I read a great deal of Greek and Latin at the British Museum of an evening.

While at University College, which is not residential, I lived alone in lodgings in the environs of London. *A Shropshire Lad* was written at Byron Cottage, 17 North Road, Highgate, where I lived from 1886 to 1905.

A Shropshire Lad was offered to Macmillan, and declined by them on the advice, I have been told, of John Morley, who was their reader. Then a friend[3] introduced me to Kegan Paul; but the book was published at my own expense.

The Shropshire Lad is an imaginary figure, with something of my temper and view of life. Very little in the book is biographical.

'Reader of the Greek Anthology' is not a good name for me. Of course I have read it, or as much of it as is worth reading, but with no special heed;

---

[1] Teacher of English literature at the Lycée d'Oran, Algeria. In the course of preparing a monograph on Housman he drew up a questionnaire (printed in Richards) which was submitted to Housman. This letter is his answer. It was published in Pollet's article *A. E. Housman. Etude suivie d'une lettre inédite*, in *Etudes Anglaises*, September 1937.

[2] National poet of Sparta (seventh century B.C.); according to tradition, an Athenian.

[3] A. W. Pollard.

and my favourite Greek poet is Aeschylus. No doubt I have been unconsciously influenced by the Greeks and Latins, but I was surprised when critics spoke of my poetry as 'classical'. Its chief sources of which I am conscious are Shakespeare's songs, the Scottish Border ballads and Heine.

'Oh stay at home' was written years before the Great War, and expresses no change of opinion, only a different mood. The Great War cannot have made much change in the opinions of any man of imagination.

I have never had any such thing as a 'crisis of pessimism'. In the first place, I am not a pessimist but a pejorist (as George Eliot said she was not an optimist but a meliorist);[1] and that is owing to my observation of the world, not to personal circumstances. Secondly, I did not begin to write poetry in earnest until the really emotional part of my life was over; and my poetry, so far as I could make out, sprang chiefly from physical conditions, such as a relaxed sore throat during my most prolific period, the first five months of 1895.

I respect the Epicureans more than the Stoics, but I am myself a Cyrenaic. Pascal and Leopardi I have studied with great admiration; Villon and Verlaine very little, Calderon and German philosophers not at all. For Hardy I felt affection, and high admiration for some of his novels and a few of his poems.

I am yours very truly   A. E. HOUSMAN

To the Countess Cave[2]

TEXT: MEMOIR

7 February 1933   [*Trinity College*]

Dear Lady Cave,

I have no reason to think that the anonymous author of the verses you mention, if still living, would have any objection to your using them,[3] and I myself, to whom they should not be attributed, have none; but I suppose that the copyright, if there is any, belongs to the editor and editorial committee of *The Bromsgrovian* . . .

I am yours sincerely   A. E. HOUSMAN

[1] James Sully's *Pessimism*, 1877 (page 399) acknowledges George Eliot's use of the term. She described her idea of it in a letter to Clifford Allbutt, 30 December 1868: 'Never to beat and bruise one's wings against the inevitable but to throw the whole force of one's soul towards the achievement of some possible better.'

[2] Ann Estella Mathews (died 1938) married George Cave (later Viscount Cave) in 1885. On his death she was granted the style and precedence of Countess.

[3] In *Ant Antics. Presented by Estella Cave. With accompaniments by Stanley Baldwin, Jack Spratt, Tom, Dick and Harry etc.*, 1933. This book for children included contributions by several eminent men of the day. The poem here mentioned, 'As I was a-walking among the grassy hay', was included in Housman's story 'A Morning with the Royal Family', published in *The Bromsgrovian*, 1882. It was apparently offered to Lady Cave by Laurence Housman, who also contributed to the book.

To Charles Wilson

MS. VIRGINIA

7 February 1933   *Trinity College*

Dear Mr Wilson,

I am very sorry to hear of your painful illness, which is even worse than the influenza now raging around me. Up to the present I have got nothing worse than a bad cold, so I ought to congratulate myself, especially when I see in *The Times* the tall columns of the deaths of people younger than me.

Yours very truly   A. E. HOUSMAN

To Pauline Hemmerde

MS. FEINBERG

16 March 1933   *Trinity College*

Dear Miss Hemmerde,

I have hitherto generally allowed anthologists to have the "Epitaph",[1] but I am getting out of patience with this endless procession of anthologies, and I refuse my permission.

Yours sincerely   A. E. HOUSMAN

To W. R. Agard[2]

MS. COLBY

22 March 1933   *Trinity College*

Dear Mr Agard,

I will not refuse you my permission to reprint my Swinburnian translation from Euripides, but if your text is that in A. W. Pollard's *Odes*[3] I will ask you to make a correction. In the second line there is a misprint, *Far-seeking*, which should be *Far seeking*, as *seeking* is noun substantive.

I am yours sincerely   A. E. HOUSMAN

To Cyril Clemens[4]

26 March 1933   *Trinity College*

Dear Mr Clemens,

Thank you very much for sending me your delightful *Josh Billings*,[5]

---

[1] i.e. 'Epitaph on an Army of Mercenaries' (*Last Poems* XXXVII).
[2] Walter Raymond Agard (born 1894), American anthologist. I have not traced his book.
[3] See p. 30, note 1.
[4] Text from Clemens' *An Evening with A. E. Housman*, 1937.
[5] Pseudonym of Henry Wheeler Shaw (1818-1885). Clemens' book was published in 1932.

Yankee Humorist which I found interesting reading. I had heard of, and enjoyed, the inimitable humour of Artemus Ward,[1] but Josh Billings was new to me, and I am indebted to you for making such a robust and characteristic Yankee known to me. I have always been interested in American humour.

Yours very truly   A. E. HOUSMAN

To Grant Richards

TEXT: RICHARDS

28 March 1933   [*Trinity College*]

Your invitation[2] is very kind and pleasant, but I dare not accept it. Until I have broken the back of that infernal lecture[3] I have no time for anything else.

I have promised our University Press to let them publish it, as they regularly do these lectures.

I don't think the story[4] is in Rabelais, whom I have read. Of Balzac I have only read a small fraction; but I don't think it is in the *Contes Drolatiques*.[5]

To Houston Martin[6]

MS. MARTIN

28 March 1933   *Trinity College*

Dear Mr Martin,

It was kind of you to write to me on my birthday. You are right in supposing that I do not look with favour on the collecting of first editions and autographs, but it is a vice which is sometimes found in otherwise virtuous persons, of whom you doubtless are one.

It is many years since I have had a photograph taken, but I have found and enclose an old one, taken about the time when I was writing *A Shropshire Lad*.

I could not say that I have a favourite among my poems. Thomas Hardy's was no. XXVII in *A Shropshire Lad*, and I think it may be the best, though it is not the most perfect.

I am yours very truly   A. E. HOUSMAN

[1] Pseudonym of Charles Farrar Browne (1834–1867).
[2] To stay with Richards in London.
[3] The Leslie Stephen Lecture for 1933, *The Name and Nature of Poetry*, which Housman delivered in the Senate House, Cambridge on 9 May.
[4] Of a rejected lover who revenged himself by sprinkling the lady's dress with a scent to attract dogs.
[5] Published in 1855.
[6] American collector and admirer of Housman's poetry, born 1914.

To Grant Richards

TEXT: RICHARDS

20 April 1933 [*Trinity College*]

The lecture is at five o'clock on 9 May in the Senate House. So far as I remember, no tickets are required for the Leslie Stephen Lecture, but I will enquire.

I shall not be able to offer you any hospitality, as I have to dine with the Vice-Chancellor.[1]

To S. C. Roberts

MS. C.U.P.

20 April 1933 *Trinity College*

Dear Roberts,

1. I enclose, signed, the two forms of agreement, though of course the index etc. referred to in section (3) are non-existent things.

2. I have quoted eight lines from a sonnet by Andrew Lang. Is that violation of copyright?

3. When do you really want the MS? In any case I should be glad if you would let me have a printed copy to read from on 9 May.

Yours sincerely A. E. HOUSMAN

To Grant Richards

TEXT: RICHARDS

22 April 1933 [*Trinity College*]

I strictly enjoin you to tell Miss Shirley Pratt[2] nothing. The sham education given at American Universities has resulted in my receiving about half-a-dozen similar enquiries from its victims.

To Percy Withers

MS. WITHERS

3 May 1933 *Trinity College*

My dear Withers,

I am going into Worcestershire on Monday 12 June, and if it would suit you that I should accept your kind invitation for Friday the 9th, that would fit in well for me.

I am sorry we shall not see you here this term. I have known certainly two

---

[1] J. F. Cameron, Master of Gonville and Caius College.
[2] American student writing an essay on Housman.

better springs, 1893, and 1894 with much more sunshine and less rain, and trees and flowers at least as much ahead of their dates.

My respectful congratulations to Audrey,[1] and kind regards to Mrs Withers.

I have grown older in the last twelvemonth.

Yours sincerely   A. E. HOUSMAN

To William Rothenstein

MS. HARVARD

4 May 1933   *Trinity College*

My dear Rothenstein,

I shall be glad to see you again, and though both the two Guest Rooms are engaged, as was to be expected this term, there are sure to be bedrooms vacated by undergraduates on a Saturday, and I have bespoken one for you. The Head Porter will direct you to it if you do not happen to find me on your arrival.

Unfortunately I shall be dining in St John's; but Bertram Thomas[2] promises to look after you in Hall and afterwards, and asks you to look him up in his rooms, staircase L in Great Court, some time before 8 o'clock.

I hope you will breakfast with me next morning, at 9 or any hour you may prefer.

My kind regards to Lady Rothenstein.

Yours sincerely   A. E. HOUSMAN

To H. E. Butler

MS. ST JOHN'S

15 May 1933   *Trinity College*

Dear Butler,

I am not proud of my lecture, which I wrote unwillingly; but I am rather afraid that Platt, as you say, would have liked it, and I will send a copy.

I made Mawer's[3] acquaintance the other day at a feast at St John's, where he was Prior's[4] guest.

Would you mind directing and posting the enclosed?

Yours sincerely   A. E. HOUSMAN

[1] Withers' daughter, later editor of *Vogue*.
[2] Arabian traveller; Fellow Commoner of Trinity College, 1932–1933.
[3] Allen Mawer (1879–1942), Professor of English at Liverpool, 1921–1929; succeeded Sir Gregory Foster as Provost of University College, London, 1929; knighted, 1937.
[4] Oliver Herbert Phelps Prior (1871–1934), Fellow of St John's College and Drapers' Professor of French in the University since 1919.

333

To Sydney Cockerell

MS. VICTORIA AND ALBERT

16 May 1933   *Trinity College*

My dear Cockerell,

Thank you for your letter. This poor old Shakespeare! Mackail came to me after the lecture and said that "Take O take those lips away"[1] was Fletcher's.

Yours sincerely   A. E. HOUSMAN

To Max Beerbohm[2]

MS. MERTON

16 May 1933   *Trinity College*

Dear Mr Beerbohm,

I am glad you were amused,[3] and thank you for writing. On the other subject, though I cannot hope to repeat the stroke and gain the sky, I yet cannot refrain from sending you, since the opportunity presents itself, the idea of a pair of cartoons which I have cherished many years.

I also have a vision of grandpapa and great-grandpapa reading the works of Mr Aldous Huxley,[4] with the legend:

T. H. Huxley Esq., P.C.
Is this how Leonard bred his brat?
The Rev. T. Arnold, D.D.
Good gracious! even worse than Matt.

Rothenstein was here the other day and told me that with advancing years you have grown too benevolent to do caricatures.

I am yours sincerely   A. E. HOUSMAN

[Enclosure]
Gladstone and Disraeli in heaven
They are seated on two clouds back to back. Gladstone is twanging his harp

---

[1] In *Measure for Measure*; quoted in the lecture as an example of Shakespeare's loveliest poetry. A slightly different version of the song occurs in *The Bloody Brother*, 1639, which is probably in part by John Fletcher (1579-1625).

[2] Essayist and caricaturist (1872-1956); knighted, 1939. He admired Housman's poetry but was not impressed by him in person. 'He was like an absconding cashier. We certainly wished he would abscond—sitting silent and then saying only "there is a bit of a nip in the air, don't you think?" ' (Quoted in *Max* by Lord David Cecil, 1964.)

[3] By the Leslie Stephen Lecture.

[4] Aldous Huxley was the son of Leonard Huxley (son of T. H. Huxley) and Julia Arnold (daughter of Matthew Arnold). Max Beerbohm made none of the drawings suggested by Housman.

334

and singing lustily out of *Hymns Ancient and Modern*. Cherubs, attracted to the spot by the intemperate piety of the novice, hover between mirth and awe. Disraeli, who was very sensitive to cold, is curling up his toes under his night-gown; he has hung his harp on a knob of his cloud, for want of a willow-tree, and the Psalms of David lie open on his knee at "Super Flumina Babylonis".

Disraeli and Gladstone in hell
Disraeli and the devil are warming themselves before a furnace full of the damned, and absorbed in mutually agreeable conversation: so much absorbed that the devil has negligently let fall the end of a red-hot poker on Gladstone's toe, who is dancing and yelling.

To Laurence Housman

TEXT: MEMOIR

20 May 1933   *[Trinity College]*

My dear Laurence,
    I am not proud of this, which I wrote against my will, and am not sending copies outside the family. But its success here has taken me aback. The leader of our doctrinaire teachers of youth is reported to say that it will take more than twelve years to undo the harm I have done in an hour. . .[1]

    Your affectionate brother   A. E. HOUSMAN

To Laurence Housman

TEXT: MEMOIR

24 May 1933   *Trinity College*

My dear Laurence,
    . . . The painful episode is closed; but I may take this sentence from a paragraph which I cut out.[2] "Not only is it difficult to know the truth about anything, but to tell the truth when one knows it, to find words which will not obscure it or pervert it, is in my experience an exhausting effort."
    I did not say that poetry was the better for having no meaning, only that it can best be detected so.
    I hear that Kipling says I am 'dead right' about the pit of the stomach.[3]

---

[1] The Leslie Stephen Lecture was widely reported and discussed. Housman's assertion that the sense of a poem is irrelevant to its value as poetry was taken as an attack on the views of Dr F. R. Leavis and his followers.
[2] From the Leslie Stephen Lecture.
[3] As one of the organs through which poetry is recognised; the other symptoms mentioned by Housman are tears in the eyes and bristling skin.

I had better tell you before I forget it that the solicitor E. S. P. Haynes,[1] who writes letters to the papers about the liberties of the subject, says in *A Lawyer's Notebook* that Belloc is the best living poet with the possible exception of you and me.

Your still affectionate brother   A. E. HOUSMAN

To Percy Withers

MS. WITHERS

7 June 1933   *The Evelyn Nursing Home,*
Trumpington Road, Cambridge

My dear Withers,

This place is very comfortable, and your kindly distress on my behalf is excessive. The misbehaviour of my heart, for which my doctor sent me here, was momentary, and I am unconscious of it; and it is now behaving with monotonous correctness. My real trouble, which I have often had before, is nervous depression and causeless apprehensions, aggravated by the fact that I am going to move into new rooms next term; the necessary alterations in the new rooms, and the making of new furniture and so forth, give me perfectly unreasonable worry to look forward to; and I have been disappointed of a companion for France in August. I leave this abode at noon on Saturday. On Monday I expect to motor into Worcestershire; may I lunch with you on the way? But do not produce port, which I am probably better without.

Kind regards and thanks to Mrs Withers.

Yours sincerely   A. E. HOUSMAN

To S. C. Roberts

MS. C.U.L.

3 July 1933   *Trinity College*

Dear Roberts,

I congratulate you on your salesmanship.

I enclose the MS,[2] which however lacks two pages. Probably I destroyed them as containing things too bad to be read.

Yours sincerely   A. E. HOUSMAN

---

[1] Edmund Sidney Pollock Haynes (1877–1949), writer on matrimonial and divorce law, eccentric, individualist and conversationalist.

[2] Of the lecture, as a gift to Roberts. It is now in the University Library, Cambridge.

To Grant Richards

MS. LILLY

7 July 1933   *Trinity College*

My dear Richards,

It distresses me that you are again in difficulties, the more so because this time I cannot relieve them. I am finding £450 a year for the education of a godson, and this will go on for four years. I am also involved in much expense in changing my rooms, making repairs and buying furniture, and a lift which has to be put in will cost £324. One incidental consequence of the change will be that your labour and kindness in arranging my books will have been to some extent wasted. These various worries may be partly accountable for the bad nervous condition in which I now am; and the doctor also says that my heart is out of order, for which this hot weather is not good. We are both of us in trouble.

Yours sincerely   A. E. HOUSMAN

To Katharine Symons

MS. LILLY

13 July 1933   *Trinity College*

My dear Kate,

I have just come across this old cutting from a newspaper, which will interest you if these Brettells are our relations.

I had pleasant stays at Tardebigge and Street, though Jeannie was taking medicine and Grace[1] was in bed all the while with weakness of the heart. Which reminds me that early in June the doctor sent me into a nursing home for a week because he said my heart was all over the place. It seems to have been behaving properly from that very day onward, but he advises me not to walk more than a little in the hot weather; and this deprives me of my usual exercise. But what is troubling me is not my heart but the nervous depression and causeless anxiety and agitation which I have suffered from half-a-dozen times already,—on two occasions, I think, when I was at Bath; and it is made worse by the fact that I have to look forward to a certain amount of real bother in moving into new rooms before Christmas.

We ran over to Shrewsbury one Sunday and found Denis and his family well. They are a nice household. I suppose you are beginning to surround yourself with grandchildren.

Your affectionate brother   A. E. HOUSMAN

[1] Jeannie Housman's eldest sister.

To Denys Kilham Roberts[1]

MS. SOCIETY OF AUTHORS

22 July 1933   *Trinity College*

Dear Mr Roberts,

As it might seem ungraceful to decline the compliment paid me by your Committee of Management,[2] I accept it with thanks, feeling equal to the discharge of purely nominal duties.

I am yours sincerely   A. E. HOUSMAN

To Witter Bynner

MS. HARVARD

4 August 1933   *Trinity College*

My dear Witter Bynner,

I have received this morning with great pleasure *Eden Tree*[3] and your photograph. I was in shirt-sleeves myself, for England at this moment of the year is trying to emulate American heat.

Many thanks.

Yours sincerely   A. E. HOUSMAN

To Percy Withers

MS. WITHERS

10 August 1933   *Trinity College*

My dear Withers,

After your lunch I had a most pleasant and tranquil ride into Worcestershire, so much so that I fell asleep before Stratford-on-Avon, and the chauffeur to my surprise, found his way without my directions. But I am sorry to say that after my holiday I am worse rather than better. In previous visitations of this nervous trouble I have been physically strong and able to take good long walks; but at present, though my heart appears to be all right again, I am feeble, partly no doubt because of this weather.

I am hoping to go to France on the 22nd and make a motor tour of about three weeks, perhaps in Anjou and Touraine, which are almost unknown to me. I expect to have a French companion, though not one of much education,

---

[1] Lawyer and author (born 1903); Secretary of the Society of Authors.
[2] Membership of the Council of the Society of Authors.
[3] A volume of poems, 1931.

and, though amiable, he may be bored. Your invitation is most kind, indeed to an agitating extent in my present hyperaesthesia; but I think it most likely that I shall not take advantage of it, so do not keep it open. I try to fortify myself by comparisons with people like yourself, who have tangible troubles (and now dental supervening).

I must congratulate you on your daughter's marriage, and I am sending her one of those cheap presents which literary men do send. I ought perhaps to apologise to you as a father, as I think I have told you that the person who at first was the head of the Richards Press threw *A Shropshire Lad* behind the fire as 'the filthiest book he had ever read.'

My kind regards and thanks to Mrs Withers.

Yours sincerely   A.E. HOUSMAN

To Katharine Symons

MS. TRINITY

18 August 1933   *Trinity College*

My dear Kate,

I intend to leave here on Monday afternoon, sleep at the Aerodrome hotel at Croydon, and cross by the aeroplane on Tuesday which leaves Croydon at 9 a.m., so do not concern yourself about the fate of the others. From Paris I shall start immediately on my tour in Touraine etc. and shall have no fixed address for about three weeks, I expect; but letters can be addressed to me care of Mm. Morgan Pope and Co., 6 Rue Caumartin, Paris IX, France, where I shall find them on my return to Paris. I shall have with me a French companion, a nice young man, not much educated, who regards me as a benefactor.

I dare not say that I am better, though last night was a good one, but I am not worse.

I hope that your Shrewsbury guests are with you, in spite of the doubts about their coming, and that they and you are enjoying things. I was glad to hear of the various achievements of your grandchildren. Love to Clemence, if she happens to be already with you. Mrs Hugh Dixon[1] was here at Girton for a week early in the month and very kindly left a card, but I told her I did not feel equal to asking her to tea or doing anything properly civil.

Your affectionate brother   A. E. HOUSMAN

[1] Jeannie Housman's sister-in-law.

To Katharine Symons

MS. TRINITY

24 August 1933   *Grand Hôtel, Blois*

My dear Kate,

I ought to tell you that though I am now better and improving I have been wretchedly ill, worse than I can ever remember having been in all my life. Just when my nervous trouble was so evidently decreasing that I was looking forward with pleasure to going abroad, I was seized by what my doctor called a catarrh of the throat, which he said might get worse or better. His remedies did not prevent it from getting worse, but I could not disappoint those who were expecting me and depending on me, and I had two days of the most violent and frequent pain I have ever undergone, though that may only mean that I have been more fortunate hitherto than most people. I could not swallow a morsel of food or a drop of drink without such pain as made me fear to repeat the action; and I could not get more than three minutes' sleep at a time because the phlegm collected and started a spasm. I have found a doctor here who has given me an inhalation which seems to be acting well, and lunch to-day, which was an exceedingly good one, is the first meal which I have eaten with more pleasure than pain. My companion has been as kind and helpful as can possibly be imagined. I am still ridiculously feeble, and the mistakes in this letter are not all due to the hotel pen.

It will be no good writing to me, as to-morrow I leave here for Tours and shall not stay there or anywhere long. I will write from time to time to relieve your anxiety.

Your affectionate brother   A. E. HOUSMAN

To Katharine Symons

MS. TRINITY

26 August 1933   *Hôtel de l' Univers, Tours*

My dear Kate,

My throat has grown so very much better that I am leaving off the inhalation, as it seems to cause thirst. Fatigue is still ever-present and annoying. I go through most of my programme, but I hope that the memory of having seen these castles will be more pleasure to me than the seeing of them at present is. My only pleasures are eating, drinking and sleeping, which would make me feel much ashamed if I were a lofty-minded man, which I am not. The third is the only one in which I indulge too much. I am ashamed to write letters which are pretty sure to cause you pain; but do not worry too much about me as I do not worry excessively about myself. To-morrow I am going on to Nantes.

Your affectionate brother   A. E. HOUSMAN

340

To Katharine Symons

MS. TRINITY

28 August 1933   *Central Hôtel, Nantes*

My dear Kate,

My throat now gives me no pain at all, though it is hardly yet all right. I think I forgot to say that I had almost lost my voice, but that is now all right. My strength improves though I can hardly in this hot weather take enough exercise to do me good. To-morrow I may go on to a watering place called Sables d'Olonne, but if there is no room in the hotels, as may be at this season, I shall go to La Rochelle.

Your affectionate brother   A. E. HOUSMAN

To Katharine Symons

MS. TRINITY

29 August 1933   *Grand Hôtel, Les Sables d'Olonne*

My dear Kate,

I have just come here from Nantes, which is a poor place, as I suspected it was, and the heat here is pleasantly tempered by the sea-breeze. I do not expect to stay more than two nights; I may then go to Royan, another watering place further south, and from thence perhaps turn north to Brittany. I am not very definitely improving so far, but the sea ought to be useful.

Your affectionate brother   A. E. HOUSMAN

To Katharine Symons

MS. TRINITY

31 August 1933   *Palace Hôtel, Royan*

My dear Kate,

This magnificent hot weather gives so much pleasure to so many that I cannot regard it as part of the general conspiracy against me because it does not happen to suit my health; but it is very mean that the English pound, which has stood at 84 francs for ever so long, should begin to sink the moment I left England and should have reached 79 when I had to change money yesterday.

I am weak and low, but my companion takes all trouble on his shoulders, and really does not seem to be bored. Here we are likely to stay two nights, and then turn towards the centre of France in the direction of Clermont-Ferrand.

Your affectionate brother   A. E. HOUSMAN

To Katharine Symons

MS. TRINITY

1 September 1933   *Palace Hôtel, Royan*

My dear Kate,

If it would amuse you to write to me at Grand Hôtel et de la Poste, Clermont-Ferrand, Puy-de-Dôme, France, I might get the letter, as I am leaving here to-morrow and shall probably stay one night at Angoulême, one at Limoges, and three at Clermont-Ferrand. Only do not write too much, and do not be misled by your beautifully compact handwriting.

This is a beastly place, all noise and mosquitoes, and the heat continues stifling. But I managed to get a very good lunch to-day with the first oysters of the season; and the first guns popping in the distance.

Your affectionate brother   A. E. HOUSMAN

To Katharine Symons

MS. TRINITY

6 September 1933   *Grand Hôtel, Clermont-Ferrand*

My dear Kate,

I was rejoiced to get your nice letter at breakfast this morning.

As my fatigue persisted without abatement I have seen a doctor here, who has given me something which makes me feel rather better, and also advice about food. He does not find anything particularly wrong with my heart.

This afternoon we have had rain and thunder, and it looks as if the weather were changing. Though cooler, it is still rather close.

I expect to leave here Friday morning, to spend one night at Nevers and one at Bourges, to return to Paris on Sunday, collect my correspondence on Monday, and return to England on Tuesday the 12th by the British aeroplane which leaves le Bourget at 12.30, reaching Cambridge in the afternoon.

Certainly you are quite welcome to keep the press-cutting which has taken your fancy.

Love to you and Clemence.

Your affectionate brother   A. E. HOUSMAN

To Katharine Symons

MS. LILLY

11 September 1933   *Hôtel Continental, Paris*

My dear Kate,

This morning I have got my three weeks' budget of letters, including your

342

two, which are touchingly kind. I cannot claim merit in the matter of air-mail, as the letters must have chosen that route without my knowledge: perhaps it depends on the hour of posting. I should not wonder if my trouble is the influenza which Cardiff and Phyllis[1] have been suffering from, though the ulcers in the mouth have not yet made their appearance. Your account of the Exmouth hotel, and the advertisement, are both attractive, but I feel as if when I get to Cambridge I should like to sit down and remain in that position. Your offer to take me into your house is too kind. Many thanks for Jerry's letter, interesting as usual.

This hotel is pleasantly quiet, and so was that in which I slept last night; but for some nights before I was waked up early by the various noises made by this early-rising nation.

Best love to you and Clemence.

Your affectionate brother   A. E. HOUSMAN

To Katharine Symons

MS. TRINITY

13 September 1933   *Trinity College*

My dear Kate,

Whether it is the cooler weather, or whether the disease is running its natural course, I feel stronger and more comfortable. My doctor is satisfied with me, says that my heart is behaving well, and thinks that my tour has probably done me good: all the same, I should not like to go through it again. Since I left, there has been a great deal of the same illness at Cambridge.

I came back by air, as I went out, and in both journeys the machine did the distance in two hours, which is a quarter of an hour less than the time advertised. I lunched on board, as it was lunch time: naturally one expected little, but one did not expect that little to be spun out almost to the length of the whole journey.

I am almost entirely ignorant of the history of England and Europe during the last three weeks, and shall have to tackle the back numbers of the *Times*. French papers contain no news, and the *Continental Daily Mail*, which I did not see regularly, very little.

Love to you and Clemence.

Your affectionate brother   A. E. HOUSMAN

[1] Wife of Denis Symons.

To Laurence Housman

TEXT: MEMOIR

14 September 1933 [*Trinity College*]

My dear Laurence,

... Many thanks for your *Victoria and Albert*[1] which I shall read when I have got through things which are awaiting on my return. Your *Palace Plays* are always entertaining, however fabulous some of them may be.

My doctor inclines to think that my disagreeable tour in France has done me good, so I hope I shall soon find it out ...

Your affectionate brother   A. E. HOUSMAN

To Grant Richards

TEXT: RICHARDS

28 September 1933 *Trinity College*

M. Pollet's essay, which I return, is certainly complimentary, and is not silly, and I should not raise objections, 'momentous' or otherwise, to its publication in an English paper, though I imagine he would find this difficult, and have no wish that he should succeed.[2]

I am still in very poor health. Just when I went to France I was seized by a form of influenza which has been prevalent here, starting with a violently painful inflammation of the throat and leaving the victim in a state of feebleness and fatigue in which I still continue, with very low spirits. You would therefore find me wretched company, and I cannot honestly recommend you to come. On the other hand if I were selfish I should be glad to see you, because your company might do me good; and I should be at liberty any day next week except the Saturday.

To Katharine Symons

MS. LILLY

25 October 1933 *Trinity College*

My dear Kate,

Thanks for your letter and the press cuttings. I enclose another one, which is amusing, because its author, T. S. Eliot, is worshipped as a god by the writers in the paper which had the only hostile review.[3]

---

[1] The third series of *Palace Plays*, just published.
[2] The *Etude* has not been published in England. In sending the essay to Richards, Pollet had written 'I hope that he [Housman] will not raise too momentous objections to it.'
[3] T. S. Eliot's very favourable criticism of the Leslie Stephen Lecture was printed in *The Criterion*, October 1933. The hostile review, by S. Gorley Putt, was in *Scrutiny*, edited by F. R. Leavis and others, September 1933.

I am glad that you are so well. I am much better than I have been. The doctor has given me a tonic which took away the horrid inward feeling of fatigue, and I am getting to walk more strongly, though very gradually and with ups and downs. But for the first fortnight after my return he left me alone, and I made no progress at all; and the monotonous misery gave the nervous trouble a chance to steal back again to some extent. I wake up too soon and have a rather disagreeable time till I get into my bath. I find too that I cannot turn with interest to work. My lectures however give me no trouble.

Jeannie wrote to me a little while ago, and evidently Grace's illness was serious and she has not got rid of it.

Your affectionate brother   A. E. HOUSMAN

To S. G. Morley[1]

MS. BERKELEY

28 October 1933   *Trinity College*

Dear Mr Morley,

I am much obliged by your kindness in presenting me with your translations from Anthero de Quental,[2] which I am reading with interest and appreciation. Modern Portuguese poetry is almost unknown to me, though I find that without having learnt Portuguese I can read Camoëns to some extent with the aid of Latin and French.

Most of the subjects which I mentioned in connection with the Art of Versification are touched on by Coventry Patmore in an essay first published, I do not know where, in 1856, and printed as an appendix to his 'third collective edition' of poems, 1887, two volumes, George Bell and Son. Its title is "Essay on English Metrical Laws".[3]

I am yours sincerely   A. E. HOUSMAN

To Grant Richards

TEXT: RICHARDS

1 November 1933   *[Trinity College]*

Your talent for practical affairs is only equalled by your amiability and readiness to help; but at present at any rate I do not look forward to changing my rooms as a likely event. If it ever occurs, I will certainly remember and take advantage of your noble offer.

[1] Sylvanus Griswold Morley (born 1878), Professor of Spanish at the University of California, Berkeley.
[2] Portuguese poet (1842–1891). Morley's translation was published in 1922.
[3] First published as 'English Metrical Critics' in *The North British Review*, 1857; reprinted in Patmore's *Poems*, 1879.

To Percy Withers

MS. WITHERS

10 November 1933   *Trinity College*

My dear Withers,

In the first place I am very sorry that you have been suffering so much this summer, in which the hot weather was hostile also to me.

Towards the end of August, when the nervous trouble had begun to relax its hold, I went to France; but just at starting I was attacked by a form of influenza which has been prevalent in Cambridge and arises in hot dry weather: it begins with an excruciating sore throat, which prevents eating, drinking, or sleeping for more than ten minutes at a time, during two days and nights, and then leaves one as weak as water.

Consequently, when the throat was cured, I had a miserable time in France, dragging myself about sightseeing and ready to drop with fatigue. My companion however was all that could be imagined in kindness and help-fulness.

When I came back my doctor left me to nature for a fortnight, because he was satisfied with the condition of my heart, and I did not improve a bit in strength all the while, so that the nervous trouble took the opportunity of stealing back to some extent. He then gave me a strong tonic (known among doctors as 'honeymoon mixture') which soon made me stronger but then had no progressive effect. I have now left it off without experiencing relapse; but I walk sluggishly and am low in spirits. My chief remaining trouble is excessive sensitiveness to noise, which prevents me from getting to sleep again if I wake when life has begun to stir in the morning.

Well! woe has made me eloquent, and you ought to be satisfied at least with the length of this egotistic letter. Your invitation is exceedingly kind, but I feel sure that I had best stay at home. My lectures are no trouble to me, but I find I cannot get up a real interest in work and study. I read chiefly novels and Lecky's history of England in the eighteenth century,[1] from which I learn much that I did not know.

My kind regards to Mrs Withers and my best wishes and hopes for your health.

Yours sincerely   A. E. HOUSMAN

Bevan[2] had a most enviable death. At luncheon that afternoon he was talking vigorously. He had advanced heart-disease of a kind which gives no warning of its existence.

---

[1] Published in eight volumes, 1878–1890.
[2] Anthony Ashley Bevan (1859–1933), Fellow of Trinity College, 1890; Professor of Arabic in the University, 1895–1933.

To Houston Martin

MS. MARTIN

20 November 1933   *Trinity College*

Dear Mr Martin,

Apparently you have been searching the Scriptures and have lighted on the 18th chapter of St Luke.[1] I am ashamed of myself for showing no more firmness of mind than the unjust judge, but such infatuation as yours is quite intimidating. I observe that your photograph wears a grin of assured success.

I gave the manuscript of *A Shropshire Lad* to the Library of this college, and that of *Last Poems* to the Fitzwilliam Museum in Cambridge.

I was not born in Shropshire at all, but near the town of Bromsgrove in Worcestershire. The Shropshire hills were our western horizon, and hence my sentiment for the county, I suppose.

I am yours sincerely   A. E. HOUSMAN

To Laurence Housman

TEXT: MEMOIR

30 November 1933   *[Trinity College]*

My dear Laurence,

. . . There was no enclosure in your letter, but I know what it was, and have already had an invitation from the people at University College, which so far as I remember, I pretty explicitly declined. No doubt I should enjoy seeing you wrestle with the King of Terrors,[2] but though I am much better than I have been and no longer actually feeble, my spirits are rather low and the visit to London would worry me in prospect if not in act. . .

Your affectionate brother   A. E. HOUSMAN

To Laurence Housman

TEXT: MEMOIR

6 December 1933   *[Trinity College]*

My dear Laurence,

Thanks for your "Pre-Raphaelitism",[3] which I am glad to have, though

[1] Verse 5: 'Yet because this widow troubleth me, I will avenge her, lest by her continual coming she weary me.' Housman now yielded to a request that he had earlier refused, and enclosed a manuscript copy of *A Shropshire Lad* II.

[2] In *Nunc Dimittis*.

[3] 'Pre-Raphaelitism in Art and Poetry' in *Essays by Divers Hands* (Transactions of the Royal Society of Literature, volume xii), edited by R. W. Macan, 1933. Macan wrote an introduction to the book in which he misspelled Laurence Housman's Christian name. Burne-Jones is not mentioned in the essay.

some of the other contents of the volume seem pretty poor. What a wretched writer is Macan! and speller too.

I think that you make too much of Morris, and that the manner of *The Defence of Guinevere* is just one of his falsettos. He dropped it like hot copper when he found it did not pay.

I should have liked to be told what to think of Burne-Jones. . .

Your affectionate brother   A. E. HOUSMAN

To Grant Richards

MS. LILLY

6 December 1933   *Trinity College*

My dear Richards,

If I did what you ask,[1] because it is painful to refuse, it would be cowardice, and I should be angry with myself afterwards, and ashamed; and you yourself would be obliged to think me weak.

Yours sincerely   A. E. HOUSMAN

To Houston Martin

MS. MARTIN

14 December 1933   *Trinity College*

Dear Mr Martin,

You are an engaging madman, and write more agreeably than many sane persons; but if I write anything of an autobiographical nature, as I have sometimes idly thought of doing, I shall send it to the British Museum to be kept under lock and key for fifty years. There is no biography of Matthew Arnold (whom I am glad to see that you read) in accordance with his own advice; so there certainly need be none of me.

Your last enquiry, though frivolous, is harmless, and I may reply that I never do sign my name in full except in documents where I am directed to do so.

Accept my best thanks for your kind Christmas gift.

I am yours very truly   A. E. HOUSMAN

[1] Presumably lending Richards money.

348

To Jeannie Housman

MS. LILLY

20 December 1933   *Trinity College*

My dear Jeannie,

Many thanks for your kind Christmas letter, which puts me two letters in your debt. I am glad to have fairly good news of Grace and Bess,[1] and though you say nothing much about your own health I hope it is satisfactory. I am so much better than I have been that I ought not to grumble at not being really myself again: I am told that I look extremely well, which naturally rather annoys me.

The enclosed is a reprint by two infatuated admirers of a lecture which I probably sent to Basil, when it was in manuscript, to read; but if you have no printed copy you may care to have this.[2] I don't autograph it, as it is not good enough. The Cambridge Press has managed to sell 12,000 copies of my Leslie Stephen lecture in England, not counting America. The Broadcasting people, no doubt at your request, have offered me £100 to deliver a discourse over the wireless next year; but you will have to do without it. However, do not let this sadden your Christmas. Kind regards to Grace, and Bess if she is arrived.

Yours affectionately   A. E. HOUSMAN

Laurence's idea sounds pleasant, but he is such a busy man that it might be difficult to make things fit.

To Percy Withers

MS. WITHERS

20 December 1933   *Trinity College*

My dear Withers,

I think that most likely you have never seen the enclosed lecture, which has just been reprinted by a couple of besotted admirers. It is no use asking me to autograph it.

It is one of my grievances against the Creator that I always look better than I am (as Emerson said of the Scotch 'Many of them look drunk when they are sober') and consequently receive fewer tears of sympathy than I deserve; but I am really so much better than I have been that I ought not to grumble much at not being really myself again.

You do not say anything about your own health, but I hope no news is good news.

[1] Jeannie Housman's sister, Mrs Thompson.
[2] The Introductory Lecture of 1892, privately printed in an edition of 100 copies for John Carter and John Sparrow.

Canon Watson of Christ Church,[1] who was with me at Oxford, on resigning his Professorship of Ecclesiastical History, has bought a house 'thirteen miles north of Oxford', therefore somewhere in the Bicester neighbourhood, I suppose.

Thanks for your Christmas good wishes, which I reciprocate, and remember me kindly to Mrs Withers.

Yours sincerely

A. E. HOUSMAN

To Thaddeus Gorecki[2]

MS. COLBY

25 December 1933   *Trinity College*

Dear Sir,

I am much obliged by your kindness in sending me the music to which you have done me the honour to set my poems. I only regret that my knowledge of music is not sufficient to enable me to appreciate it adequately.

I am yours sincerely

A. E. HOUSMAN

To Seymour Adelman

TEXT: MEMOIR

30 December 1933   *[Trinity College]*

Dear Mr Adelman,

. . . The paragraph in the catalogue, as you surmise, contains a great deal of error. It was only one publisher who was offered *A Shropshire Lad* and declined it. The firm which published it at my expense was the joint firm of Kegan Paul, Trench, Trübner and Co., which had published a good deal of belles lettres. The number of copies printed was 500, and the time it took to sell them (at 2/6 each) was rather more than two years. There was no contract about republishing: I kept Mr Grant Richards waiting until Kegan Paul and Co. signified that a second edition would have to be printed again at my own expense. It is a great exaggeration to talk about a boom in connexion with the second edition: such boom as there was began with the war of 1914 . . .

Yours sincerely

A. E. HOUSMAN

To Sydney Cockerell

MS. PRINCETON

1 January 1934   *Trinity College*

Dear Cockerell,

It delights me to see in the paper the King's recognition of your services

[1] The Rev. Edward William Watson (1859–1936); Professor of Ecclesiastical History at King's College, London, 1904–1908; and at Oxford, 1908–1934.

[2] An American composer. He had sent Housman photocopies of manuscript settings of *A Shropshire Lad* II, XI, XV, XVII and XX.

and achievements;[1] and let me wish you a happy new year in which to enjoy your honour.

Yours sincerely   A. E. HOUSMAN

To A. S. F. Gow

MS. TRINITY

12 February 1934   *Trinity College*

Dear Gow,

As the meaning of a poem is what it conveys, not anything else which its author may or may not have wished it to convey, I don't think that this poem,[2] considered as a whole, has a meaning. It seems to be a rather random assemblage of pretty words, or words which he thinks pretty, without much to express but a vague agitation of mind.

Yours sincerely   A. E. HOUSMAN

To Grant Richards

MS. CONGRESS

2 March 1934   *Trinity College*

My dear Richards,

No, do not protest: I think this sort of quotation is unobjectionable; and besides there is no American copyright. As to 'Housman', it is for Laurence to object if he likes.[3]

Yours sincerely   A. E. HOUSMAN

To Katharine Symons

MS. TRINITY

18 March 1934   *Trinity College*

My dear Kate,

I am glad to have news of you, and good news, and to hear that your history is nearing harbour.[4] I have no photograph later than one taken when I was 35, which you probably have already. The one you have seen in print I sat for to oblige the artist, as he called himself and perhaps was, and I never had any copies.

---

[1] By a knighthood.

[2] Submitted for the Chancellor's Medal. Gow, one of the awarders, had asked Housman's opinion.

[3] An advertisement in *The New Yorker*, 7 November 1931, printed two lines from *A Shropshire Lad* XLII, attributing them to 'Housman' *tout court*.

[4] *The Grammar School of Edward VI, Bath*, 1934.

It is no good pretending that I am well, for I have made no progress at any rate since the beginning of the year, and am neither strong nor comfortable. However, life is endurable, and my heart seems to be steady enough. The spring has been pleasant so far, and wonderful for flowers: last year's heat seems to have suited the bulbs.

The Librarian shows no wish to have a portrait of A. J. Macleane,[1] but I will also enquire of the Memorials Committee.

I meant to tell you, in case you had not seen it yourself, that Bertie Millington died last September, and Dr George Fletcher in December. The latter you may just remember as a ginger young man sitting a few pews in front of us in church. I found him in practice in Highgate when I went there; and he was *the* Old Bromsgrovian.

I probably stay here for Easter.

Your affectionate brother   A. E. HOUSMAN

To Houston Martin

MS. MARTIN

14 April 1934   *Trinity College*

Dear Mr Martin,

I have never seen the misprint 'tramping' in no. vii of *A Shropshire Lad*. Perhaps you have come across it in some of the pirated American editions. Even in the authorised edition by Holt there are disgraceful misprints.

I know nothing of Mr Edmund Wilson's translation of my Latin poem.[2]

The stanza prefixed to no. L of *A Shropshire Lad* is traditional. One version is 'drunkenest'.

At Buildwas there is the ruin of an abbey church, not large but fairly complete, of Norman date.

I am Worcestershire by birth: Shropshire was our western horizon, which made me feel romantic about it. I do not know the county well, except in parts, and some of my topographical details are wrong and imaginary. The Wrekin is wooded, and Wenlock Edge along the western side, but the Clees and most of the other hills are grass or heather. In the southern half of the county, to which I have confined myself, the hills are generally long ridges running from north to south, with valleys, broad or narrow, between. The northern half is part of the great Cheshire plain. The Wrekin is isolated.

I gave the manuscript of my lecture to the Secretary of our University Press, who asked for it.

---

[1] See p. 292, note.
[2] English version of the dedication to Manilius I, published in *The Bookman*, New York, October 1927 and reprinted in Richards.

352

As you know Mr Basil Davenport,[1] perhaps, if you meet him, you will give him my thanks for sending me a telegram on my birthday. I could not respond because I had not his address.

You will not expect me to approve your project. I am appalled to hear of your copying my articles in the *Classical Quarterly*.

I am yours very truly   A. E. HOUSMAN

To Percy Withers

MS. WITHERS

18 April 1934   *Trinity College*

My dear Withers,

You sometimes honour Cambridge with a visit in May, and perhaps you might be inclined to make it coincide with our Ascension Feast on Thursday the 10th, though that is rather early in the season and would involve the bother of bringing a dress suit.

I hope that you and yours are well. I am better than I was last year, but neither strong nor comfortable, and I do not progress. This last term I have had as a holiday,—not on account of my health, but in view of my length of service. I had intended to spend part of it in Africa, but did not feel brave enough.

This spring, not a model in most respects, has made a wonderfully rich display of flowers here: I suppose last year's heat penetrated to the bulbs and other roots.

My kind regards to Mrs Withers.

Yours sincerely   A. E. HOUSMAN

To Percy Withers

MS. WITHERS

20 April 1934   *Trinity College*

My dear Withers,

That is right. As this is a regular Feast, most people will be wearing tail-coat and white tie. The hour is eight o'clock. If you would like to sleep in college I could probably secure you a room; but I thought probably you would prefer an hotel, as if you should be ill in the night, as you once were after dining with me, attendance and assistance are hard to obtain in a college.

I should be delighted to come and see you in June, which I know is the month in which you like to show your garden, and I could stay the inside of

[1] American author and editor (born 1905); translator of Rostand's *L'Aiglon*, 1927; wrote the introduction to the 'Centennial' edition of Housman's poems, New York, 1959.

a week, if that would not try you too much. What of Monday the 11th to Saturday the 16th? But be sure to tell me if this would cut into other guests' week-ends.

Your account of your own health is vague but does not seem to be good, I regret to infer. I am distressed at the plague among Michael's dogs. I expect to go into Worcestershire in July and to France near the end of August,— probably Lorraine and that region, which is unknown to me. I hope to take a French friend with me.

Thanks and kind regards to Mrs Withers.

Yours sincerely   A. E. HOUSMAN

To Charles Wilson

MS. LILLY

25 April 1934   *Trinity College*

Dear Mr Wilson,

Many thanks for the pretty book on Rossetti[1] which you have been kind enough to send me.

A. C. Benson, the late Master of Magdalene, is buried here in the Huntingdon Road Cemetery. I believe that an ornamental tombstone was erected by a rich Swiss lady who was an admirer of his.

Yours very truly   A. E. HOUSMAN

To Viscount Halifax[2]

MS. LILLY

26 April 1934   *Trinity College*

My Lord,

The generous intention of the Hebdomadal Council to propose that the degree of Doctor of Letters should be conferred upon me is one which they formed and communicated to me in the year 1928; and I then, with due expression of gratitude and appreciation, begged that it might not be fulfilled. Their renewed proffer of the honour in increasing my obligation to them increases also my embarrassment; but my reluctance to accept such distinction even from my own University persists, and I trust that neither she nor

---

[1] Probably the one by Lucien Wolff, Paris, 1934.

[2] Edward Frederick Lindley Wood (1881–1959), created Baron Irwin, 1926; third Viscount Halifax, 1934; created Earl of Halifax, 1944; Viceroy of India, 1926–1931; President of the Board of Education, 1932–1935; subsequently Lord Privy Seal, Lord President of the Council, Foreign Secretary and Ambassador to the United States; appointed to the Order of Merit, 1946; Chancellor of Oxford University, 1933–1959. He had written personally to ask Housman to accept an honorary degree. This draft reply is written on the back of his letter.

her Chancellor will think me ungrateful or ungracious if I still adhere to a resolution which was taken long ago for reasons which, though they are not easy to formulate, still seem to me sufficient.

I am your Lordship's loyal and obedient servant.

To Blanche Trollope[1]

MS. LILLY

30 April 1934   *Trinity College*

Dear Blanche,

I thought that very likely you would be kind enough to write and tell me more about Ted[2] than I could learn from the *Times*. I saw him last in last July, when he looked well and strong; and he wrote to me at Christmas. His has been a most valuable life, and I don't know what the village will do without him.

I hope that you are keeping well. I had a sort of influenza last summer and am not properly well yet.

Yours very truly and with thanks   A. E. HOUSMAN

To Percy Withers

MS. WITHERS

3 June 1934   *Trinity College*

My dear Withers,

I will come then on Monday the 11th, and ought to arrive by 4.45. I shall not be travelling onward, so the Bletchley car which brings me can take me back on the Saturday.

I shall be pleased to meet Gordon[3] again, the more so as I was disappointed of seeing him when he was lecturing here.

One of the places I should like to go to is Brill, which will be within easy reach by your car.

My kind regards to Mrs Withers.

Yours sincerely   A. E. HOUSMAN

Our Vice-Master[4] is dangerously ill. Three of the younger fellows are getting married in a lump.

[1] Neighbour and close friend of the Wise family in Woodchester.
[2] Edward Tuppen Wise died at Woodchester on 24 April 1934.
[3] George Stuart Gordon (1881–1942), President of Magdalen College, Oxford, 1928–1942; Professor of Poetry, 1933–1938.
[4] R. St J. Parry.

To John Sparrow

MS. SPARROW

19 June 1934   *Trinity College*

Dear Mr Sparrow,

In the second edition of *A Shropshire Lad*, which was not sent to me in proof, there are consequently a number of petty corruptions; but I accepted the even margin of XXXI as a lesser evil than the over-running of lines, which is apparently the only alternative on an ordinary page. The Alcuin edition was printed from the first.

I have made only two real alterations, in XXXVIII 10 and LII 9, which were meant to appear in 1922 simultaneously with *Last Poems* but were belated by the publisher's fault. All other changes, very few, are trifles of spelling or printing.

Some of the plagiarisms in your list[1] I thought imaginary and non-existent, but a much greater number escaped your notice, and in particular I see that you are not such a student of the Bible as I am.

Mr Houston Martin, though I am always telling him how silly he is, cannot be repressed, and is now pestering my brother for things which he has no hope of extracting from me.

Yours sincerely   A. E. HOUSMAN

To Laurence Housman

TEXT: MEMOIR

20 June 1934   [*Trinity College*]
My dear Laurence,

... The more I think of the ——[2] the less I like it. That narrow street sees and hears the passage of more motors than almost any other in England, and the noise must begin early and cease late; and noise has been a trouble to me for the last twelvemonth.

I return the great poem corrected. 'Peter piper' does not come up to my exalted notion of my genius, nor the stanza added to Cousin Agnes's poem.[3]

Mr Houston Martin is a lunatic, but not unintelligent. I have expressed so much contempt of his aims and activities that he has now let me alone for some time.

I do not know what is the poem of which he has the unique MS...

Your affectionate brother   A. E. HOUSMAN

[1] 'Echoes in the Poetry of A. E. Housman' in *The Nineteenth Century*, February 1934.
[2] A hotel (name omitted by Laurence Housman).
[3] These *juvenilia* have not been printed.

356

To Grant Richards

MS. CONGRESS

2 July 1934   *[Trinity College]*

My dear Richards,

P. 5[1] is chiefly hallucination. I do not believe that I have ever entertained you at Verrey's.[2] Anyhow it was in April 1922 that I first told you, by letter, that I should be having a book ready for the autumn.

P. 6. The specimen pages did not exhibit any of the text of *New Poems*,[3] if I remember right, and I can hardly have sent you the MS so early. But printed slips of the whole were in my hands in August, if not July.

I have been amused by a book called *Swan's Milk* by Louis Marlow,[4] about Radley, Oxford, Cambridge, and literary men in 1895–1910, with minute personal details which I should have thought libellous.

I am no better than I was at the beginning of the year.

Yours sincerely   A. E. HOUSMAN

Postcard to Grant Richards

MS. CONGRESS

2 July 1934   *Trinity College*

You had intended, until discouraged by the booksellers, to print 5,000 copies as a first edition of *New Poems*; I had advised 10,000: the number printed before the end of the year was 21,000.

            A.E.H.

My heart bleeds when I read your account of the domestic scene at Cookham Dean,[5] especially for poor Geoffrey and Hélène.

To Percy Withers

MS. WITHERS

7 July 1934   *Trinity College*

My dear Withers,

Your news is surprising to me and I suppose it ought to be pleasing, as you presumably wished a house which you offered for sale to be sold, and I am

---

[1] In the proofs of Richards' *Author Hunting*, 1934.
[2] The restaurant in Regent Street. Housman gave Richards dinner there on 31 May 1922.
[3] i.e. *Last Poems.*   [4] Pseudonym of Louis Wilkinson (1881–1968).
[5] On the first reading aloud of *Last Poems*. Richards had taken the manuscript home to read to his family. He subsequently cut down the description of the 'domestic scene'.

glad that you find a preponderance of advantages on that side. Changing your abode is not a novelty to you, and not so dismaying as it would be to me. I hope that the new house may be in Buckinghamshire rather than Wiltshire, for nearness to Cambridge.[1]

My sister-in-law still lives, and is in little pain or distress, and on the 16th I am going with my brother Laurence to Droitwich for a week to motor about the county and pay her visits.

I wish fortitude and luck to Mrs Withers in her quest.

Yours sincerely   A. E. HOUSMAN

I don't know what the village will do without you

To Sydney Cockerell

MS. PRINCETON

8 July 1934   *Trinity College*

My dear Cockerell,

Needless to say that I am flattered and grateful;[2] but when I turned 70 I made up my mind that I would not sit any more, and I have already declined one similar proposal.

Yours sincerely and obliged   A. E. HOUSMAN

To Stephen Gaselee

MS. LIVERPOOL

14 August 1934   *Trinity College*

Dear Gaselee,

I shall be much pleased to enjoy your succulent repast on Michaelmas Day. That date is safer for me than a week earlier.

When I was in the Patent Office, I remember a trade-mark showing a 'procession of the Emperor and Empress Nero'. Nero was not, as you might perhaps fancy, doubling the part: they were two figures.

Yours sincerely   A. E. HOUSMAN

---

[1] Withers, who had formerly lived in Oxfordshire, now moved to Epwell Court, Warwickshire.

[2] Cockerell had apparently proposed that Housman should sit for a portrait for the Fitzwilliam Museum.

To Katharine Symons

MS. TRINITY

18 August 1934   *Trinity College*

My dear Kate,

I shall leave here on Tuesday afternoon, sleep at Croydon, and cross to Paris by the 9.30 plane thence on Wednesday; from Paris I shall take the 1.45 train to Nancy. So you need not concern yourself about the fate of any other vehicles.

Laurence was here for two or three days, and his lecture seems to have been lively and much appreciated by its rather contemptible audience. These 'Summer Meetings' consist of people who should never be allowed to enter a University town, and on this occasion I am told that the majority were foreigners,—who to be sure were probably the better educated part.[1]

The latest news of Jeannie seemed to have been rather more satisfactory. I am not better, either in strength or tranquility, than I was at the beginning of the year. The part of France I am going to is Alsace-Lorraine, quite new to me. Strasburg is the chief sight, and the scenery of the Vosges; also there is a good deal of first-rate food and second-rate drink.

I hear that Clemence has benefited by her stay with you, and I hope you are well yourself, and capable of dealing with the grandchildren who I suppose have by now descended on you.

Your affectionate brother   A. E. HOUSMAN

To Katharine Symons

MS. TRINITY

15 September 1934   *Trinity College*

My dear Kate,

I came back last Wednesday after just three weeks abroad, and the pound, which dropped from 75 to 74 francs on the day of my departure, immediately recovered. However, I must have economised a good deal by hiring local cars instead of taking one from Paris. The weather was almost perfect throughout. Nancy and Strasburg and the Vosges were well worth seeing; and in returning, besides Franche-Comté and Burgundy, where I had been before, I went to Troyes in Champagne, where the cathedral is much finer than I had ever suspected, and there are several interesting churches. I think on the whole I am a bit better; certainly the difference from my last tour is very great.

The chief ambition of my life has long been to be invited to the Colchester

[1] Laurence Housman spoke extensively at this time in support of pacifism.

Oyster Feast. This year it has happened; but to teach us that earthly hopes are dust and ashes, I have a lecture that will keep me in Cambridge.

I am glad to have your good news of Jeannie, and I hope that you have enjoyed all your visitors at Exmouth. I saw the review of your book in the *Times Literary Supplement*,[1] and I hope it will bring you repute as it evidently will be of value to the historical and antiquarian public. Our University Library is closed till October, as it is moving into a great new building, which takes four months.

Your affectionate brother   A. E. HOUSMAN

To Grant Richards

MS. CONGRESS

22 September 1934　　　　　　　　　　　　　　　　　　　*Trinity College*

p. 28 Sedgwick] Sidgwick[2]
  55 apothegm] apophthegm
  124 Auteuil] Longchamp
  128n. common] combination
  201 Danielli] Danieli
  219n. mnie] mine
  224 'I did not have' is American.
  255 'reconcile' is at any rate not English.
  271 There should be no 'à la' after *barbue*.

I have told you already that your account of our first acquaintance is wrong: I called in Henrietta Street by appointment, and you took me out somewhere in a cab to lunch; and I first met you at Laurence's in Marloes Road.

I have found your publishing intrigues rather slow reading, but the rest is bright and interesting.

Yours sincerely   A. E. HOUSMAN

To Houston Martin

MS. MARTIN

26 September 1934　　　　　　　　　　　　　　　　　　　*Trinity College*

Dear Mr Martin,

You ought to have known better than to send me the copy of *A Shropshire Lad*. American publishers have a perfect right to issue unauthorised copies,

---

[1] A full-column review, praising the book as 'a fine piece of research', in the issue for 6 September 1935.

[2] Further corrections to *Author Hunting*. Richards had sent Housman a copy of the published volume.

but for me to sign them would be an indignity or an excess of magnanimity. I am also deaf to fantastic requests that I should write my name in full or add special stuff for you. One thing I am prepared to do, which might gratify your depraved mind: if you like to send me 'New Year's Eve'[1] I can make and initial a correction which I was too late to make before it was printed. If I possess a copy of 'Parta Quies',[2] which I do not know to be the case, I do not know where to find it. *A Shropshire Lad* and *New Poems* will never be joined together while I am here to prevent it, and I think it a silly notion.

I congratulate you on your twentieth birthday and your approach, I hope, to years of discretion. I did not realize how frightfully young you were: it explains and perhaps excuses much.

I thank you for your good wishes and you have mine.

I am yours sincerely   A. E. HOUSMAN

To John Sparrow

MS. SPARROW

16 October 1934   *Trinity College*

Dear Mr Sparrow,
    G. B. Shaw lately advised a young man of my acquaintance to specialise in collecting unautographed copies of authors' works, which bid fair to become rarities; so my name probably detracts from the value of this book.

Yours sincerely   A. E. HOUSMAN

To Houston Martin

MS. MARTIN

17 October 1934   *Trinity College*

Dear Mr Martin,
    I have had to make more than one correction in the copy of 'New Year's Eve' which I return.

'*New Poems*' was only a slip of my senile pen.

'Fragment composed in a dream'[3] I do not know, or have forgotten.

I suppose it would be impossible to explain to you, perhaps to any American, the impropriety of your conduct in writing, as you seem to have done, to ask famous writers their opinion of me. I hope that some of them, at any rate, have ignored your letters.

---

[1] Published in *Waifs and Strays*, November 1881; reprinted in *Collected Poems*, 1939. Housman's correction was 'Once' in place of 'Then' in verse 12, line 4.

[2] Published in *Waifs and Strays*, March 1881; reprinted in *More Poems*, 1936.

[3] An unauthorised printing (by John Carter and John Sparrow), circulated as a Christmas card in 1930, of 'When the bells justle in the tower' (*Additional Poems* IX).

Bredon Hill is in Worcestershire on the edge of Gloucestershire. That poem was written early, before I knew the book would be a Shropshire book. Abdon Burf is the highest part of the Brown Clee, which is the highest hill in Shropshire, but will soon cease to be so, as they are quarrying the top away.

I am yours sincerely   A. E. HOUSMAN

To David Emrys Evans[1]

24 November 1934   *Trinity College*

Dear Principal Emrys Evans,

I thank you for the terms in which you conveyed to me the generous proposal of the Council of your University to confer on me the degree of Doctor in Litteris honoris causa.

I have a high sense of the honour designed for me, and am correspondingly grateful; and if I nevertheless ask leave to decline it, as I have declined similar distinctions placed within my reach by the kindness of other Universities, I trust that I may not be deemed thankless in thus adhering to a resolution taken long ago and founded on reasons which still seem to me sufficient, though they could not be briefly or easily expressed.

I am yours very truly   A. E. HOUSMAN

To Percy Withers

MS. WITHERS

24 November 1934   *Trinity College*

My dear Withers,

I had begun to think of trying to find you by letter and discover which of the counties you meditated had caught and fixed you. It turns out to be none of them, but I am glad to hear that you have secured a spot which in some respects at any rate is so much to your taste. I regret to observe that my convenience has not been your prime consideration and that I shall have a much longer journey between me and your Domain of Arnheim. I am at liberty to hope that both of you are fairly well, as you say nothing to the contrary.

My tour in Alsace and Lorraine was pleasant, and the weather almost perfect, and I suppose it did me some good. But improvement is infinitesimal, and the perpetual recurrence of discomfort every morning between waking and finishing my toilet is wearisome in the extreme, apart from the feeling of physical fatigue which is frequent and is probably a natural sign of old age.

[1] Born 1891; Principal of the University College of North Wales, 1927–1958; Vice Chancellor of the University of Wales, 1933–1935; knighted, 1952. Text from a copy in the possession of the University of Wales.

My life is bearable, but I do not want it to continue, and I wish it had ended a year and a half ago. The great and real troubles of my early manhood did not render those days so permanently unsatisfactory as these. At Trinity we have suffered a great loss in R. V. Laurence, whom I expect you remember. He was ill for nearly two years, but so brave that he had arranged and intended to lecture on the day he died. He talked so much about me to his nurse that she has written to bespeak me for her next death-bed.

My kind regards to Mrs Withers: I suppose you are temporarily cut off from the rest of your family.

Yours sincerely   A. E. HOUSMAN

To Laurence Housman

TEXT: MEMOIR

29 November 1934   *[Trinity College]*

My dear Laurence,

. . . Many thanks for *Victoria Regina*:[1] there are several pieces which I had not read before. What impresses me most is your cleverness in inventing detail. Perhaps Palmerston, as you think, is the best, though I think you take his side too much, and also make him too superior. There is a story by an eyewitness of his being reduced to tears by a jobation from the Prince Consort.

The verses come back to me, but I feel as if I wrote 'stays' and not 'leaves',[2] which may be an emendation of Clemence's prompted by her dislike for the harmless letter *s*. Also I don't use notes of admiration . . .

Your affectionate brother   A. E. HOUSMAN

To Sydney Cockerell

MS. TEXAS

2 December 1934   *Trinity College*

My dear Cockerell,

Many thanks for letting me look at Landor's Horace, returned herewith. He has written 'beautiful' or 'very good' against most of my favourites. In one place he has anticipated a detail of correction, probably not quite right, put forward by a German editor a good many years later.

Yours sincerely   A. E. HOUSMAN

[1] The first volume of Laurence Housman's *Palace Plays*, published in 1934.

[2] In the second verse of Housman's song for Lady Jane Grey, written at the age of 15: 'For the reaper stays his reaping.' The poem was printed by Laurence Housman in *The Unexpected Years*, 1937.

To Jeannie Housman

TEXT: MEMOIR

3 December 1934 [*Trinity College*]

. . . Here is December, bringing round the sad time when we lost Basil, but bringing also this year to me in a letter from Kate the good news that you are wonderfully better in health and have kicked your nurse out of doors. I do beg you to keep it up and not to be weary in well doing. The winter, thus far, is being quite nice to invalids, of whom, however, we have rather a large number here among my friends and acquaintances. One of my best boon-companions died a few months ago, and apparently spoke so much and so well of me in his last illness that his nurse has written to me to engage herself for my death-bed. People, however, are always telling me that I look exceedingly well; so that, I fear, must be a pleasure deferred.

To Katharine Symons

MS. TRINITY

3 December 1934 *Trinity College*

My dear Kate,

I am glad that your history seems to be proving a best-seller. I have not consulted it in the new Library, which I rather seldom visit, as it is more than twice as distant as the old one. The outside, I agree, is ill-favoured; the interior spacious and well-arranged, though I have yet to learn my way about it. The weak point seems to be the lifts, which sometimes stick or do not act, and may imprison you. If you are a lady you then scream till released, and collapse in hysterics on your rescuer.

I am just about the same, with frequent feelings of fatigue, occasional sinkings at the heart and continual uneasiness at beginning to get up in the morning. I can bear my life but I do not at all want it to go on, and it is a great mistake that it did not come to an end a year and a half ago. This period has been a serious subtraction from the total pleasure (such as it was) of my existence. I am not doing anything important, but putting together notes from my margins to print from time to time. I am much annoyed by being told by everyone how well I look, and being admired for my comparative youthfulness and my upright carriage.

It is surprisingly good news about Jeannie. Laurence has sent me his Victoria book, a good deal of which I had not read before, and I have found it entertaining,—very clever in the invention of fictitious details and conversations.

It is pleasant to hear that your respectably numerous progeny are well and that you are comfortable. I am looking forward to my usual Christmas gluttony. Which reminds me of a great calamity. For years it had been my chief ambition to be invited to the Colchester oyster-feast: this year I was invited, but had a lecture which prevented me from going.

Love from your affectionate brother   A. E. HOUSMAN

To an Unnamed Correspondent[1]

MS. B.M.

11 December 1934   *Trinity College*

Dear Sir,
Messrs Carter and Sparrow's reprint of the introductory lecture consisted of 100 copies, none for sale. Some were presented to me, but I have now so few left that I think I ought to keep them for persons having special claims on me who may wish to possess them. In any case I should not autograph the lecture, as I do not think well enough of it.

Yours very truly   A. E. HOUSMAN

To David Emrys Evans

MS. LILLY[2]

16 December 1934   *[Trinity College]*

On 23 November you kindly wrote to inform me that your Council had resolved to propose that the degree of *Doctor in Litteris honoris causa* should be conferred upon me, and you enquired whether I would allow my name to go forward. In reply I asked leave to decline this honour, and mentioned that I had previously declined similar honours offered me by the generosity of other Universities.

I now find in newspapers of the 13th inst the announcement, apparently official, that the University of Wales on 12 December awarded me the honorary degree of D. Litt. I suppose that this announcement is the blunder of a subordinate; but it is unfortunate, and places me in a most invidious position. What must be thought of me by those Universities, half-a-dozen in number, which in the last 30 years have offered me honorary degrees—one of them quite recently repeated the offer, and with special urgency—when they see me apparently accepting from your University a distinction which I declined to receive from them!

[1] Probably Thomas J. Wise. This letter is in his collection, the Ashley Library, now in the British Museum.
[2] Housman's draft.

To the Editor of The Sunday Times[1]

[circa *18 December 1934*]   *Trinity College*

Sir,

I have been asked by scholars at Oxford to answer a note by 'Atticus' on p. 13 of *The Sunday Times* of the 16th inst. concerning the election of Dr Eduard Fraenkel[2] to the Corpus Professorship of Latin, where he makes the shade (which he represents as indignant) of Conington[3] (whom he describes as a great Latinist) inquire: 'Is, then, Oxford so barren in Latinity that she has to choose an ex-professor from Freiburg University to fill the chair and occupy the rooms which once were mine?'

The question is invidiously put, and would not have been put by Conington, who was a modest man; but 'Atticus' gives the answer in his next words: 'Herr Fraenkel is a Latinist of European reputation.' I do not know who the other candidates were, but they cannot have been Latinists of European reputation; for no Englishman who could be so described was young enough to be eligible.

                                                                    A. E. HOUSMAN

To Percy Withers

MS. WITHERS

30 December 1934   *Trinity College*

My dear Withers,

This is just to thank you for your kind letter and to wish a happy new year to you and your wife and children. On your expert advice I left off alcohol for a week, with no effect except the production of gouty symptoms, or symptoms which I am accustomed to regard as such. Your other recipe, a cold douche after my warm bath, is impracticable, because my bath is cold.

My sister-in-law, whose death we were told to expect almost daily a year ago, has just been pronounced healed, and only needs to recover health and strength.

I hope you will continue to find amusement in building your new house, and will bring it into satisfactory being.

Yours sincerely   A. E. HOUSMAN

[1] Printed in *The Sunday Times*, 23 December 1934.

[2] 1888–1969; Professor of Latin at Berlin, 1920; Kiel, 1923; Göttingen, 1928; Freiburg, 1931; Bevan Fellow of Trinity College, Cambridge, 1934; Corpus Christi Professor of Latin at Oxford, 1935–1953.

[3] John Conington (1825–1869), famous for his commentary on Virgil and verse translation of *The Aeneid*, was Professor of Latin at Oxford 1854–1869.

To Geoffrey Tillotson[1]

MS. U.C.L.

23 January 1935   *Trinity College*

Dear Mr Tillotson,

My part in the reprint[2] to be issued by your press is strictly permissive, and I express none of the preferences which you kindly suggest: I only want it to be as unassuming as possible. Six copies for me, since you are good enough to offer copies, will be ample, as no one outside my own family will be likely to want one. I naturally am quite willing that your assistant should have copies.

Yours sincerely   A. E. HOUSMAN

To Charles Wilson

MS. VIRGINIA

14 February 1935   *Trinity College*

Dear Mr Wilson,

I have to thank you for your usual kind enquiries and invitations, and to reply that I am not very well nor disposed to stir away from Cambridge.

Though I do not altogether approve of your political activities, I am sorry that they have brought upon you a chill and consequent illness.

Yours very truly   A. E. HOUSMAN

To G. M. Lee[3]

MS. TRINITY

18 February 1935   *Trinity College*

Dear Mr Lee,

I suppose it is you whom I must chiefly thank for the gift of *Nineteen Echoes and a Song*, where you fill two parts; but I am also indebted to your associates. I do not pass judgment on the works of my contemporaries, being neither a qualified critic of literature nor immune from the moral vices of jealousy and envy; so let me content myself with congratulating you on winning the Davies Scholarship.

Yours very truly   A. E. HOUSMAN

---

[1] 1905–1969; Lecturer in English at University College, London, 1931; Professor of English at Birkbeck College, London, 1944.

[2] Of *Three Poems* ('The Parallelogram', 'The Amphisbaena' and 'The Crocodile') previously printed in *The University College London Union Magazine*, 1904, 1906 and 1911.

[3] George Mervyn Lee, at this time an undergraduate at Trinity College, collaborated with H. M. Dymock and others in the production of *Nineteen Echoes and a Song*, published by the college, 1935.

To Geoffrey Tillotson

MS. U.C.L.

5 March 1935   *Trinity College*

Dear Mr Tillotson,

I return the proofs, with such misprints as I have noticed corrected. As to 'changing any of the types' I am not competent to have an opinion, but I think that the 'or' in all three titles should be in capitals.

Yours sincerely   A. E. HOUSMAN

To Katharine Symons

MS. LILLY

31 March 1935   *Trinity College*

My dear Kate,

As to my precious health, about six weeks ago I had a turn of not being able to sleep lying down, and consequently four sleepless nights in succession. That soon passed away, but the result is that I am less well than I have been since I came back from France last September, in point of strength for walking and studying, and also I have not much appetite. However, owing I suppose to the magic of your letter on my birthday, I have been walking much more strongly since that date. I do not much mind things which properly belong to old age, but the nervous annoyance every morning, and undue sensitiveness to noises which I used not to mind, are extras, and do not show any sign of leaving off. My work is no tax on me, except that I have had to write the University's Address to the King on this so-called jubilee,[1] which was a worry, though there was no reason why it should be. I am very sorry that you have had trouble with your eyes, a thing which I should not like at all; and it is lucky that you could find some solace in wireless. This reminds me that the great new wireless station near Droitwich puts the apparatus at Tardebigge out of order. Jeannie wrote to me at the beginning of the year, very cheerfully and hopefully. I am glad you are occupying and amusing yourself again with your archaeology. This early and flowery spring has been pleasant here, especially the good days lately, though March has been a mixed month. Our Trinity crocuses were outshone by a bed at Queens'.

No more, except love from your affectionate brother

A. E. HOUSMAN

---

[1] Celebrated on 6 May 1935, the twenty-fifth anniversary of King George V's accession. The Address was printed by the University Press on 29 April, and first published in *The Cambridge University Reporter*, 14 May 1935.

To an Unnamed Correspondent

TEXT: MEMOIR

12 April 1935 [*Trinity College*]

... I have received several guesses at the order of some or all of the stanzas, but I do not let the truth be known, because then everyone would begin to pretend that it was obvious to them. If I had to guess myself, I am sure I could not tell which was last and which last but one; though I think I could guess which two came first. ...[1]

To Geoffrey Tillotson

MS. U.C.L.

28 April 1935 *Trinity College*

Dear Mr Tillotson,
I am content with your proposal for the title page, and have no ideas of my own.

Yours sincerely A. E. HOUSMAN

To Percy Withers

MS. WITHERS

4 May 1935 *Trinity College*

My dear Withers,
I am indignant to hear what inconvenience you have been put to by your builders—what a perfidious race they are we have learnt from our experience in repairs to the College—but glad to know that the worst trouble is now over.

My sister-in-law has made a miraculous recovery and has invited not only me but one of my sisters to stay with her in the summer. I shall most likely be going there on Saturday 29 June, and if I may pay you my visit in the week which ends then, that should suit me well.

For the last two months and more I have been less well, physically weaker and with less mastery over my nerves. Sometimes I have found it difficult to sleep lying down, owing to a sort of failure of breathing when dozing off; but a very short use of sleeping tablets puts that right. The doctor, whenever

---

[1] In the Leslie Stephen Lecture Housman had given an account of the composition of *A Shropshire Lad* LXIII, leaving the audience to guess which of the stanzas had come spontaneously and which had to be composed. Laurence Housman, in his old age, stated that the first two were the spontaneous ones, the last had come soon after, and it was the third that it took a year to get right.

I see him, tells me that my heart is stronger and steadier, but he always wants to see me again in a week's or fortnight's time. I fear I shall not be a worthy walking-companion for you, although (not to forget my blessings) I have suffered much less than usual from corns this last winter.

My kind regards and thanks to Mrs Withers.

Yours sincerely   A. E. HOUSMAN

To Percy Withers

MS. WITHERS

20 May 1935   *Trinity College*

My dear Withers,

One advantage of living in this charming world is that however bad one may think one's own lot it is always easy to find someone whose lot is worse; but I am sorry that the person to provide me with this poor sort of consolation should be you. I hope that there is no cause beyond your unsettled life in these last months, and that as this experience recedes you will grow better.

Cambridge is at its best just now except for this ferocious cold. I have not heard whether the fruit is ruined in Worcestershire as it seems to be in Kent. I look forward to seeing you after midsummer.

My kind regards to Mrs Withers.

Yours sincerely   A. E. HOUSMAN

To Laurence Housman

TEXT: MEMOIR

9 June 1935   *[Trinity College]*

My dear Laurence,

. . . Since the end of February I have grown much weaker, and more liable to shortness of breath and occasional thumping of the heart. The doctor does not want me to take walks of much more than a mile, and I myself am often inclined not to do much more than twice that amount. I still go up my 44 stairs two at a time, but that is in hopes of dropping dead at the top. As a tour in Yorkshire would be very pointless unless one could walk a fair amount, and up steeper gradients than those of Cambridgeshire, I no longer cherish the idea: otherwise it would have been very pleasant. I may be going to France in the autumn, but there I should be chiefly in towns.

I saw some notices, generally favourable, of your *Palace Plays*[1] and am glad

---

[1] Produced under the title *Victoria Regina* at the Gate Theatre, 1 May 1935.

that the acting satisfied you and that there is a promising future for them in our revolted colonies[1] . . .

Your affectionate brother   A. E. HOUSMAN

To Henry Tonks

MS. TEXAS

9 June 1935   *Trinity College*

Dear Tonks,

I am always glad to get a letter from you; but the few people pretending to artistic taste or knowledge whom I know here belong to schools which do not much revere the Pre-Raphaelites, and some of them think that the affair is Oxford's job.[2] For my own part, when I remember how much defaced the frescoes were more than fifty years ago, I think that restoration could not avoid being falsification, and something like restoring Leonardo's Last Supper.

I have not come across Cockerell lately, and I have not applied to him, as I understand that he is likely to be out of humour with the Pre-Raphaelites, the Fitzwilliam Syndicate having recently bought a Holman Hunt against his wish.[3]

Did you ever hear the story that Rossetti, having been rebuked by Holman Hunt for his loose living, affected to believe that Hunt had been unduly intimate with the Scapegoat, and that Hunt drew up and circulated a formal denial of the scandal?

I hope you are well. I am suffering from what no doubt is partly old age and only partly heart.

Yours sincerely   A. E. HOUSMAN

To Percy Withers

MS. WITHERS

18 June 1935   *The Evelyn Nursing Home*

My dear Withers,

I am grateful for the information in your letter, though I wish it were more cheerful.

[1] A highly successful American production opened six months later at the Broadhurst Theatre, New York.

[2] An appeal for £500 for the restoration of the murals by Rossetti, Burne-Jones and William Morris in the Oxford Union was launched in *The Times*, 17 May 1935. The response was poor, and Tonks wrote to *The Times* on 31 May to protest at the lack of public interest.

[3] Portrait of Cyril B. Holman Hunt.

The doctor has sent me here 'for a fortnight or perhaps a week'. I hope for the latter, but even so I am afraid I should not be able to come to you before Wednesday the 26th. In the state in which I have been for the last week I could not have gone to stay in your or any man's house. You probably know all about Cheyne-Stokes breathing, described in Arnold Bennett's *Clayhanger*:[1] sleepless nights spent in recurrent paroxysms of failure of breath, which can be combated if one is broad awake, but which overwhelm one if one dozes. Last night they conquered it with morphia and I slept long and almost continuously, but to-day I have been rather sick in consequence, and the treatment is to be varied, with oxygen in readiness as a second string. The specific trouble has not yet recurred to-day.

If I were in proper health I should at this moment be representing Cambridge at the tercentenary of the French Academy.

Kind regards and excuses to Mrs Withers.

Yours sincerely

A. E. HOUSMAN

To Percy Withers

MS. WITHERS

23 June 1935   *The Evelyn Nursing Home*

My dear Withers,

Your proposal to fetch me is very kind, and though I am ashamed to accept it its simplicity is an element which adds to its attraction, as relieving me of thought. But I cannot yet fix a day with certainty. I have written to my sister-in-law suggesting to postpone for a few days my visit to her, which was to have been next Saturday; and I want you to tell me whether it would be less inconvenient to you for me to come to you, say, on Friday, or a fortnight later, on my return to Cambridge. This of course may possibly be quite inconsistent with your engagements.

My heart does not trouble me, but this breathing makes my nights unquiet and has to be countered by drugs; and there is no prospect of a real cure.

Kind regards to Mrs Withers.

Yours sincerely

A. E. HOUSMAN

To Geoffrey Tillotson

MS. U.C.L.

24 June 1935   *The Evelyn Nursing Home*

Dear Mr Tillotson,

I believe I have not yet thanked you for the six copies of *Three Poems*

---

[1] Published in 1910.

which I have received from you since the doctor sent me here. I must therefore do so without delay, and add, though I am no judge, that they look very nice to me. I certainly shall not crave for any more.

Yours sincerely   A. E. HOUSMAN

To Mrs Withers

MS. WITHERS

3 July 1935   *Lower House, Tardebigge*

Dear Mrs Withers,

I was glad to hear that you said I seemed happy while with you, for indeed the fact was so, and everything conspired to give me peace and enjoyment, and I make warm returns of thanks to you and your husband for your care and kindness.

I find my sister-in-law apparently little weaker than when I stayed here two years ago.

I noticed the celebrated kennels as I passed them and saw Michael at his work.

Yours with every good wish and thought   A. E. HOUSMAN

To Geoffrey Tillotson

MS. U.C.L.

17 July 1935   *Trinity College*

Dear Mr Tillotson,

As I have been unwell lately, and part of the time in bed, my correspondence has been somewhat neglected, and I am apprehensive that I may have omitted to thank you for the six copies of *Parallelogram* etc. which you were kind enough to send me.

The typography, though I am not competent to judge it, seems to me agreeable. The third line on p. 8 ought to begin a new paragraph. This has probably gone wrong because the proofs were sent to me in two detached parts, and not simultaneously.

I am much behoven to you and your associates for squandering your pains on producing what Martial I am afraid would call 'difficiles nugas'[1] adding perhaps 'Stultus labor est ineptiarum'.[2]

Yours sincerely   A. E. HOUSMAN

[1] Obscure trifles.
[2] Folly to toil at trivialities.

373

To Katharine Symons

MS. LILLY

19 July 1935   *Trinity College*

My dear Kate,

It was very pleasant to see you again, and I was glad that we were able to manage it, and in such pleasant circumstances. Jeannie's recovery seems miraculous, and except that she does not come down to breakfast I can see no difference between now and two years ago.

I don't think I ever congratulated you on all the news in your last letter, such as the King's favouritism towards your three sons, and the demand for your historical work in America.

I enclose a copy of the address to the King which you wanted to see. I have been complimented to an absurd extent, but not enough to repay me for the bother of composing it.

Laurence is going to bring his car and driver here on 11 August and stay for a week. I expect to go to France on 27 August for about three weeks.

I hope that you have pleasure ahead of you at your sea-side residence.

Your affectionate brother   A. E. HOUSMAN

Having written this letter I remember that you wrote me another with kind plans for me in connexion with Jerry, but I cannot lay hands on it.

To Grant Richards

MS. CONGRESS

30 July 1935   *Trinity College*

My dear Richards,

It is kind of you to suggest coming to see me, but I think I am best left alone, though Laurence will be here for a week in the middle of August. At the end I think of going to France for three weeks, which last year seemed to do me some good.

So many people have worse troubles than mine that I am ashamed to dwell on them; but the recurrence of disquiet and agitation every morning is wearisome and disheartening.

Yours sincerely   A. E. HOUSMAN

To A. S. F. Gow

MS. TRINITY

7 August 1935   *Trinity College*

Dear Gow,

I should like very much to dine with you on Tuesday, and so I am sure
would my brother. But he is not likely to have evening things with him, and
he has already left his home.

Yours sincerely   A. E. HOUSMAN

Postcard to Katharine Symons

MS. TRINITY

28 August 1935   *Lyon*

I have given myself a nasty knock on the head in entering a taxi. I went
to a hospital and had the wound sewn up and bandaged (and also, to ease
your anxiety, took an injection against tetanus), and it will require medical
attention off and on for some eight days. It does not prevent me from getting
about; the pain is not much, and the mosquitoes annoy me much more. Do
not expect bulletins: death or grave illness will be duly notified to you and
the Head Porter of Trinity. I am going to Grenoble to-morrow.   A.E.H.

Pencil because no ink is handy.

To Katharine Symons

MS. TRINITY

3 September 1935   *Splendid Hôtel, Annecy*

My dear Kate,

In this pretty spot and comfortable hotel I shall probably stay at least four
days; but do not go on writing just to say that you are sorry for the top of my
head. On the 13th I shall return to the Hôtel Savoie, Grenoble, Isère, and
letters addressed there will be kept for me.

My head is healing so well that it makes doctors exclaim. I ought perhaps
to add that I am weaker than usual, but that may be due to eating too much.

Your affectionate brother   A. E. HOUSMAN

The weather has been good except the first day.

To Percy Withers

21 September 1935   *Trinity College*

My dear Withers,

To allay your kind anxiety I had better begin by saying that the doctor paid me an uninvited visit this morning and told me that I was very well. In point of fact I am rather weaker than before I went abroad; but the tour itself was pleasant, and the scenery of Dauphiné and Savoy more magnificent than I had guessed; and the works of man, in the engineering of roads up and over the hills, rival the works of God. From several points I had good views of Mont Blanc, and saw it turn rose-colour in the sunset. There are also many good restaurants and some excellent Rhone wine. On the first day, at Lyon I knocked my head very hard in getting into a taxi. I went to a hospital and had the wound sewn up and bandaged, which was done very well, and it has healed so quickly that doctors exclaim at it. It did not interfere with my movements, and I continued in the same taxi the outing I had planned for the day.

I had a disagreeable journey home from Paris on Tuesday, as I had to wait three hours at Le Bourget before the aeroplane could pluck up courage to start, and the crossing was twenty-five minutes longer than usual. The machine was not particularly unsteady, except in taking off and landing.

I now have my hands full, and see no prospect of taking advantage of your kind invitation. I hope you for your part are well. Thanks and kind regards to Mrs Withers.

Yours sincerely

A. E. HOUSMAN

To Houston Martin

MS. MARTIN

27 September 1935   *Trinity College*

Dear Mr Martin,

Your questions, though frivolous, are not indecent, so I suppose I must humour you.

I do not admire the oracle poem[1] quite so much as some people do. The italics, as elsewhere, are equivalent to inverted commas, and give the supposed words of the oracle.

Alterations were made by the printer in the second edition of *A Shropshire Lad*. The proofs were not sent to me for correction.

[1] *Last Poems* XXV.

I certainly shall not issue my preface to Manilius separately. The Introductory Lecture of 1892 was reprinted in 1933 by two young men named John Carter and John Sparrow in an edition of 100 copies, not for sale. I shall not reprint it.

Hardy and I never talked about my poems. I think it was Mrs Hardy who told me his opinion.

Certainly I have never regretted the publication of my poems. The reputation which they brought me, though it gives me no lively pleasure, is something like a mattress interposed between me and the hard ground. The lectures I care very little about.

With all good wishes for your health and sanity, I am yours sincerely

A. E. HOUSMAN

To Neilson Abeel[1]

MS. PRINCETON

4 October 1935   *Trinity College*

Dear Mr Abeel,

My heart always warms to people who do not come to see me, especially Americans, to whom it seems to be more of an effort; and your preference of the Cam to the Hudson, which I have always understood to be one of the finest rivers, is also an ingratiating trait.

If you think this note a reward, I shall be pleased.

Yours sincerely   A. E. HOUSMAN

To Witter Bynner

MS. HARVARD

12 October 1935   *Trinity College*

My dear Witter Bynner,

I shall not do anything to enable you to get hold of the nonsense verses you mention, and if they dwell in Laurence's too retentive memory I shall not authorise him to communicate them to you. He is bringing out a volume of reminiscences[2] early next year, in which I have allowed him to print a piece which is rather better.

His address is Longmeadow, Street, Somerset.

With best wishes I am yours sincerely   A. E. HOUSMAN

---

[1] 1902–1949. His *Poems* were published by Princeton in 1951.
[2] *The Unexpected Years*, 1937, which contains A.E.H.'s 'At the door of my own little hovel'.

To A. S. F. Gow

MS. TRINITY

15 October 1935   *Trinity College*

Dear Gow,

As I am encouraged to hope that the Classical Board will grant my request that I may be allowed to nominate a deputy to examine for the University Scholarships and Chancellor's Medals I write to ask whether you think that you could come to my assistance in this capacity. I would rather it were you than anyone else, and I have ascertained that you are not being nominated as one of the appointed examiners or as the Vice-Chancellor's deputy. On the other hand you are not a young married man, with greed for your ruling passion, and have probably more than enough to do already, and are no more inclined to undertake the job for the money than I myself should be if I were in your place.

Yours sincerely   A. E. HOUSMAN

To A. S. F. Gow

MS. TRINITY

16 October 1935   *Trinity College*

My dear Gow,

I should not think of urging you, nor of making it a question of you or me; and I should not have taken any step towards nominating a deputy before I had the permission of the Board unless I had heard that you had not been snapped up, which made me anxious not to miss the chance if there was one.

It will be proper for me to delay my arrival at the meeting to-morrow till after the fourth item of agenda.

Yours sincerely   A. E. HOUSMAN

To Katharine Symons

MS. TRINITY

24 October 1935   *The Evelyn Nursing Home*

My dear Kate,

I suppose I was spoiled while I was abroad by living in hotels and always using lifts, but anyhow since I came back I have been going downhill at a great pace, the chief blame for which is being laid on my 44 stairs, which give my heart more work than it can manage, so that I have breathlessness, weakness, and dropsical swelling in the ankles and knees. I lecture without difficulty, but the ten minutes' walk to and fro was so exhausting that I now have a lecture room within the walls of the College. I am to change into a ground-floor set of rooms, and one of the younger Fellows has nobly made over his set to me; but it will be a great nuisance and will raise grave and probably insoluble problems about accommodating my books. At present I have gone to stay in this nursing home for a week or more, which the doctor hopes will get me into a state from which a start of recovery can be made. I shall taxi into College for my lectures twice a week. The University has relieved me of the examination which is the chief terror of the winter. People are very kind in taking trouble on my behalf.

I had hoped to induce Jerry to stay here for a day or two, but that is now out of the question. I hope that he is enjoying himself, and you with him.

The red ink is an accident and has no lurid significance.

Your affectionate brother   A. E. HOUSMAN

To Laurence Housman

MS. LILLY

28 October 1935   *The Evelyn Nursing Home*

My dear Laurence,

Thanks for your offer to help with my books, but I do not think it is a task on which I ought to employ your energies, nor on which you would find very much to do. The boys of the college Library seem to be experienced in such matters, and Gow is very kindly giving an eye to the matter. He told me that you were coming here next month and suggested that I might wish to consult you about discarding or retaining books, but I do not think this will prove much of a problem. Probably nothing which I am discarding is anything which you would wish to take. The main difficulty is to find space in the new rooms.

I shall be here probably at least ten days more, and at this moment I am reduced to great weakness by sleepless and distressed nights, the sedatives having failed; so that even if I were back in College I could not offer you hospitality or society. None the less I am grateful to you for offering to sacrifice so much of your time. Love to Clemence.

Your affectionate brother   A. E. HOUSMAN

To Katharine Symons

MS. TRINITY

2 November 1935   *The Evelyn Nursing Home*

My dear Kate,

I have had four tranquil nights in succession, partly due to champagne: the doctor, though he did not suggest it, approves of the results. I manage my lectures without difficulty, and the change of rooms is being carried out very competently so far as I can judge from the reports I receive. The dropsy seems to have vanished; and by the way it was not this which hindered my walking, but general feebleness, which continues.

Your affectionate brother   A. E. HOUSMAN

To H. G. Broadbent[1]

MS. SHREWSBURY

4 November 1935   *The Evelyn Nursing Home*

Dear Mr Broadbent,

Yours is the second application which I have received about printing the words in the programme of this recital of the 'Wenlock Edge Song Cycle', and I have already sent a refusal: it is a thing I happen to dislike. I am very generous to composers who want to set my poems, and I ought not to be worried in consequence. There is too, if I remember right, a particular reason why neither this composer nor I should wish to see the words in the programme.[2]

I am yours very truly   A. E. HOUSMAN

To Katharine Symons

MS. TRINITY

10 November 1935   *The Evelyn Nursing Home*

My dear Kate,

I have been going on satisfactorily with very good and quiet nights. Always lying in bed makes me weak on my legs when I do sally forth for lectures or revelry, as I am going out to luncheon to-day to meet scholars from Oxford and abroad. My new rooms are much admired, especially as to bathroom and lavatory, by those who have properly examined them, and are said to be the last word in luxurious and scientific plumbing. Did you ever hear of a thermo-

---

[1] Assistant Master at Shrewsbury School.
[2] See p. 181, note 8.

stat? a thing which watches the thermometer and sends the temperature up when it begins to fall. I expect to move in early this week.

I abandoned Christianity at thirteen but went on believing in God till I was twenty-one, and towards the end of that time I did a good deal of praying for certain persons and for myself. I cannot help being touched that you do it for me, and feeling rather remorseful, because it must be an expenditure of energy, and I cannot believe in its efficacy.

The college has insisted on paying for most of the expense in the new rooms.

Your affectionate brother   A. E. HOUSMAN

To A. F. Scholfield

MS. TRINITY

12 November 1935   *The Evelyn Nursing Home*

Dear Scholfield,
    I have received encouragement to hope that you will carry me to Babraham on Saturday night, and am grateful and expectant.

Yours sincerely   A. E. HOUSMAN

To A. F. Scholfield

MS. TRINITY

17 November 1935   *The Evelyn Nursing Home*

Dear Scholfield,
    We had a very pleasant dinner, saddened only by your absence, and the news that Lady Wemyss's[1] entire household has given her a month's notice: which she sustains with gaiety in affiance on a Miss Wilkinson. I hope you are going on all right and will appear faithfully next Friday.

Yours sincerely   A. E. HOUSMAN

To A. F. Scholfield

MS. TRINITY

25 November 1935   *Trinity College*

Dear Scholfield,
    Perhaps this may serve. In any case I am ashamed to have kept you waiting so long.

Yours sincerely   A. E. HOUSMAN

[1] Mary Constance Wyndham (died 1937) married the 11th Earl of Wemyss in 1883.

Qui in hoc armario seruantur apud Indos extra Gangem conquisiti codices Vniversitati Cantabrigiensi secundum testamentum Roberti Forsyth Scott, equitis, Collegii S. Ioannis Magistri, donati sunt anno MDCCCCXXXIII.[1]

To Percy Withers

MS. WITHERS

[*Late November 1935*]   *Trinity College*

My dear Withers,

If you have not engaged yourself to someone else I should hope you will dine with me in hall on Friday 6 December, if the food and drink are suitable to your dietary requirements. I regularly dine there myself and sometimes proceed to Combination Room.

I have not very recent news of your health, nor you of mine. When I came back from France I was in fair fettle, perhaps due to living in motor cars and hotels and always using lifts; but I soon began to go rapidly down hill, so that I have had to abandon my old rooms, where the 44 stairs were too much for me, and come to B 2 (ground floor) in the Great Court, which would have removed an annoyance of Bridges's. I spent about three weeks in the Evelyn Nursing Home while the change was making, but motored in twice a week for my lectures. I am much weaker generally than in July, and you would not have to check me in walking up hill over broken ground.

I met Lady Wemyss the other day and gave her your new address. I am to meet Madame de Navarro at luncheon on Saturday.

My kind regards to Mrs Withers.

Yours sincerely

A. E. HOUSMAN

To Percy Withers

MS. WITHERS

30 November 1935   *Trinity College*

My dear Withers,

It is quite plain to me that your troubles of health are greater than mine, which, apart from the annoying feebleness which is now added, consist in nervous uneasiness. I am at present, now that hot water has at last been laid on, more comfortable in my new rooms than in my old, though I foresee that in summer there will be some lack of air.

I will be in my rooms after five on 6 December, and you will come again for dinner.

Kind regards to Mrs Withers.

Yours sincerely

A. E. HOUSMAN

[1] Inscription for the Scott Collection of Burmese books in the University Library.

To Jeannie Housman

TEXT: MEMOIR

11 December 1935   *[Trinity College]*

... I was very glad to get your long and early Christmas letter, with the news, among other things, that your family is soon to indulge again in its favourite recreation of marriage.[1] I hope the young couple will be happy and will find some means of livelihood.

My present rooms are the warmest and cosiest that could be well imagined; and the bath-room, which has been equipped by the College, is the admiration and envy of all beholders. I myself walk very feebly and do not sleep very well, and my breathing is apt to be troublesome; but the comforts around me make me more cheerful than I should otherwise be. I can get through all the work that is required of me, and I go out to dinner when invited. One of the medicines I am taking is champagne, which however is not a wine I am very fond of.

To F. W. Oliver[2]

MS. HARVARD

14 December 1935   *Trinity College*

Dear Oliver,

We were indeed on the Council together at the critical period, and though all else may fade from memory the meeting of July 1900, when Horsburgh[3] was dismissed, is branded on my soul. I was at Henley, whence I was brought up by an S.O.S. from Micaiah,[4] and Lord Reay[5] asked me to keep the minutes while Horsburgh was out of the room: consequently I had to stay afterwards and enter them in the minute-book, and you kindly took to the Post Office a telegram to my friends warning them that I should not be back till late.

I cannot take to myself much credit for any of my actions in the reforming movement, for I was only a partisan and occasionally a mouth-piece, not a convinced reformer nor a statesman with any prevision of the great success which resulted.

When you were here in June I was in a nursing-home. My descent to the grave has brought me down a staircase of 44 steps to the ground-floor, where

---

[1] Jeannie Housman's niece had become engaged.

[2] Francis Wall Oliver (1864–1951), Quain Professor of Botany at University College, London, 1888–1929; thereafter Emeritus Professor. His recollections of Housman are reprinted in Richards.

[3] Secretary of University College, 1886–1900.

[4] Micaiah John Muller Hill (1856–1929), Professor of Mathematics at University College, 1884–1923.

[5] See p. 401, note 3.

I am stuck at present and my heart has less opportunity of making itself a nuisance.

Ker's successor and (I suppose) your colleague R. W. Chambers has been giving the Clark Lectures[1] here this term, and I have met him several times; and Lyde[2] has sent me a book on Pindar of all subjects in the world. Tonks I met three years ago in Scotland.

I hope climate and surroundings allow you to be happy.

Yours sincerely

A. E. HOUSMAN

To E. H. Blakeney

MS. B.M.

20 December 1935   *Trinity College*

Dear Mr Blakeney,

Many thanks for the specimen of your private printing.[3] If Watson had gone on writing things like 'Wordsworth's Grave' and some other things which he wrote when he was thirty, he would have been one of the first poets of the age. But he swallowed the praises of *The Spectator* and wrote a lot which he ought to have known was quite second-rate, and when early in this century he made a fresh start, the merit of his writing, which was sometimes considerable, was that of epigram rather than of poetry.

Thanks too for your enquiry after my health. It is weak and declining, and I have already lived more than two years too long.

Yours very truly

A. E. HOUSMAN

To Katharine Symons

MS. TRINITY

27 December 1935   *The Evelyn Nursing Home*

My dear Kate,

Christmas in a nursing home, so I must write to you. From the doctor's point of view it is not much, but for the patient indigestion and nausea are the worst things in the world. I have been nursing myself in College on soup, hot milk and brandy in great discomfort, and finally have come here where I receive great attention. I am fed on toast, chicken-broth, orange juice,

---

[1] On *English Prose from Chaucer to Raleigh*.

[2] Lionel William Lyde (1863–1947), Professor of Economic Geography at University College, 1903–1928, published *Contexts in Pindar, with reference to the meaning of φέγγος* in 1935.

[3] Sir William Watson's sonnet 'The Yesterdays and the Morrows', printed in an edition of 25 copies, Winchester, 1934.

champagne, breast of turkey, Brand's essence of chicken. I am very weak. The other night they gave me an injection of heroin instead of my usual soporific, and I learnt what it is to be totally deprived of intellect. My College fellows sympathise with me more than my family could, knowing more of my gluttony.

Yours   A.E.H.

To Laurence Housman

MS. LILLY

10 January [1936][1]   *The Evelyn Nursing Home*

My dear Laurence,
    Days fly and I am little better at conducting business, so I shall be grateful if you will take it upon you to say that I am not prepared to give permission about 'Hell Gate'. I am not conscious of any strong objection, and perhaps I am foolish, but I am not strong enough to decide affirmatively.

Your affectionate brother   A. E. HOUSMAN

To Katharine Symons

MS. LILLY

18 January 1936   *Trinity College*

My dear Kate,
    I am very sorry that you have been obliged to lay yourself down officially on a bed of medical attention, and it is good news that you seem to have got from it all that you required and that the pleasure of your stay at Jerry's was not materially spoilt. Thanks for your enquiries, which I heard of from the matron. I was in bed three weeks, leaving letters unanswered, and unable to write a cheque without advice and assistance in the early days of the year. My weakness is no longer bodily and mentally such a nuisance, but all my strength is needed for my actual work. I lectured yesterday with comfort to myself, except in crossing the Court to the room, and the hearers could hear me all right. Almost every physical action is a labour. I sleep fairly well, with the usual aids, and, best of all, my inside is getting right.

Love from your affectionate brother   A. E. HOUSMAN

[1] Housman wrote 1925 in error. The whole letter is in a very feeble hand.

To the Richards Press

MS. B.M.

18 January 1936   *Trinity College*

Dear Sirs,

I have been ill for some weeks and unable to answer letters; and I regret that I seem to have lost the letter you sent me on 23 December from Mr Bhawani Shankar.[1] Can you apologise to him from me and ask him to repeat it, if you do not sufficiently remember its purport?

Faber and Faber wish to reprint in England a trashy American book by Babette Deutsch.[2] She was of course entitled to quote in America as much as she liked of *A Shropshire Lad*, and I am always willing to see quotation from any book made for 'criticism or review'; but the amount quoted from this work, of which I forbid the reproduction wherever I can, does seem to me inordinate, and the book is trashy.

To Mr Moore[3] you may say that I refuse him permission to publish his illiterate alterations of my verses, and that I regard his request as an act of incivility.

Yours faithfully   A. E. HOUSMAN

To Grant Richards

TEXT: RICHARDS

20 January 1936   *[Trinity College]*

I was three weeks in the Nursing Home unable to answer letters. I am now back here and lecturing but with no strength for anything beyond my actual work. I am having your books returned and I thank you for sending them but I cannot bear to look at them; and I should not approve of anything of that sort under any circumstances. I am not a descriptive writer and do not know Shropshire well.[4]

The chief trouble was digestive.

To Percy Withers

MS. WITHERS

23 January 1936   *Trinity College*

My dear Withers,

Your letter is so extravagantly kind and wrong-headed that I am obliged,

---

[1] Lecturer in English at the University of Allahabad.   [2] *This Modern Poetry*, 1936.

[3] G. V. Moore of Burton-on-Trent wrote to the Richards Press on 14 January 1936 for permission to quote poems by Housman in an article for *The London Quarterly and Holborn Review*. The article was not published.

E. V. Lucas wanted to publish a book on the country of *A Shropshire Lad* and had sent similar books published by Methuen containing work by the illustrator they proposed to employ.

weak as I am, to lift the pen. Although my physical weakness is depressing and prostrating, my misery is much less than it has been for two years and a half. My own diagnosis for much of my discomfort before Christmas was obstruction in what I suppose to be the upper intestine: there was a protuberance above the navel which has now vanished, and my inside is that of a new man. My nerves are not restored but are quieter than at any time since June 1933. I am surrounded by more comforts, luxury and attention than ever in my life, and take quite an interest in ordering my meals. Lecturing is far less labour than walking across the court to the lecture room: my only worry in the matter is that my preparation, which usually occupies the vacation, has because of my illness been curtailed, and is not so much ahead as is usual and desirable. A weak soporific and a glass of champagne, followed by a cup of tea at 7.30 p.m., procure me a peaceful night, except that the champagne has not a very quieting effect on the bladder. Do therefore be at peace and persuade Mrs Withers, to whom all thanks and good wishes, to imitate you.

Yours sincerely   A. E. HOUSMAN

To Percy Withers

MS. WITHERS

28 January 1936   *Trinity College*

My dear Withers,

I am sorry to have written tartly: my intention was not so; and indeed the extreme and undeserved kindness and generosity of your letters move me almost to tears. On my part, perhaps the facts do not quite justify the account I gave of my surroundings, as you would think me to be pitied for being alone at night with only a telephone for company. But, so far as I can analyse my feelings and separate bodily weariness from condition of soul, I am in better spirits than I have been for two years and a half, although particular ailments rather tend to increase.

Yours sincerely   A. E. HOUSMAN

To G. V. Moore[1]

MS. SPARROW

[29 January 1936]   *[Trinity College]*

Permission to quote is one thing, permission to misquote is another. First you take certain verses of mine and disfigure them with illiterate alterations, then you ask me to let you attribute them publicly to me, and now, because I

---

[1] Draft written on the back of Moore's letter.

do not abet you in injuring my reputation, you think it rather hard. Why was Burton built on Trent?[1]

To Jeannie Housman

TEXT: MEMOIR

31 January 1936   *[Trinity College]*

... I am sorry to hear that you have been ill and laid up, and I hope your recovery is proceeding as it should. As you say nothing of Grace I suppose that she is despising us both and exulting in good health. When your letter reached me I had strength to read it but not to answer it; and this is one of my pieces of correspondence which I am trying to overtake. In several respects I am much more comfortable and cheerful than when I went into the nursing home at Christmas, but my physical weakness (chiefly due to lying so long in bed) is extreme and very vexatious; and next to walking, writing seems to be what tires me most. On the other hand my lectures are no trouble. Some shadow is cast over the pleasure with which I look forward to visiting you in the summer by perplexity how I am to manage your stairs. True there are not 44 of them, but they are precipitous; and the days when I used to take them two at a time are not likely to return.

To Mrs Wilson[2]

MS. COLBY

7 February 1936   *Trinity College*

Dear Mrs Wilson,
  Your request[3] is one which I have sometimes received from Americans, but I have not acceded to it, as it seems to me unwarrantable.
  There arrived here this morning what appeared to be your copy of *A Shropshire Lad*, but I returned it to the post office.

    Yours very truly   A. E. HOUSMAN

To Cyril Clemens[4]

2 March 1936   *Trinity College*

Dear Mr Clemens,
  My forefinger has a small fracture and is in plaster of Paris, so please excuse my handwriting and my brevity.
  I am deeply sensible of the honour which your Society does me by the

---

[1] 'And why was Burton built on Trent?' (*A Shropshire Lad* LXII).   [2] Not identified.
[3] To write out a poem in her copy of *A Shropshire Lad*.
[4] Text from *Poet Lore* LIII, 1947.

offer of its Silver Medal, and I shall always remember it with gratitude. Nevertheless I beg you to allow me to decline it, as, in pursuance of an early resolve, I have in the course of my life already declined a considerable number of honours, even when offered me by my own two Universities and by the King of England with the same excess of kindness and over-estimate of desert.

Yours sincerely and gratefully   A. E. HOUSMAN

To Katharine Symons

MS. TRINITY

3 March 1936   *Trinity College*

My dear Kate,

My forefinger is in plaster of Paris, so do not expect much. A month ago I slipped and fell and sprained my hand, and as the swelling and pain did not much decrease it was X-rayed on Saturday and a small fracture of a bone was found. I am to go on like this for a fortnight. It does not interfere with other things so much as writing.

Your affectionate brother   A. E. HOUSMAN

I hear that I am lecturing better than ever.

To Laurence Housman

TEXT: MEMOIR

11 March 1936   *[Trinity College]*

My dear Laurence,

... I rejoice that you have made a fortune.[1] Do not squander it as you did the proceeds of *The Englishwoman*.[2]

When you wrote to me about the setting of 'Hell Gate' I was very ill and could not make up my mind to say yes; but I now do not mind consenting. The orchestra will *drown* the words, which must be pretty bad if a composer had an overwhelming admiration for them.

> Brightness falls from the air;
> Queens have died young and fair;
> Dust hath closed Helen's eye.
> > T. Nashe
> > 'In time of plague'[3]

Your affectionate brother   A. E. HOUSMAN

[1] Out of *Victoria Regina*.
[2] *An Englishwoman's Love Letters*, 1900, earned Laurence Housman over £2,000.
[3] Laurence Housman had asked A.E.H. to complete and identify the quotation.

To Houston Martin

MS. MARTIN

22 March 1936   *The Evelyn Nursing Home*

Dear Mr Martin,

I was very ill at the beginning of the year, and I am now again in a nursing home. I hope that if you can restrain your indecent ardour for a little I shall be properly dead and your proposed work will not be by its nature unbecoming. But the hope is not more than a hope, for my family are tough and long-lived, unless they take to drink.

Do not send me your manuscript. Worse than the practice of writing books about living men is the conduct of living men in supervising such books. I do not forbid you to quote extracts from my letters.

I think you should ask yourself whether you are literary enough for your job. You say that I may think it 'indignant and presumptious' for an American to write such a book before an English one has appeared. By *presumptious* you mean *presumptuous* and what you mean by *indignant* I have no idea.

The best review I ever saw of my poems was by Hubert Bland the Socialist[1] in a weekly paper *The New Age* (1896). The American who called them (I do not know where) the best poetry since Keats is endeared to me by his amiable error.

When an athletic performance, previously the best, is excelled, the *record* is said to be *broken* or *cut*. I am not sure if the latter is really good English, but it was common in sporting circles in my youth.

In philosophy I am a Cyrenaic or egoistic hedonist, and regard the pleasure of the moment as the only possible motive of action. As for pessimism, I think it almost as silly, though not as wicked, as optimism. George Eliot said she was a meliorist: I am a pejorist, and also yours sincerely

                                                                A. E. HOUSMAN

To Katharine Symons

MS. TRINITY

24 March 1936   *The Evelyn Nursing Home*

My dear Kate,

I use pencil because it is easier. I am not nearly so bad as I was at Christmas, but shortness of breath and indigestion cause me a good deal of annoyance. I fear I shall live to be seventy-seven.

Your affectionate brother   A. E. HOUSMAN

[1] See p. 37, note 1.

To Katharine Symons

MS. TRINITY

2 April 1936 *The Evelyn Nursing Home*

My dear Kate,

After the great turn for the better I took on Thursday my birthday I have not looked back. My doctor was away but his substitute managed me very well with his opiate, and the Regius professor came to see me and seemed quite satisfied. Sleep and digestion are both satisfactory and I have reading to fill my hours. I have heard from Jeannie not very good news.

I did think of asking Venn[1] if he would like to know anything of Fletcher Housman[2] who probably would be more interesting than our grandfather. But probably he was not at Cambridge.

Your affectionate brother A. E. HOUSMAN

7 April 1936

You see why the Post office has returned this letter.[3] I am going on well, and so I hope are you. A.E.H.

To Percy Withers

MS. WITHERS

2 April 1936 *The Evelyn Nursing Home*

My dear Withers,

I am sorry that your experiment has been attended by pain, but I hope it will prove a success. My term was conducted to a triumphant end, but finally I had such bad nights that I was obliged to resort to the Nursing Home and the 24th and 25th were very wretched, on the 26th I was wondrously renewed by morphia and am going on well.

Yours sincerely A. E. HOUSMAN

Postcard to S. C. Roberts[4]

[Postmark 20 April 1936][5] *[Trinity College]*

I trust that I responded to your Family invitation. I still hope to be there, though I am not so sanguine as I should like to be.[6] A.E.H.

---

[1] John Archibald Venn (1883–1958), University Lecturer in the History and Economics of Agriculture, 1921; President of Queen's College, 1932–1958; University Archivist, 1949; part-author of *Alumni Cantabrigienses*.

[1] Cousin of A.E.H.'s grandfather; biographer of the Rev. Robert Housman.

[3] The envelope is not preserved, but it was presumably wrongly addressed.

[4] Sold by Messrs Sotheby, 7 December 1966.

[5] Housman dated this card in error 22 April 1936.

[6] Though obviously very ill, Housman attended this dinner party on 24 April.

To Houston Martin

MS. MARTIN

21 April 1936   *Trinity College*

Dear Mr Martin,

If I were well I could make a long reply to your kind but irrelevant letter of the 2nd inst., but I am so ill that I am not fit to discharge the functions of my office or of ordinary life, and my doctor is trying hard to send me back into a nursing home.

    I am yours very truly   A. E. HOUSMAN

To R. A. Scott-James[1]

21 April 1936   *Trinity College*

I am obliged by your letter, but my career and it is to be hoped my life are so near their close that it is to be hoped they will concern neither of us much longer.

Postcard to Katharine Symons

MS. TRINITY

25 April 1936   *[Trinity College]*

Back to Evelyn nursing home to-day (Saturday).

    Ugh.   A.E.H.

By the time of his final return to the nursing home Housman was obviously a dying man. His heart disease was so far advanced that he could scarcely walk or even breathe. All that could be done was to relieve the pain with morphia and assure that he was properly attended at night.

In his last few days he mellowed. When he was told that the nurses were praying for him, he thanked them and said that their prayers did him good. His doctor was impressed by his self-control. Housman did not complain, but in the end he asked that he should not be allowed to suffer any more. The doctor promised that he should not, and gave him an injection. As he was leaving he told Housman an improper story. Housman was delighted. 'Yes, that's a good one,' he said, 'and to-morrow I shall be telling it again on the Golden Floor.' They are his last recorded words. Soon afterwards he sank into unconsciousness, and lay holding the nurse's hand until the morning of 30 April, when his life ended.

After a memorial service in Trinity College Chapel on 4 May, Housman's

---

[1] Rolfe Arnold Scott-James (1878–1959), editor of *The London Mercury*, 1934–1939. This letter, answering a request for a contribution, was published in the issue for June 1936.

body was cremated in London. The ashes were finally buried in the church-yard at Ludlow on 25 July. A cherry tree was planted near the grave and a bronze tablet placed in the church wall above it.

In his will Housman appointed Laurence his literary executor and gave him permission to publish any of his manuscript poems that were not below his average. This collection, *More Poems*, came out in October 1936. It con-tained some good things, but also many poems that added little to Housman's reputation.

Laurence did not keep Housman's library together. He gave a number of the books to Gow and to Trinity College Library, and had the rest sent to Oxford and sold in Blackwell's bookshop. He instructed that pencilled notes should be rubbed out before the books were put up for sale, and for several days assistants in the shop filled their spare time with the task, while cus-tomers hovered to snap up any volume with annotations that had escaped the eraser.

The manuscript books in which Housman had kept the drafts and fair copies of his poems met an odder fate. Ordered by his brother's will to destroy all poems that he decided to leave unpublished, Laurence was in a quandary. The unpublished material in Housman's notebooks was so mixed up with the rest that to destroy it would have meant destroying the lot. He therefore compromised. He destroyed the pages containing only unpublished matter; on about 140 others, on which unpublished verses were written on the reverse of published work, he scored out the forbidden matter and pasted it down on mounting sheets.

In this form in 1939 he sold the notebooks. Bought first by an American dealer, they eventually reached the Library of Congress, where they now repose—though hardly in peace. To modern science the task of uncovering their secrets was no problem. The gummed sheets were separated, the dele-tions penetrated by infra-red photography, and the cancelled words revealed. The results, somewhat doubtfully transcribed, appeared in *The Manuscript Poems of A. E. Housman*, edited by Tom Burns Haber, 1955.

That his brother should first have flouted his wishes by publishing poems that might have been better forgotten; then, three years later, by authorising the issue of *A Shropshire Lad* and *Last Poems* in a single volume; then by failing to destroy the unpublished poems; then by condoning their appear-ance in a less than scholarly text—all this would surely have infuriated Housman if he had foreseen it. But there is a mystery: he never thought much of Laurence's judgment and must have guessed that he would fail to carry out his instructions. Had he wanted an obedient executor he could easily have found one. So perhaps it should be concluded that Housman cared less than he pretended what happened when he was gone, and even amused himself with the likelihood that for him and his works death was not quite the end to acrimony.

Part II
Letters on Classical Subjects

'MY TRADE is that of professor of Latin.' Housman spent a hundred hours on his academic work for every one that he gave to his poems, and, if the choice had been his, he would probably have wished to be remembered as a scholar rather than as the author of *A Shropshire Lad*.

The letters that follow are those that deal primarily with the technicalities of his studies. I intended at first to add translations of all Greek and Latin words, together with enough commentary to make the grammatical, prosodic, palaeographic and astronomical points intelligible to the general reader; but I have come to the conclusion that to do so would be to weigh the text down with an inordinate load of elucidation, which would irritate scholars but still inevitably leave much obscure to everyone else. They are printed therefore as they stand, encumbered, I hope, only with enough footnotes to send the interested reader to the right source of information.

To W. Aldis Wright[1]

MS. CAMBRIDGE

28 December 1887   *17 North Road*

Dear Sir,

The authority of the best and oldest MSS both Greek and Latin is all in favour of the orthography Clytaemestra, Hypermestra etc., and most of the best Latin texts for some years past have spelt the names so.[2] In Greek the progress of reform is slower as usual, but Wecklein in his Aeschylus of 1885 always has Κλυταιμήστρα with the Medicean MS, and I believe there is a paper of his in the *Philologische Wochenschrift* for 1885 or 1886 stating the evidence on the point.

The detail however is a minute one, and if you think the spelling looks pedantic I shall have no vehement objection to the change.

I am yours very truly   A. E. HOUSMAN

[1] William Aldis Wright (1831–1919); Joint Editor of *The Journal of Philology* from 1868; Vice-Master of Trinity College, Cambridge, 1888–1912.

[2] Wright had questioned Housman's spelling in his article 'The Agamemnon of Aeschylus', printed in *The Journal of Philology*, 1888.

To the Editor of The Academy[1]

7 March 1891   [*17 North Road*]

The fragment of the "Antiope" published by Professor Mahaffy[2] in the last number of *Hermathena* is emended in this month's *Classical Review* by two distinguished Grecians. Their emendations are numerous and intrepid. Dr Rutherford[3] "would restore" to Euripides the senarius σὺ μὲν χερῶν τὸ πνεῦμ' ἐκ πολεμίων λαβών, which Euripides, I think, would restore to Dr Rutherford. Professor Campbell[4] proposes to enrich the tragic vocabulary by the importation of ἄχρι, in accordance with his opinion that it is not yet 'time to cease from guessing and to begin the sober work of criticism.' When that time arrives it will occur to someone that l. 18 of fragment C, ὁλκοῖς γε ταυρείοισιν διαφερουμένη, is neither verse nor Greek, and should be amended ταυρείοισι διαφορουμένη: there is, of course, no such verb as διαφερῶ. It surprised me that the first editor did not correct this obvious blunder, and I looked to see it removed by the first critic who took the fragment in hand; but our scholars seem just now to be absorbed in more exhilarating sport, so I will perform this menial office, at the risk of incurring Professor Campbell's censure for premature sobriety.   A. E. HOUSMAN

To the Editor of The Academy[5]

22 March 1891   [*17 North Road*]

If Professor Campbell will turn to v. 1100 of the *Aiax* of Sophocles, he will see what comes of assuming that any correction, however trivial, can be 'too much a matter of course to be worth mentioning.' He will find that he and his brother-editors—Dindorf, Wunder, Schneidewin, Nauck, Jebb, Blaydes, Wecklein, Paley, and, in short, the whole goodly fellowship—have printed in that verse the non-existent word λεῶν. They mean it for the genitive plural of λεώς; but the genitive plural of λεώς is λεών. And it looks as if another false accentuation were about to gain a foothold in our fragment of Euripides. The text is given in *Hermathena* without accents or breathings, but Fragment B has been twice invested with these perhaps superfluous ornaments—in the *Athenaeum* of 31 January, and again by Professor Campbell in the *Classical Review* for March; and in both places v. 4 begins with ἵκται . Now ἵκται is the nominative plural of ἵκτης, and makes no sense whatever: the word meant

---

[1] Printed in *The Academy*, 14 March 1891.

[2] John Pentland Mahaffy (1839–1919), Professor of Ancient History at Trinity College, Dublin, 1869; Provost, 1914; knighted, 1918.

[3] William Gunion Rutherford (1853–1907), Headmaster of Westminster School, 1883–1901.

[4] Lewis Campbell (1830–1908), Professor of Greek at St Andrews, 1863–1902.

[5] Printed in *The Academy*, 28 March 1891.

is ἷκται. The reason why I do not descend so far as to correct the spelling of vv. 40 and 57 in Fragment C is that Nauck[1] or Wecklein,[2] whichever gets hold of the fragment first, can be trusted not to miss the chance of observing "ἄστεως scripsi" and "εὐνατήριον scripsi," and they derive more pleasure from these achievements than I do.

The further fragments of Professor Campbell's *Antiope* (a drama which I much admire and hope to see completed), published in last week's *Academy*, have been slightly corrupted by the scribes, and I would venture to restore the poet's hand by the following emendations: for πούσθ' read ποῦ 'σθ', for στεγή read στέγη, for ἔνοντας read ἐνόντας and for ἰθαγένους read ἰθαγενοῦς.

A. E. HOUSMAN

To Robinson Ellis

MS. BODLEY

30 October 1891   *17 North Road*

Dear Mr Ellis,

I am glad to be able to make any sort of return for the information you have given me, so I write to tell you that on examining the defloratio Brit. Mus. 18459[3] I find that your report of it is in error in one particular. It contains the verses 39 and 40 (quam mihi . . . rupta tuis), and it does not contain the verses 35 and 36 (et noua . . . ira pyra). This explains the absence of any statement in your app. crit.[4] as to its reading *quem* or *quam* in 36.

Yours very truly   A. E. HOUSMAN

It has *tibi sit* for *sit tibi* in 109, but this perhaps is not worth mentioning.

To the Editor of The Athenaeum[5]

[May 1899]   *[17 North Road]*

Juvenal, Sat. VI.—In the new fragment of Juvenal's Sixth Satire published in this month's *Classical Review*[6] the following emendations should be made.

---

[1] August Nauck (1822–1892), editor of Sophocles.

[2] Nicolaus Wecklein (1843–1926), German classical scholar, who in 1892 supported Housman's candidature for the Chair of Latin at University College, London.

[3] Of Ovid's *Ibis*, which Housman was editing for J. P. Postgate's *Corpus Poetarum Latinorum*, volume I, 1894.

[4] In Ellis' edition, 1881.

[5] Printed in *The Athenaeum*, 13 May 1899.

[6] In an article by J. P. Postgate.

Lines 1–3 should read:

In quacumque domo vivit luditque professus
Obscenum, tremula promittit et omnia dextra,
Invenies omnis turpes similesque cinaedis.

Quacumque is relative, as usual.

Lines 12, 13:—

                                                  Pars ultima ludi
Accipit has animas aliusque in carcere nervos.
Nervŏs is nominative singular.

Line 27:—
Quem rides? aliis hunc mimum!

A. E. HOUSMAN

To P. G. L. Webb

MS. LILLY

7 December 1899   *17 North Road*

My dear Webb,

I remember E. J. Webb's[1] article on Postgate's Manilius:[2] I was particularly pleased to see that he knew astronomy, which modern scholars are often very ignorant of. It did not dawn upon me that he was your brother: there is another Webb going about, whose initials are C.C.J.,[3] and I had got it into my head that that was the one. I suppose Providence has not showered *two* classical brothers upon you?

When I shall get to the end of Manilius I do not know. I have just been reading through the Latin translators of Aratus in order to throw light upon him; and I find that they also are in a shocking state and will want editing. For example, Germanicus prognostica II (III) 16 is believed to have written

'*binos* Gradivus perficit orbes', i.e. Mars goes round the $\begin{Bmatrix} \text{earth} \\ \text{sun} \end{Bmatrix}$ twice in one

year. The editors don't know that Mars goes round the $\begin{Bmatrix} \text{earth} \\ \text{sun} \end{Bmatrix}$ about once in

two years, and therefore don't see that it ought to be *bimos*, i.e. biennes.

Yours very truly   A. E. HOUSMAN

---

[1] Edmund James Webb (1852–1945), classical scholar, astronomer and writer on history.

[2] Review of Postgate's *Silva Maniliana* in *The Classical Review*, July 1897.

[3] Clement Charles Julian Webb (1865–1954), Fellow of Magdalen College, Oxford, 1889; Professor of the Philosophy of the Christian Religion, 1920; also an occasional contributor to *The Classical Review*.

Address to the University of Sydney[1]

Universitati Sydneiensi Collegium Londinense Universitati
Affine

S.P.D.

Litteris vestris humanissimis in communionem laetitiae vocati, qua
natalem Universitatis Sydneiensis quinquagensimum celebraturi estis, etsi
quominus animo obsequamur et ex nostro numero aliquem ad vos mittamus
obstiterunt tanta itinerum interjecta spatia, tamen invenimus quomodo
Horatianum illud, nequiquam terras Oceano dissociabili abscissas esse, novo
comprobemus exemplo. Nam civem vestrum, alumnum nostrum, Angelum
Money, M.D., B.S.[2] virum in medica arte sollertissimum rogavimus ut
Londinensis Londinensium legatus esse velit, quinquaginta annos cum
maxima doctrinae laude feliciter peractos Sydneiensis Sydneiensibus gratule-
tur. Hunc igitur testem habetote academias tanto locorum intervallo divisas
animo tamen ac mente conjunctissimas esse et artissimo communium
studiorum vinculo cohaerere.

Scriptum Londini, die XX. mensis Junii, anni MDCCCCII.

REAY,[3]

Collegii Praeses

To G. F. Hill[4]

MS. B.M.

23 March 1903   *University College*

My dear Sir,

Your brother, my colleague,[5] encourages me to hope that you will let me
trouble you with the following enquiries.

A. von Sallet, *Beiträge z. gesch. u. numism d. Könige des Cimmer. Bosp.* (1866)
pp. 69–70 mentions a coin of Pythodoris queen of Pontus, struck in 14 A.D.,
which has Tiberius' head on the obverse and the constellation Libra on the
reverse: apparently it is also mentioned in a work which I have not seen,
Ch. Giel, *Kl. beiträge z. antiken Numismatik Süd-Russlands* (1886) pp. 12–18.

Since the constellation Capricornus, which often accompanies Augustus'
head, is known to have been his natal star, it is natural to infer from this coin
that Libra was the natal star of Tiberius; and I think that certain passages in

---

[1] Text from *Record of the Jubilee Celebrations of the University of Sydney*, Sydney, 1903.

[2] Angel Money graduated at University College, London, in 1880.

[3] The eleventh Baron Reay (1839–1921), formerly Governor of Bengal and Under-
Secretary of State for India; President of University College, London, 1897–1921.

[4] George Francis Hill (1867–1948); employed at the British Museum in the Department
of Coins and Medals since 1893; Deputy Keeper, 1911; Keeper, 1912; Director of the
British Museum, 1931–1936; knighted, 1933.

[5] M. J. M. Hill (see p. 383, note 4.)

Manilius point the same way. The points on which I want light are these.

1. Is the coin genuine? W. von Voigt in *Philologus* vol. 58 p. 176 speaks as if this were not certain.

2. Is the head certainly that of Tiberius, and the figure on the reverse certainly Libra?

3. Does Libra elsewhere appear in company with *either* Tiberius *or* Augustus? (for some think that this constellation also was connected with Augustus.)

I beg you will not trouble yourself seriously with a matter so unimportant: I only venture to apply to you because it is possible that a numismatist may be able to answer easily questions which a layman might fumble at for a long time without result.

I am yours very faithfully   A. E. HOUSMAN

To G. F. Hill

MS. B.M.

25 March 1903   *University College*

My dear Sir,

I am very much obliged by your kind reply to my letter, which tells me just what I wanted to know.

If I find I cannot get Reinach's work[1] in the Reading Room I shall be glad to avail myself of your offer to use the departmental library.

Yours very truly   A. E. HOUSMAN

To J. W. Mackail

MS. LILLY

31 July 1903   *17 North Road*

Dear Mackail,

Many thanks for your notes,[2] which I will perpend (odious word). I put down here some remarks on some of them.

34 I meant the words 'notitiae congruenter' to forestall your objection: the names were not revealed by Mercury directly, but they owe their existence to his revelation of the properties which they indicate. 30 and 31 were placed after 37 by Stoeber; but the three lines 35–37 cannot belong to the sentence 'quis foret ... conatus?'; they evidently describe the purpose of the gods in unfolding astronomy to men.

[1] *L'Histoire par les Monnaies* by Théodore Reinach.
[2] On Housman's edition of Manilius I, 1903.

88 I don't think there is any Latin word in which *inter* is prefixed to another preposition. The first ship might naturally be supposed to be a *linter*, a hollowed trunk.

214 was ejected by Bentley; but first we want to know in what form the interpolator wrote it, for at present it will not construe.

You say that '259, 261 seem to go better after 260'; but then 260 will refer to the zodiac and be foolish: and you go on 'the *signa* of 255 includes both the fixed stars *omnia quae caelo possis numerare*'—but in your order of verses, as I say, these words refer to the zodiac only— 'and the planets'—but Manilius never elsewhere calls the planets *signa*.

288 *diuerso cardine* means the two opposite poles, and answers to Arat. 24 καί μιν περαίνουσι δύω πόλοι ἀμφοτέρωθεν.

340 But did Leda ride on Jupiter's back? Europa did.

355 I think Germanicus 199 shows that *relictam* must be kept and referred to Andromeda.

407–9 'An ample guarantee that she possesses these powers is the colour and motion of the star that glitters at her mouth. It is hardly less than the sun himself, only it is placed far off and darts with its blue-green countenance a light that conveys no heat.'

417 Is there any objection to *una*? Coruus and Crater are closely connected by the fact that they are both perched on the poor long-suffering Anguis, and by the story told in Ovid Fast. II 243–266.

571 'Why *medio*?' Because only at midsummer does the sun touch the tropic of Cancer.

588 may not be a pretty line, but Manilius cannot have mentioned the distance between all the other circles and omitted the distance between these two; especially if he was going to add up the numbers and give the total as 30 in 594. I don't think he would be likely to write *per ter denas* when he might have written *per tricenas*. Why do you say that the objection that the *fines tempora signantes* are three, not five, applies equally to 598? That verse means that the circles keep pace with one another in their diurnal revolution and that they rise in the east as fast as they set in the west.

680 'The zodiac is not the *culmen*'; no, nor is the milky way at 714: the *culmen* is the sky overhead, which these circles decorate. *caelare* takes two sorts of accusatives: the material on which the *caelatura* is imposed (caelare argentum), and the figure which the *caelatura* imposes (caelare centauros). *caelatum culmen* answers to the first of these, and *caelatus Delphinus* to the second, but *caelatum lumen* to neither. The *lumen* is neither the material chiselled (that is *tenebrae* rather) nor the form created by chiselling: it is the touch of the chisel itself.

766 The society in the milky way was much too select to admit either *castra* or *Troia*.

788 Yes, *prior palma*. Marcellus was the third winner (Virgil 'tertia palma Diores') of the *spolia opima*, Cossus was *prior palma*, and Romulus *prima*.

825 If you want a participle to agree with *fine* I think it will have to be masculine in Manilius.

I am very much pleased and flattered that you should have read the commentary through. So little did I venture to hope that you would, that originally I did not think of sending you a copy of the book: it was your sending me your Odyssey[1] shortly before that brought it down on your devoted head.

Yours very truly   A. E. HOUSMAN

To Gilbert Murray

MS. BODLEY

4 November 1904   *17 North Road*

Dear Murray,

Many thanks for your Euripides,[2] which came just in time to prevent me from buying a copy. It is much the pleasantest edition and clearest apparatus to use; and I have been looking through the earlier part of the Heracles in general agreement with your selection of readings. Turning over the pages at random, it strikes me that Verrall[3] has exerted a baleful influence: e.g. ⟨τί⟩ at suppl. 149 is what I should call a perfectly impossible reading. Why didn't Porson make the conjecture? Not from any lack of fondness for palaeographical neatness: he had that taste, and it sometimes led him too far (as when he proposed κριταί ⟨τε⟩ at Aesch. cho. 37), but not so far as this. In fact Attic tragedy has been studied so long and so minutely by such great men that all the corrections which consist in iteration of syllables, or separation of letters or the like, must almost necessarily have been made already; and when one at this date makes a conjecture of this sort one ought to do it with one's hair standing on end and one's knees giving way beneath one; because the odds are a hundred to one that it is a conjecture which our betters were withheld from making by their superior tact. Such chances as remain for us are practically confined to cases like Horace serm. I 9 39, where I thoroughly believe in Verrall's *sta re*; cases where there was some special obscuring cause, such as ignorance of the form *ste = iste*, which was first brought to light by Lachmann[4] in 1850.

---

[1] Translated into English, 1903.

[2] The second volume of the Oxford edition, 1904.

[3] Arthur Woollgar Verrall (1851–1912); Fellow of Trinity College, Cambridge from 1874. He had read the proofs of Murray's edition.

[4] Karl Konrad Friedrich Wilhelm Lachmann (1793–1851), regarded by Housman as the greatest of the German classical scholars.

One detail which has just caught my eye: at Her. 1351 the order of the names 'Wilamowitz et Wecklein' is neither alphabetical nor chronological. But *suum cuique* is a precept which it is hardly any use trying to keep: e.g. I observe that the Duchess of Sutherland[1] thinks that you are a professor and I only a gentleman. Your poem and mine, by the way, according to Horatio Brown, are the gems of the volume: I think I preferred Mackail and the Irishman who has my initials.

> Yours very truly   A. E. HOUSMAN

On p. 27 of the collection there is an easy emendation to be made, quite devoid of palaeographical or neographical probability, but certain none the less.[2]

To J. D. Duff[3]

MS. SHAW-SMITH

15 July 1905   *17 North Road*

Dear Mr Duff,

I am glad you have had Munro's book[4] reprinted and am much obliged to you for the copy you have sent me. I think though that his recantation of the remarks on 68 68[5] should have been among the matter added.

I do not suppose that you overlooked anything of importance in T;[6] but I mean, as I say, that we have all the variants of certain MSS registered and not all the variants of T. For example, if it anywhere has a *quotiens* in agreement with P, I do not feel sure that this would necessarily appear in your notes.

The *tituli* were the very first thing I threw overboard. Are they any use? In Martial they are, no doubt.

I have been pleased to see that you expel from your text most of the things which I had crossed out in Lindsay's.[7] As you do not accept your own

---

[1] In *Wayfarer's Love* the table of contents names Murray as Professor (though he had resigned the Chair of Greek at Glasgow in 1899) and Housman as 'Mr.' Murray's contribution was a translation from Theocritus; Brown's was 'The Stones of Stanton Drew'; Mackail's a quatrain from Maeterlinck's *La Princesse Lointaine*; 'A.E.' (pseudonym of George Russell) contributed 'The Wind of Angus'.

[2] In 'Horace. Ode XXVIII. Lib. I', translated by A. C. Lyall. Almost certainly line 11: 'To the sacred harbour that Neptune loves.' The last word should be 'guards'.

[3] James Duff Duff (1860–1940), Fellow of Trinity College, Cambridge from 1883.

[4] *Criticisms and Elucidations of Catullus* by H. A. J. Munro (1819–1885), first published in 1878; second edition, with a prefatory note by Duff, 1905, containing three additional papers and further illustrations from Munro's manuscript notes.

[5] In *The Journal of Philology* VIII, 1879.

[6] In his recension of Martial in the second volume of Postgate's *Corpus*, 1905. Housman contributed emendations to Duff's text as well as editing Juvenal for the volume.

[7] Published in 1900.

emendation of IX 3 14[1] I suppose I shall be driven to edit Martial myself, much against my will, in order that it may come to its rights.

I am yours very truly   A. E. HOUSMAN

To J. W. Mackail

MS. LILLY

22 May 1912   *Trinity College*

Dear Mackail,

You well describe as extraordinary the pleasure with which you are kind enough to say you read my commentary.[2] I don't believe anyone in Cambridge will read it, whether with pleasure or with agony: the Latinists here are very well disposed towards me but terribly afraid of Manilius.

I return your notes, which I am obliged to you for sending me, and I add remarks on some of them.

3 I don't think it admits of dispute that *sub* with the abl. in Manilius can mean 'in the person of'. There is another example at IV 766, about which I wrote on p. lxxi of the first volume; and in IV 25 no other interpretation is possible, for Troy, except as embodied in Aeneas, was overthrown. That *non euersa* means the opposite of *uicta* is a circumstance which does not affect the question. Of course *tutam sub Hectore* is also quite good in itself: I only prefer *uictam* because I think it more appropriate.[3]

23 The nymphs in Stat. Theb. IV 684 are *fluuiorum numina* because they belong to the rivers, but the rivers do not belong to them. *ustic* is not very like *at*.

55 *durato ore* = beak.

90 *haec seditio* 'cesd eux mouvemens opposés de l'océan', Pingré. Stat. Theb. IX 141–2 Siculi ... seditione maris, the tides of the straits of Messina.

193 If you came across *superest, quaeritur alterum*, it would surprise you a good deal more than *superest et quaeritur unum*.

246 You understand the phrase much as I do; my only difficulty is the lack of an exact parallel.

324 *sequentum* surely would not make sense, for the *partem summam* belongs only to the fourth sign. *sequentis* is wanting in precision, but so is *prioris*; and the defence, as I say in my note, is that only the signs where the angles come are taken into consideration.

328 I don't think there is any ellipsis of the subject of *duplicat*: its subject is the nearest preceding substantive.

[1] *Quo* for *quod*.   [2] On Manilius II.
[3] Housman adopted this suggestion in the *editio minor*, 1932.

337 The angle in question is 90°, not 60°.

419–21 (and 718 and 774–81). If you are going to rid Manilius of redundant ornament, you have your work cut out for you: even his admirer Scaliger confesses that he does not know when to leave off. Here you will have to remove 422 as well, because *sic* etc. will have nothing proper to refer to; and if you eject the description of summer and winter you ought not to spare its pendant, the description of spring and autumn which follows.

521 The four tropical signs are the leaders of the four triangles, and the opposition of triangle to triangle is effected by the two diameters which join those signs. The other four diameters, joining the subsidiary signs (e.g. Taurus and Scorpius), can only say ditto.

534 (*quid*) *mirer*, I agree, is not Manilius' usual way of talking, but it is inoffensive in itself and can hardly be got rid of without great expense. In your conjecture I think *neu* should be *ne*, as no conjunction is in place.

574 *que* unites the participle *defixa* and the clause *quod . . . feruntur*, both of which are causal. So in Ouid. met. V 367 *que* unites *postquam exploratum satis est* and *deposito metu*, both of which are temporal.

544 *dant* would certainly have the advantage of making the construction of *Pisces* clear, and *Scorpius acer* would quite account for the change to *dat*.

552 The Centaur is called geminus (IV 784) as being *bimembris*.

566 *fugata* seems to me not only more violent but less suitable than the *fugiens* I conjectured in 1903. With a passive participle one would expect *uirtute* or *a uirtute* rather than *sub*.

615 If you like *uellere* better than *corpore* I think you ought to like *tergore* better still.

644–5 It is desirable to procure a *stellarum* for *uagarum*, but what *parte* wants is the genitive *mundi*, and I don't think the sense of your supplement is admissible.

699 Of course *ecce* much oftenest stands at the beginning of a verse, but it has no native repugnance to the end, and stands there in Verg. Aen. III 219.

745 (Lucr. VI 85). *quŏque* does not seem to be found except in quoqueuersus.

826 If *quae* is right, *at caeli* is probably as good as anything else; but *qui* is supported by the parallels I quoted.

860 The future participle of *nascor*, so far as it exists at all, is nasciturus; and the sense which you procure is not germane to the matter in hand.

891 *que* is not attached to words ending in *c* by poets earlier than the fourth century (Madvig Cic. de fin. V 40, Haupt opusc. III pp. 508–10): the exception, Ouid. fast. IV 848, is one of those which prove rules. *huice* is not used in the classical period at all.

917 If we had *thea* here I should have expected *theos* in 909–10.

Yours very truly   A. E. HOUSMAN

To D. A. Slater[1]

MS. LILLY

17 September 1913   *Hôtel Terminus, Paris*

Dear Slater,

I have been travelling about in Normandy beyond the reach of letters, and yours is one of a batch which has been forwarded here.

So far as I remember, all I did at the British Museum MSS of the metamorphoses was to consult them in the 15th book and the destitute parts of the 14th, at those places where Korn's apparatus[2] gave variants. My only reason for consulting them was that Postgate had sent me in proof his article on book XV,[3] and I have no recollection of examining them in the earlier books; nor do I know that anyone else has done so. As they are none of them eminent even among the poor MSS containing book XV, I should not expect them to be of any use beside the better MSS in the earlier books; but of course one never can tell.

If you do as you suggest about the Tours MS of the Ibis I shall be very grateful for a sight of the photographs.

It so happens that next term I am lecturing on book I of the metamorphoses; so it would be no trouble to me to look through that part at any rate of your text and apparatus.

Your proposal at XIV 671[4] does not seem to me better than some others (I have seen *tam digna* somewhere, perhaps only in my own margin) nor very likely on general grounds. I am not at all sure that *audacis* wants changing: Ulysses was *audax* (though he had other characteristics more prominent and more often mentioned) and I believe I have noted down another place where he is called so. Further, a reading like *timidi aut audacis*, giving correct metre and grammar and a clear though foolish sense, suggests to me interpolation rather than a confusion of letters.

I am returning to Cambridge at the end of the week.

Yours sincerely   A. E. HOUSMAN

---

[1] David Ansell Slater (1866–1938) was a friend of Laurence Housman's and had been AEH's pupil in the Sixth Form at Bromsgrove School, 1881–1882; worked as a schoolmaster, 1890–1900; Lecturer, 1900, and Professor of Latin, 1903, at Cardiff; at Bedford College, London, 1914; at Liverpool, 1920. He had undertaken to edit Ovid's *Metamorphoses* for the Oxford edition but did not complete the task.

[2] Published in 1878.

[3] In *The Journal of Philology*, 1894.

[4] In his article 'On Three Passages of Ovid' in *The Classical Review*, 1913. Slater abandoned the suggestion of *tam digna* in his *Towards a Text of the Metamorphosis of Ovid*, 1927.

To D. A. Slater

MS. LILLY

23 October 1913   *Trinity College*

Dear Slater,

Ar. Thesm. 1070 τί ποτ' Ἀνδρομέδα περίαλλα κακῶν / μέροσ ἐξέλαχον. In Latin I think the only piece of direct evidence is Germ. phaen. 201, where the variants *-e*, *-ae*, *-a*, *-am*, in a context which requires the nominative, certainly point to *Andromeda*; but the indirect evidence of the accusative *Andromedan*, attested by metre in Ouid. her. XVIII 151 and met. IV 757, is better.

I am glad you will stay here.

Yours sincerely   A. E. HOUSMAN

To A. S. F. Gow

MS. TRINITY

11 February 1914   *Trinity College*

Dear Gow,

In the cod. Lemovicensis[1] and some other MSS, which have Servius' commentary without Servius' name, there is a quantity of additional matter largely antiquarian and mythological, sometimes called *scholia Danielis* because first edited by P. Daniel in 1600, sometimes *Seruius auctus* or *plenior* or the like. It is not by Servius, but is at least as old, and more valuable. This is what Thilo[2] prints in italics.

Yours sincerely   A. E. HOUSMAN

To F. J. H. Jenkinson

MS. CAMBRIDGE

8 March 1914   *Trinity College*

Dear Jenkinson,

The MS called 1 by this collator[3] is pretty clearly Vat. 5951, one of the two best; none of his MSS correspond to the other, Med. plut. 83, but seem to belong to the inferior class.

His date, I should think, cannot be much earlier than 1800, as he seems not

---

[1] Of Virgil.
[2] In his edition of Servius, 1881–1887.
[3] Of Celsus' *De Medicina*.

to use the long *s* except when *t* follows. He therefore is not, as I thought for the moment he might be, the collator and editor Targa (1769); and moreover he designates his MS by a different set of signs.

I return the book with many thanks.

Yours very truly
A. E. HOUSMAN

To Stephen Gaselee

MS. BIRKBECK

8 January 1915
Trinity College

Dear Gaselee,

We were enjoying ourselves so much that Amaryllis[1] was left weeping on the doorstep. I think your second interpretation is right,—that what she now loves is something more valuable than any nuts, chestnuts or otherwise; but I think the right punctuation is that of Heinsius and Burman,[2] who put no stop in the pentameter. If we had scholia on the poem they would say '*castaneas nuces ἀπὸ κοινοῦ*'. By writing 'aut castaneas nuces, quas Amaryllis amabat' Ovid would have affronted his most intelligent readers; by writing 'aut nuces quas Amaryllis amabat (sed nunc eas non amat)' he might have left his least intelligent readers in the dark: by mentioning the species casually in the second clause he avoids both.

I hope you did not lose much at bridge.

Yours very truly
A. E. HOUSMAN

To A. S. F. Gow

MS. TRINITY

23 February 1916
Trinity College

Dear Gow,

The -*it* of the perf. was originally long in the 4th as in the other conjugations, and remains so in Plautus; but by Virgil's time it had become short in the regular verbs, as is shown by audiït and ambiït in the 5th foot at Aen. VII 516 and X 243: its lengthening is artificial in Ouid. met. XII 392. On the other hand in *eo* and *peto* it is never shown by the metre to be short and often shown to be long, for it occurs where artificial lengthening is not allowed, as in Ouid. met. II 567. The source of all wisdom on this subject is Lachmann's note on Lucr. III 1042:[3] the only material addition that I find in my margin is

---

[1] See Ovid *Ars Amatoria* II. 268.

[2] Heinsius' Ovid appeared in 1652, Burman's in 1713. An edition combining their texts was published by Lemaire in 1819.

[3] In his edition, 1850.

Stat. Theb. XII 396 *te cupiit unam* (so the best MS is now reported: *cupiens* cett.), which may seem to show natural length, as Statius does not elsewhere allow artificial lengthening except at the caesura in the 3rd foot.

Yours sincerely   A. E. HOUSMAN

To J. W. Mackail

MS. TRINITY

4 May 1916   *Trinity College*

Dear Mackail,

Many thanks for your notes.[1] What I say at 113 is that political oratory (*rostris*) has no business in the middle of forensic matters. As to *numerosis* in 172, although I think *pro spatio magna* can mean 'of a length proportioned to the distance', I do not think that *magnus* could mean 'great or small' without help, nor *numerosus* 'many or few; and if it could, what a thing to think of saying! *longa dies* in 482 is the long day of midsummer. At 325 as a parallel to *gradus* perhaps you would prefer Soph. Ai. 7–8 εὖ δέ σ᾽ἐκφέρει . . . βάσις. It is not for equality but for sense that I adopt the future in 361, as in 333.

Yours sincerely   A. E. HOUSMAN

To A. S. F. Gow

MS. TRINITY

30 October 1916   *Trinity College*

Dear Gow,

1. For *-cque* see Madvig Cic. de fin. V 40[2] and Haupt opusc. III p. 508 = Herm. V p. 38. The only classical example is Ouid. fast. IV 848[3] '*sic*' *que*, where *sic* is said by one person and *que* by another. Where *tuncque* occurs, as at Manil. III 841, it should be *tumque*; *hancque* etc. don't occur except in inferior MSS.

2. Adjectives are allowed, though rarely, at the end of pentameters, as in her. X 138 *grauis*, amor. II 6 58 *pias*, trist. IV 3 42 *piae*, and I don't think it makes any difference whether they are predicates. In fast. I and II, omitting numerals, 2 are predicates (I 168, 230), 4 are not (I 222, II 56, 114, 546).

3. In Ibis 223 I suppose *in aduerso culmine* means 'on a house-top (or other eminence) opposite'. Ibis was born out of doors, as you see from what follows.

---

[1] On Housman's edition of Manilius III.
[2] In his edition, 1839.
[3] Published 1875–1876.

4. *uirides campos* or the like is quite common, *niueos campos* or the like very rare, but not unexampled, e.g. amor. I 9 19 *graues urbes*, art. II 594 *insidias illas*, fast. II 300 *graues imbres*, ex Pont. I 4 56 *dis ueris*. But an exception is made for possessive pronouns, and *nostris oculis, suos annos* etc. are pretty frequent.

Yours sincerely

A. E. HOUSMAN

To Charles Sayle

MS. LILLY

14 December 1917   *Trinity College*

My dear Sayle,

It was in a review by Parry of Hodgkin's life in a recent number of the *Cambridge Review*.[1] Mrs Creighton, poor thing, had printed *Juveni patiem*, which has to be emended *Inveni portum*, and is the opening of an epigram quoted at the end of *Gil Blas*, book IX.[2] But in this form I don't think it is classical, and some attribute it to Ianus Pannonius saec. XV. The Greek original is anth. Pal. IX 49: the ancient Latin version, found more than once in inscriptions (C.I.L. VI 11743, anth. epigr. Buech. 1498, carm. Lat. epigr. Engstroem 324), is

evasi, effugi. Spes et Fortuna valete.
nil mihi vobiscum est, ludificate alios.

There is also a translation by Grotius.[3]

Yours very truly

A. E. HOUSMAN

To H. F. Newall[4]

MS. YALE

7 February 1918   *Trinity College*

My dear Newall,

I told you a lie across the table last night, for the Burman who collected the anthology was the nephew of Bentley's Burman.[5] They were both christened Pieter.

[1] In the number for 6 December 1917 R. St J. Parry reviewed Louise Creighton's *Life and Letters of Thomas Hodgkin*.

[2] 'Inveni portum: Spes et Fortuna, valete.
   Sat me lusistis. Ludite nunc alios.'

[3] In his edition of the Greek Anthology, 1795.

[4] Hugh Frank Newall (1857–1944), Fellow of Trinity College, Cambridge; Professor of Astrophysics, 1909–1928.

[5] Pieter Burman I (1668–1741) supported Bentley in his controversy with Le Clerc and published Bentley's corrections of Le Clerc's edition of Menander and Philemon in 1710. His nephew, Pieter Burman II, lived from 1714 to 1778.

The ancient Copernicus whose name I could not remember was Aristarchus of Samos, third century B.C. The Farnese globe, judging from the places in which it puts the equinoctial points, is near the same date.

Circle is one of those English words (like *salt*) on which you men of science have laid hands and wrested them out of their original meanings. The Latins called the zodiac and even the milky way a *circulus*; and Gray calls the hoop which he trundled at Eton a *circle*,[1] though it must have had three dimensions.

Yours sincerely   A. E. HOUSMAN

To Percy Withers

MS. WITHERS

5 March 1919   *Trinity College*

My dear Withers,

The vaunt of Archimedes, 'give me where to stand, and I move the world' is quoted by the geometer Pappus (VIII 1060) as δός μοι ποῦ στῶ καὶ κινῶ τὴν γῆν, by the Aristotelian commentator Simplicius (Physic. VII 250a) as δός μοι πᾶ βῶ καὶ κινῶ τὰν γᾶν, which, being Doric, is more likely to be what Archimedes said: the only difference in sense is that στῶ means 'stand' and βῶ 'set foot'.

I cannot call to mind at this moment a verse to suit your purpose, but if any occurs to me I will let you know.

I am a very bad correspondent, or I should have thanked you before now for your letter of a fortnight ago. I hope you and Mrs Withers are both well and enjoying your home. Cambridge already has half its regular number of undergraduates, and Whewell's Court and various other places are filled up with young naval officers.

Yours sincerely   A. E. HOUSMAN

To A. S. F. Gow

MS. TRINITY

11 February 1920   *Trinity College*

Dear Gow,

Some scholars are under the impression that Lachmann investigated the frequency of elisions in which the elided syllable ends in *m* and is immediately preceded by a long vowel or diphthong, such as Verg. Aen. V 328 *Ledaeam*

---

[1] 'To chase the rolling circle's speed,
      Or urge the flying ball.'
—'Ode on a Distant Prospect of Eton College.'

Hermionen. He did not; but one might think he ought to have done so in his note on Lucr. III 374, because one would hardly suppose these elisions to be less harsh than those on which he discourses. I have sometimes thought of seeing about it, and perhaps it might be worth your while.

Or you might take I. Hilberg's *Gesetze des Wortstellung im Pentameter des Ovid*[1] and try how far they apply to the pentameters of other poets, if true.

Or the employment, in Attic tragedy for instance, of forms mostly used for metrical convenience, in places where metre does not require them: e.g. λαός in Eur. frag. 21 2 (Nauck ed. 2). Elmsley[2] would have to be consulted.

The seal looks like Boreas flying off with Orithyia; but what is she doing with a lyre?

Yours sincerely

A. E. HOUSMAN

To A. S. F. Gow

MS. TRINITY

15 February 1920   *Trinity College*

Dear Gow,

I have filled in the form and will give it to Deighton and Bell.[3]

As to the spondee in the 4th foot, I examined the usage of Propertius in Journ. Phil. vol. XXI pp. 150 sq., and Meineke has some remarks on Horace's in his 2nd edition[4] (I have not got the 1st) pp. XXIII sq. I do not think a full collection would lead to anything definite: it is quite clear that there was no hard and fast rule, and Cortius[5] made a fool of himself in trying to rob Lucan of variety in the matter.

Yours sincerely

A. E. HOUSMAN

To J. W. Mackail

MS. TRINITY

28 February 1920   *Trinity College*

Dear Mackail,

I agree that χειρὶ παχείῃ is not parallel to *ingenti manu* nor τρήρωνα πέλειαν to *uolucrem columbam*, but I do think that XI 556 *dextra ingenti* is parallel to the one and Soph. Ai. 140 πτηνῆς πελείας to the other. *ingenti* no doubt is

---

[1] Published in 1894.

[2] Peter Elmsley (1773–1825) published editions of Euripides in 1821 and Sophocles in 1826.

[3] Cambridge bookshop.

[4] Published in 1854; the first edition appeared in 1834.

[5] Gottlieb Cortius (1698–1731) edited Lucan, 1726.

tumid, but in reading Virgil I often cry 'Out, hyperbolical fiend! how vexest thou this man!'; and *uolucrem* is useless, but if epic poets are debarred from useless epithets they will never fill their 12 or 24 or 48 books. The magnitude of Serestus' ship is not much to the point, so long as the mast itself was tall, which we are told in 489.

From what I see in the papers, you are to be congratulated on your son's connexion with *The Dynasts* at Oxford.[1]

Yours sincerely   A. E. HOUSMAN

To W. H. D. Rouse[2]

MS. DUBLIN

2 January 1921   *Trinity College*

Dear Dr Rouse,

In Lucr. III 83 I think your *hic . . . hic*, which Heinze and Merrill assign to one Bergson, may quite well be right; but I do not see anything wrong with Munro's reading. *hunc . . . hunc* divide up the *homines* of the verse which he inserts, and may get support of one kind from Verg. georg. II 505–12 and of another from Aen. X 9 sq.

IV 418–9 is a passage I have often broken my head over without avail. The lections of the MSS are as you say: *caelum ut* A, *caelum* B, *corpora* AB. *caeli ut* (with other changes) was proposed by Bergk, and Giussani adopts it without other changes. I only feel clear that *mirande* was not Latin in the time of Lucretius, if it ever was, and that *caelum* cannot be right in *both* verses. Also I do not think he would say *mirando caelo*. What I should expect is something like 'et *mole* ut videare videre corpora *miranda*'.

I am yours very truly   A. E. HOUSMAN

To J. D. Duff

MS. TRINITY

30 June 1921   *Trinity College*

Dear Duff,

I have looked at Lucr. I 657 and I think it ridiculous that the subject of the verbs *cernunt, fugitant, metuunt, amittunt, cernunt, credunt, reparcunt*, should

---

[1] Denis Mackail designed the scenery for the production which opened on 10 February 1920.
[2] William Henry Denham Rouse (1863–1950); Fellow of Christ's College, Cambridge, 1888–1894; Headmaster of the Perse School, Cambridge, 1902–1928. His edition of Lucretius in the Loeb Classical Library was published in 1924.

be the title of a book, the alternative title of a book, and the title of two other books,—the history of Herodotus and the epistles of Aeschines. The subject must be the same as the subject of *faciant* 655, namely *qui materiem rerum esse putarunt ignem.*

It is a further absurdity of Ernout's[1] to fancy that the names Μοῦσαι and περὶ Φύσεως were given to Heraclitus himself.

Yours sincerely

A. E. HOUSMAN

To A. S. F. Gow

MS. TRINITY

22 February 1922   *Trinity College*

Dear Gow,

Ovid does not in point of fact use *nesciŏ* except in *nescioquis*, but it cannot be supposed that he would feel any scruple, when Catullus had already used it 85 2, and he himself has *conferŏ* ex Pont I 1 25 and *oderŏ* amor. III 11 35.

I may be in Eton at the end of term, as that Minotaur (or Μινώκριος[2] rather) the Essay Society is bleating for a new victim.

Yours sincerely

A. E. HOUSMAN

To J. D.Duff

MS. TRINITY

27 July 1922   *Trinity College*

Dear Duff,

μοῦσαι in Plat. Soph. p. 242 D is a generic term: Ἰάδες μοῦσαι is *the literary Ephesian* and Σικελαὶ μοῦσαι is the literary Agrigentine, and Clement copies the phrase. The result of considering these passages is that I do not believe Μοῦσαι was the title of anything which Heraclitus wrote, and when Diog. Laert. gives it as an alternative to περὶ φύσεως he is merely misunderstanding Plato's phrase. And this is the opinion of Wellmann in Pauly-Wissowa VIII i p. 505.

Yours sincerely

A. E. HOUSMAN

[1] In his edition of Lucretius, 1920.
[2] i.e. A. B. Ramsay (see p. 241, note 2), Lower Master of Eton College and host to the Essay Society; nicknamed The Ram.

To Ernest Harrison[1]

26 March 1923   *Trinity College*

Dear Harrison,

uersant in Iuu. VI O 18 is not the word for turning in a particular direction: that would be *uertunt: animum uersant* would naturally mean the same as Hor. serm. I 8 19 *uersant . . . humanos animos*. Nor ought *magistris* to stray outside the clause in which *discunt* is. But, quite apart from these two points, I do not see how anyone could guess that the sense of the words is what R.[2] says it is. 'Heavy irony' is litotes, and 'characteristically' and 'Juvenalian' are libel.

You have spotted two of the metrical points in the C.R.:[3] the others are these.

p. 12[a]. It would not be a Sophoclean elision[4] unless the preceding syllable were long; it would not even be possible; because, until one foot is full, nothing can overflow into the next.

p. 13[b]. Do you know of any place where the first vowel of 'Ιόνιος is short?

p. 16[a]. Ag. 239 has no 'metrical flaw' except in the imagination of the ignorant and immodest Agar,[5] and similar folk.

Yours sincerely   A. E. HOUSMAN

To A. S. F. Gow

21 October 1923   *Trinity College*

Dear Gow,

Regiomontanus' is the edition[6] I want, and I did authorise Sotheby's[7] to bid for me up to £40 (the highest price it had yet fetched) on the occasion when it was bought for £60; but that was rather an act of extravagance on my part, as I can really get all I want out of it by paying a visit to the British Museum when I am about to produce a volume. Books that I want more, if you should happen to see them, are on the opposite page; I should be ready

---

[1] Harrison became editor of *The Classical Review* in 1923.

[2] Not identified; presumably author of an article submitted to *The Classical Review* and rejected on Housman's advice.

[3] In his article on *Frogs 1203* in *The Classical Review*, February–March 1923.

[4] Between lines in Greek iambics, to avoid a final tribrach.

[5] T. L. Agar, author of 'Suggestions on the Agamemnon of Aeschylus' in *The Classical Review*, February–March 1923.

[6] Of Manilius, published in 1472.

[7] The auctioneers.

to pay any price which is likely to be asked for them. Do not bother to keep a look out for them: it is very kind of you to make the offer you do.

Yours sincerely   A. E. HOUSMAN

Manilius, Scaliger ed. 1600
    ,,   ,, E. Burton ed. 1783
    ,,   ,, J. Creech transl. 1697 or 1700
Paulus Alexandrinus, Witebergae, 1586
Salmasius, de annis climactericis, 1648
'Procli in Ptolemaei Quadripartitum enarrationes, accedunt Porphyrii introductio etc., Basileae, 1559.' (The full title is longer.)

To the Editor of The Times[1]

20 September 1924   *Trinity College*

Sir,

In to-day's *Illustrated London News* there are reproduced in facsimile the four lines which Dr Max Funke says that Dr di Martino-Fusco allowed him to copy from the MS shown to him. When a few slight and necessary corrections have been made, they will run as follows:

Ubi multitudo hominum insperata occurrit audire Gallum de sancti Martini virtutibus locuturum.

This reference to Dr di Martino's patron saint cannot plausibly be assigned even to the prophetic books of Livy. The Provost of Eton[2] may know where the words come from—I do not: but clearly they are an abridgment of what Sulpicius Severus relates in his Dialogus II (III) 1 5:

Quid, inquam, tam subito et *insperati* tam ex diversis regionibus tam mane *concurritis*? Nos, inquiunt, hesterno cognovimus *Gallum* istum per totum diem *Martini* narrasse virtutes, et reliqua in hodiernum diem, quia nox oppresserat, distulisse: propterea maturavimus frequens auditorium facere de tanta materia *locuturo*.

German scholars, who have had the facsimile before them ever since 12 September, must have found out this more than a week ago.

Yours faithfully   A. E. HOUSMAN

[1] Printed in *The Times*, 22 September 1924 under the heading 'Not Livy'.
[2] M. R. James, who was an authority on hagiology.

418

To the Editor of The Times[1]

22 September 1924   *Trinity College*

Sir,

I can now complete the identification of the supposed excerpt from Livy. In Vol. XXXII of the *Mémoires de l'Institut National de France* (*Académie des Inscriptions*), at the end of a paper (pp. 29–56) read in 1884 by Léopold Delisle, there is printed a facsimile (Plate III) of a page from a manuscript now at Quedlinburg, but written early in the ninth century in St Martin's own abbey at Tours. There may be seen the four lines transcribed by Dr Funke: the hand is very similar, the divisions identical, the text a trifle more correct. They constitute the first item in a table of contents prefixed to the dialogue of Sulpicius, which I quoted in my former letter.

Yours faithfully   A. E. HOUSMAN

To A. C. Pearson

MS. KING'S

12 October 1924   *Trinity College*

My dear Pearson,

I am very grateful for the gift of your Sophocles[2]. To what you say in your note I must reply that if your judgment is not worth more than mine you ought not to be editing Sophocles nor sitting in the Greek chair. From turning over your pages I should say that it is rather about Nauck's conjectures than mine that I should differ from you. The two first places I look at to form an opinion on an editor are O.T. 597 and 795, and I give you a good mark at the one and a bad one at the other. Your own emendations, some of which are very neat, I have already seen, or most of them. I might be tempted to a good deal of discussion but that I must really stick to my desk and finish my Lucan. One observation: O.C. 1212 πάρεκ was proposed before Verrall by Badham,[3] Euthydemus p. 93.

If this is the end of the Oxford series, I think it comes to a very distinguished close.

Yours sincerely   A. E. HOUSMAN

---

[1] Printed in *The Times*, 23 September 1924. The identification was also given in a letter by F. W. Hall in the same issue.

[2] In the Oxford edition.

[3] Charles Badham (1813–1884), Professor of Classics and Logic in the University of Sydney, 1867–1884. His edition of Plato, *Euthydemus* and *Laches*, was published in 1865.

To the University Registrary[1]

MS. TRINITY

28 October 1924   *Trinity College*

My dear Registrary,

I gather from this gentleman's attempt at translation that by *education* he means not the process but that which it confers; so perhaps his two sentences may be rendered as over the page.

I strongly hold the opinion that the Public Orator is the proper person to molest on such occasions, though possibly he may not.

Yours sincerely

A. E. HOUSMAN

1. *Nulla sine moribus doctrina,* or *nihil doctrina sine moribus proficit.*
2. *Non discendi sed agendi causa vivimus* (or *vivitur*). (*Finis vitae,* though correct, would be ambiguous.)

To Ernest Harrison[2]

MS. JACOBS

[*17 January 1925*]   [*Trinity College*]

I do not think that the Greeks imagined that the acromychal rising of a star was particularly bright, and if they did they were of course quite wrong. But a star is brighter near the horizon than when it is higher, and I should say that this is why παμφαίνων is used in Hes. op. 567, and that πρῶτον signifies simply emergence into sight *(προλιπὼν ῥόον ᾿Ωκεανοῖο)* and does not conflict with the fact that an ἐπιτολὴ ἑσπερία is a last and not a first appearance.

To J. W. Mackail

MS. TRINITY

22 February 1925   *Trinity College*

Dear Mackail,

With *optandum*[3] you require something like *quicquam*, which Estaço[4] obtained by writing *dicere quid*. With *optandam* of course you can supply *uitam* from *uita*; but yet the MS reading is *optandus*. Because Catullus once

---

[1] John Neville Keynes (1852–1949); University Lecturer in Moral Science, 1884–1911; University Registrary, 1911–1925; father of Lord Keynes and Sir Geoffrey Keynes.
[2] Draft reply written on the back of Harrison's note, dated 16 January 1925.
[3] In Catullus 107. 8.
[4] i.e. Achilles Statius (1524–1581), whose edition of Catullus was published in 1566.

elides que at the end of a verse it cannot safely be inferred that he would elide anything else. I have seen nothing better than Munro's *magis aeuom optandum hac uita,*[1] though it is not all the heart could desire.

Yours sincerely   A. E. HOUSMAN

To A. S. F. Gow

MS. TRINITY

26 March 1925   *Trinity College*

Dear Gow,

If anyone knows what Catull. 104 4 means, I do not; and the commentators are no good. But I see no reason to think it corrupt.

I wish you would make a correction on my p. XV:[2] the date of Creech's translation should 1697: 1700 was the second edition.

No, I am not well, though in my case it is bronchial tubes and not a leg.

Yours sincerely   A. E. HOUSMAN

To A. D. Nock[3]

27 January 1926   *Trinity College*

Dear Nock,

To say seriously that the stars follow the moon's course[4] is of course absurd, as they move in the opposite direction; so I surmise that this is an ornate expression of Genesis I 16, that the Moon is confused with Night (they both ride in a coach and pair) as in Ovid fast. VI 233 and Luc. I 218, and that then one may compare Eur. Ion 1151 ἄστρα δ' ὡμάρτει θεᾷ, Theocr. II 166, Tibull. II 1 87 sq.

Yours sincerely   A. E. HOUSMAN

If the moon's δρόμος is her visible motion from her rising in the east to her setting in the west, then the herd of stars may seem to be following a great leader, if the observer is not sharp enough to notice that they are always overtaking her.

[1] Proposed in *The Journal of Philology* IX, 1880.
[2] Of Manilius I.
[3] Text from *The Harvard Theological Review*, January 1952.
[4] In the *Epistle to Diognetus* VII. 2.

Postcard to J. W. Mackail

MS. TRINITY

24 July 1926   *Trinity College*

coniux is rather commoner in inscriptions, but *coniunx* occurs earlier, and is rather commoner in the earliest MSS; Priscian and the other grammarians generally inculcate *coniunx*, though they mention the other.

A.E.H.

To A. C. Pearson

MS. KING'S

14 October 1926   *Trinity College*

Dear Pearson,

Is it good Greek to say τοῖν δυοῖν Κάστωρ μὲν ἱππεὺς ἦν, Πολυδεύκης δὲ πύκτης, or τῶν Ἀθηναίων Θεμιστοκλῆς ... Περικλῆς ... Ἀλκιβιάδης? The corresponding genitive, without *alter* ... *alter* or the like, is good Latin, though apparently not Ciceronian.

Hunt[1] has sent me some new Callimachus from the next Oxyrhynchus volume,[2] and I am making a manful pretence of knowing the language; but you see I require your assistance.

Yours sincerely

A. E. HOUSMAN

To A. C. Pearson

MS. KING'S

15 October 1926   *Trinity College*

Dear Pearson,

The particular case is this. Callimachus, descanting on his favourite theme that small things are often better than great ones, has a couplet which I have filled up thus: [τοῖν δὲ] δ[υ]οῖν, Μίμνερμοσ ὅτι γλυκὺσ, ἅ[μμε τὸ μεῖον] [βιβλίον] ἡ μεγάλη δ᾽οὐκ ἐδίδαξε γύνη,[3] 'we have learnt the sweetness of Mimnermus from the smaller of his two books, not from the portly Nanno': that he did write two is stated by Porphyrion at Hor. epist. II 2 101. Now in an ill-written and ill-preserved scholium there are traces of the name of the

---

[1] Arthur Surridge Hunt (1871–1934), Fellow of Queen's College, Oxford, 1894; Professor of Papyrology, 1913–1934.

[2] Part XVII, published in 1927, containing a fragment from the Prologue to the *Aetia*.

[3] This proposal was not adopted. Hunt left the missing words blank, though Housman is thanked in the preface for 'several illuminating suggestions'.

other book, and it may turn out to be μέλισσαι. It therefore occurs to me that he may have written, more smartly, ἄ[μμε τὸ μικρὸν θηρίον] (see Theocr. XIX 5 sq, τυτθὸν θηρίον ἐντὶ μέλισσα), and, though I feel inside me that the genitive is right enough, I have no quite parallel passage.

Thanks for your letter. The number of good Greek scholars whom I have deceived into thinking that I know Greek is mounting up, and I add your scalp to Platt's and Headlam's.

Yours sincerely   A. E. HOUSMAN

To J. W. Mackail

MS. TRINITY

20 January 1927   *Trinity College*

Dear Mackail,

Virgil's besetting sin is the use of words too forcible for his thoughts, and the *moritura* of Aen. XII 55 makes me blush for him whenever I think of it; but I think that the defence of *ulta uirum*[1] put forward by Seruius and elaborated by Donatus is not bad, and that it has some support from Virgil's phrase I 363 sq. *auari Pygmalionis opes.*

Yours sincerely   A. E. HOUSMAN

To Frank E. Robbins[2]

MS. CLEMENTS

28 October 1927   *Trinity College*

Dear Mr Robbins,

Many thanks for your letter and for the offprints of your paper.

Like you, I have not come across the business of the epicycles elsewhere, nor any similar method of determining the ὅρια. The chief interest and importance of the papyrus is that it is the oldest astrological script, except a few genitures, which has come into our hands, and we therefore cannot suspect its doctrines of being Byzantine or medieval in origin.

I enclose a copy of my paper with corrections of two or three misprints.

I am yours sincerely   A. E. HOUSMAN

---

[1] In *Aeneid* IV. 656. Mackail was preparing the edition which he published in 1930.

[2] Frank Egleston Robbins (born 1884) of the University of Michigan. His paper on the Michigan Astrological Papyrus appeared in *Classical Philology* XXII, 1927. Housman's review was printed in the same volume.

To A. S. F. Gow

MS. TRINITY

8 February 1928 [*Trinity College*]

Mart. XII 82 4. It appears from Isid. orig. XVIII 69 2 that if a ball was sent out of bounds a spectator who caught it might take his place in the game. I suppose Menogenes makes over this right.

XII 87 6. *excalciatus* is no more than 'unshod', as in the Graeco-Latin glossaries *excalcior* is ὑπολύομαι and *calciatus sum* ὑποδέδεμαι. In Gell. XIII 22 1 the same persons are described as *gallicis calceati* and *soleati*.

XIV 4 6. *nobilibus* 'earning renown', like those of Polybius VII 72 11. *sinistrae*, whatever substantive is supplied with it, means strokes, not hands, so that *mobilibus* does not properly suit it.   A.E.H.

To J. W. Mackail

MS. TRINITY

23 May 1928 *Trinity College*

Dear Mackail,
    Scholia under the name Iulius Pomponius Sabinus were published by G. Fabricius in his edition of Virgil 1561. They were then supposed to be ancient but are now referred to the early renascence.

Yours sincerely   A. E. HOUSMAN

To J. W. Mackail

MS. TRINITY

11 February 1929 *Trinity College*

Dear Mackail,
    Χειμερινὸς ὄνειρος[1] etc. is in Lucian I 17.
    The reading which you advocate in Verg. Aen. XII 648 is the reading which I proposed.[2]

Yours sincerely   A. E. HOUSMAN

---

[1] Quoted (without source) on the title-page of Pater's *Marius the Epicurean*, 1885.
[2] In 'Prosody and Method' in *The Classical Quarterly*, 1927. Mackail correctly attributes the conjecture in his edition.

To A. S. F. Gow

MS. TRINITY

3 March 1929   *[Trinity College]*

The constellation is called Τρίγωνον for instance in Ptol. synt. VII c. 5 (Heiberg vol. I ii p. 82), schol. Arat. 236, Vett. Val. p. 13 13. I do not find *Trigonum* in Latin: in schol. Germ. ed. Breys. p. 109 8 sq. it is *Triangulus*.

A.E.H.

To Frank E. Robbins

MS. CLEMENTS

17 November 1929   *Trinity College*

Dear Mr Robbins,

I shall be very glad to look through your proofs,[1] though I cannot promise a profound or prolonged examination, as I am now concentrated on finishing the last volume of my Manilius.

The octatropos, wherever it occurs, *is* simply an incomplete dodecatropos: it never divides the circle into eight equal parts. Cumont in *Revue de Philologie* 1918 p. 74 has a probable theory of its origin, confirmed by your papyrus.

At 3 B 13 the name of an astrologer is required, and Ἑρμῆσ[2] seemed to fit the space.

I am yours very truly   A. E. HOUSMAN

To H. E. Butler

MS. ST JOHN'S

3 January 1930   *Trinity College*

Dear Butler,

As what happens when *es* follows a vowel is aphaeresis rather than elision, it would be logical for the vowel to retain its quantity; and a long vowel does so in Anth. Lat. Ries. 462 28 impius hoc *telo es, hoc* potes esse pius. The poem is a correct piece of verse, of the first century after Christ at the latest I should say, and possibly Seneca's.

About the lacus Vmber[3] I have long had the suspicion you mention.

---

[1] Of further corrections to the Michigan Astrological Papyrus.
[2] Proposed by Housman in his review.
[3] In Propertius IV. 1. 124. Housman conjectured *non tepet* for *intepet*. See also p. 427.

Bredon is the Worcestershire hill; the Shropshire Breidden is very different, covered with bracken. The poem[1] is one of the earliest, written before I knew the book would be Shropshire.

Yours sincerely   A. E. HOUSMAN

To J. W. Mackail

MS. TRINITY

27 January 1930   *Trinity College*

Dear Mackail,
   torquet in Verg. Aen. IX 402 was suggested by Ribbeck in 1862, but I do not like it, because it takes *suspiciens* away from the verb *precatur*, to which in sense it belongs.
   Your objection to *amens*[2] is one which I have heard before; but similarly *amens* in XII 742 is followed by *tum uero amens formidine* in 776.

Yours sincerely   A. E. HOUSMAN

To W. H. Shewring[3]

MS. SAMUELS

27 March 1930   *Trinity College*

Dear Sir,
   I should guess doubtfully that the man was loosely girt, so that a purple undergarment showed down the front between the two borders of the overgarment, themselves also purple, I presume. The Greek translator seems to have understood somewhat thus.[4]
   Certainly *discinctatus* is not correctly formed from a noun of the fourth declension, and apparently can mean no more than *discinctus*, which you cite from another MS, and which should perhaps be read. One of the vagaries of scribes is to dilate words by inserting syllables, as in Livy 45. 28. 3 *nobilitatemplo* for *nobili templo*.

I am yours very truly   A. E. HOUSMAN

---

[1] *A Shropshire Lad* XXI, written in 1891.
[2] In Housman's conjecture at IX 403 *suspicit altam amens lunam* proposed in the preface to Manilius I.
[3] Classical scholar and poet; author of *The Water Meads*, 1927.
[4] The reference is to the *Passio SS Perpetuae et Felicitatis*, which Shewring edited and translated in 1931. Housman's suggestion was adopted and acknowledged.

there is, why a pause should make a cacophony greater rather than less. Incidentally you commit yourself to the opinion that the cacophony of *quisquis is* is diminished by the immediate addition of a word containing a fourth sibilant. If the next Bentley or Scaliger came along and told me that *uincunt* in 114 is no improvement on *uictum*, I should be discomposed and begin to examine myself; but when one of you gentlemen says it I only think of him what you think of me, that he ought to be more modest. Two of the conjectures which you select for dispraise have been selected for praise by Heraeus.[1]

Several people want me to produce an edition or else a text of Horace's odes: a text perhaps I may; but it is about time that I gave up writing and tried to improve my mind in leisure.

I am yours very truly   A. E. HOUSMAN

To J. W. Mackail

MS. TRINITY

17 December 1931   *Trinity College*

Dear Mackail,
    Why is *namque* 'intensive' in Verg. Aen. V 733 and VII 122? it seems to me the regular 'for' with finite verb, postponed as in buc. I 14, and in your edition you do not seem to take it otherwise. In Juvenal IV 79 I did think of *nempe*, which is often confused with *namque*, but *quippe* seemed nearer.

    I hope you have not been buying my second edition,[2] which our press sells at an absurd price: they over-pay their workmen and therefore over-charge their customers. I would have sent you a copy (I will now if you have not got one), but it has only about 20 pages of new matter.

    I see from reviews that literature has broken out in another of your family.[3]

Yours sincerely   A. E. HOUSMAN

To S. C. Roberts

MS. PRIVATE

6 February 1932   *Trinity College*

My dear Roberts,
    For the second time your overpaid underlings refuse to print my apparatus

---

[1] Karl Wilhelm Heraeus (1862–1938).
[2] Of Juvenal.
[3] Mackail's daughter Angela Thirkell (1890–1961), later a successful novelist, had just published her first book, *Three Houses*. Her brother, Denis Mackail, produced the first of his many novels in 1920.

criticus as I wrote it, and insist on running together lines which I carefully separated.

There is also a detail in which the type is not satisfactory. The signs Ω and ς, since they mean MSS, ought to be of the same stature and obesity as GLM; though I must say that these three seem to me to be too obese. Matters were better in the Juvenal, though even there the signs Ψ and Σ were not fully equal in size to PSAFGLOTU. In any case Ω and ς should be larger or thicker than they now are, for now they are on an equality with the surrounding letterpress.

Yours sincerely   A. E. HOUSMAN

I do not mean that ς should be as *big* as Ω, but that it should belong (as now it does) to the lower case of the same fount.

To Kenneth Wellesley[1]

MS. WELLESLEY

12 February 1932   *Trinity College*

Dear Mr Wellesley,
    The other judges for the Montagu Butler prize,[2] which I congratulate you on winning, have asked me to see you about certain modifications which they think should be made before the poem is published. I shall be here and pleased to talk with you any day next week between six and seven in the evening, if you will give me notice beforehand. You had better bring a copy of the poem.

Yours very truly   A. E. HOUSMAN

To Kenneth Wellesley

MS. WELLESLEY

20 February 1932   *Trinity College*

Dear Mr Wellesley,
    We have neglected to observe that *modero*, except in the past participle, appears to be only ante- and post-classical, so that 'quaeque ipsa domum moderauerat olim' should be 'cuique ante domus parere solebat' or some-things else.[3]

Yours very truly   A. E. HOUSMAN

[1] Now in the University of Edinburgh.
[2] For Latin hexameters.
[3] The printed version reads 'quaeque ante domus moderamen habebat'.

To F. H. Fobes[1]

MS. GOTOFF

24 June 1932 *Trinity College*

Dear Mr Fobes,

I am much obliged by your kindness in sending me your little book of Benner Greek.[2] I am not altogether a worthy recipient, for I have no more appreciation of what typographers call beauty than of the 'elegance' of a mathematical proof or the points of a bull-terrier; and moreover I seem to find that thick type prevents me from reading quickly.

The reform most needed in Greek type, now that the double sigma has been got rid of, seems to me to be the abolition of the subscript iota and the substitution, not simply of the adscript, which often causes ambiguity, but of the diminished adscript, as in Porson's last edition of the Hecuba.[3]

Yours very truly A. E. HOUSMAN

To E. H. Blakeney

MS. B.M.

3 October 1932 *Trinity College*

Dear Mr Blakeney,

You should get Hosius *Die Moselgedichte des Decimus Magnus Ausonius* (N. G. Elwertsche Verlagsbuchhandlung, Marburg 1. H.),[4] which has a useful commentary and is quite cheap. In any case I have little authority to 'settle' difficulties in Ausonius or give 'decisions' on them.

Yours very truly A. E. HOUSMAN

To J. D. Duff

MS. TRINITY

21 November 1932 *Trinity College*

Dear Duff,

'Ex murorum ruina nouus altiorque agger oriebatur, qui obstabat, et impediebat pugnantes: u. 374 *iacens uallum* dicitur. Lucani est locus simillimus III 508 *procubuit maiorque iacens apparuit agger*' Ernesti.[5] As *certatim*

---

[1] Professor of Greek, Amherst College (died 1957).
[2] A Greek font devised by Fobes.
[3] Published in 1800.
[4] First published in 1894, though the title-page description here given is that of the second and third editions, 1909 and 1926.
[5] In his edition of Silius, 1791–1792.

with *prorutus* would be foolishly irrelevant, I suppose it must mean that each part of the débris tried to rise higher than the rest.

Yours sincerely   A. E. HOUSMAN

To J. D. Duff

MS. TRINITY

9 January 1933   *Trinity College*

Dear Duff,

Thanks for Conington's letter,[1] which I return.

I think that *fastigatur*[2] signifies the narrowing (tapering would be too strong) of the island at toe and heel.

Yours sincerely   A. E. HOUSMAN

To F. V. M. Cumont[3]

MS. TRINITY

20 Mars 1933   *Trinity College*

Monsieur,

Je vous remercie beaucoup d'avoir bien voulu m'envoyer votre étude, savante comme de coutume, sur Adonis et Sirius.[4] Je me permets cependant de vous faire remarquer que dans la note (2) p. 260 vous vous trompez en matière de chronologie. C'est moi qui est le devancier (1903) et qui ai induit en erreur mes élèves parfois trop dociles Breiter (1908) et van Wageningen (1921), et c'est moi aussi qui ai proposé (1930) la solution que vous répétez p. 261.

Croyez je vous prie, Monsieur à l'expression de mes sentiments les plus distingués (or sympathiques).

To J. D. Duff

MS. TRINITY

15 July 1933   *Trinity College*

Dear Duff,

In Sil. XIII 106 sq. I think *nodis ferroque* is ἐν διὰ δυοῖν.

In XIII 261 I suppose *mussat* means much the same as in Verg. Aen. XII

---

[1] To H. A. J. Munro, 1 December 1864, about his edition of Lucretius.

[2] In Silius XII. 356.

[3] Franz Valéry Marie Cumont (1868–1947), Belgian orientalist and historian of religion. The text is taken from Housman's draft.

[4] *Adonis et Sirius* in *Mélanges G. Glotz*, 1932.

657, and indicates that Virrius lost confidence and nerve. Summers's[1] *coetuque* seems good and even necessary: the invitation must have been issued to a limited audience, and *turba comitante* in 276 must be restricted to it; and a *que* is needed to get rid of such an asyndeton as *mussat, docet*.

Yours sincerely   A. E. HOUSMAN

To J. D. Duff

MS. TRINITY

22 July 1933   *Trinity College*

Dear Duff,

I think that Silius would be very ill-pleased with you for wanting to alter XIII 681 *Libyci quas fecerat auri*, which is possessive, like Liu. 33 13 8 *eas populi Romani factas esse*. Barth[2] renders 'mancipauerat eas auro'.

Yours sincerely   A. E. HOUSMAN

To J. D. Duff

MS. TRINITY

24 July 1933   *Trinity College*

Dear Duff,

sui exercitus fecerat would I suppose be partitive genitive: this, as I said, is possessive, and the sense is given by Barth: literally 'had rendered them the property of Punic gold', 'the slaves or creatures of his bribery', so that they had no independence.

Yours sincerely   A. E. HOUSMAN

To J. D. Duff

MS. TRINITY

28 July 1933   *Trinity College*

Dear Duff,

This ship, even under press of sail, moved so slowly, because of its enormous size, that you would have thought it was only propelled by oars.[3] But

---

[1] His recension of Silius was included in Postgate's *Corpus*, volume II, 1905.

[2] In *Adversaria*, 1624, by Caspar von Barth (1587–1658).

[3] Duff printed this interpretation of Silius XIV. 389–391 verbatim.

I think that in XIV 391 the right reading is Withof's[1] *quasi*, mistaken for *qua si* and the *qua* then omitted.

Thanks for your kind wish, but the heat has been against me.

Yours sincerely

A. E. HOUSMAN

To J. D. Duff

MS. TRINITY

2 October 1933   *Trinity College*

Dear Duff,

I should think that *in cornua* IV 318 means that they are trying to outflank one another, and that *glomerata volumina* means massed ranks in motion; but I am not at all sure.

I am sorry for the cause of your regretted absence. All sorts of colds are hateful things.

Yours sincerely

A. E. HOUSMAN

To C. M. Bowra[2]

MS. BOWRA

18 November 1933   *Trinity College*

Dear Mr Bowra,

Thanks for your note: you are probably right. I see from Weir Smyth[3] that Ilgen[4] had the idea of pot and kettle.

Yours sincerely

A. E. HOUSMAN

To H. E. Butler

MS. ST JOHN'S

6 December 1933   *Trinity College*

Dear Butler,

Many thanks for your half of the gift of *The Elegies of Propertius* which I received this morning. As yet I have only glanced through it, but I make one

[1] In *Kritische Anmerkungen über Horaz und andere Römische Schriftsteller*, 1791–1802.

[2] (Cecil) Maurice Bowra (born 1899); Fellow of Wadham College, Oxford, 1922; Warden, 1938; Professor of Poetry, 1946; knighted, 1951. He had read a paper at Cambridge, Housman had questioned a point in it, and Bowra had written him a note to supplement the answer he gave on the spot.

[3] In *Greek Melic Poets*, 1900.

[4] In his *Opuscula*, 1797.

remark before I forget. I am tired of saying that Craugidos in IV 3 55 is not Buecheler's.[1] I told Postgate whose it was, and he told the world; and I have at last dinned the truth into Hosius.[2]

Yours sincerely   A. E. HOUSMAN

To J. W. Mackail

MS. TRINITY

12 December 1933   *Trinity College*

Dear Mackail,

Verg. g. I 513 is a verse on which I have thought much and vainly; but MSS and scholia and testimonia are together in favour of *in spatio*, so I am afraid of your conjecture.[3]

I am so much better than I have been in the course of this year that I do not like to boast myself 'very poorly', but I am uncomfortable, and depressed by slow progress.

Yours sincerely   A. E. HOUSMAN

To Frank E. Robbins

MS. CLEMENTS

8 February 1934   *Trinity College*

My dear Dr Robbins,

I am very grateful to you for sending me your improved text of the papyrus, and I congratulate you on the progress which has been made. If, as you kindly offer, you also send me your commentary and translation, that will increase my gratitude.

I am yours sincerely   A. E. HOUSMAN

To Frank E. Robbins

MS. CLEMENTS

21 March 1934   *Trinity College*

Dear Mr Robbins,

I congratulate you on the production of a most instructive commentary,

---

[1] The conjecture was Bergk's (MSS *Graucidos* or *Grancidos*). It was correctly attributed in Postgate's *Corpus*, volume I, 1894. The second edition of C. Hosius' Propertius, 1922, gives the credit to Buecheler, and Butler and Barber repeated the attribution, even though Hosius had corrected it in his third edition, 1932.

[2] In his review of Hosius' second edition in *The Classical Review*, 1923.

[3] Apparently not published.

and on the progress made in deciphering the papyrus, and I am much in your debt for sending me the documents and allowing me to keep them.

I enclose a few notes which have occurred to me.[1]

Yours sincerely   A. E. HOUSMAN

To Frank E. Robbins

MS. CLEMENTS

14 April 1934   *Trinity College*

Dear Dr Robbins,

Again I have to thank you for great and laborious kindness in copying out and sending your latest results. In XIV 34–5 I should think ἀγόνους καί στεί [ρους] is indicated.

Whatever way you may choose of making acknowledgment to me I shall be well content.

I am yours sincerely   A. E. HOUSMAN

To Frank E. Robbins

MS. CLEMENTS

28 April 1934   *Trinity College*

Dear Dr Robbins,

I am much obliged by your kindness in sending me the new corrections of the papyrus, and I enclose some remarks[2] on the questions which you raise in your letter.

Many thanks also for your chronology of Trollope, the ingenuity of which reminds me of Ronald Knox's[3] and Michael Sadleir's[4] researches into the topography of Barsetshire. I read Trollope chiefly when I am suffering from sleeplessness; but he certainly makes some very warm friends.

Yours sincerely   A. E. HOUSMAN

[1] These notes are preserved with the letter.
[2] Preserved with the letter.
[3] In *Essays in Satire*, 1928.
[4] His *Trollope: A Commentary*, 1927, contains three maps of Barsetshire.

To Otto Skutsch[1]

MS. U.C.L.

Ottoni Skutsch iuueni doctissimo A. E. Housman s.

Non subito nec compecto poetae Latini *Achilles* et *Vlixes* nomina a quinta declinatione (nam *Achilli* sic dicitur ut *dii facii fami* cetera Gell. IX 14) ad tertiam traduxerunt, multisque post annis quam Horatius serm. II 3 193 *Achillē* ablatiuum protulit Ouidius ex Pont. III 3 43 *Achillē* retinuit, etsi ipse ib. I 3 74 *Achillis* scripsisse pariter numeris conuincitur; eundem her. I 84 *Vlixis* posuisse metrum, at met. XIV 159 *Vlixei* Priscianus G.L.K. II p. 277 testatur, qui etiam Horatii libris epist. I 6 63 in eadem forma adstipulatur. uetustioris figurae uestigia, quae plura quam commemoras apud Vergilium et posteriores supersunt, eo magis seruanda iudico quod librarios ad -*is* substituendum proniores fuisse et ex Prop. II 9 13 et ex pluribus Vergilii locis apparet. praeterea in utroque Propertii uersu antecedit, quod etiam Vergilio (georg. III 91, Aen. I 30, II 275, III 87, VI 839, II 7, 90, 436, III 613, 691) Horatio (epist. I 6 63, 7 40) Ouidio (met. XIV 159, 671) suasisse uidetur ut has formas eligerent, uocabulum *s* littera terminatum. Ouidium certe eodem quo adhuc soliti sumus modo illa *tanti* . . . *Achilli* accepisse colligitur ex met. XII 615 sq 'de *tam magno* restat *Achille* | nescioquid paruam quod non bene compleat urnam': adde Il. Lat. 1062 'inque leues abiit tantus dux ille fauillas' et Sen. H.O. 1758 sqq. 'tam paruus cinis | Herculeus, huc huc ille decreuit gigans. | o quanta, Titan, ad nihil moles abit': haec autem *corpus Achilli* (gen.) coniuncta redeunt carm. epigr. Buech. 1233 3. omnino sic sentio: fieri non potuisse quin Cynthia Propertium, si id uoluit quod tu eum uoluisse censes, quamuis docta puella, falso interpretaretur. Latinum esse ut non confido, neque enim exempla noui, ita negare non ausim. Illud deprecor, ne Midan tibi aliquem pro Rhadamanthye arbitrum sumpsisse uidearis.[2]

ann. 1934 mens. Iun. d. 5.   coll. Trin. Cantabr.

---

[1] Born 1906; at the time of this letter a post-graduate student at Göttingen; Professor of Latin at University College, London since 1951. This letter answers a suggestion that in *foedavit . . . tanti corpus Achilli* (Propertius II. 9, 13) *Achilli* should be taken as dative and *tanti* as genitive of value.

[2] Mr Skutsch's letter, also in Latin, was headed with the verse 'Ante tuum venio, linguae Rhadamanthe, tribunal'.

To E. H. Blakeney

MS. B.M.

21 September 1934   *Trinity College*

Dear Mr Blakeney,

I am much obliged by the gift of your edition of Julius Africanus' letter,[1] which was worth doing.

In ἔκρουσα it is surely a note and not a blow which is struck. Africanus may for aught I know have pronounced σχίνον, but not πρίνον and πρῖνον both.

Yours very truly   A. E. HOUSMAN

[1] *A Letter to Origen on the Story of Susanna*, the Greek text, edited with introduction translation and notes by E. H. Blakeney, 1934.

438

SELECT BIBLIOGRAPHY

WORKS BY HOUSMAN

1. *Introductory Lecture*, printed for distribution to members of University College, London, 1892.
   (a) Reprinted privately, 1933.
   (b) First published edition, 1937.
2. *A Shropshire Lad*, 1896.
   (a) Second edition, 1898; followed by numerous reprints.
   (b) Illustrated editions, 1908, 1929, 1940.
   (c) *The Making of A Shropshire Lad. A Manuscript Variorum* by Tom Burns Haber, 1966.
3. *M. Manilii Astronomicon Liber Primus*, 1903. The four succeeding books appeared in 1912, 1916, 1920 and 1930.
   (a) Second edition, 1937.
   (b) Editio minor, 1932.
4. *D. Iunii Iuuenalis Saturae*, 1905.
   (a) Second edition, 1931; reprinted 1938.
5. *Last Poems*, 1922; frequently reprinted.
6. *M. Annaei Lucani Belli Ciuilis Libri Decem*, 1926.
   (a) Second edition, 1927.
7. *The Name and Nature of Poetry*, 1933; several times reprinted.
8. *More Poems*, 1936.
9. *The Collected Poems*, 1939; frequently reprinted.
   (a) The best text is that of the Penguin edition, 1956, which has an excellent introduction by John Sparrow. A small number of printing errors, pointed out by William White in *The Bulletin of Bibliography*, Vol. 22, No. 4, 1957, were corrected in the subsequent reprints.
10. *The Manuscript Poems*, edited by Tom Burns Haber, 1955. The best comment is that of the review (by John Sparrow) in *The Times Literary Supplement*, 29 April 1955 (reprinted in no. 24 *infra*).
11. *Selected Prose*, edited by John Carter, 1961.
    A most useful collection containing nos 1 and 7 *supra* and selections from

Housman's prefaces, reviews and other contributions to books and periodicals.

12. *The Confines of Criticism* (Cambridge inaugural lecture, 1911), with notes by John Carter, 1969.

BIOGRAPHICAL WORKS

13. *A. E. Housman. A Sketch* by A. S. F. Gow, 1936.
An authoritative and scholarly memoir, with a list of Housman's writings. (a) Addenda to the bibliography were published by G. B. A. Fletcher in *The Durham University Journal* XXXVIII, 1946.

14. *A. E. Housman. Recollections* by Katharine E. Symons and others, 1936.
A miscellaneous volume containing many useful details.

15. *The Unexpected Years* by Laurence Housman, 1937.
An autobiography which is the main source of knowledge of AEH's early life.

16. *A.E.H.* by Laurence Housman, 1937.
The memoir is an indispensable supplement to Gow (no. 13 *supra*); approximately 120 letters are quoted at length, together with the best of Housman's humorous verses (apart from his 'Fragment of a Greek Tragedy').

17. *A Buried Life* by Percy Withers, 1940.
The author's personal recollections of Housman, with numerous quotations from his letters.

18. *Housman: 1897–1936* by Grant Richards, 1941.
The author, though not an intimate friend, knew Housman longer and better than anyone outside the family. Nearly 500 letters are quoted, and the book gives a vivacious account of their business dealings and of Housman as a travelling and eating companion.

19. *A. E. Housman. A Divided Life* by George L. Watson, 1957.
The first formal biography, concentrating mostly on Housman's early life, with much useful family history.

20. *A. E. Housman: Man Behind a Mask* by Maude M. Hawkins, 1958.
Extended talks with Laurence Housman, wide reading and patient research enable the author to add considerably to what is known of Housman. But her book is not dependable; it suffers from inaccuracy, confusion between fact and conjecture, and an over-stimulated imagination.

21. *A. E. Housman's 'De Amicitia'* by Laurence Housman, annotated by John Carter (in *Encounter*, October 1967).
The author here gives details, omitted from his earlier writings, of A.E.H.'s relations with Moses Jackson, together with the complete text of his diary entries relating to Jackson, 1888–1890.

22. *A. E. Housman. Scholar and Poet* by Norman Marlow, 1958.
A detailed and scholarly examination of the literary influences, Classical and English, on Housman's poetry, together with a survey of critical writing on him.
23. *'Fool's-errand to the Grave' : the Personality and Poetry of Housman* by F. L. Lucas (in his collection of essays, *The Greatest Problem*, 1961).
The best critical account.
24. *A. E. Housman. A Collection of Critical Essays* edited by Christopher Ricks, 1968.
Useful more as a guide to recent academic opinion than for information on Housman. The 'Chronology of Important Dates' mis-dates his death by six months.

BIBLIOGRAPHIES

25. *A Bibliography of Alfred Edward Housman* by T. G. Ehrsam, 1941.
Useful chiefly for numerous references to articles on Housman in periodicals.
26. *A. E. Housman. An Annotated Hand-List* by John Carter and John Sparrow, 1952.
27. *Published Letters of A. E. Housman: A Survey* by William White (in *The Bulletin of Bibliography*, Vol. 22, No. 4, 1957).
28. Catalogue of the Housman Centenary Exhibition at University College, London, 1959.
29. Catalogue of the Collamore Collection of Housman manuscripts, letters, first editions etc. exhibited in the Lilly Library, Indiana University, 1961.
Contains a description of the Woodchester Visitors' Book with numerous entries by Housman.

(See also the List of Writings in no. 13 and the List of Sources in no. 20 *supra*.)

INDEX OF RECIPIENTS

Abeel, Neilson, 377
Academy, The, 398
Adams, H. M., 235, 427
Adelman, Seymour, 264, 267, 350
Agard, W. R., 330
Asquith, H. H., 236
Athenaeum, The, 399

Barnes, George, 312
Barrie, Sir James, 262
Beerbohm, Max, 334
Blakeney, E. H., 302, 319, 384, 431, 438
Bowra, C. M., 434
Bridges, Monica, 294, 303, 310
Bridges, Robert, 158, 173, 213, 214, 221, 222, 231, 258, 272, 282, 287
Broadbent, H. G., 380
Brockington, A. Allen, 290
Brown, Horatio F., 59
Brussel, I. R., 308
Butler, H. E., 63, 118, 231, 244, 247, 333, 425, 427, 434
Butler, Mrs H. E., 231
Butler, H. M., 130
Bynner, Witter, 65, 70, 108, 117, 211, 221, 229, 338, 377

Cambridge University, Registrary, 420
Carter, John, 290
Cave, Countess, 329
Chambers, R. W., 37, 308
Clemens, Cyril, 246, 277, 313, 318, 330, 388
Cockerell, Sydney, 117, 135, 190, 192, 194, 207, 350, 315, 334, 358, 363
Collingwood, E. F., 303
Country Life, 92
Cross, Wilbur, 153, 252
Cumont, F. V. M., 432

Drinkwater, John, 194, 205, 209, 254, 255, 281
Duff, J. D., 405, 415, 416, 427, 431, 432, 433, 434

Eliot, T. S., 235, 262
Ellis, Robinson, 399
Eton College, Headmaster, 220
Evans, David Emrys, 362, 365

Fobes, F. H., 431
Frazer, Lady, 234
Frazer, Sir James George, 184

Gaselee, Stephen, 154, 255, 358, 410
Garrod, H. W., 121, 167
Gosse, Edmund, 114, 133, 136, 149, 151, 157, 159, 205, 220
Gosse, Lady, 266
Gosse, Philip, 275
Gorecki, Thaddeus, 350
Gow, A. S. F., 126, 133, 172, 190, 197, 218, 229, 238, 260, 351, 375, 378, 409, 410, 411, 413, 414, 416, 417, 421, 424, 425

Hackforth, Reginald, 309
Halifax, Viscount, 354
Hall, F. W., 210, 226, 240, 241, 242
Hardy, Thomas, 127
Harrison, Ernest, 417, 420
Hemmerde, Pauline, 330
Hill, G. F., 401, 402
Hinkson, Katherine Tynan, 80
Housman, Basil, 257
Housman, Edward, 13
Housman, Jeannie, 349, 364, 383, 388
Housman, Laurence, 31, 34, 36, 37, 38, 39, 40, 41, 67, 88, 92, 94, 96, 97, 100, 110, 116, 117, 118, 132, 149, 168, 207, 208, 230, 232, 276, 277, 280, 296, 318, 327, 335, 344, 347, 356, 363, 370, 379, 385, 389
Housman, Lucy, 5, 7, 11, 12, 19, 23, 24, 42, 43, 45, 46, 47, 53, 55, 56, 59, 72
Hudson-Williams, A., 287

Ishill, Joseph, 299, 306, 319

Jackson, Henry, 64, 84, 86, 97, 130, 162
Jenkinson, F. J. H., 153, 409

Lee, G. M., 367
Leippert, Mr, 253, 263
Lemperly, Paul, 50
Lucas, E. V., 216
Lulham, P. Habberton, 70

Mackail, J. W., 153, 162, 198, 199, 200, 289, 304, 402, 406, 411, 414, 420, 422, 423, 424, 426, 429, 435
Maclagan, Eric, 111
Macmillan and Co., 26, 223
Macmillan, Frederick, 245
Makin, Walter, 308
Marsh, Edward, 125

Martin, Houston, 331, 347, 348, 352, 360, 361, 376, 390, 392
Masefield, John, 296
Meakin, Annette, 51
Meyerstein, E. H. W., 326
Monroe, Harriet, 189
Moring, Messrs Alexander, 87
Moore, G. V., 387
Morley, S. G., 345
Murray, Gilbert, 51, 68, 69, 75, 99, 105, 106, 205, 404

Newall, H. F., 412
Nock, A. D., 421

O'Brian, Delos, 326
Oliver, F. W., 383
Owlett, F. C., 219, 298, 300
Oxford and Asquith, Earl of, 236
Oxford University, Registrar, 265

Parry, R. St J., 170, 233
Patent Office, Registrar of Trade Marks, 27
Payne, L. W., 202, 309, 318
Pearson, A. C., 189, 273, 419, 422
Phillimore, J. S., 167
Platt, Arthur, 144
Platt, Mrs, 50, 108, 114, 126, 127, 145, 182, 249, 250, 289, 291
Pollet, Maurice, 328
Postgate, J. P., 94
Priestley, J. B., 193, 222

Quiller-Couch, Arthur, 281

Rackham, Harris, 284
Ramsay, Lady, 115, 147
Rice, Virginia, 324
Rice, Wallace, 77
Richards, Mrs E. Grant, 79
Richards, Grant, 46, 48, 49, 50, 51, 60, 61, 62, 63, 64, 65, 66, 67, 68, 70, 71, 72, 74, 76, 78, 79, 80, 81, 82, 83, 84, 85, 86, 87, 89, 90, 91, 93, 95, 96, 98, 99, 101, 102, 103, 104, 105, 106, 107, 109, 111, 112, 113, 114, 115, 116, 119, 120, 122, 123, 124, 125, 128, 131, 134, 135, 136, 137, 138, 139, 140, 141, 142, 143, 144, 145, 146, 147, 148, 152, 156, 157, 160, 161, 163, 164, 165, 166, 167, 169, 171, 172, 174, 175, 176, 177, 178, 179, 181, 183, 184, 185, 186, 187, 188, 189, 191, 192, 193, 194, 196, 197, 198, 201, 203, 204, 206, 210, 211, 212, 214, 216, 223, 225, 228, 230, 234, 242, 245, 247, 248, 254, 256, 258, 259, 264, 267, 268, 270, 274,

278, 284, 291, 293, 294, 307, 309, 311, 313, 314, 315, 317, 320, 321, 323, 327, 331, 332, 337, 344, 345, 348, 351, 357, 360, 374, 386
Richards, Mrs M. Grant, 163, 169
Richards, Messrs Grant, 218
Richards Press, The, 255, 264, 266, 268, 269, 270, 272, 274, 279, 290, 291, 292, 294, 297, 298, 299, 300, 301, 302, 305, 307, 311, 313, 322, 323, 324, 386
Robbins, Frank E., 423, 425, 435, 436
Roberts, Denys Kilham, 338
Roberts, S. C., 234, 241, 243, 244, 248, 250, 251, 282, 283, 296, 300, 304, 305, 315, 316, 317, 322, 325, 332, 336, 391, 429
Rothenstein, Alice, 92, 94, 102, 104, 108, 110, 111, 115, 118, 128, 130, 147, 152, 155, 171, 246, 307
Rothenstein, William, 87, 89, 101, 109, 132, 173, 182, 260, 261, 262, 319, 333
Rudge, W. E., 227
Rouse, W. H. D., 415

Sayle, Charles, 188, 412
Scholfield, A. F., 181, 190, 237, 238, 239, 279, 281, 304, 306, 323, 381
Scott-James, R. A., 392
Secker, Martin, 156, 247
Shewring, W. H., 426
Skutsch, Otto, 437
Slater, D. A., 408, 409
Sparrow, John, 223, 356, 361
Spicer-Simson, Theodore, 199, 202
Stamfordham, Lord, 277
Standard, The, 30
Stevens, P. P., 206
Stewart, Hugh, 428
Stewart, William, 77
Sunday Times, The, 366
Sydney University, 401
Symons, Edward, 255
Symons, Katharine, 121, 129, 140, 176, 178, 180, 195, 211, 215, 217, 221, 228, 233, 237, 238, 243, 252, 253, 269, 278, 279, 283, 286, 292, 296, 312, 321, 324, 337, 339, 340, 341, 342, 343, 344, 351, 359, 364, 368, 374, 375, 378, 380, 384, 385, 389, 390, 391, 392

Thicknesse, Lily, 52, 103, 129, 136, 138, 218
Thomson, J. J., 227
Thring, Herbert, 225, 226
Tillotson, Geoffrey, 367, 368, 369, 372, 373
Times, The, 219, 271, 325, 418, 419
Tonks, Henry, 297, 371
Trollope, Blanche, 355

University College, London, 29
Unnamed Correspondents, 169, 191, 225, 240, 258, 259, 260, 282, 311, 365, 369

Webb, P. G. L., 123, 400
Wellesley, Kenneth, 430
Wiggins, G. H., 295
Williams, Charles, 285, 286, 293
Wilson, Charles, 245, 299, 310, 316, 330, 354, 367

Wilson, Mrs, 388
Winstanley, D. A., 185
Wise, Mrs, 27, 78
Withers, Mrs, 154, 248, 266, 373
Withers, Percy, 154, 170, 174, 183, 185, 187, 196, 203, 209, 213, 216, 224, 229, 232, 236, 239, 240, 249, 256, 263, 273, 275, 280, 288, 289, 295, 306, 314, 326, 332, 336, 338, 346, 349, 353, 355, 357, 362, 366, 369, 370, 371, 372, 376, 382, 386, 387, 391, 413

GENERAL INDEX

Where there is a biographical footnote the reference to it is placed first.

Abeel, Neilson, thanked for not visiting H., 377
Abercrombie, Lascelles, 252, 302
Adair, A. H., 294
Adam, Mr, 278
Adams, Captain, 3
Adeane, C. R. W., 289
'A.E.' (George Russell), 405
Aeschines, 416
Aeschylus, 30, 76, 144, 150, 397, 404, 417; H's favourite Greek poet, 328
Agar, T. L., 417
Agard, W. R., 330
Agate, James, *L. of C.*, 177
Alington, C. A., 220
Allbutt, Clifford, 329
Allen, Mrs Grant, 320
Andrea (gondolier), 58–9, 237–9
Aratus, 400, 425
Archer, William, *Poets of the Younger Generation*, 48
Archimedes, 413
Aristarchus, 413
Aristophanes, 409, 417
Armstrong, Thomas, 172
Arnold, E. V., 210, 242, 309
Arnold, Matthew, xi, 334, 348; 'The Church at Brou', 39
Arnold, Thomas, 334
Ashburner, Walter, 107
Asquith, H. H. (Earl of Oxford and Asquith), address on Scaliger, 236; 133, 148, 228
Asquith, Margot, *Autobiography*, 188
Aulus Gellius, 437
Ausonius, 431
Austin, Alfred, 16–17

Badham, Charles, 419
Bainbridgge, P. G., *Jocundus Robertus*, 257
Baldwin, Stanley, 260, 329
Balfour, A. J., 208
Balzac, *Contes Drolatiques*, 331
Banting, Sir F., 213
Barber, E. A., *The Elegies of Propertius*, 434–435
Barnes, George, 312
Barrie, J. M., 262, 260, 302
Barth, C. von, *Adversaria*, 433
Baumann, A. A., 15

Baumeister, Denkmäler, 93
Bax, Belfort, 139, 160, 188
Becker, Sophie, 27, 3
Beddoes, T. L., *The Bride's Tragedy*, 41
Beerbohm, Max, H. suggests caricatures, 334; caricature of Watson, 71; *Seven Men*, 172; exhibition, 186; 159, 267, 320
Belloc, Hilaire, 336
Bennett, Arnold, *Milestones*, 126; *Clayhanger*, 372
Benson, A. C., 230, 254
Bentley, Richard, edition of Manilius, 36, 403, 429
Bergk, 415, 435
Best, C. H., 213
Bevan, A. A., 346
Binyon, Laurence, 300, 302
Birch, F. L., 133
'Birdie', 78
Blackett, Spencer, 36, 46
Blackwell, B. H., 116, 230
Blakeney, E. H., stanza on Watson, 302; prints sonnet by Watson, 384; edition of Julius Africanus, 438
Bland, Hubert, 37, 390
Blunden, Edmund, 205, 302
Blunt, W. S., 135; *My Diaries*, 161; found H. dull, 187
Boswell, *Life of Johnson*, 251
Boulestin, X. M., dinner in honour of H., 294
Bowra, C. M., 434
Bradley, A. C., 159
Bramah, Ernest, *Kai Lung Unrolls his Mat*, 270
Breiter, T., 432
Bresci, 54–5
Bridges, M. M., 294
Bridges, Robert, edits G. M. Hopkins, 158; first meeting with H., 133; foreword to Hardy presentation volume, 162; *Shorter Poems*, 173, 294, 308; *October*, 173; blamed for Withers' illness, 196; approves of *Last Poems*, 205; visits H., 214; 'an unscrupulous character', 216; 'an amazing old man', 217; prints poems by H. without permission, 218; back from America, 221; and 'Beatus Martinus', 224; *New Verse*, 231; his

447

Bridges, Robert, (*contd.*)
  'new-fangled stuff', 249; 'fierce interest' in prosody, 252; *The Testament of Beauty*, 258, 273, 287; congratulated on O.M., 282; *A Critical Introduction to Keats*, 285; the 'boom', 288; death, 294; epitaph, 303, 310
Bright, John, 208
Broadbent, Henry, 228
Brockington, A. A., 290
Brown, Horatio F., 59, 107, 405
Browning, Robert, 290
Buecheler, F., 435, 437
Buhrer, Albert, *Rosetta*, 275
Bunting, W. L., 98
Burman, Pieter, namesakes distinguished, 412
Burnaby, Rev. John, 133
Burrows, F. R., 15
Butler, H. E., 63, 118, 172, 242, 251; *The Elegies of Propertius*, 425, 427, 434-5
Butler, H. M., rumoured to have gone mad, 127; eightieth birthday, 130; memorial inscription, 185
Bynner, Witter, admires H.'s poems, 65; Canticle of Pan, 211; *Caravan*, 229; *Eden Tree*, 338
Bywater, Ingram, 98, 159

Calderon, G., *Tahiti*, 186
Callimachus, new fragments, H.'s suggestions, 422-3
Calverley, C. S., translations of Horace, 209
Cameron, D. Y., 93
Cameron, J. F., 332
Campbell, Lewis, 'not yet time to cease from guessing', 398; 'his' *Antiope*, 399
Cartault, Augustin, edition of Persius, 181
Carter, John, 290; 285, 293, 349, 365, 377
Cassagnac, *Les Vins de France*, 294
Catullus, 80, 144, 405, 416, 420-1
Cave, Countess, *Ant Antics*, 329
Cave, George, 226
Celsus, *De Medicina*, 409
Chamberlain, Joseph, 84; in L. Housman's *Dethronements*, 208; H.'s recollection of his maiden speech, 325
Chambers, R. W., recommended as librarian, 37; obituary of Platt, 245; Clark Lectures, 227, 384
Chesterton, G. K., 'Ballad of the White Horse', 126
Chitty, Sir J. W., 20
Church, Dean, 17
Churchill, Lord Randolph, 208
Cicero, 181
Clark, A. C., 116

Cleland, John, *Fanny Hill*, 139
Clemens, Cyril, 246; proposed biography of H., 313, 318; *Josh Billings, Yankee Humorist*, 330-1; *An Evening with A. E. Housman*, 330; offers H. silver medal of Mark Twain Society, 389
Cockerell, Sydney, offers to show H. Fitzwilliam Museum, 117; supervises Hardy presentation volume, 162; knighted, 350; proposes portrait of H., 358; out of humour with Pre-Raphaelites, 371
Cocteau, Jean, 196
Coleridge, S. T., parodied, 150
Colette, 293
Collie, Professor, 250
Collingwood, E. F., 303
Collins, Wilkie, 235, 262
Conington, John, 366; translation of Horace, 209; letter to Munro, 432
Cornford, F. M., 246; 'drawing' of him, 129
Cornford, Frances, *Poems*, 109; H.'s parody, 109, 320; *Death and the Princess*, 129
Cornforth, Fanny, 190
'Corvo, Baron' (F. Rolfe), *The Desire and Pursuit of the Whole*, 256; essay by Symons, 257; Venice letters, 257, 264
Cornwallis, Admiral, 277
Coulton, G. G., 195
Creighton, Louise, *Thomas Hodgkin*, 412
Cross, Wilbur, asks for contribution to *Yale Review*, 153; prints 'Fragment of a Greek Tragedy', 252
Cumont, F. V. M., *Adonis et Sirius*, 432; 425
Cunningham, Rev. William, 127

Darley, George, *Sylvia* and *Nepenthe*, 41
Darling, W. Y., *Private Papers of a Bankrupt Bookseller*, 314
Darrow, Clarence, defence of Loeb and Leopold, 257
Darwin, Erasmus, H.'s paper on, 220; *The Loves of the Plants*, 220
Davenport, Basil, 352
Davey, Norman, *The Hungry Traveller in France*, 314
Davidson, John, *New Ballads*, 38; *The Triumph of Mammon* and *The Theatrocrat*, 90
Defoe, Daniel, *Tour thro' Great Britain*, 283
de la Mare, Walter, 91, 162, 302
Deutsch, Babette, *This Modern Poetry*, 386
Disraeli, Benjamin (Lord Beaconsfield), 14-17, 116; *Endymion*, 204; his complexion, 325; H.'s suggestion for caricature, 334-5

Dixon, Mrs Hugh, 339
Dobell, Sydney, 285
Dobree, Peter Paul, 274
Dodd, Francis, drawing of H., 240–1, 246
Douglas, Lord Alfred, *Collected Poems*, 188; and Wilde, 267
Doumergue, Gaston, 224
Draper, Rev. W. H., 'An Armistice Day Anthem', 216
Dreiser, Theodore, *A Traveller at Forty*, 138
Drinkwater, John, *Seeds of Time*, 194; *Selected Poems*, 194; visits H., 255–6
Drummond, William, *The Cypress Grove*, 83
Duff, Charles, *A Handbook of Hanging*, 271
Duff, J. D., recension of Martial, 405; a conjecture, 406; edition of Juvenal, 116; to complete H.'s Lucan, 230; edition of Silius, 427, 431–4
Duse, Eleanora, 69

Edward VII, King, not introduced to H., 98
Elgar, Edward, 302
Eliot, George, 329, 390
Eliot, T. S., asks H. to write on Wilkie Collins, 235; *For Lancelot Andrewes*, 271; reviews *Name and Nature of Poetry* 344
Ellis, Robinson, H.'s contempt, 67; supports H.'s candidature, 29; edition of *Ibis*, 399; 113, 116
Ellwood, Fanny, 312
Elmsley, Peter, editions of Sophocles and Euripides, 414
Emerson, R. W., 349
Engledow, F. L., 303
Epistle to Diognetus, 422
Ernout, Alfred, edition of Lucretius, 181, 416
Ettrick, H. H., 66
Euripides, H.'s conjectures, 51; Elmsley's edition, 414; Murray's edition, 51–2, 404–5; Murray's translations, 69, 75–6, 168; *Antiope* (fragments), 398–9; Hecuba (Porson), 404, 431
Evans, David Emrys, 362, 365
Ewing, Robert, 11, 20

Faure, Elie, *The Soul of Japan*, 306
Feuchtwanger, Lion, *Jew Süss*, 247
Firbank, Ronald, 196
Fisher, H. A. L., 155
FitzGerald, Edward, 103; *see also* Platt, *Nine Essays*
Fletcher, George, 98, 352
Fletcher, John, *The Bloody Brother*, 334

Fletcher, W. M., 133
Fobes, F. H., 431
Forster, W. E., 14
Foster, Gregory, 220
Fothergill, J. R., *An Innkeeper's Diary*, 314
Fowler, R. H., 306
Fraenkel, Eduard, 366
Fraser, Claud Lovat, drawings for *A Shropshire Lad*, 181, 265
Fraser, James (Bishop of Manchester), 18
Frazer, James George, *The Golden Bough*, 184; 114, 235
Frazer, Lilly, 114, 234
Freeman, John, article on H., 179
Frood, Hester, 93, 142
Fry, C. B., distinguished from Roger Fry 251
Funke, Max, 418–19

Gadd, C. J., 121
Galsworthy, John, 110, 260, 282, 302
Gardiner, Balfour, 87
Gardner, E. A., 93
Garrod, H. W., Commentary on Manilius, 11, 121; *Worms and Epitaphs*, 167
Gaselee, Stephen, 154
Gasquet, Cardinal, *Monastic Life in the Middle Ages*, 195
George V, King, letter from Asquith and Bridges, 133; does H. no harm in Paris, 134; O.M. offered to H., 277, 389; favours appointment of Kipling as Poet Laureate, 295; Silver Jubilee, 368, 374
Germanicus, 400, 403
Gide, André, 156
Gladstone, W. E., at Oxford, 14, 16; burned in effigy, 17; treatment of Queen Victoria, 21; defeat, 25; prolixity, 188; H.'s suggestion for caricatures, 334–5
Glaisher, J. W. L., 139
Gleadowe, R. M. Y., drawing of H., 246
Goodford, Rev. C. O., 21
Goodwin, Alfred, 29
Gordon, G. S., 355
Gosse, Edmund, 114, 260; dinner party for Asquith, Bridges and H., 133; trouble with the Censor, 136–7; *Life of Swinburne*, 149–52; Swinburne's *Letters*, 157–8; private memoir of Swinburne, 159–60; Hardy presentation volume, 162; reviews *Last Poems*, 205; looks through Danish translation of *Last Poems*, 220, 259; death, 266; letters to H., 275; diaries, 276; *Life and Letters*, 276
Gosse, Philip, *The Pirates' Who's Who*, 221; collecting E. Gosse's letters, 275

449

Gow, A. S. F., *A. E. Housman: A Sketch*, 126, xii; master at Eton, 134; asked to apply for Liverpool professorship, 172; query on Rossetti, 190; invited to Family dinner, 218; invited to return to Trinity, 229-30; compiles list of H.'s writings, 238, 302; sorts out H.'s articles, 240; birthday telegram to H., 281; to see Manilius V through the press, 297; invites H. and Laurence H. to dinner, 375; deputy examiner for H., 378 and H's library, 379, 393

Grattan, J. H. G., 308
Gray, Thomas, 108, 413
Greek Anthology, influence on H., 328; Grotius' edition, 412
Grey, Edwin, 269
Griggs, F. L. M., etchings for H.'s poems, 275, 278
Gurney, Ivor, 95

Haber, Tom Burns, 393
Hackforth, Reginald, 309
Halifax, Viscount, 354
Hall, A. W., 16, 20-1
Hall, F. W., and the 'bone of contention', 210, 242; subscription for Cave's portrait, 226; sends H. photographs of Dodd's drawing, 240-1
Hanbury, R. W., 17
Harcourt, Sir William, 16; defeated in by-election, 20-1; his pedigree, 214
Hardy, Thomas, 127; meets H., xx; H. invited to Dorchester, xx; at Cambridge, 130; presentation volume, 162, 166; Rothenstein asks H. to write on, 173; selection of poems, 192, 194; portrait medallion, 199; funeral, 260-2, 266; H.'s admiration, 329; on H.'s poems, 331, 377; *The Dynasts*, 415
Harris, Frank, descends on H., 113; 'sincere and characteristic beliefs', 136; found H. rude, 187; controversy with Richards, 215; *My Life and Loves*, 284, 291, 315, 320
Harrison, Ernest, 283, 417, 420
Hartington, Marquess of, 208, 325
Haupt, Moritz, 69, 411
Havet, Louis, 181
Hayn and Gotendorf, *Bibliotheca Erotica*, 323
Haynes, E. S. P., *A Lawyer's Notebook*, 336
Headlam, Walter, 'Restorations of Menander', 94; deceived into thinking H. a Greek scholar, 423
Healy, Maurice, *Irish Wine*, 268
Hedges, Frank, 20-1

Heenan, J. C., 159
Heine, Heinrich, translations, 123; influence on H., 265, 328
Helena, Princess, 21, 212
Hemmerde, Pauline, 256, 330
Hemsley, Thomas, *Latin Elegiac Verse-Writing*, 113
Henderson, Mrs A. M., *Attractive Readings in Prose and Verse*, 311
Henley, W. E., 'comical', 35; no companion for H. in anthology, 91
Heraclitus, 416
Heraeus, K. W., 429
Herodotus, 416
Hesiod, 420
Hewlett, Maurice, 110
Hicks, R. D., 237
Hicks, Beach, M., 208
Hilberg, I., *Gesetze*, 414
Hill, G. F., 401-2
Hill, M. J. M., 383, 401
Home, Percy, 198
Homer, *Odyssey*, 404, 420; *Iliad*, 437
Hopkins, Gerard Manley, *Poems*, 158
Horace, H.'s paper, 23; Mackail's, 153; on wine and poetry, 160; translations, 209; dread of recitation in schools, 254; on avarice, 270; H. asked to edit, 429; 401, 404-5, 414, 422, 428, 437
Horton, Reginald, 12
Hosius, C., edition of Ausonius, 431; of Propertius, 435
Houghton, Lord, influence on Swinburne, 160; and text of Keats, 219
Housman, A. E. Writings (principal references); *see also* pp. 439-40
A Shropshire Lad, composition, 35, 328; rejected by Macmillan, 35, 223, 328-9, 350; published by Kegan Paul, 35, 328, 350; cover, 36; sent to Wilde, 267; price of first edition, 46, 230, 232, 292, 318; reviews, 36, 39, 390; H. visits Shropshire, 39; never saw Hughley, 233; H.'s sentiment for Shropshire, 328, 347; proposal from Richards to take over, 46; transferred to Richards, 48, 350; reprints, 49, 50, 61, 64, 70, 78, 86-7, 90, 193, 203, 261, 289; illustrated editions, 83, 96-8, 101, 135, 169, 227, 265, 275, 288, 306; American editions, 83-4, 225-7, 299, 352, 360-1; in Smaller Classics series, 70, 87, 157; growing popularity, 113, 350; limited editions, 135-6, 223, 274-5, 278, 288, 315; in Braille, 141; increased price, 148-9; a spectacular advertisement, 149; alterations, 193, 210, 356; royalties, 46, 70, 210,

245, 261, 270; translations, 171, 218, 220, 228, 259–60; manuscript given to Trinity, 235, 347; use in anthologies, 63, 77, 80, 91, 140, 216, 218, 254, 281, 311, 313, 324–5, 386; use by composers, 66, 78, 87, 95, 101, 105–6, 113, 124, 152, 172, 181, 184, 198, 211, 214–15, 247, 265, 350, 380; misprints, 50, 70, 71, 98, 135–6, 157, 203, 248, 268; called a 'filthy' book, 276, 339; not to be published together with *Last Poems*, 223, 225, 227, 361; H.'s attitude to publication, 65, 377; H. has no favourite poem, 331

Last Poems, 46, 179, 192, 193, 357; manuscript sent, 197; read by Richards, 357; cover, 198; proofs, 199–201; reviews, 205–6; sales, 211, 357; manuscript given to Fitzwilliam Museum, 207, 347; American editions, 225–7; cheaper edition, 257, 264, 268, 288; limited edition, 275, 288, 306; in Braille, 210; misprints, 204, 206, 282

More Poems, 393

Collected Poems, 393

Single poems: 'Sir Walter Raleigh', 7; 'The Death of Socrates', 7; contributions to *Odes from the Greek Dramatists*, 30, 330; 'The Oracles', 67, 376; 'Astronomy, 68, 405; 'The Olive', 70; 'Illic Jacet', 141; 'The Deserter', 214; 'Revolution', 234; 'Epitaph on an Army of "Mercenaries"', 255, 295, 330; 'R.L.S.', 274; 'Eight o'clock, 319; 'Is my team ploughing?', 331; 'Loveliest of trees', 347; 'New Year's Eve', 361; 'Parta Quies', 361; 'When the bells', 361; Song for Lady Jane Grey, 363; 'I hoed', 369; 'Hell Gate', 385, 389

Comic poems: contributions to *Rounde Table*, 10, 14, 19; copied in letters, 41, 45, 47, 48; 'Fragment of a Greek Tragedy', 52, 116, 252; 'Fragments of a Didactic Poem', 220; 'As I was walking', 329; *Three Poems*, 367–9, 372–3; 'At the door of my own little hovel', 377

Articles: 'Horatiana', 23; 'Emendationes Propertianae', 26; 'The manuscripts of Propertius', 26, 35; list of early papers, 30; 'Corrections and Explanations of Martial', 86; 'Greek Nouns in Latin Poetry', 105; 'Application of Thought to Textual Criticism', 186, 285; 'Notes on the *Thebais* of Statius', 210, 242, 309; review of Pearson's Sophocles, 226; 'Praefanda', 309; 'The Agamemnon of Aeschylus', 397; 'The Michigan

Astrological Papyrus', 423; Gow's list, 238

Introductory Lecture (1892), 29, 285, 290, 349, 365, 377

Cambridge Inaugural (1911), 113, 285, 286, 293

The Name and Nature of Poetry (1933), 265, 331–3; Beerbohm amused, 334; Kipling and Leavis, 335; manuscript given to Roberts, 336; Eliot's review, 344; sales, 336, 349

Selected Prose, 290

Manilius: I, 36; slow progress, 400; a query, 401–2; text and notes sent, 60; price, 61; Vatican manuscript, 62; proofs, 62; dedication, 64, 68, 352; cost of printing, 66, 74; legal difficulties, 78, 85; reviews, 80, 90; Mackail's comments, 402–4; out of print, 254; preface not to be printed separately, 377; corrections, 421, 432

II, photographs of Madrid manuscript, 109, 111, 113, 119–20; proofs, 122; delay, 123; free copies, 124; Mackail's comments, 406–7

III, 'a classy work', 139; finished, 141; Richards reminded not to go to sleep, 142; Mackail's comments, 411

IV, 164–7, 172, 174–5; delay, 178; advertisement, 179; reviews, 186

V, H. equipped, 171; still to be done, 226, 272; offered to Richards Press, 274; 279, 282, 291–2, 294, 297–9, 301, 302, 304, 307; Stewart's review, 428

Editio minor, 304–5, 315–17, 319, 322, 325

Juvenal: H.'s text in *Corpus*, 405; H.'s edition, 46; sent to Richards, 71; cost of printing, 72, 74; advertisement, 79; delay, 80; review, 90; 'no use to students', 116; bill for binding, 137; second edition, 282, 296, 301, 304–5, 312, 429–30

Lucan: offered to Macmillan, 223; rejected, 224; nearly finished, 226, 419; published by Blackwell, 224, 232, 245; Macmillan repents, 245; 'scientific, not literary', 263

Miscellaneous: projected edition of Propertius, 10, 22, 23, 26; text of *Ibis*, 36, 399; obituary of Vesey, 204; paper on Erasmus Darwin, 220; preface to Platt's *Nine Essays*, 234, 244, 248, 258; 'A Morning with the Royal Family', 329; University Address to George V, 368, 374. Conjectures: Euripides, 51; Germanicus, 400; Keats, 219; A. C. Lyall,

405; Martial, 405; Propertius, 425, 427; Virgil, 424, 426. Miscellaneous writings not to be reprinted, 302

Housman, Basil Williams (brother), 4, 253; coming to London, 24; health, 211, 244, 312, 324; looking older, 283; retirement, 286; death, 326, 364; his 'diabolism', 327

Housman, Clemence (sister), 4, 6, 23, 359; in London, 37; advised to read *Ann Veronica*, 110; *The Werewolf*, 4, 132; telegram to H., 280; living in Somerset, 322; emendation of early poem by H., 363

Housman, Edward (faher), first marriage, 3; neglects family, 4; remarries, 5; illness, 22; death, 35

Housman, Eva (second cousin), 47

Housman, Fletcher, 391

Housman, Rev. Henry ('Cousin Henry'), 6, 47

Housman, Herbert (brother), 4, 36

Housman, Jeannie (sister-in-law), 121, 286, 337, 358–60, 364, 366, 368–9, 373–4, 388

Housman, Katharine (sister), *see under* Symons, Katharine

Housman, Laurence (brother), character, 4; sends a postcard, 23; *Green Arras*, 31–35, 38; in London, 37; *All-Fellows*, 40; *Gods and Their Makers*, 41, 100; *Spikenard*, 45, 92, 100; introduces Richards to H., 360; sends Richards' proposal to take over *A Shropshire Lad*, 46; asks H. to write on Patmore, 67, 318; edits *The Venture*, 67; 'a great artist', 78; bad behaviour in theatre, 88; *Selected Poems*, 92, 94–5; overpowering celebrity, 92; warned he would never illustrate book by H., 97; *The Chinese Lantern*, 97, 327; Suffragist declaration, 110; *Pains and Penalties*, 116–18; *King John of Jingalo*, 132, 149; *Return of Alcestis*, 149; *The Royal Runaway*, 149; *The Wheel*, 168; *Little Plays of St Francis*, 195, 244, 327; *Dethronements*, 207–8; *Angels and Ministers*, 207; *Odd Pairs*, 232; thriving, 237; in America, 265; broadcast of H,'s poems, 276–8, 280; essay on Florence Nightingale, 318; living in Somerset, 322; *Nunc Dimittis*, 327, 347; gramophone record, 327; offers Lady Cave story by H., 329; *Palace Plays*, 344, 370; 'Pre-Raphaelitism', 347; 'a busy man', 349; pacifist lectures, 359; *Victoria Regina*, 363–4; *The Unexpected Years*, 363, 374; and *A*

Shropshire Lad LXIII, 369; to visit Cambridge, 374; offers to move H.'s books, 379; advised not to squander his fortune, 389; as H.'s literary executor, 393; *A.E.H.*, 440; presents H.'s diary to British Museum, 313

Housman, Lucy (step-mother), 3, 5, 10, 88

Housman, Mary Brettell ('Aunt Mary'), 8

Housman, Mary Theophania ('Cousin Mary'), 5

Housman, Rev. Robert (great-grandfather), 3, 391

Housman, Robert (brother), 4, 96

Housman, Sarah Jane (mother), 3–5

Housman, Rev. Thomas (grandfather), 3, 239, 279, 321

Hudson, W. H., *El Ombu*, 89

Hueffer, F. M. (F, M. Ford), 314

Hunt, A. S., 422

Hunt, William, 195

Hunt, William Holman, 371

Huxley, Aldous, 310, 334

Huxley, T. H., 334

Hyde, William, illustrations to *A Shropshire Lad*, 96–7, 101, 265

Ilgen, *Opuscula*, 434

Ingpen, Roger, 293

Ireland, John, 184

Ishill, Joseph, proposal to produce limited edition of *A Shropshire Lad*, 299; *Free Vistas*, 319

Jackson, Adalbert, 23

Jackson, Henry, 64; 28, 29, 127, 170; appointed Regius Professor, 84; O.M., 97; 80th birthday, 162; death, 187; miscellaneous papers, 191

Jackson, Moses, shares lodgings with H., 22; in London, 23; marriage, 28; dedication of Manilus I, 64, 67; entries in H.'s diary, 313

James, M. R., 127, 418

Jebb, R. C., 61, 99, 398

'Jerry', *see* Symons, N. V. H.

Jewell, Lucina, 101

Jonson, Ben, *The Alchemist*, 133

Jowett, Benjamin, 99

Joyce, James, *Ulysses*, 291

Julius Africanus (Blakeney), 438

Juvenal (*see also* Housman, A. E.), 429; new fragment, 399–400, 417

Kahane, Jack, 315

Kains-Jackson, Charles, article on L. Housman, 98

Keats, John, 158, 219–20, 240, 245, 265, 390

Kenealy, E. V., 9
Kennerley, Mitchell, 84
Ker, W. P., 200; 36, 384; consulted on *Last Poems*, 197, 200–1; memorial fund, 220
Keynes, J. N., 420
Kidd, H. Cameron, 42
King, Canon, 17
Kipling, Rudyard, at Hardy's funeral, 260; proposed as Poet Laureate, 295; Watson appeal, 300, 302; says H. is 'dead right', 335
Knight, Joseph, 190
Knox, R. A., *Essays in Satire*, 436
Krupp, F. A., at Capri, 137

Lachmann, Karl, 410, 413
Lamb, Charles, 219
Lamb, Henry, portrait of H., 104–6
Lambert, E. Frank, 105
Landor, W. S., 227, 363
Lane, Hugh, 140
Lane, John, publishes *Green Arras*, 34; drawn by Beerbohm, 71; and *A Shropshire Lad*, 83–4
Lang, Andrew, 332
Laurence, R. V., 295, 363–4
Lawrence, D. H., *Lady Chatterley's Lover*, 291
Leader, B. W., 112
Leavis, F. R., and *The Name and Nature of Poetry*, 335, 344
Lee, Lieutenant, 194
Lee, G. N., *Nineteen Echoes and a Song*, 367
Le Gallienne, Richard, 34
Lejay, Paul, 181
Lemprière, *Classical Dictionary*, 328
Leopardi, 329
Leslie, Shane, *Poems*, 268
Lewis, T. C. ('the other Lewis'), 237
Lewis, W. J., 209, 232, 236, 241
Liddon, Canon, 18
Livy, 418–19, 426, 433
Lloyd, George D., 133, 148, 302
Louis (chauffeur), 267, 284
Lucan (*see also* Housman, A. E.), 414, 421, 427, 431
Lucas, E. V., *The Open Road*, 91; the Queen's Doll's House, 212; writes to H., 216; proposed book on Shropshire, 386
Lucian, 424
Lucretius, 410, 414–15, 421; H.'s lectures, 258; (Ernout), 181; (Merrill), 143; (Munro), 432; (Rouse), 415
Lulham, E. P. H., *Devices and Desires*, 70
Lutyens, Edwin, 212
Lyall, A. C., 405

Lyde, L. W., *Contexts in Pindar*, 384
Lymington, Lord, 15
Lynd, Robert, 189

Macan, R. W., *Essays by Divers Hands*, 347
Macaulay, T. B., *Critical and Historical Essays*, 18; 255
MacDonald, Ramsay, at Hardy's funeral, 260; advises appointment of H. as Poet Laureate, 295
Macdonnell, Annie, 40
Machen, Arthur, advised on wine, 182; *The Secret Glory*, 191
Mackail, Denis, 415
Mackail, J. W., 66, 302, 334; congratulates H. on his publisher: paper on Horace, 153; *Latin Literature*, 154; consulted on *Last Poems*, 197–200; 'a remarkably handsome man', 309; comments on H.'s Manilius, 402–4, 406–7, 411; translation of *Odyssey*, 404; contribution to *Wayfarer's Love*, 405; edition of *Aeneid*, 423–4, 426, 429; advised against conjecture, 435
Mackenzie, Compton, 136
Maclagan, Eric, 105, 109, 111
Macmillan & Co., 93; reject H.'s Propertius, 23, 26; reject *A Shropshire Lad*, 35, 328; reject H.'s Lucan, 224; repent, 245
Macmillan, Sir F., letter to H., 245
Madvig, J. N., 69, 168
Mahaffy, J. P., 398
Mais, S. P. B., 204, 230
Manilius (*see also* Housman, A. E.), 125, 144, 222; early editions, 418, 421; (Regiomontanus), 237, 417; (Scaliger), 36, 236, 429; (Bentley), 36, 429; (Valpy), 145
Marillier, Christabel, 214
Marie Louise, Princess, 212
Marlow, Louis (Louis Wilkinson), *Swan's Milk*, 357
Marsh, Edward, asks H. to contribute to *Georgian Poetry*, 135
Marsh, Richard, *The Beetle*, 125
Marston, P. B., 39
Martial, Duff's text, 405; (Lindsay), 405; H. threatens to edit, 406; Gow's queries, 424
Martin, Houston, 331; persuades H. to copy poem, 346; advised not to write biography of H., 348, 390; copying H.'s articles, 353; a 'lunatic', 356; 'fantastic requests', 361; H. sends good wishes for his sanity, 377
Martin, S. S. and T. L., 121

Martin, Theodore, translation of Horace, 209
Martino-Fusco, Dr di, 418–19
Mary, Queen, 212
Mary Tudor, Queen, pregnancy, 249
Masefield, John, 105, 205; *Captain Margaret*, 109; *Multitude and Solitude*, 109; *Tragedy of Nan*, 111; appointed Poet Laureate, 295–6; Watson appeal, 300, 302
Massingham, H. J., *The Great Victorians*, 318
Maugham, W. Somerset, 67
Mawer, Allen, 333
Maycock, John, letter to H., 28
Mayor, J. E. B., 113
Meakin, Annete, 51
Menken, Adah Isaacs, 159
Meredith, George, 67, 124
'Meredith, Owen', 106
Merrill, W. A., edition of Lucretius, 143
Meyerstein, E. H. W., *Four Elegies of Propertius*, 326
Meynell, Alice, 40; *A Father of Women*, 162
Meynell, Wilfrid, 174
Millay, Edna St Vincent, *Fatal Interview*, 315
Miller, W. H., 222
Millerand, A., 224
Millington, Bertie, 352
Millington, Herbert, 42, 98
Milton, John, 200–1
Mimnermus, 422
Money, A., 401
Monroe, Harriet, 189
Montaigne, 102
Moore, G. V., 386–7
Moore, T. S., 271
Moring, Alexander, 87, 124
Morley, John, *On Compromise*, 206; said to have advised rejection of *A Shropshire Lad*, 328
Morley, S. G., translations from Quental, 345
Morris, Dr, 88
Morris, William, worth 144 poems; *Defence of Guinevere*, 348
Moss, Richard, 21
Mulock, D. M., *Agatha's Husband*, 175
Munro, H. A. J., H. corresponds with, 10; *Criticisms and Elucidations of Catullus*, 405; a conjecture, 421
Murray, Gilbert, sends H. *Andromache*, 51; edition of Euripides, 51–2, 404–5; invited to music hall, 52, 68; Euripides translations, 69; *Hippolytus*, 75–6; appointed Regius Professor, 99; sends

H. *Rose and Vine*, 106, 219; Pre-Raphaelite style, 168

Nauck, A., 398–9, 419
Navarro, J. M. de, 154; Madame de, 382
Newall, H. F., 412
Newbolt, Henry, 295; 162, 300
Nicoll, W. Robertson, reviews *A Shropshire Lad*, 37; on H. and Catullus, 80, 144
Nook, A. D., 287, 421
Norris, Rev. W. F., confuses H. with Laurence Housman, 232

O'Brian, Rev. Delos, H.'s ambition of decorating his vestry, 326
Oldmeadow, Ernest, 142; *Antonio*, 166
Olive, Edyth, 76
Oliver, F. W., recollections of H., 383
Ombiaux, Maurice des, *Le Vin*, 264
Orr, C. W., 215
Osborn, E. B., 183
Osma, G. de, 111
Ovid, H.'s text of *Ibis*, 399; *Metamorphoses* (Slater), 408; 403, 407, 409, 411–12, 414, 416, 421, 427–8, 437
Owen, S. G., edition of Juvenal ignored by H., 81
Owlett, F. C., *Kultur and Anarchy*, 219; *Chatterton's Apology*, 298; Watson appeal, 300

Palgrave, F. T., *The Golden Treasury*, 41
Palmer, H. R., 256, 312
Parry, R. St J., proposal that H. should be Public Orator, 170; *Henry Jackson O.M.*, 191; Platt's *Nine Essays*, 233–4, 251; at Lewis's funeral, 237; dangerously ill, 355; review of *Thomas Hodgkin*, 412
Pascal, 329
Pater, W. H., *Marius, the Epicurean*, 424
Patmore, Coverntry, H. asked to write on, 67, 318; essay on metre, 318, 345
Pattison, Mark, essay on Scaliger, 236
Paul, Kegan, publishes *A Shropshire Lad*, 35, 328, 350; feelings to be considered, 46; 'not lacerated', 48
Pauly-Wissowa, *Real-Encyclopädie*, 323, 416
Payne, L. W., 202; 'courteous and amiable letter', 309; H. avoids reading things written about him, 318
Pearson, A. C., 189, 187, 306; his Sophocles, 226, 419; deceived into thinking H. knows Greek, 423
Pearson, Karl, 52
Peel, Graham, 124
Peel, Sir Robert (the younger), 16

Persius, Cartault's edition, 181; no new edition greatly needed, 319

Phillimore, J. S., 'The Revival of Criticism', 167; not to be sent Richmond's *Propertius*, 242

Pius IX, Pope, 18

Platt, Arthur, 'knows everything', 50; 36, 64, 115, 118, 145; translation of *Agamemnon*, 114; paper on Cervantes, 144; married for 35 years, 182; candidate for Cambridge Professorship, 187, 189; *Nine Essays*, 233–4, 243–4, 247–51; sonnets, 250; 'a dear and wonderful creature', 258; would have liked *The Name and Nature of Poetry*, 333; deceived into thinking H. knew Greek, 423

Pliny, Scaliger's epigram, 236

Pollard, A. W., *Odes from the Greek Dramatists*, 30; shares lodgings with H., 22; revises *A Shropshire Lad*, 35; introduces H. to Kegan Paul, 328; and *Last Poems*, 197

Pollet, Maurice, article on H., 328, 344

Polson, J. R., 215

Polybius, 424

Porson, Richard, 162, 274, 404, 431

Postgate, J. P., 94, 172; *Select Elegies of Propertius*, 26; *Corpus Poetarum Latinorum*, 71, 399, 405, 433, 435; article on new fragment of Juvenal, 399; *Silva Maniliana*, 400; article on *Metamorphoses* XV, 408

Price, Rev. J. W., 209

Priestley, J. B., *Brief Diversions*, 193; *Figures in Modern Literature*, 222

Prince, John, *Worthies of Devon*, 129

Prior, Joseph, 185

Prior, O. H. P., 333

Priscian, 422, 437

Propertius (*see also* Housman, A. E.), 26, 241, 326, 415, 425, 427, 434–5, 437

Proust, Marcel, Richards advised not to publish, 166; *Le Côté des Guermantes*, 196

Putt, S. Gorley, the only hostile review of *The Name and Nature of Poetry*, 344

Quiller-Couch, Arthur, 91, 161

Quilter, Harry, *Universal Review*, 232

Quintilian, 271

Rabelais, 331

Rackham, Harris, on pronunciation of 'Milan', 284

Raleigh, Walter, edits *Times Broadsheets*, 140; recipient of Gosse's private memoir, 159; lecture on Landor, 227

Ramsay, A. B., 'a desirable acquaintance', 241; at Hardy's funeral, 260; and the Eton Essay Society, 416

Ramsay, Sir William, 115, 147

Rattenbury, R. M., 241

Read, Herbert, 318

Reay, Lord, 401, 383

Reinach, Théodore, *L'Histoire par les Monnaies*, 402

Rendall, G. H., admires Laurence Housman, 40

Ribbeck, a conjecture in Virgil, 426

Richards, Charles, graph of Housman's sales, 178

Richards, Gerard, 147

Richards, Grant, *Housman 1891–1936*, 46; introduced to H., 360; offers to publish successor to *A Shropshire Lad*, 39, 51; proposal to take over *A Shropshire Lad*, 46, 350; publishes second edition of *A Shropshire Lad*, 35, 48–9, 230; sales, 49; later editions, 49, 50, 61–2, 64, 70–1, 78, 82–3, 86–7, 90, 96–8, 101, 134–6, 148, 157, 169, 193, 203, 210, 248, 261, 268, 278; publishes H.'s Manilius, 60–8, 72, 74, 80, 85–6, 90, 99, 109, 111, 119–20, 122–4, 139, 141–2, 164–5, 167, 172, 174–5, 179, 254; publishes H.'s Juvenal, 71–2, 74–6, 79–81, 137; bankrupt, 76; father's death, 78; lectured on unauthorised permissions, 91; resumes business, 98; and outside brokers, 101; letters from his authors, 124; urged not to edit Manilius or write poetry, 125; *Caviare*, 125, 225; *Valentine*, 131; with H. on Riviera, 138, 188; *Bittersweet*, 139; remarried, 140; prevented from travelling to France, 143; bad at answering letters, 145; death of son, 147; in France, 160; advised not to publish Proust, 166; *Double Life*, 175; 'a skilled epicure', 182; solicitude for the corruption of H.'s mind, 196; *Last Poems*, 179, 183, 192–5, 197–8, 201–4, 206, 208, 223, 242, 257, 259, 261, 268, 278, 357; told not to prosecute Queen Mary, 212; not to prosecute Bridges, 216; *Every Wife*, 225; bankrupt again, 234; tours France with H., 252; *The Coasts of Pleasure*, 258; *Memories of a Misspent Youth*, 320; *Author Hunting*, 357, 360

Richards, Mrs E. Grant, 79, 84, 98

Richards, Mrs M. Grant, 140, 143, 148, 156, 161, 163, 169

Richards, Herbert, 98, 106, 143

Richmond, O. L., edition of Propertius, 241

Ridgeway, William, 427
Robbins, F. E., Michigan Astrological Papyrus, 423, 425, 435–6; chronology of Trollope, 436
Roberts, Cecil, paragraph about H., 182
Roberts, S. C., and Platt's *Nine Essays*, 234, 243–5, 248, 250–1; and Richmond's *Propertius*, 241–2; and Young's *English Prosody*, 251–2; second edition of H.'s Juvenal, 282, 296, 300–1, 304–5; *editio minor* of H.'s Manilius, 315–17, 322, 325, 429; *The Name and Nature of Poetry*, 332, 336; entertains Family, 391
Robertson, D. H., 133
Robertson, D. S., 274
Robinson, A. Mary F., use of 'insensate', 33
Rogers, Thorold, 'the Beaumont Street Gorilla', 14
Ross, Robert, 136; recites H.'s poems to Wilde, 267
Rossetti, D. G., 'indecent', 35; the 'menagerie', 190, 354; and Holman Hunt, 371
Rossetti, W. M., reminiscences of D.G.R., 190; edition of Shelley, 285–6
Rothenstein, Alice, 88–9, 101, 109, 132, 173, 183, 261, 320, 333; on the telephone, 102; in France, 104; invites H. too often, 108; holding Rothenstein on a cliff, 110; happy, 111; painted by Rothenstein, 112; congratulates H., 115
Rothenstein, Betty, 246
Rothenstein, John, 104
Rothenstein, William, 87, 102, 314; gives H. a drawing, 92; to join H. in drinking Jackson's health, 97; admires Laurence Housman's play, 98; lecture on British art, 101; and the vices of Paris, 104; sends Frances Cornford's *Poems*, 109; painting on a cliff, 110; painting in India, 115; in America, 119; moves to Gloucestershire, 129; allows drawing of H. to be reproduced, 132; behaves nicely at Cambridge, 147; exhibition of war drawings, 155; called up, 156; gives H. celestial globe, 171; as a character in Beerbohm's *Seven Men*, 172; asks H. to write on Hardy, 173; his drawings of H. a 'venomous libel', 179–80; never gets a likeness, 240, 261; loses monopoly of H.'s features, 246; proposed group portrait, 260–2; knighted, 307; celebratory dinner, 309; drawing of H. not to be reproduced, 313; *Men and*

Memories, 319–20; to hear H.'s lecture, 333, on Beerbohm, 334
Rousseau, J.-J., 159
Ruskin, John, 12, 57
Russell, Bertrand, 128
Rutherford, Ernest, 202, 306
Rutherford, W. G., 398

Sacher-Masoch, 159
Sade, Marquis de, 159–60
Sadleir, Michael, *Trollope : A Commentary*, 436
Saintsbury, George, distinguishable by the shabbiness of his hat, 224; *History of English Prosody*, 252
Sala, G. A., admired by Swinburne, 160
Salisbury, Marquess of, 25
Sallet, A. Von, *Beiträge*, 401
Sanders, Edith, 22
Sandys, Sir John, his oratory, 188; *History of Classical Scholarship*, 236
Sankey, Mrs and G. M., 19
Santley, Charles, 7
Sassoon, Siegfried, 162, 313
Sayle, Charles, 188
Scaliger, J. J., editions of Manilius, 36, 236, 429
Scholfield, A. F., 181; and list of H.'s writings, 238; birthday telegram, 281
Schücking, L. L., *Anthology of Modern English Poetry*, 311, 313
Scott, Rev. C., 142
Scott, Sir Walter, *Lord of the Isles*, 314
Scott, W. B., 190
Scott-James, R. A., 392
Searancke, Mr, 21
Secker, Martin, *Women*, 156
Semple, W. H., 239
Seneca, 425, 437
Servius, 409, 423
Sewell, J. E., 11
Seymour, Rev. A. E., 25
Shakespeare, 329, 334
Shankar, Bhawani, 386
Shaw, G. B., sends bill to Richards, 49; and the Queen's Doll's House, 212; refuses O.M., 277; advice to a collector, 361; 124, 260, 262, 302
Shelley, P. B., dislike of revising, 49; 'O World', 285–6, 293; 199, 200, 219, 271, 284
Shewring, W. H., 426
Shorter, C. K., 144
Silius Italicaus, Duff's edition, 427, 431–4; (Ernesti), 431; (Summers), 433
Simon, André, *Wines and Spirits*, 166
Skutsch, Otto, 437

Slater, D. A., 408–9, 172

Smith, Horace and James, *Rejected Addresses*, 200

Sophocles, 411, 417; (Elmsley), 414; (Jebb), 61; (Nauck), 399, 419; (Pearson), 226, 419

Sparrow, John, 223, 285, 293, 349, 365, 377; 'Echoes in the Poetry of A. E. Housman', 356; *see also* 439–40

Spicer-Simson, Theodore, portrait medallion of H., 199, 202; *Men of Letters of the British Isles*, 227

Stamfordham, Lord, H.'s refusal of O.M., 295

Stanley, Dean, 'Absolution', 17

Statius, 406, 411; H.'s paper, 210, 242, 309

Steenstrup, H. Troller, ('Hans Tiransil'), 220, 259

Sterne, Laurence, *Tristam Shandy*, 137

Stevenson, W. H., 240

Stewart, H. F., 273

Stillman, W. B., 22

Stock, G. St H., *Revelations of the School and Bedroom*, 152

Story, Sommerville, *Paris à la Carte*, 201

Stuart, C. E., 133, 428

Sudermann, Hermann, *Magda*, 69

Sully, James, *Pessimism*, 329

Sulpicius Severus, 418–19

Sutherland, Duchess of, *Wayfarer's Love*, 68, 405

Symons, A. D. (nephew), 176, 217, 253, 269, 312, 324, 337

Symons, A. J. A., *Frederick Baron Corvo*, 257; 'magnificent handwriting', 259, 271; *A Book of Nineties Verse*, 271; and 'R.L.S.', 274

Symons, C. A. (nephew), 141

Symons, Edward (brother-in-law), 121, 141, 195, 217, 237, 269, 283, 286, 312

Symons, Katharine (sister), 4; early letter to H., 19; prefers H.'s verse to his sentiments, 37; and memorial to Robert Housman, 96; letter on family history, 321; *The Grammar School of Edward VI, Bath*, 351, 360, 364

Symons, N. V. H. ('Jerry') (nephew), 141, 195, 211, 217, 228, 253, 292, 374, 379, 385

Symons, Phyllis, 343

Swinburne, A. C., his women have 'flanks', 33; Laurence Housman accused of imitating, 35; expected to write 144 poems on Morris, 39; biography by Gosse, 149–52; *The Whippingham Papers*, 151; his letters, 157–60; Gosse's private memoir, 159–60; and the text of Shelley, 285–6

Taylor, H. M., 260

Taylor, Rachel Annand, *Rose and Vine*, 106–107, 219; *Aspects of the Italian Renaissance*, 212

Taylor, Sedley, 185

Theocritus, 4

Thicknesse, Lily, *Collected Poems*, 52; advice on a literary career, 103–4

Thicknesse, Ralph, 52; *Rights and Wrongs of Women*, 103

Thirkell, Angela, *Three Houses*, 429

Thomas, Bert, caricature of H., 203

Thomas, Bertram, 333

Thomas, Edward, *Pocket Book of Poems and Songs*, 91

Thomas, L. H., 241

Thomson, J. J., 202; H. declines Clark Lectureship, 227

Tibullus, 421

Tillotson, Geoffrey, reprint of H.'s *Three Poems*, 367–9, 372–3

Tonks, Henry, 297, 312, 384; appeal for Oxford Union murals, 371

Trim, Mrs, 81

Trinick, J. B., *The Dead Sanctuary*, 199

Trollope, Anthony, 235, 436

Turner, Reginald, 267

Tyler, Royall, *Spain*, 103

Tyrtaeus, 328

Twain, Mark, *Huckleberry Finn*, 247, 277

Umberto I, King, 54

Untermeyer, Louis, *Including Horace*, 169

Valéry, Paul, 255

Valliant, O. M., thesis on H., 309, 318

van Vechten, Carl, 196

Vaughan, Williams, Ralph, *On Wenlock Edge*, 106; permitted to print poems by H. on concert programme, 152; mutilates poems, 181, 198; gramophone royalties, 215

Venn, J. A., *Alumni Cantabrigienses*, 391

Verlaine, Paul, 329

Vernon, H. F., 22

Verrall, A. W., supports H.'s candidature, 29; 'a baleful influence' on Murray, 404; 419

Vesey, W. T., obituary written by H., 204

Victoria, Queen, Gladstone's behaviour, 21; Golden Jubilee, 181; Diamond Jubilee, 42–3, 158

Villon, François, 329

Virgil, 404, 410, 413–15, 423–4, 426, 429, 435, 437; scholia, 409, 423–4

Wageningen, J. van, 432

457

Walker, E. M., 260
Ward, A. W., 242
'Ward, Artemus', 331
Warren, T. H., 12
Watson, Canon, 350
Watson, William, *The Purple East*, 71;
    appeal, 300, 302; privately printed
    sonnet, 384
Watts, Irene L., article on H., 322
Watts-Dunton, Theodore, 150
Webb, C. C. J., 400
Webb, E. J., article on Postgate's Manilius,
    400
Webb, P. G. L., in a Patent Office dispute,
    27; *Translations*, 123
Webster, Ben, 76
Wecklein, N., 29, 397–8, 405; edition of
    Aeschylus, 397
Weir Smyth, H., *Greek Melic Poets*, 434
Wells, H. G., *Ann Veronica*, 110
Wemyss, Lady, 381–2
Whall, J. C., 178
Whibley, Charles, 223
Whistler, J. M., 150
Wicksteed, P. H., 249
Wilamowitz-Moellendorf, U. von, 94, 405
Wilde, Oscar, arrest, 35; sent *A Shropshire
    Lad* by H., 267
William II, Emperor, 137
Williams, Rev. A. T. P., 234
Williams, Charles, 285–6, 293
Willoughby, Véra, 278
'Willy' (H. G. Villars), *Le Troisième Sexe*,
    293
Wilson, Charles, *Collected Poems*, 245; his

pamphlet, 299; invites H. to Willington,
    299, 319, 367; ill, 330
Wilson, Edmund, translation of dedication
    in H.'s Manilius, 352
Winstanley, D. A., 185–6, 190
Wise family, 3, 27, 130, 253, 269, 355
Wise, T. J., 151, 365
Withers, Percy, 154; moves to Oxfordshire,
    174; convulsion in his cellar, 183; sends
    marmalade, 196; enquiry about *Last
    Poems*, 203; enthusiasm, 209; *Friends in
    Solitude*, 213; reviewed, 217; better
    health, 240; abuses H. for not writing,
    273; persuades H. to allow limited
    edition of poems, 275; H.'s most
    acrimonious correspondent, 314; sent
    Introductory Lecture, 349; moves to
    Warwickshire, 358; offers to fetch H.
    from Cambridge, 372; 'extravagantly
    kind', 386; query about Archimedes,
    413
Withof, *Kritische Anmerkungen*, 434
Wolff, Sir H. D., 16
Wolff, Lucien, 354
Wordsworth, William, his 'perpetual tinker-
    ing', 49; misquoted by Gosse, 150; 219
Wright, W. Aldis, 397
Wyse, William, 29

Yeats, W. B., 311
Young, Desmond, *Hun Hunters*, 148
Young, Filson, *Sands of Pleasure*, 83; *When
    the Tide Turns*, 93
Young, Sir George, *English Prosody*, 252;
    Homer and the Greek Accents, 272